The Political Economy
of Armed Conflict

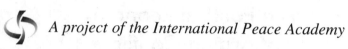 *A project of the International Peace Academy*

The Political Economy of Armed Conflict

Beyond Greed and Grievance

edited by
Karen Ballentine
Jake Sherman

LYNNE
RIENNER
PUBLISHERS

BOULDER
LONDON

Published in the United States of America in 2003 by
Lynne Rienner Publishers, Inc.
1800 30th Street, Boulder, Colorado 80301
www.rienner.com

and in the United Kingdom by
Lynne Rienner Publishers, Inc.
3 Henrietta Street, Covent Garden, London WC2E 8LU

Library of Congress Cataloging-in-Publication Data
  The political economy of armed conflict : beyond greed and grievance /
Karen Ballentine and Jake Sherman, editors.
      p.   cm.
  "A project of the International Peace Academy."
  Includes bibliographical references and index.
  ISBN 1-58826-197-2 (alk. paper)
  ISBN 1-58826-172-7 (pbk. : alk. paper)
  1. Civil War—Economic aspects—Case studies. 2. War—Economic
aspects—Case studies. I. Ballentine, Karen. II. Sherman, Jake.
III. International Peace Academy.
HB195.P634   2003
303.6'4—dc21   2003046717

British Cataloguing in Publication Data
A Cataloguing in Publication record for this book
is available from the British Library.

Printed and bound in the United States of America

     The paper used in this publication meets the requirements
 ∞   of the American National Standard for Permanence of
     Paper for Printed Library Materials Z39.48-1992.

  5 4 3 2 1

Contents

Foreword

DAVID M. MALONE,
PRESIDENT, INTERNATIONAL PEACE ACADEMY

THE QUESTION OF HOW BEST TO EFFECTIVELY ASSIST TRANSITIONS FROM PRO-tracted war to lasting peace is of tantamount importance to the international community. Throughout the 1990s, it became increasingly clear from the United Nations' experiences in Angola, Cambodia, and Sierra Leone that the economic dimensions of contemporary internal conflicts, highlighted by—but scarcely limited to—the role of so-called conflict diamonds and other easily exploitable natural resources, have acquired new relevance to peacemaking and peacebuilding. We know that globalization has enabled rival factions, through licit and illicit commercial networks, to better access international markets, and thus to finance civil wars. But until recently, there were few answers for policymakers as to what kinds of tools and strategies could be deployed by the international community to address the flow of economic resources that feed conflict or to engage the economic interests of elites, their internal supporters, and their external economic clients to support the conditions in which peace could be achieved.

Recognizing that a greater understanding of the role of economically driven behavior in generating and sustaining internal armed conflicts was critical, the International Peace Academy (IPA) cosponsored a conference in London in 1999, out of which flowed the now widely cited volume *Greed and Grievance: Economic Agendas in Civil Wars.* The conference and volume proved instrumental in highlighting the importance to conflict resolution of this vector of policy research, as well as the need for further empirical study and policy development. In response, the IPA initiated the three-year Economic Agendas in Civil Wars (EACW) project in September 2000.

The first phase of the project, of which this volume is the culmination, focused on empirical and conceptual research into the economic strategies of belligerents and the relationship between global and regional resource flows and conflict. As these case studies make clear, while combatant dependence on globalized resource flows has become a common feature of contemporary conflicts, and in some cases has profoundly altered the character and goals of armed struggle, the pursuit of economic self-interest and of redress for legitimate grievances are neither mutually exclusive nor static goals. Because so few conflicts qualify as pure examples of greed-driven resource wars, the assumption that reducing or depriving combatant access to economic resources will induce them to negotiate a peaceful end to hostilities, therefore, stands in need of qualification. More attention also needs to be paid to the conflict-promoting economic behavior of state actors. Indeed, the greater risk of conflict observed for countries with high dependence on natural resource exports is largely a function of poor state capacity for governance.

Building on the outcomes of this research, the second phase of the EACW project will focus on policy development, specifically on identifying and assessing the existing and emerging policy, legal, regulatory, and financial mechanisms that may be applied to more effectively redress the conflict-promoting aspects of economic activity in vulnerable or war-torn states. While the development of effective policy responses to the economics of conflict is still nascent, the promotion of a more concerted global regulatory effort is indispensable to effective conflict prevention. It is our hope that this volume will make a modest contribution to that end.

Policy actors, notably the UN Security Council, have increasingly been compelled to reflect and act on economic factors in contemporary civil wars. We have sought, in all of our work on this topic, to generate perspectives of use to them. We hope this volume will be no exception.

Such an endeavor would not be possible without the foresight and dedication of our funders to supporting policy development and research on this groundbreaking topic. In particular, the IPA is deeply grateful to the Canadian Department of Foreign Affairs and International Trade, the Canadian International Development Agency, the Department for International Development of the United Kingdom, the International Development Research Centre, the Government of Norway, the Government of Switzerland, the Government of Sweden, the Rockefeller Foundation, and the United Nations Foundation for their support in developing the conceptual and practical foundation upon which the ensuing volume is built.

Acknowledgments

THE EDITORS WOULD LIKE TO ACKNOWLEDGE THE GENEROUS SUPPORT OF OUR funders. We would also like to thank the many individuals who have contributed to the conceptual design and implementation of the Economic Agendas in Civil Wars program and to the realization of this volume. Above all, Virginia Gamba, Colin Keating, Leiv Lunde, Andrew Mack, and the members of the Advisory Group have provided invaluable intellectual guidance and enthusiasm. Neclâ Tschirgi played a vital role, first as a funder and later as vice president of the IPA. For their invaluable and well-informed comments on draft chapters, we would like to thank our reviewers and Alexandra Guáqueta. For their patience and their dedication, we thank Heiko Nitzschke, Karin Wermester, and Jason Cook, who assisted us in the often challenging but ultimately rewarding editorial work that all such collaborative volumes demand. Clara Lee, our publications coordinator, ensured an effortless transition to press. We also wish to thank Lynne Rienner and her team for seeing the volume through to fruition.

—*Karen Ballentine,*
Jake Sherman

1

Introduction

KAREN BALLENTINE AND JAKE SHERMAN

WAR-MAKING, LIKE ANY OTHER FORM OF ORGANIZED SOCIAL ACTIVITY, RE-
quires financial and other resources to proceed. This fact has long
informed analyses of interstate wars.[1] Yet although intrastate or "civil"
wars have been the dominant mode of conflict since 1945, their economic dimensions were long overshadowed by conflict analyses shaped
first by superpower competition and then by the ethnonationalist insurgencies that accompanied the end of the Cold War. Where the economic
factors of intrastate conflicts were taken into account, investigation
tended to focus on the role played by economic deprivation or resource
scarcity in the eruption of violent conflict. Since the late 1990s, however, increasing scholarly and policy attention has been paid to the economic dimensions of contemporary armed conflict. Whether conducted
under the rubric of war economies, economic agendas in civil wars, or
resource wars, the analytic emphasis has shifted from a consideration of
deprivation and scarcity to an examination of the conflict-promoting
aspects of resource abundance. In all, these efforts have been directed
both at improving understanding of the character and dynamics of
intrastate conflicts and at developing more effective policies for conflict
prevention and conflict resolution.[2]

Perhaps more than any other single factor, this new focus on the
economics of intrastate conflicts was prompted by an observable
increase in the *self-financing* nature of combatant activities in intrastate
wars. As many scholars have noted, this development is deeply connected to shifts in the global political and economic order.[3] The end of
the Cold War marked a precipitous decline in foreign state patronage for
state and nonstate combatants throughout the globe, while also diminishing the ideological programs for which they had fought. In some
cases, such as Mozambique, El Salvador, and Nicaragua, the withdrawal

1

of external support helped induce combatant parties to enter peace agreements. In others, however, it merely impelled active and aspiring combatants to seek out alternative modes of financing for their military campaigns, including the traditional fallbacks of pillage and plunder of local civilians, extortion of local businesses, smuggling, capture of relief aid, and rudimentary systems of war taxation.

Furthermore, rapid economic globalization and the replacement of state-led development by market-driven free trade have created new and abundant opportunities for more systematic forms of combatant self-financing. In conditions of socioeconomic underdevelopment and political instability, locally available assets, particularly natural resources such as timber, precious and semiprecious gems, oil and other mineral wealth, and also lucrative cash crops, particularly narcotics such as opium and coca, have become a major source of war revenues, contributing to a vicious cycle of poor governance and conflict. The ability of combatants to transform these captured assets into revenues and war matériel has been facilitated by a parallel increase of their access to poorly regulated global trade and investment markets, both licit and illicit, through often overlapping business, criminal, and diaspora networks.

The reassessment of the character and purposes of armed conflicts in terms of civil war economies and of combatants as economic actors with economic interests and agendas has led some scholars to a new understanding of how many of today's wars are being fought as well as of the changing nature of armed conflict. One important insight concerns the conceptualization of civil war itself. Whereas conventionally, intrastate war was seen as engendering complete economic breakdown and anarchy, now it is understood as having the potential of creating "an alternate system of profit, power and protection."[4] Even as violent conflict contributes to massive human suffering and societal devastation, it engenders patterns of distribution and redistribution that realign interests and actors in ways that are consequential to the course of armed conflict as well as to the opportunities for its resolution.

Like all war economies, "civil war economies" are distinguished by the militarization of economic life and the mobilization of economic assets and activity to finance the prosecution of war. But recent scholarship has identified several features unique to the economies of civil war: they are parasitic, because they are dominated by rent-seeking and the extraction and trade of primary products, rather than by value-adding economic activities; they are illicit, insofar as they depend heavily on black and gray markets that operate outside and at the expense of legal and formal economic activity of the state; and they are predatory—that is, they are based on the deliberate and systematic use of violence to acquire assets, control trade, and exploit labor. They are also highly dependent on external financial and commodity networks that provide access to the globalized marketplace.[5] Unlike the war economies of classical interstate wars, civil war economies rarely contribute to state capacity or economic development. Indeed, they are a particularly malignant form of production and exchange that both reflects and perpetuates a vicious cycle of underdevelopment and poses severe immediate and longer-term threats to the security and well-being of war-torn societies.

A second important insight concerns the functions of violence in armed conflicts. As evidenced in conflicts such as those in Angola and Sierra Leone, the turn to self-financed conflict has expanded the purposes—as well as the targets—to which violence is directed. Parallel to attacks on capitals and military installations, fighting has also been directed at capturing or protecting natural resource endowments, diverting humanitarian aid, and controlling trade routes. While combatants have continued to mobilize around political, communal, and security objectives, increasingly these objectives have become obscured—and sometimes contradicted—by their more businesslike activities. On various occasions, erstwhile foes have been found collaborating in money-making pursuits, whether in the diamond fields of Sierra Leone or in the timber tracts of Burma.[6]

Greed and Grievance

For some scholars, renewed attention to the economic behavior of combatants, particularly the predation of abundant natural resource wealth, may reveal not only how internal conflicts are being fought but also *why*. David Keen has suggested that where combatants exploit conflict to engage in crude resource accumulation, "there may be more to war than winning."[7] The pursuit of war, in short, may be economically rational for some of those individuals who participate in it, notwithstanding its cumulative societal destructiveness. This view has found its most systematic and influential formulation in a series of quantitative studies undertaken by the World Bank. Using a statistical analysis of all civil wars occurring since 1965, Paul Collier and his team assessed a range of variables to determine which were most salient to the risk of violent conflict.[8] They found that factors commonly identified as conflict causes—such as ethnic heterogeneity, the level of political rights, economic mismanagement, and regime type—have no statistical bearing on the incidence or outbreak of civil wars. Instead, they found that economic factors were more salient to the risk of civil war, and in ways that may appear counterintuitive. For example, while low incomes and low growth rates put countries at high risk of civil war, no robust correlation was found between socioeconomic inequality, either between or within groups, and conflict risk. The data also revealed a high risk of conflict for those countries with a strong dependency on primary commodity exports and a high number of poorly educated young men. This led Collier and his colleagues to conclude, first, that objective political grievances have no direct link to the onset of conflict and, second, that where there are accessible natural resources and a mass of ill-educated youth, rebel movements have a powerful incentive to use violence to acquire wealth and the opportunity and means to do so.[9]

These statistical findings have been subject to varying interpretations. In their initial strong formulation of the "greed theory" of rebellion, Collier and his team offered a rational actor account that focused on the *motives* of rebel actors, arguing that greed or loot-seeking rather than grievance or justice-seeking was the key factor in the onset of violent rebellion. This suggested that economic resources are not simply pursued to sustain war, but rather that war is pursued in order to capture resources. More recently, Collier's team has offered a weaker formulation of the greed thesis that places increased emphasis on the *opportunity* for organized violence, the feasibility of rebellion, and the way that access to finances (especially lucrative natural resources), diaspora networks, and high levels of poorly educated youth contribute to this opportunity, regardless of motivation.[10]

Both the motive and the opportunity formulations of economic agendas in intrastate armed conflicts offer some useful analytical insights to understanding the economic dimensions of armed conflict. By underscoring the fact that violent conflict can yield economic benefits for some actors, the motive formulation has drawn attention to the importance for conflict resolution of employing a "stakeholder analysis"[11] of civil war that seeks to identify which actors benefit from war, and hence, who may act as spoilers to its peaceful resolution. Likewise, attention to the opportunities that natural resources create for violent conflict holds the promise of improving structural prevention by designing new tools and strategies for more effective resource management and equitable economic governance, both locally and globally.

Yet the assertion that contemporary armed conflicts are predominantly caused by greed rather than grievance, and in the ways postulated by some of its proponents, has provoked an ongoing, sometimes heated debate and raised a number of important analytical and normative questions.[12] While there is growing agreement that economic factors matter to conflict dynamics, there is little consensus as to how they matter, how much they matter, or in what ways. In part, this disagreement has stemmed from the loaded normative connotations of the terms "greed" and "grievance," the stark opposition in which they were presented, and a continued lack of clarity as to what variables these terms are meant to capture.[13] From the outset, however, a key issue of contention has been the relative explanatory weight of economic factors vis-à-vis the role played by other political, cultural, and strategic factors in shaping the incidence, duration, and character of intrastate conflicts. Does the fact that combatants in many of today's armed conflicts finance themselves through the exploitation of natural resources warrant the wholesale reconceptualization of their conflicts as "resource wars"? Are political, social, and ethnic grievances merely a narrative deployed by combatants to obscure their true pecuniary motives? Is resource capture an end in itself rather than simply a means of enabling combatants to continue campaigns begun for other reasons? Should policy efforts be limited to reducing the economic opportunities for violence that are available to rebel groups, or extended as well to regulating the economic activities of state and corporate actors in conflict zones? Can the behavior of combatants be meaningfully understood outside the particular historical, social, and political environments that shape them and allow them to thrive?

In its narrowest formulation, the greed theory of civil war answers these questions in the affirmative. It is worth stressing, however, that the greed account is the product of a quantitative statistical analysis. As such, its propositions regarding the high salience of economic factors— whether cast in terms of motive or opportunity—are probabilistic statements of conflict risk rather than factual descriptions of actual conflict dynamics in the specific real-world instances that preoccupy policymakers. In general, while statistical methods are a useful way of identifying key variables across a class of cases, at best they generate broad correlations that illuminate only part of the picture. Clarifying whether and how economic factors promote or sustain particular armed conflicts requires more careful empirical investigation and comparative assessment of the relative applicability of these and other explanations of armed conflict in specific cases.

For those seeking to devise more effective policies of conflict regulation and prevention, such clarification is essential. Correctly identifying those actors who are engaged in war for profit may also help to identify opponents to and spoilers of peace settlements. Likewise, an improved understanding of the factors that shape an opportunity structure favorable to organized violence and large-scale armed conflict may yield policy measures that can more effectively reduce combatant access to finances and perhaps alter their cost-benefit calculus in favor of peace. No less important, however, is the need to correctly identify those who are fighting wars for other reasons—and who may be comparatively more impervious to economic sanctions and inducements—as well as those who participate in war economies out of necessity, and whose livelihoods may suffer as much from untrammeled predation as from ill-conceived efforts to end it. Just as the costs and benefits of war are borne differently by different participants in war economies, so too are the costs and benefits of peace.

Objectives and Design of the Book

The studies contained in this volume were undertaken with precisely these objectives in mind. In inquiring into the economic dimensions of specific armed conflicts, they proceed from a recognition that conceptualizing explanations of armed conflict in terms of greed or grievance has imposed an unnecessarily limiting dichotomy on what is, in reality, a highly diverse, complex set of incentive and opportunity structures that vary across time and location. While informed by the insights and propositions that this debate has generated, the overall approach of these studies can be characterized as one of theoretical agnosticism: whether economic factors are causal to the conflict in question or merely facilitating to other more fundamental causes—such as repression, political exclusion, contests over power or ideology, or the insecurity born of ethnic animosity—is approached as a question to be investigated. Accordingly, the objective of these studies is not to vindicate or disqualify the paradigm of "resource wars" or the greed thesis but to qualify them by examining the actual extent to which and the manner in which economic factors may have contributed to the onset, persistence, intensity, and character of specific conflicts. In contrast to quantitative methods, which assess the salience of economic variables either in isolation or in stylized multifactor regressions, these qualitative case studies seek to ascertain the causal impact on specific conflicts of economic factors relative to and in combination with other potentially significant political, ideological, ethnic, and security factors. While necessarily lacking the methodological rigor of large-number quantitative studies, the virtue of this case-specific approach is that it offers a more accurate understanding of how economic incentives and opportunities fuel conflict, the extent to which a particular conflict may be explained by these economic factors, and hence the kinds of policy responses that may be merited under both economic approaches to conflict.

Throughout these analyses, economic factors are construed broadly. In addition to identifying the economic behavior and agendas of conflict actors, they also examine the impact on conflict of prior economic conditions, such as low growth and socioeconomic inequality within and between groups, and the economic policies of national governments and international actors on creating opportunities and incentives for armed conflict. Regarding the economic behavior of conflict actors, the key subjects of inquiry include the identification of the economic activities in which conflict actors are engaged, the determination of key economic beneficiaries, and the identification of the sources and networks by which they derive financial and material support, including linkages to regional and global financial, commodity, and arms markets, licit as well as illicit. These studies also seek to explore whether access to different forms and amounts of financial and material resources has shaped the relative balance of war-making capacities among combatant groups, their relationship to opponents, allies, and civilians, their military goals and conduct, as well as their predispositions to resolve conflict through negotiation. Where feasible, this inventory was undertaken through field-based research as well as examination of relevant primary and secondary sources. However, given the illicit and hence unrecorded nature of the activities in question and, in some instances, the context of ongoing hostilities, in most cases there are insufficient data to reliably ascertain precise amounts of combatant financing or the full scope of income-generating activities that contributed to the conflict in question. While none of these case studies can thus pretend to have achieved a comprehensive inventory of combatant economic transactions, they do provide a coherent estimation of the most central sources of financing and the most commonly deployed methods to access them.

Likewise broadened is the range of conflict actors studied. To date, most of the influential studies of the economics of conflict have focused exclusively on the predatory behavior of rebel or insurgent groups. Moreover, they have tended to treat rebel groups as unitary actors with a common interest in predation. This approach has proven problematic in a number of respects. First, limiting the inquiry to the predatory activity of rebel groups yields a partial view that not only risks casting all insurgencies as an extreme form of common criminality, but effectively forecloses examination of the conflict-promoting effects of corruption and rent-seeking on the part of state agents and other important actors. To correct for this bias, these studies seek to examine the economic behavior of all relevant conflict actors, including rebels, state agents, private-sector actors, transnational criminal organizations, and private-sector security companies involved in conflict zones. Second, by inadequately distinguishing between rebel leaders, their core cadres, and other followers and supporters, treating rebel groups as unitary actors fails to capture the ways that economic opportunities and incentives may interact with a range of other motivations to shape the behavior of differently situated rebel actors and their commitment to the insurgency. While followers on all sides may be attracted by the prospect of material gain in the absence of few other economic opportunities, they may also be attracted by ideological zeal, ethnic loyalty, or aspirations to power. Alternatively, they may be coerced by the use or threat of force.[14] Overall, the motivations of conflict actors are never static. In actual conflict situations, individual motivations may vary widely and may also change over time in response to changing opportunities and constraints. For these reasons, it is important to examine the internal dynamics of combatant groups, including the patterns of economic redistribution within them.

Another important parameter of these studies is their effort to contextualize the economic dimensions of specific conflicts historically, geographically, and in relation to the degree of national state capacity. As a main concern is to ascertain the relative import of economic factors to the onset as well as the duration of conflict, a historical perspective is indispensable. As many scholars have observed, conflict dynamics are highly fluid.[15] In the face of evolving constellations of opportunity, constraint, resources, ideas, and leadership, conflicts transform, mutate, degenerate, or consolidate. The longer the conflict, the more likely that it has evolved through many stages and the more likely that the factors that sustain it are different from those that provided the initial trigger. For example, conflicts that begin as national liberation struggles may, as a result of protracted violence, provoke new grievances as well as create new incentives for predation, thereby transforming and multiplying the points of conflict. An analysis of the shifting interplay between economic and other factors over time is thus essential to understanding the relative salience of economic opportunities and incentives, both in terms of the initial conditions of conflict and in shaping the processes by which conflict proceeds.

Placing armed conflicts in their global and regional geographic context is also critical to understanding their dynamics. While often referred to by the shorthand of "civil" or "intrastate" war, most contemporary armed conflicts do not observe sovereign boundaries. This is particularly true of their economic dimensions. As observed above, a distinguishing feature of these war economies is their intimate connection to the increasingly decentralized nature of global aid, trade, and finance. Both the supply and demand sides of war-making have become internationalized as combatants have exploited the opportunities inherent in weakly regulated national and global marketplaces to trade lucrative natural resources for war matériel and financing. Armed conflicts also exhibit varying degrees of regional economic embeddedness, depending on the will and capacity of national governments and neighboring states to control transborder movements. In most cases, such capacities are too weak to prevent the conventional spillover effects of refugee flows, rebel or state military incursions into border zones, and the consequent disruption of normal trade routes. In cases such as West Africa, the Democratic Republic of Congo (DRC), and Afghanistan, where mutually reinforcing transnational conflicts coalesce into regional conflict formations,[16] however, the integration of combatant groups and civilians into regional trade and commercial networks can acquire a more systematic character. Very often, these regional economic networks are an important avenue of access to global markets, a factor that multiplies the number of economic stakeholders in conflict, thereby posing an additional challenge for conflict resolution.

Finally, these studies seek to situate the economic dimensions of armed conflicts in relation to the degree of national state capacity. As has been widely observed, the relative capacity of the state to perform core functions, including the provision of security, effective governance throughout its territory, and the equitable distribution of public goods, has a direct bearing on the incidence of armed conflict. Indeed, weak and failing states have been identified as both cause and consequence of armed conflict. While the defining condition of a weak or failing state is subject to competing definitions among scholars, such states are minimally characterized by a loss of legitimacy and a loss of governing effectiveness in all or significant parts of their territory. These infirmities may give rise to conflict in a variety of ways, such as by unleashing security dilemmas or by revitalizing ethnic and communal competition.[17] Importantly, state weakness is a critical component of the opportunity structure that makes violent challenges militarily and economically feasible. At the most basic, where weak states are accompanied by a decline in military strength, the costs of insurgency borne by would-be challengers are less and the prospects for a relatively rapid victory are greater. Where state weakness is further associated with incomplete territorial reach and already large informal economies, the feasibility of launching and sustaining an insurgency is enhanced because of the expanded access it affords to income-generating resources and opportunities. From this perspective, the high risk of armed conflict that is now commonly attributed to natural resource–dependent countries is not a direct relationship, but one that is mediated by a critical failure of economic governance. As Jeffrey Herbst further suggests of recent cases of

conflict in Africa, resource-driven rebellions, with their attendant looting and predation, may be more a function of weakened states than of
the physical presence of lootable resources.[18]

As this last point highlights, to date, most of the scholarly and policy
attention to the economic dimensions and drivers of armed conflict has
focused on conflicts in Africa, notably Sierra Leone, Angola, Liberia, and
the DRC. Indeed, these conflicts have become the paradigmatic examples
of "greed-driven rebellion" and "resource war." Readers who have
already consulted the table of contents may well wonder why African
conflicts are not also the central focus of this volume. One reason is that
there is already a fairly large and well-developed body of empirical
research on these cases, which is widely familiar to conflict analysts and
policymakers.[19] Another, perhaps more intellectually compelling reason,
is that many of the main theoretical propositions regarding the role of
economic factors and the onset and duration of conflict—such as the role
of natural resources and the impact of globalization—claim to apply
beyond Africa to the current generation of armed intrastate conflicts. Yet
aside from a few studies of the economics of conflict in Indonesia and
Afghanistan, the relevance of this framework for understanding conflicts
in the rest of the world remains largely unexplored. On the one hand,
extending empirical investigations on the economic dimensions of conflicts in Europe, South and East Asia, South America, and the Pacific
may help to shed further light on the nature of these conflicts and their
resolution. On the other hand, because the historical, institutional, cultural, and economic endowments of these regions are distinct from each
other, as well as from those in Africa, they may offer new insights for
our understanding of the economic dynamics of armed conflict.

The majority of studies included in this volume concern separatist
conflicts. To date, theoretical and empirical investigations of the economic dimensions of conflict have been overwhelmingly confined to
classic insurgencies, where the central axis of conflict is the defense or
capture of state power, rather than the wholesale reconfiguration of the
boundary and identity of the state that defines separatist conflicts. In
turn, separatist conflicts have generally been analyzed under paradigms
in which identity politics, group dynamics, and state behavior are the
predominant explanatory variables.[20] In part, this conceptual and analytical gap may be due to the fact that there have been few separatist
conflicts in Africa, where attention to the economics of conflict first
emerged. It may also be a function of the fact that, in their most reduc-
tivist monocausal formulations, the ethnic conflict and the resource war
paradigms appear as mutually exclusive explanations. If wars are seen
to be caused by "ancient ethnic hatreds," there appears to be little room

for an independent role for economic factors, whether stylized as greed, grievance, or something else. However, separatist conflicts, no less than insurgencies, require economic resources and a favorable opportunity structure to proceed. Far from suggesting that all separatist conflicts are fundamentally contests over resources, an inquiry into the way that economic factors shape the emergence and progress of separatist conflicts may tell us something new about how these wars are being fought as well as something about the theoretical and empirical limitations of the resource war model.

This volume is divided into three parts. Part 1 consists of two comparative analytical studies that address some of the key propositions concerning the relationship between economics and conflict. In Chapter 2, Charles Cater revisits Angola, the Democratic Republic of Congo, and Sierra Leone—the paradigmatic African cases of "resource wars"—in order to provide a critical assessment of the relative merits of four explanatory frameworks—economic predation, kleptocracy, political protest, and weak states—for understanding the political economy of conflict as well as their implications for international policy and practice. In turn, he offers a modified conceptual framework that not only examines the interrelationship between economic and political causes, but also integrates complementary state-centric and rebel-centric theories. In Chapter 3, Michael Ross draws upon evidence from fifteen recent conflicts to develop and test a set of preliminary hypotheses concerning the varying impact of different types of natural resource endowments on the incidence and duration of conflict. In doing so, he draws out the different ways that natural resource exploitation affects separatist and nonseparatist conflicts. Ross's research indicates that certain natural resources are associated with a higher incidence of conflict than others and that lootable and nonlootable resources are associated with different types of conflict.

Part 2 is comprised of country-based case studies. Alexandra Guáqueta's analysis of the Colombian conflict in Chapter 4 shows how changes in the global and regional economies during the last decade have enabled both insurgent and paramilitary groups to capitalize upon the illegal narcotics trade, as well as kidnapping and extortion, to expand their military capacities as well as the territory under their control. While the conflict continues to be dominated by ideological differences and the deep-seated grievances of economically marginalized rural populations, her analysis demonstrates how the transformation of armed groups into "formidable money-making machines" has escalated the level of political violence and conflict-related crime, while also making this conflict one of the most resistant to peaceful resolution. In Chapter 5, John Bray, Leiv Lunde, and Mansoob Murshed examine the recent Maoist insurgency in Nepal. An impoverished country with few natural resource endowments, Nepal stands well outside the resource war model. In this case, the economic drivers of conflict stem from ethnic- and caste-based social frustration with chronic poverty, inequality, corruption, and the as yet unrealized promises of democratic reform. Yet as the authors also show, there are already signs of recourse to extortion and plunder among rank-and-file insurgents. Unless this conflict is resolved early, it has the potential of degenerating into predatory violence.

The subsequent chapters all deal with various aspects of the political economy of separatist conflicts. In Chapter 6, Anthony Regan looks at the case of Bougainville in Papua New Guinea, a classic instance of conflict in which a multinational mining venture has been at the center of a violent separatist struggle. As he demonstrates, this was a conflict in which economic, political, and ethnic agendas proved mutually reinforcing. While the violence unleashed by the Bougainville Revolutionary Army arose from grievances about the inequitable distribution of mine revenues, natural resource wealth did not make rebellion more feasible, nor have continuing disagreements over the future of mining precluded the peaceful resolution of the conflict. Bougainville's experience is in part consistent with Ross's analysis of how nonlootable resources may feed grievances that give rise to separatist conflict. However, in contrast to Ross, Regan suggests that the goal may not be for a redistribution of mining revenues, but for an end to mining altogether. In his examination of the Kosovo conflict in Chapter 7, Alexandros Yannis likewise demonstrates how political, ethnic, and economic exclusion coalesced into armed rebellion by the Kosovar Albanians against both the Serbian state and the Serbian inhabitants of Kosovo. While ethnic exclusion was the primary and enduring cause of this conflict, Yannis indicates how diaspora networks, state breakdown in neighboring Albania, and the already well-established shadow economy of Kosovo itself contributed to the Kosovo Liberation Army's capacity to mobilize against the Serbian state. He also offers an assessment of the internationally managed transitional administration, showing that, while laudable in most respects, it has been slow to address the economic criminality and illicit networks that, even in peacetime, continue to sustain nationalist militants, thereby undermining the larger international peacebuilding effort. In Chapter 8, the connection between international financial flows and separatist conflict is examined in the context of Sri Lanka. In this analysis, Rohan Gunaratna shows how the Tamil Tigers have skillfully exploited diaspora remittances as well as legitimate business ventures to sustain their conflict, while becoming a transnational corporation in their own right. Finally, in Chapter 9, Jake

Sherman explores how, in the case of Burma, certain ethnic minority insurgents as well as state and military agents have systematically exploited natural resources to further their military objectives and pecuniary interests. Following the logic of the resource war paradigm, Burma's abundant wealth of timber, gems, and opium would seem to provide ample fuel for violent struggle and would suggest a conflict impervious to peaceful resolution. In fact, however, the military regime has managed to secure cease-fire agreements with a majority of ethnic insurgent groups, some of which have endured for over a decade. It has done so not by cutting off insurgent access to economic resources, but by making their continued economic activities a quid pro quo for the cessation of hostilities. Backed, as these cease-fires are, by a credible threat for renewed counterinsurgency, and absent a comprehensive peace accord, the result has been a situation of "negative peace." As Sherman's analysis makes clear, however, economic inducements can be a powerful factor in ending violent conflict.

As stated at the outset, the purpose of undertaking these studies was to extend our empirical understanding of the economic dimensions of conflict so as to contribute to better-informed policy responses. Thus far, there is little agreement among conflict analysts as to whether gaining an analytical purchase on the economic dimensions of conflict makes the task of conflict resolution by outside intermediaries easier or more complex. This discussion is taken up in the concluding chapter, by Karen Ballentine, together with a synthetic distillation of the major policy implications of the chapter studies.

Notes

1. R. T. Naylor, *Economic Warfare: Sanctions, Embargo Busting, and Their Human Cost* (Boston: Northeastern University Press, 2001).

2. Seminal studies include Mats Berdal and David Malone, eds., *Greed and Grievance: Economic Agendas in Civil Wars* (Boulder: Lynne Rienner, 2000); Stephen Ellis, *The Masks of Anarchy: The Destruction of Liberia and the Religious Dimension of an African Civil War* (New York: New York University Press, 1999); David Keen, *The Economic Functions of Violence in Civil Wars,* Adelphi Paper no. 320 (Oxford: IISS/Oxford University Press, 1998); Michael Klare, *Resource Wars: The New Landscape of Global Conflict* (New York: Metropolitan Books, 2001); and William Reno, *Corruption and State Politics in Sierra Leone* (Cambridge: Cambridge University Press, 1995).

3. Mark Duffield, *Global Governance and the New Wars: The Merging of Security and Development* (London: Zed Books, 2001); and Mary Kaldor, *New and Old Wars: Organized Violence in a Global Era* (Stanford: Stanford University Press, 1999).

4. Mats Berdal and David Keen, "Violence and Economic Agendas in Civil Wars: Some Policy Implications," *Millennium: Journal of International Studies* 26, no. 3 (1997): 797. See also Duffield, *Global Governance*, pp. 137–140; Keen, *The Economic Functions of Violence*, p. 11; and Phillipe Le Billon, "The Political Economy of Resource Wars," in Jakkie Cilliers and Christian Dietrich, eds., *Angola's War Economy: The Role of Oil and Diamonds* (Pretoria: Institute of Security Studies, 2000), p. 30.

5. Kaldor, *New and Old Wars*, p. 11.

6. See Adekeye Adebajo, *Building Peace in West Africa: Liberia, Sierra Leone, and Guinea-Bissau* (Boulder: Lynne Rienner, 2002); and Chapters 4 and 9 in this volume.

7. David Keen, "Incentives and Disincentives for Violence," in Berdal and Malone, *Greed and Grievance*, p. 26.

8. Paul Collier, "Doing Well Out of War," in Berdal and Malone, *Greed and Grievance*, pp. 90–111; Paul Collier and Anke Hoeffler, "On the Economic Causes of War," *Oxford Economic Papers* 50, no. 4 (October 1998): 563–573; and Paul Collier and Anke Hoeffler, "Greed and Grievance in Civil War," October 21, 2001, available online at http://econ.worldbank.org/files/12205_greedgrievance_23oct.pdf (accessed January 2, 2003).

9. Collier, "Doing Well Out of War," p. 14.

10. Collier and Hoeffler, "Greed and Grievance in Civil War," pp. 3–7.

11. Koen Vlassenroot and Hans Romkema, "The Emergence of a New Order? Resources and War in Eastern Congo," *Journal of Humanitarian Assistance*, October 28, 2002, p. 1, available online at www.jha.ac/articles/a111.htm (accessed December 13, 2002).

12. For fuller consideration of this debate, see Ted Robert Gurr, "Containing Internal War in the Twenty-First Century," in Fen Osler Hampson and David M. Malone, eds., *From Reaction to Conflict Prevention: Opportunities for the UN System* (Boulder: Lynne Rienner, 2002), pp. 48–50; and João Gomes Porto, "Contemporary Conflict Analysis in Perspective," in Jeremy Lind and Kathryn Sturman, eds., *Scarcity and Surfeit: The Ecology of Africa's Conflicts* (Pretoria: Institute of Security Studies, 2002), pp. 6–16.

13. Most commonly, Collier's team has used "grievance" to designate political factors such as exclusion and repression, whereas "greed" refers to economic motivations. But "grievance" has also been associated with economic factors such as inequality. Some scholars have pointed out that a surfeit of undereducated young men, which Collier's team uses as an indicator of greed, may also be read as an indicator of grievance, thereby leaving unclear whether the terms capture mutually exclusive phenomena. To complicate matters, in the opportunity formulation, "greed" is now used as shorthand for a constraints-based theory of rebellion, as distinct from preference-based theories. See Macartan Humphreys, "Economics and Violent Conflict," August 2002, p. 4, n. 29, www.preventconflict.org/portal/economics/essay.pdf (accessed November 15, 2002); and Gomes Porto, "Contemporary Conflict Analysis," p. 15.

14. For a fuller discussion of how rebel leaders motivate followers, see Jeffrey Herbst, "Economic Incentives, Natural Resources, and Conflict in Africa," *Journal of African Economies* 9, no. 3 (2000): 270–294.

15. See D. Sandole, *Capturing the Complexity of Conflict: Dealing with Violent Ethnic Conflicts in the Post–Cold War Era* (London: Pinter, 1999); and Frances Stewart, "Horizontal Inequalities as a Source of Conflict," in Hampson

and Malone, *From Reaction to Conflict Prevention,* p. 107. See also Chapter 2 in this volume.

16. On regional conflict formations, see Peter Mwangi Kagwanja and Gloria Ntegeye, "Regional Conflict Formations in the Great Lakes of Africa: Dynamics and Challenges for Policy," Summary Report of the Nairobi Conference, November 2001, Center on International Cooperation, www.nyu.edu/pages/cic/pdf/rcf_nairobi.pdf (accessed December 17, 2002).

17. Sebastian von Einsiedel, "State Failure and the Crisis of Governance: Making States Work," Background Paper for the conference "Making States Work," International Peace Academy, November 2002, p. 4.

18. Jeffrey Herbst, "Economic Incentives," p. 286.

19. See endnote 1. Seminal policy-oriented analyses on the role of economic resources in African conflicts include Ian Smillie, Lansana Gberie, and Ralph Hazleton, *The Heart of the Matter: Sierra Leone, Diamonds, and Human Security* (Ottawa: Partnership Africa–Canada, January 2000); Global Witness, *A Rough Trade: The Role of Companies and Governments in the Angolan Conflict* (London: Global Witness, December 1988); Amnesty International, *Making a Killing: The Diamond Trade in Government-Controlled DRC* (London: Amnesty International, October 2002); Christian Aid, *The Scorched Earth: Oil and War in Sudan* (London: Russell Press, March 2001); and the UN Panels of Experts and Monitoring Mechanisms reports on sanctions violations in Sierra Leone, Angola, and Liberia, and on the illicit exploitation of natural resources in the DRC.

20. One notable exception is Kaldor, *New and Old Wars.* For a survey of dominant approaches to ethnic and separatist conflicts, see Michael E. Brown, *Nationalism and Ethnic Conflict* (Cambridge: MIT Press, 1997).

PART I

Economics and Conflict:
Exploring the Relationship

2

The Political Economy of Conflict and UN Intervention: Rethinking the Critical Cases of Africa

CHARLES CATER

THE END OF THE COLD WAR HAS GREATLY IMPACTED PATTERNS OF WAR AND peace in developing countries. In some cases, the end of military and financial support by the United States and the Soviet Union for proxy wars provided new opportunities for the resolution of previously intractable conflicts. In other cases, often in authoritarian client states, the withdrawal of external sources of patronage appears to have exacerbated instability, indirectly precipitating a new generation of civil wars. Conventional approaches to security studies typically concentrate on the military strategies combatants pursue to attain political goals, yet many of these "new wars" also seem to show explicit patterns of economically motivated violence.[1] Accordingly, Carl von Clausewitz's dictum has been rephrased to claim "war has increasingly become the continuation of economics by other means."[2] To many outsiders, some civil wars in Africa have become identified with an emerging economic, resource-based conceptual model of armed conflict. Notably, the *New York Times* has described the conflicts in Angola, Sierra Leone, and the Democratic Republic of Congo (DRC) as "Africa's diamond wars."[3]

Through reference to these three cases, this chapter examines the relative utility of competing explanations for the causal roles of economic factors in civil wars and highlights their implications for policy and practice by the UN and other international actors. The experience of UN intervention in the cases highlights not only the complexity and intractability of these wars, but also the hazards of policymaking influenced by potentially misleading assumptions about the nature of armed conflict, particularly excessive reliance on a paradigm of economic predation. Despite much contemporary debate regarding the relative merits of economic versus political approaches for explaining civil war, the cases suggest that a modified "political economy" approach more accurately reflects the realities of contemporary armed conflict. This conceptual framework not only examines the interrelationship between economic and political causes, but also integrates complementary state-centric and rebel-centric theories regarding economic predation, kleptocracy, political protest, and weak states. The cases also suggest that the interrelationships between political and economic dynamics change over the duration of the conflict and are therefore not easily captured by such shorthand as "resource war." Analogous to past academic trends that viewed African conflicts through one-dimensional prisms of either Cold War ideology or ethnicity, one must be wary of natural resource–centric reductionism. To adequately explain aspects of conflict like intensity and duration, other concepts must also be considered, including regionalization, privatization, and globalization.

This chapter is organized into the following sections: first, an overview of four theories on the causes of civil war; second, a brief history of conflict in Angola, Sierra Leone, and the DRC; third, an evaluation of the literature with reference to the case studies; fourth, an analysis of three relatively underemphasized dimensions of conflict within mainstream debate (regionalization, privatization, and globalization); and finally, an examination of four types of UN intervention (humanitarian assistance, mediation, peacekeeping, and sanctions) in the three cases.

Economic and Political Causes of Civil War

As a starting point, I have selected four of the leading theories for the causes of civil war. Two are predominantly economic in focus—economic predation and kleptocratic states—while two place greater emphasis on political factors—horizontal inequalities and weak states. Assessed independently, none of these theories is entirely economic or political in orientation. However, for the comparative purposes of this chapter, they have been categorized as either economic or political in relation to each other. The immediate goal is to outline the competing claims of economic versus political explanations for contemporary civil war in countries such as Angola, Sierra Leone, and the DRC.

Economic Causes

According to research by Paul Collier of the World Bank, civil wars are primarily caused by the feasibility of economic predation and the rational pursuit of economic self-interest, while having no relation to objective grievances.[4] The underlying assumption is that all societies have grievances, but only where there are opportunities for rebellion do societies experience civil war. In contrast to most academic research, Collier's analysis of forty-four civil wars from 1960 to 1999 finds relatively little correlation between the incidence of armed conflict and factors such as inequality, lack of democracy, and ethnic diversity. Rather, the most powerful risk factor is a high dependence upon primary commodity exports.[5] Natural resources are particularly salient because they typically remain a viable source of revenue during war (in contrast to most services and manufacturing), and as exports they may be more easily looted or taxed by rebels. According to Collier's model, other significant positive correlations with the probability of conflict include large diaspora populations, geographic dispersion, a prior history of war, low levels of education, high population growth, low average income, and economic decline.

William Reno argues that the chronic diversion of state economic resources through patronage networks leads to the creation of a "shadow state" and increases the risk of civil war.[6] The origins of contemporary intrastate conflicts can be traced to the Cold War, when political elites deliberately undermined formal bureaucratic institutions but were nonetheless kept in office by repression and the financial and military support of the superpowers. As these kleptocrats accrued massive personal wealth through state channels, the standard dichotomy between the private and the public realms effectively dissolved. In order to maintain power, rulers deliberately withdrew the provision of public goods such as security and economic stability—thereby instrumentalizing coercion and corruption. Initially, this minimized the material resources available to potential challengers, while creating loyalty among subject populations in exchange for continued access to patronage networks. According to Reno, fragmentation of shadow states—characterized by the rise of warlords—occurs when a ruler is no longer able to maintain control over these channels of wealth accumulation and distribution. In an insecure environment, rebel leaders have often organized their insurgencies through utilizing extortion in a manner analogous to those tactics employed by state rulers. As Reno notes, with the end of the Cold War, declining external support and increasing internal pressures led to the outbreak of new civil wars.

Political Causes

Frances Stewart proposes that civil wars are frequently caused by group perceptions of "horizontal inequality" that lead to organized violence for political purposes, particularly securing (or retaining) state power.[7]

Group identity may be constructed in terms of region, ethnicity, class, or religion. There are also four general sources of economic and political differentiation between groups: political participation, economic assets, employment and incomes, and social access and situation. A collective perception of an intergroup disparity within one or more of these dimensions constitutes horizontal inequality. Group mobilization for conflict usually results from situations of relative deprivation vis-à-vis other groups, but in some cases violence may be instigated by groups motivated to maintain their position of relative privilege. Stewart makes a clear distinction between horizontal inequality and vertical inequality, noting that the latter only accounts for inequality in private income distribution among individuals and therefore fails to capture the full range of underlying economic and political sources of violent conflict. Stewart concludes by placing horizontal inequality within a broader context, acknowledging that private costs and benefits, state capacity, and the availability of resources are also relevant explanatory variables.

Finally, Mohammed Ayoob theorizes that the erosion of legitimate authority and a lack of capacity for effective governance offer the best explanation for the cause of civil war in developing countries.[8] His theory is based upon an analysis of state formation, a process that is dependent upon a state's ability to monopolize the means of coercion, maintain order within its territory, and extract resources to finance the provision of public goods such as administration. State formation in developing countries has been characterized by disproportionate financial allocations to the military, an inability of political institutions to check military power, and a tendency to implement coercive strategies when confronted with problems of domestic insecurity. However, the underlying cause of disorder in these weak states stems from a lack of legitimate authority, not an excessive resort to the use of force per se (i.e., strong states can maintain order without resorting to the use of violence because they possess legitimacy). In some circumstances, the accelerated pace of contemporary state formation has caused crises that often exceed the capabilities of governments, which then leads to the generation of more conflicts and the further erosion of legitimacy among postcolonial regimes. Thus Ayoob concludes that the relationship between state failure and internal conflict is often cyclical, rather than merely a linear progression from the former to the latter.

Angola, Sierra Leone, and Zaire/DRC

The civil wars in Angola, Sierra Leone, and Zaire/DRC have deeply influenced current understandings by scholars and practitioners of the causal role played by economic factors in civil wars. At the same time, the severity of these conflicts and the failure of many outside interventions calls for a critical reassessment of theory, policy, and practice in this area. The following narratives provide a historical frame of reference.

Angola

Although Angola has been in a nearly constant state of war during the last four decades, characterizations of the conflict have changed over time, from a struggle for national liberation (1961–1974), to Cold War proxy conflict (1975–1991), to a resource-based civil war (1992–2002). During the 1960s the illegitimacy of Portuguese rule prompted the creation of three rival nationalist movements: the União Nacional para a Independência Total de Angola (UNITA), the Frente Nacional para a Libertação de Angola (FNLA), and the Movimento para a Libertação de Angola (MPLA). These insurgent groups competed for control of the capital and the country as November 11, 1975, the date for official Portuguese withdrawal and Angolan independence, approached. Military support for the FNLA and UNITA by the United States, South Africa, and Zaire prompted Cuban and Soviet support for the MPLA—resulting in a protracted conflict where a relatively fluid transition to independence had once been at least hypothetically possible. With the end of the Cold War, the drying up of superpower financing, the withdrawal of foreign troops, the signing of the Bicesse Accords in 1991, and the establishment of a UN presence, there was hope that Angola's civil war would finally be resolved.

However, rather than achieving sustainable peace, the country returned to war in September 1992 after "free and fair" UN-supervised democratic elections in which Eduardo Dos Santos of the ruling MPLA defeated Jonas Savimbi of UNITA for the presidency. The belligerent parties replaced financing from external state patronage by expanding multibillion-dollar exports of natural resources, with UNITA deriving income from diamonds and the state receiving funds from oil. Facing subsequent military reversals against a rearmed MPLA regime, UNITA then agreed to the Lusaka Protocol in November 1994. The number of casualties during this two-year phase of combat, estimated at 300,000 deaths, may have been more than the total from the entire Cold War era of conflict from 1975 to 1991.[9] The next four years were marked by sporadic low-intensity conflict—particularly in the diamond-producing areas of the country—but an absence of the previously dominant type of total warfare. In December 1998, frustrated with UNITA's failure to abide by the terms of the peace agreement, the state resumed all-out war. With the death of Jonas Savimbi in February 2002 and the surrender of

UNITA, the government appears to have resolved the conflict through armed force.

Sierra Leone

Unlike Angola, Sierra Leone's independence from the United Kingdom in 1961 was followed by a period of relatively stable democratic governance until a series of three coups d'état in 1967 and 1968. Siaka Stevens, who initially entered into office through the ballot box, eventually regained power and then remained in office for seventeen years, officially creating a one-party state in 1977. In 1985, Stevens was followed by Major-General Joseph Momoh, his military commander and handpicked successor. Both the Stevens and Momoh regimes were highly kleptocratic, coercive, and unpopular. Sierra Leone's situation became progressively worse in the latter half of the 1980s as fiscal crisis led to a deterioration of the public infrastructure, increased unemployment, and the near total collapse of core state institutions such as the educational system and the military. The violent end of U.S. client Samuel Doe's brutal reign and the outbreak of civil war in nearby Liberia then provided the catalyst for the instigation of rebellion in Sierra Leone.

The Revolutionary United Front (RUF), led by Corporal Foday Sankoh and supported by Liberian warlord Charles Taylor, invaded Sierra Leone in March 1991. In April 1992, Captain Valentine Strasser staged a military takeover, while the RUF escalated its offensives in diamond-producing areas and recruited more rebels. In January 1996, Brigadier-General Julius Maada Bio took power and then ceded control to President Ahmed Kabbah after democratic elections in March 1996. In January 1997, under pressure from the International Monetary Fund (IMF), President Kabbah ended the contract of the corporate mercenary firm Executive Outcomes, which had been employed by successive regimes since 1995. Kabbah promptly lost power in a coup d'état four months later to Major Johnny Paul Koroma of the Armed Forces Revolutionary Council (AFRC), who then formed an alliance with the RUF. It was not until February 1998 that troops of the Economic Community of West African States Cease-Fire Monitoring Group (ECOMOG) were able to retake Freetown and reinstate Kabbah. By 1999 the war in Sierra Leone had caused 75,000 deaths (mostly civilians), more than 500,000 refugees, and the internal displacement of half the country's 4.5 million population.[10] In July 1999, Kabbah and Sankoh signed the Lomé Peace Accord, but combat resumed as the RUF tried to capture the capital city. The UN Assistance Mission in Sierra Leone (UNAMSIL), substantially reinforced by British troops, eventually managed to establish control over most of the country. Kabbah was reelected in May 2002.

Zaire/DRC

Upon independence from Belgium in 1960 the Congo descended into civil war. Independence leader Patrice Lumumba was assassinated with the collusion of the CIA in 1961, and Washington's client, General Joseph Mobutu, managed to consolidate his hold on power by 1965. Over the next three decades, the Mobutu regime both created and perpetuated cycles of popular opposition and state repression through its own omnipresent practices of coercion and theft.[11] Unsuccessful challenges to Mobutu's power included a rebellion by mercenaries in 1967 and secessionist insurrections in the mineral-rich Shaba region in 1977 and 1978. Mobutu's reign managed to survive these threats at least partially due to the continued military aid and diplomatic backing of his patrons—Belgium, France, and the United States.[12] However, by the end of the Cold War, due to decades of human rights abuse, widespread poverty, and a nearly total collapse of state functions, including the security sector, Zaire was on the verge of political and economic implosion. The genocide in Rwanda and the subsequent refugee crisis in eastern Zaire precipitated the outbreak of civil war in 1996 and the eventual downfall of Mobutu in 1997.

Rebel leader Laurent Kabila and the Alliance des Forces Démocratiques pour la Libération du Congo (AFDL) were backed militarily by Uganda and Rwanda (both of which had border security concerns in the wake of genocide), financially supported by the mining company American Mineral Fields (which wanted to protect its concessions and expand its opportunities), and joined by local ethnic groups, including the Tutsi, Katangans, and Mai-Mai.[13] The rebellion faced markedly little opposition from the Zairian armed forces and seized Kinshasa in May 1997. After a brief interlude, war restarted in August 1998 when Kabila cut domestically unpopular ties with former patrons Rwanda and Uganda. The two countries invaded the now renamed DRC in support of incipient anti-Kabila rebel coalitions, the Rassemblement Congolais pour la Démocratie (RCD) and the Mouvement de Libération du Congo (MLC). Zimbabwe, Angola, and Namibia sent troops in defense of the DRC state. Approximately 30,000 foreign troops (about 15,000 soldiers on each side) have been deployed during this second phase of war.[14] In July 1999 the parties agreed to the Lusaka Peace Accord and in February 2000 the UN Security Council authorized a mission with about 5,000 peacekeepers (later reduced to 3,000). The humanitarian cost of this conflict has been staggering: an estimated 2 million Congolese have died from war-related disease and starvation. Despite a recent peace agreement between Rwanda and the DRC, the crucial issue of disarming tens of thousands of Interahamwe and former members of the Rwandan military responsible for genocide in 1994 has not been adequately addressed.[15]

State Failure, Insurgency, and Transformation

In this section, the four economic and political theories summarized above are assessed in light of the three African cases. Reno and Ayoob explain the political economy of state failure, which provides a structural opportunity for civil war. In contrast, Collier and Stewart explain the political economy of mobilizing the requisite human and material resources for insurgency (i.e., why, how, and when people rebel). As the cases demonstrate, both state-centric and rebel-centric models are complementary. Furthermore, because processes of social, economic, and political change during civil war cannot be adequately explained by static models, theories and analysis of conflict transformation are also considered.

State Failure

The concept of the shadow state proposed by Reno is relevant to all three cases outlined above. This is perhaps not surprising, as Reno's theory was developed to explain the decades of kleptocracy during the Stevens and Momoh regimes, which created a context of economic decline and state collapse conducive to the instigation of Sierra Leone's RUF insurgency in 1991.[16] Likewise, Mobutu was perhaps the world's prototypical kleptocrat, reportedly having personal control over U.S.$6 billion as of 1992, an amount larger than Zaire's annual economic output at the time.[17] According to political scientist Michael Schatzberg, insecurity and scarcity became the "twin motors driving a dialectic of oppression."[18] In both Sierra Leone and the DRC, growth of the shadow state ultimately weakened important formal institutions including the military, created widespread opposition to incumbent regimes, and served as the source of its own collapse. In Angola, the systematic diversion of state funds by an unaccountable MPLA military and political elite has precluded the provision of public goods and services necessary for good governance, social welfare, and economic growth. However, the rise of a shadow state in Angola may have primarily been a result rather than a cause per se of internal conflict.

Like Reno, Ayoob argues that the fundamental source of disorder in developing countries is structural. He observes a cyclical relationship between state failure, precipitated by a lack of legitimate authority, and internal conflict. This appears to be applicable in the cases of Angola, Sierra Leone, and the DRC—for instance, the decline of formal institutions of the Zairian state, the fall of Mobutu, and the rise of Kabila during the 1996–1997 civil war. However, rather than fundamentally reforming the state and attaining a measure of domestic legitimacy, Kabila engaged in many of the same tactics of oppression as his predecessor. This triggered the formation of new opposition groups opposed to the government and to the reemergence of conflict in 1998. Likewise, in Sierra Leone, only one of five different leaders during the 1990s came to power through a democratic process—nor could the other four claim a popular mandate within the country. Finally, while Angola is clearly less of a failed state than either the DRC or Sierra Leone, it nonetheless serves as a stark reminder that many African countries still do not pass the primary criteria of empirical (as opposed to juridical) statehood: monopolizing the means of coercion, maintaining order within its territory, and extracting resources for the provision of the public good. From a macrohistorical perspective, as Ayoob reluctantly concludes, this does not bode well for the future prospects of peace on the continent.

Insurgency

The work of Frances Stewart provides a useful framework for discerning aspects of group mobilization for rebellion. Horizontal inequality does a very good job of accounting for the outbreak of anticolonial war in Angola during the 1960s, but with a nearly exclusive focus upon domestic actors it is considerably less convincing for explaining the perpetuation of conflict in the country since independence in 1975. In Sierra Leone, construction of identity in terms of class may have been most salient, although the most important sources of differentiation leading to RUF mobilization likely included unemployment and a lack of access to education. In Zaire/DRC, identity was primarily constructed according to regional and ethnic criteria, although sources of differentiation leading to rebel mobilization were probably factors, such as poverty and a lack of personal security. Horizontal inequality also explains some aspects of the large-scale violence in Rwanda and Liberia that subsequently served as a catalyst for the outbreak of conflict in Zaire and Sierra Leone. These observations highlight both the main asset and the biggest liability of Stewart's theory. Horizontal inequality is so broadly construed that it can potentially be applied to virtually any intrastate conflict, but having such conceptual breadth can also entail a trade-off in terms of sacrificing analytic utility.

Explaining the mobilization of material resources for insurgency requires adaptation of the economic predation model proposed by Paul Collier. His regression analysis of forty-four civil wars during the period from 1965 to 1999 appears to have some predictive utility with regard to the incidence of conflict in Angola, Sierra Leone, and the DRC. Of the variables identified as having a positive correlation with the incidence of war, including high resource dependency, high geographic dispersion, low levels of education, fast population growth, and economic decline, these countries score high in every category except one (they do not have large diaspora populations residing in developed countries to fund an insurgency). All three states are heavily dependent upon primary commodity exports, which were ultimately used to finance armed conflict. However, whereas Collier's tabulation of statistical probabilities may be convincing, the causal arguments advanced to explain these correlations are nonetheless flawed. Collier is correct to suggest that all insurgencies require material resources, but his a priori assumption that all societies have grievances and would therefore erupt into civil war if given the right mix of opportunities ignores a crucial variable: governance. Arguably, this may be the essential difference between peaceful resource-rich developing states, such as Botswana, and those that have been prone to civil war. As Jeffrey Herbst argues, the viability and form of a rebel movement can only be properly determined in relation to the capacity of the state it is challenging.[19]

Transformation

The preceding analysis of theories based on state failure and insurgency suggests that, although they are not without flaws, both have some relevance to explanations of armed conflict in Angola, Sierra Leone, and the DRC. Rather than insisting upon an artificial dichotomy between political and economic causes of conflict maintained by rival academic disciplines, both must be viewed as part of the political economy of armed conflict. Empirical evidence suggests a high degree of market and state interdependence at the macro level, as well as a complex mix of economic and political motivations at a micro level.[20]

Yet the political economy of civil wars also continually changes over time, yielding different functions of violence at different points throughout the duration of the conflict. As David Keen notes, "Increasingly, civil wars that appear to have begun with political aims have mutated into conflicts in which short-term economic benefits are paramount."[21] Thus, conflicts could be conceived as changing from one type to another type (e.g., from national liberation to Cold War proxy to resource-based conflict in Angola). However, it is also important to recognize that civil wars are neither unilinear nor teleological. In other words, conflicts do not always proceed along the same trajectory, from one stage to another stage, toward a common predetermined outcome. A case in point: few analysts or policymakers anticipated the apparent reemergence of RUF political ambitions in 2000, as shown by their rejection of a lucrative peace process and the launch of a risky military offensive to capture the capital city of Sierra Leone. RUF motivations appeared to transition from political to economic then back to political. If economic and political motivations had not been regarded as an "either or," but as concurrent, this chain of events would likely have been far less surprising.

As implied above, the armed conflicts examined herein cannot adequately be explained by the uniform logic implied by such shorthand as "resource war." Contrary to some prevailing arguments, conflict in these countries was not *caused* by the exploitation of natural resources by rebel groups. In Angola, high levels of commodity dependence did not initially cause civil war; instead, increasing reliance upon natural resources by both the state and UNITA has been a consequence of protracted conflict as other sectors of the economy were progressively destroyed. In Sierra Leone and the DRC, chronic mismanagement of natural resources by the state did contribute to grievances and generate opposition, but only later did the commonly asserted pattern of natural resource exports financing insurgency become a salient dimension of these conflicts. Conventional wisdom suggests that commodity-based conflicts will intensify commensurate with increasing dependence upon natural resource exploitation for funding. This has been true in some cases, such as Angola from 1992 to 1994. Yet as the following section of this chapter shows, closer examination yields a more ambiguous relationship where commercial collusion often coexists with ostensible military goals. This again implies that economic and political motivations for armed conflict are not mutually exclusive. As for conflict duration, the conventional wisdom appears to have proved correct for these three cases: natural resource exploitation by rebel, government, and external forces did "fuel" these civil wars.

Regionalization, Privatization, and Globalization

The generally accepted definition of a "civil war" is an intrastate conflict of at least one year in length, with at least 1,000 combat-related deaths, where both state and rebel forces sustain casualties. According to this definition, patterns of conflict in Angola, Sierra Leone, and the DRC easily exceed the minimum technical standards for what constitutes a civil war. Analyses of civil wars also typically operate under the core assumption that a "civil war" is a closed system of violence between domestic actors. However, explaining certain aspects of *internal* conflict, including intensity and duration, also requires exploring dynamics contingent upon linkages with *external* processes of regionalization, privatization, and globalization.

Regionalization

Regional dimensions of conflict are highly evident in these three cases. War in Zaire/DRC demonstrates significant regionalization and a corresponding erosion of territorial sovereignty among African states. While Laurent Kabila's rise to power in Zaire depended upon the active participation of regular Ugandan and Rwandan troops, subsequently there have been no fewer than five external states actively involved in the second phase of this conflict. Angola's intervention in the DRC, undertaken in order to deprive UNITA of a rear base, demonstrates how civil wars can spill over into regional conflict complexes. Likewise, the fate of Sierra Leone has been inextricably linked to Liberia's own civil war and Charles Taylor's backing of the RUF insurgency, as well as to the intervention by Nigeria, the regional hegemonic power, in the form of an ECOMOG peacekeeping operation. There are also other more covert but equally important regional dimensions of these conflicts, including the intervention of South African mercenary firms and the involvement of continentwide criminal brokerage networks engaged in sanctions evasion and war profiteering. Nonetheless, as the political economy of the Great Lakes region illustrates, not all cross-border trade of goods is necessarily based on a military objective or a profit motive: for many Congolese civilians, the extraction and trafficking of commodities is the only means available for survival.[22]

Regionalization among these three conflicts is significant for several reasons. Large-scale violence in one country may exacerbate tensions in a nearby state and subsequently facilitate the outbreak of an interrelated civil war (e.g., Rwanda/Zaire and Liberia/Sierra Leone). The cause of instability need not be directly military; for example, Kabila's insurgency was initially triggered by large-scale refugee flows from neighboring countries. Direct military intervention by regional states, as in the DRC, not only increases the number of actors, but also inherently increases the complexity of the conflict, with the result that diplomatic efforts to resolve conflict are considerably more difficult.

Furthermore, the cross-border trafficking of natural resources, arms, and other commodities may lead to a "mutually profitable stalemate" and cycles of conflict perpetuation.[23] Finally, as an organization composed of juridically sovereign states, the UN has only recently recognized the regional dimensions of these civil wars and the complicity of its own member states. Thus the transnational criminal networks that both satisfy and sustain market demand for the means of war in Africa remain a problem.

Privatization

The personal pursuit of financial incentives by rebel groups and state elites can create situations where economic and political collusion between supposed rivals can coexist with armed conflict. In Angola, much of the violence witnessed in the diamond fields since the Lusaka Protocol, often directed at civilians dependent upon illicit mining for subsistence, reflects the aim among rebel and government elites to control production and trade in these areas.[24] Some individual military commanders have prioritized commercial collusion over prosecution of their respective war efforts—at times resulting in enclaves of relative peace between UNITA and the Angolan armed forces.[25] Assessing conflict in Sierra Leone strictly in terms of military criteria could be likewise misleading. The RUF often attacked farmers and miners rather than directly engaging government forces or Nigerian ECOMOG peacekeepers. At the same time, government troops frequently collaborated with the rebels for personal profit—thus giving rise to the expression "sobels" (i.e., "soldiers by day, rebels by night"). The net effect of these patterns is that violence is often directed at civilians to extort their labor and property, yielding a lengthy self-financing conflict with high civilian casualties. Economic opportunities may also create command and control problems within state militaries and rebel groups, making conflict resolution and peacekeeping efforts more difficult. The pursuit or protection of such activities may contradict the aims of the combatant party as a whole, potentially undermining a group's cohesion.

As for private-sector actors, the rise of corporate mercenary firms and their linkage with "junior" natural resource extraction corporations has been primarily a post–Cold War development. The South African company Executive Outcomes (EO) worked for the Angolan state from 1993 until 1996 and for successive governments in Sierra Leone from 1995 to 1997. In each case, EO reportedly leveraged the insecurity of the state in order to obtain mining concessions below market rate for resource extraction firms with its corporate network, such as Branch

Mining. Upon EO's departure from each country of operation, affiliated security firms such as Life Guard were then put into place to protect newly acquired material assets.[26] Rival security-service/resource-extraction networks include the pairing of International Defence and Security (IDAS) and American Mineral Fields (AMF). AMF financing in the former Zaire was instrumental in Kabila's overthrow of Mobutu in 1997. Interestingly, AMF was backing both sides, as it had just previously negotiated a mining deal with Mobutu as well. Not to be outdone, Kabila reneged AMF's concessions and kept the money after attaining state power.[27] There are two main conclusions to be drawn: corporate mercenary firms and "junior" resource extraction corporations may work for states, but they also won't hesitate to abandon or undermine them if profitable; and governments often risk mortgaging the long-term development prospects of their countries in exchange for short-term security assistance.

Globalization

War in Angola, Sierra Leone, and the DRC has also shown a high degree of integration into the global economy. Yet rather than positively influencing economic growth and national development, these ties may be increasing both the intensity and the duration of violence.[28] In order to maintain world price levels, the DeBeers cartel has had a long and controversial history of buying "conflict diamonds" originating from rebel-held territories in countries such as Angola and Sierra Leone—diamonds purchased overwhelmingly by Western consumers. Likewise, coltan, a crucial mineral used in the production of cell phones and laptop computers, has become a main commodity in the war economy of the DRC.[29] Most prominently, oil exports from Angola have financed capital-intensive militarization by the state, while filling the bank accounts of corrupt political elites. The nongovernmental organization Global Witness estimates that nearly one-third of Angola's multibillion-dollar annual oil revenue is routinely being diverted into "parallel budgets of the shadow state."[30] Moreover, some of the largest transnational corporations (TNCs) in the world, including ChevronTexaco and Total-FinaElf, have a considerable financial stake in Angola, consequently influencing the foreign policy of their home governments. Washington and Paris apparently consider oil exports from Angola to be a matter of national interest: the U.S. government has facilitated state-backed loans, political risk insurance, and corporate mercenary contracts for U.S. oil TNCs, while the French government has been implicated at the highest levels in the arms-for-oil "Angolagate" scandal.[31]

Mark Duffield has suggested that violent conflict in countries such as Angola, Sierra Leone, and the DRC is not the temporary result of a "developmental malaise," but rather indicative of a "durable disorder" where insecurity and underdevelopment are inseparable and cyclical aspects of globalization.[32] The natural resources exported from these wars, including oil, diamonds, and coltan, have little intrinsic worth; it is only within the context of the international market that they have value. Likewise, the arms used in these wars are typically not manufactured in Africa, but rather in the industrialized countries of the world, including the permanent five (P-5) members of the UN Security Council. Hence in examining the causes of conflict, one must not only concentrate on the supply of natural resources and the demand for arms among developing countries, but also examine the demand for natural resources and the supply of arms among developed countries. Emphasizing the political dimensions of this global equation, David Keen has recently noted: "'Interventions' are not simply something that 'the West' or the 'international community' does to remedy humanitarian disasters once they occur; more often than not, interventions occur prior to the disaster, perhaps helping to precipitate it."[33] Recognizing the economic and political interests at stake (or conversely, the lack thereof) among powerful states is thus a prerequisite for assessing UN intervention in Africa and the prospects for reform.

UN Intervention

There are serious questions to be considered with respect to how well the UN is suited for intervention in conflicts such as Angola, Sierra Leone, and the DRC. Past experience suggests that policymaking in the Security Council is typically subject to the priorities of dominant member states, particularly the P-5. A nebulous conception of the common good (as implied by frequent reference to the "international community") is not without some basis, but it is most often subordinated to P-5 national interests. Likewise, the organizational culture of the UN Secretariat often leads to defining conflicts according to the limited means available for intervention and pursuing expedient rather than durable solutions to complex problems.[34] As the following discussion indicates, UN interventions in Angola, Sierra Leone, and the DRC need to be improved. But this requires a realistic grasp of the obstacles to be overcome—not only in Africa but also in New York.

Humanitarian Assistance

As earlier sources of Cold War patronage for states and rebel groups declined during the 1990s, competition for scarce resources in conflict zones increasingly led to the appropriation of humanitarian assistance by combatants. According to critics, the provision of aid supplies and their subsequent diversion for commercial benefit by state militaries and rebel groups have often served to perpetuate violent conflict. In response, some practitioners have suggested that humanitarian aid should instead be selectively distributed according to political criteria, arguing that unintended consequences could thus be avoided and humanitarian assistance could instead be a force for peacebuilding. However, according to David Shearer, both critics and proponents of international humanitarian assistance may have overstated their cases: relief aid neither perpetuates war nor contributes to peacebuilding to the degree typically claimed.[35]

The refugee crisis in the former Zaire has been mistakenly cited as a clear example of how relief aid perpetuates or even causes conflict. In the wake of the Rwandan genocide, more than 1 million Hutus fled across the border—including innumerable Interahamwe militia members and former government troops. Since no effort was made to separate these armed elements from the general refugee population, the *genocidaires* substantially benefited from the distribution of humanitarian aid. Meanwhile, the refugee camps were used as a staging ground for attacks against nearby Zairian ethnic Tutsis as well as for periodic incursions back into Rwanda. In response, international actors merely continued to defer to the ill-equipped, underpaid, and often complicit Zairian armed forces. Thus, growing border insecurity became a plausible rationale for Rwanda's crucial military backing of Kabila's AFDL rebellion to overthrow Mobutu. In retrospect, the fundamental mistake by international actors was not the provision of humanitarian aid per se, but an unwillingness to undertake the steps required for security in the refugee camps.

While the example above indicates some of the risks involved with providing relief aid in the absence of adequate security, Angola and Sierra Leone highlight both the limits and the necessity of humanitarian assistance. In these conflicts, diamonds were a far more lucrative source of financing for continued military activity than the appropriation of relief aid, implying the potential ineffectiveness of manipulating relief supplies as a lever for peacebuilding where viable alternative resources exist. When humanitarian aid to Sierra Leone was cut off by comprehensive Economic Community of West African States (ECOWAS) sanctions, the most significant impact was civilian starvation, not rebel capitulation.[36] Likewise, the inability of humanitarian agencies to gain access to much of Angolan territory since 1998 (combined with a regional drought and the destruction of crops by government troops) has currently put the lives of between 500,000 and 1 million people at serious risk of death by starvation.[37] Both cases therefore illustrate the unacceptably high humanitarian cost of failing to provide relief assistance during conflicts. At best, humanitarian aid remains a necessary but insufficient form of intervention—analogous to treating the symptoms rather than the causes of civil war.

Conflict Resolution and Mediation

During the Cold War, mediation of intrastate conflicts often hinged upon the relevant commitment to peace (or war) of superpower patrons who could exert pressure upon their local proxies. In contrast, contemporary civil wars with comparatively autonomous sources of financing, including natural resource extraction, appear to be particularly resistant to the effects of outside mediation.[38] Furthermore, coupled with the lack of an ideological rationale that once held together earlier anticolonial movements, proliferating opportunities for war profiteering have resulted in erratic command, control, and cohesion among contemporary forces. This unpredictability can make determinations of leadership and motivation even more difficult to discern. For example, do members of rebel groups engage in the extraction of commodities for survival, profit, political change, or some combination of these factors? The answer has important implications for third-party mediation; if the analysis is flawed, the peace proposals probably will be as well.

The future management of natural resources is a core dilemma for conflict mediation in states dependent upon commodity exports. Faced with the withdrawal of Nigerian ECOMOG troops and under heavy pressure from U.S. envoy Reverend Jesse Jackson, President Kabbah of Sierra Leone signed the Lomé Peace Agreement in July 1999. The agreement was essentially premised on a twofold Faustian bargain to buy peace: granting an "absolute and free pardon" to all combatants and rewarding RUF elites with continued access to the country's diamonds.[39] The deal was particularly advantageous for Foday Sankoh, as his death sentence was commuted and he became chair of the Commission for the Management of Strategic Resources, National Reconstruction, and Development. To observers who saw Sankoh as an avaricious warlord, the agreement reached at Lomé may have been repugnant, but from an economic predation paradigm it nonetheless seemed logical. However, rather than being content with the substantial peace dividend, the RUF shortly thereafter abandoned the peace process, attacked UN peacekeepers, and launched an assault on Freetown in a bid to capture full political power. A poorly conceived peace agreement—concluded under conditions where President Kabbah had few other viable options—led to neither peace nor justice for the people of Sierra Leone.

In Angola, throughout negotiations for the 1994 Lusaka Protocol, the issue of diamond revenue allocation was considered too sensitive for inclusion in the peace agreement. Instead the government and UNITA preferred to hold these discussions on a purely bilateral basis. The mediators (the UN and the troika of the United States, Russia, and Portugal) concurred on the grounds that the Lusaka Protocol would not have been possible otherwise.[40] Unfortunately, this unresolved point of contention subsequently served to undermine the peace process: UNITA resisted the extension of government administration into diamond-producing territories and the government restarted the war in December 1998. Devolution to the warring parties on the issue of future diamond revenue allocation may have made peace possible in the short term but unsustainable in the long term.

Peacekeeping

The review of UN peace operations, chaired by former Algerian foreign minister Lakhdar Brahimi, identified several challenges for peace implementation, including the presence of "three or more parties, of varying commitment to peace, with divergent aims, with independent sources of income and arms, and with neighbors who are willing to buy, sell, and transit illicit goods."[41] The experience of the UN in Angola, Sierra Leone, and the DRC must have directly affected this observation. As implied above, the regionalization, privatization, and globalization of these conflicts rendered them problematic for UN intervention—particularly peacekeeping operations. Unfortunately, the Security Council, consistent with a pattern of severe global inequity in terms of peacekeeping expenditures, has typically authorized underfinanced and inadequate deployments in response to African wars. The disjuncture between extremely demanding mission requirements and limited capabilities affects all UN peacekeeping operations to some degree, yet it has been exceptionally acute in these three conflicts.

With an intensification of natural resource exploitation in Angola, the level of military expenditures increased and the prospects for an effective UN peacekeeping intervention correspondingly decreased. After the 1992–1994 war, the third UN Angolan Verification Mission (UNAVEM III), a peacekeeping operation of more than 7,000 troops, was established to implement the Lusaka Protocol. UNAVEM III was meant to be a significant improvement over its predecessor, which had shown little ability to deter the outbreak of war in 1992. However, during the mid-1990s the Angolan government and UNITA continued military procurements worth several billion dollars through the export of diamonds and oil to the global market. Thus UNAVEM III, understaffed and comparatively ill equipped, was unable to pressure either side to comply with the peace agreement, let alone serve as a credible deterrent force. Due to UN financial constraints, UNAVEM III was replaced with the skeletal 1,000-member UN Observer Mission in Angola (MONUA) in 1997. Full-scale war resumed the following year.

The privatization and regionalization of conflict have proved to be significant obstacles for UNAMSIL and the UN Organization Mission in the Democratic Republic of Congo (MONUC). Following the Lomé Peace Agreement, the initial deployment of 6,000 UNAMSIL peacekeepers could adequately protect neither Freetown nor themselves. RUF rebels, funded through diamond exports and sponsorship from Charles Taylor's regime in Liberia, attacked UN forces and maimed civilians with extreme brutality. The peace process in Sierra Leone was salvaged only through the subsequent intervention of UK troops. In the DRC, the active participation of Rwanda, Uganda, Zimbabwe, Angola, and Namibia has prompted some observers to call the conflict "Africa's first world war."[42] Struggles to control and exploit natural resource–rich areas of eastern DRC have led to fragmentation of the Uganda/Rwanda alliance opposing Kabila. Exports of gold, diamonds, coltan, and other natural resources have dramatically increased during what Rwandan president Paul Kagame has termed a "self-financing war." Zimbabwean defense officials and troops also have an economic stake in perpetuating the war, having received mining concessions and bonuses in exchange for their support of the DRC government.[43] Most important, the presence of thousands of Hutu Interahamwe militia and former members of the Forces Armées Rwandaises (FAR) responsible for the genocide remains a significant challenge to the peace effort in the DRC.[44] It is unclear how MONUC, with a few thousand peacekeepers, will effectively guarantee the peace.

Sanctions Regimes

Prior to 1990, the UN had only authorized sanctions twice—for Rhodesia in 1966 and for South Africa in 1977. During the 1990s, the Security Council approved sanctions relating to conflicts in twelve different countries.[45] Due to evidence that comprehensive sanctions are often counterproductive or inefficient, the use of targeted or "smart" sanctions is increasingly thought of as an attractive option within UN circles. They are perceived as a way for the UN to influence intrastate conflicts without overtly jeopardizing the institution's public stance of impartiality or incurring the risks and costs associated with alternative forms of intervention, such as peacekeeping operations. Some targeted sanctions, particularly those related to the export of natural resources, represent an explicit effort on the part of the UN to influence the economic incentives of combatants, particularly insurgent groups. The underlying logic appears to be that civil wars can best be resolved through influencing the decisionmaking calculus of rebel leaders and the flow of commodities upon which (it is assumed) they depend to perpetuate conflict.

Sanctions have not been authorized or implemented with regard to war in the DRC, but the UN's expert panel report does merit scrutiny. The panel's inquiry defined "illegality" and its mandate in terms of existing regulatory frameworks, widely accepted business practices, principles of international law, and national sovereignty. The last point has been the most politically contentious: "All activities—extraction, production, commercialization, and exports—taking place in the Democratic Republic of Congo without the consent of the legitimate government are illegal . . . only non-invited forces and their nationals are carrying out illegal activities in the Democratic Republic of Congo."[46] The panel recommended a full range of sanctions: an embargo on selected natural resource exports from Rwanda, Uganda, and Burundi; the freezing of financial assets for rebels, companies, and individuals involved in illegal commerce; and a weapons embargo on rebel groups as well as their state patrons. Not surprisingly, Rwanda and Uganda strenuously objected to the findings of the report, protesting that their client rebel groups were being victimized by the UN's state-oriented bias (a point only heard clearly in international diplomatic circles because Rwanda and Uganda are themselves members of this club of sovereign states). As for why the panel's recommendations have not yet been adopted, one theory is that the Security Council has realized that the proposed sanctions regime would not be an effective step toward peace in the DRC. Alternatively, the governments identified as targets for sanctions, Rwanda and Uganda, are supported militarily by a P-5 member, the United States.

Sierra Leone has been subjected to a series of ECOWAS and UN sanctions dating back to the military coup d'état in 1997. More recently, in an attempt to cut off the revenue base of the RUF, the Security Council prohibited member states from importing all rough diamonds from Sierra Leone with Resolution 1306 in July 2000.[47] According to a UN estimate in December 2000, the value of RUF trade in diamonds ranged from U.S.$25 million to U.S.$125 million per year.[48] As discussed earlier, most of the RUF export of diamonds has been trafficked through

Liberia in exchange for arms and other supplies. In response, Resolution 1343 approved sanctions on Liberia in March 2001—the first time the UN Security Council imposed "secondary sanctions" against a state for violating a sanctions regime relating to another state. This could signify the UN's effective adaptation to regional conflict dynamics. The sanctions regime and a new governmental certification scheme for rough diamonds may have helped curtail the RUF's income, but smuggling still persists on a large scale. Nonetheless, facing battlefield setbacks against British forces and diminishing support from Taylor in Liberia, the RUF has been more amenable to negotiation, signing a cease-fire in November 2000 and ceding territory to UNAMSIL the following year.[49]

As for Angola, in September 1993 the Security Council passed Resolution 864—an embargo of oil and arms imports to UNITA intended to induce rebel participation in negotiations for the Lusaka Protocol. Subsequent sanctions—the diplomatic isolation of UNITA with Resolution 1127 in August 1997 and the prohibition on the export of diamonds from UNITA-held territory with Resolution 1173 in June 1998—were initially meant to compel UNITA to comply with the terms of the peace agreement. Yet this changed with the launch of a state military offensive in December 1998; the Angolan sanctions regime in essence became a component of the government's new war effort. Strictly in terms of efficiency, the sanctions regime was somewhat effective: the prohibition on the sale or supply of petroleum to UNITA reportedly reduced its combat ability, and the embargo on diamonds forced the rebel group to accept below-market rates on its illicit exports. Nevertheless, it was not possible to entirely cut off the arms transfers that sustained the insurgency.[50] Thus it appears that sanctions contributed to the transformation of UNITA from a formidable opponent of state power equipped with conventional combat capacity into a guerrilla group on the defensive. In other words, sanctions probably facilitated a coercive resolution rather than a peaceful solution to Angola's civil war.

Unfortunately, evaluations of sanctions regimes are often framed within the limited terms of how efficiently they have been implemented, rather than within the broader context of their relative effectiveness within an overall peace process. With the advent of expert panels and monitoring mechanisms, the Security Council has begun to take some necessary technical steps in terms of efficiency. However, sanctions regimes targeting the flow of so-called conflict diamonds have only been somewhat effective for two basic reasons: the inherent difficulties of supply-side interdiction, and a false premise that profit motivates insurgency and that therefore the denial of resources will alter the

incentive of rebel groups. More important, the opportunity cost of imposing sanctions has not been properly considered. Sanctions regimes effectively criminalize rebel groups and end any pretense of impartiality—
potentially eliminating diplomatic channels for mediation. Thus sanctions
regimes often amount to de facto UN involvement in fighting wars, rather
than resolving them peacefully. As Jeffrey Herbst has commented:

> Demanding such sanctions is an implicit call for the military defeat of
> the rebels by the government. As calls for military victory appear to be
> politically incorrect in the current age, the vocabulary of victory and
> defeat has been transferred to the more neutral and technocratic lan-
> guage of sanctions and restraints on the trade of natural resources.[51]

This "neutral and technocratic language" has served to obfuscate a fundamental question about the purpose of sanctions: Are targeted sanctions regimes intended to facilitate the peaceful resolution of conflict or
to assist the pursuit of coercive war termination? The answer may vary
according to the situation, but policymakers should at least be fully cog-
nizant of the potential strategic, humanitarian, and normative implications for their chosen course of action.

Conclusion

Although it is often difficult to discern direct connections between how
conflict is understood and how intervention is pursued, there are several
points that are worth examination. Practitioners typically view the
world through a conceptual prism implicitly shaped by their own place
within a global hierarchy, thus placing the most explanatory weight on
the rational decisions made by other elites and the readily identifiable
factors assumed to influence these choices. Consequently, strategies for
intervention by the UN and other actors have focused on a limited range
of measures intended to influence the flow of natural resources and the
decisionmaking calculus of elites, rather than more comprehensive
approaches that tackle the macrolevel processes and structures that generate and sustain intrastate wars. UN policymaking with regard to
Angola, Sierra Leone, and the DRC appears to have been guided by
assumptions based upon an economic predation paradigm (i.e., rational
pursuit of profit motive facilitated by lootable commodities). As discussed earlier, strategies predominantly extrapolated from this conceptual prism have met with decidedly mixed results.

This chapter has sought to illustrate how civil wars in countries
such as Angola, Sierra Leone, and the DRC are much more complex

than some scholars have suggested. These intrastate conflicts appear to be caused by cyclical patterns of state failure and mobilization of resources for insurgency—each having interrelated economic and political dimensions. State failure can be understood as a declining state capacity or desire to provide public goods (e.g., administration, economic opportunity, and security) and an increasing erosion of legitimacy. Insurgency requires the mobilization of both human and material resources—thus often leading to ambiguous and evolving combinations of justice-seeking and loot-seeking over the course of a conflict. The intensity and duration of internal wars appear to be strongly influenced not only by lootable resources, but also by linkages with external processes of regionalization, privatization, and globalization. Accordingly, conflict analysis also needs to incorporate a wider range of public- and private-sector actors than typically considered relevant: adjacent states, criminal networks, mercenary firms, resource extraction corporations, and powerful industrialized states.

This suggests that a more comprehensive and effective strategy for UN intervention in African civil wars would need a mutually reinforcing combination of three components: structural prevention, enhanced peacekeeping capacity, and supranational regulation. First, structural prevention would entail mitigation of the underlying causes of violence such as state failure. This would include a substantial increase in foreign aid, comprehensive debt relief, and the lowering of trade barriers among developed countries to exports from developing countries. It would also require the commitment of the international financial institutions (IFIs) to a revised approach for promoting "good governance"—one that actually enhances rather than undermines state institutional capacity to manage resources and provide public goods. Second, substantially improved UN peacekeeping capacity in African conflicts is necessary in order to facilitate the trust required for mediation; enable the disarmament, demobilization, and reintegration of combatants; manage challenges posed by a multiplicity of nonstate and regional actors; and provide an adequate deterrent against those who may oppose peace processes. Finally, the establishment of a comprehensive supranational regime for the regulation of natural resource extraction in conflict zones may be required to deal with the privatized and globalized aspects of war economies. This could include increased financial transparency by the extractive and financial sectors; monitoring (and potentially restricting) the flow of commodity exports; creating a common set of operational guidelines for firms in unstable or conflict areas; and enacting internationally binding legislation for the conduct of corporate mercenary firms.

Unfortunately, what may be most needed may also be the least probable. The scale of structural prevention required in Africa would necessitate an outlay of financial resources and a level of commitment that the developed countries have thus far only matched with rhetoric. Likewise, effective UN peacekeeping operations on the continent would require an unlikely combination of rectifying global expenditure inequities and deploying forces from states with significant military capacity. Finally, proposals for creating a comprehensive global regulatory regime for natural resource extraction in conflict zones face a number of political hurdles, above all the opposition of developing states concerned about the erosion of sovereignty and developed states protecting corporate interests. At the risk of cynicism, the P-5 and G-8 countries that establish the respective agendas of the UN and the IFIs appear to be focused more on their own national security and commercial interests than on preventing and resolving civil wars in Africa. Given this reality, the prospects of fundamental reform appear unlikely.

Notes

I would like to sincerely thank Karen Ballentine, David Keen, and Jake Sherman for their very insightful and helpful comments on earlier drafts of this chapter.

1. Mary Kaldor, *New and Old Wars: Organized Violence in a Global Era* (Stanford: Stanford University Press, 1999).

2. David Keen, *The Economic Functions of Violence in Civil Wars*, Adelphi Paper no. 320 (London: Oxford University Press, 1998), p. 11.

3. Blaine Harden, "Africa's Diamond Wars," *New York Times*, April 6, 2000.

4. Paul Collier, "Economic Causes of Civil Conflict and Their Implications for Policy," in Chester A. Crocker, Fen Osler Hampson, and Pamela Aall, eds., *Turbulent Peace: The Challenges of Managing International Conflict* (Washington, D.C.: U.S. Institute of Peace Press, 2001), pp. 143–162.

5. The study found that in countries where primary commodity exports account for 26 percent of gross domestic product (GDP), the risk of violent conflict is highest. Presumably, at much lower percentages of dependency there are insufficient natural resources for rebel groups to extort, while at much higher percentages the state can finance a better deterrent to insurgency.

6. William Reno, "Shadow States and the Political Economy of Civil Wars," in Mats Berdal and David M. Malone, eds., *Greed and Grievance: Economic Agendas in Civil Wars* (Boulder: Lynne Rienner, 2000), pp. 43–68.

7. Frances Stewart, "Horizontal Inequalities as a Source of Conflict," in Fen Osler Hampson and David M. Malone, eds., *From Reaction to Prevention: Opportunities for the UN System* (Boulder: Lynne Rienner, 2002), pp. 105–136.

8. Mohammed Ayoob, "State Making, State Breaking, and State Failure," in Crocker, Hampson, and Aall, *Turbulent Peace*, pp. 37–51.

9. Human Rights Watch, *Angola Unravels: The Rise and Fall of the Lusaka Peace Process* (New York: Human Rights Watch, 1999), p. 15.

10. Ian Smillie, Lansana Gberie, and Ralph Hazleton, *The Heart of the Matter: Sierra Leone, Diamonds, and Human Security* (Ottawa: Partnership Africa–Canada, 2000), p. 9.

11. Michael Schatzberg, *The Dialectics of Oppression in Zaire* (Bloomington: Indiana University Press, 1988).

12. Michael Schatzberg, *Mobutu or Chaos: The United States and Zaire, 1960–1990* (Lanham, Md.: University Press of America, 1991).

13. James Fairhead, "The Conflict over Natural and Environmental Resources," in E. Wayne Nafziger, Frances Stewart, and Raimo Väyrynen, eds., *War, Hunger, and Displacement: The Origins of Humanitarian Emergencies,* vol. 1 (Oxford: Oxford University Press, 2000), pp. 154–159; and Johan Peleman, "Mining for Serious Trouble: Jean-Raymond Boulle and His Corporate Empire Project," in Abdel-Fatua Musah and J. 'Kayode Fayemi, eds., *Mercenaries: An African Security Dilemma* (London: Pluto Press, 2000), pp. 155–168.

14. Adekeye Adebajo and Chris Landsberg, "Back to the Future: UN Peacekeeping in Africa," in Adekeye Adebajo and Chandra Lekha Sriram, eds., *Managing Armed Conflicts in the Twenty-First Century* (London: Frank Cass, 2001), p. 180.

15. BBC, "Congo and Rwanda Sign Peace Deal," July 30, 2002, available online at http://news.bbc.co.uk/1/hi/world/africa/2160522.stm (accessed September 18, 2002).

16. William Reno, *Corruption and State Politics in Sierra Leone* (Cambridge: Cambridge University Press, 1995).

17. Reno, "Shadow States," p. 46.

18. Schatzberg, *Dialectics of Oppression,* p. 135.

19. Jeffrey Herbst, "Economic Incentives, Natural Resources, and Conflict in Africa," *Journal of African Economies* 9, no. 3 (October 2000): 270–294.

20. See, for example, William Reno, *Warlord Politics and African States* (Boulder: Lynne Rienner, 1998); and Keen, *Economic Functions of Violence.*

21. Keen, *Economic Functions of Violence,* p. 12.

22. Musifiky Mwanasali, "A View from Below," in Berdal and Malone, *Greed and Grievance;* and Blaine Harden, "A Black Mud from Africa Helps Power the New Economy," *New York Times,* August 12, 2001.

23. In contrast to situations characterized by I. William Zartman's "mutually hurting stalemate" and conflict resolution, a "mutually profitable stalemate" and conflict perpetuation occurs when the shared material benefits of violence continue to outweigh the anticipated rewards of peace. See I. William Zartman and Saadia Touval, "International Mediation in the Post–Cold War Era," in Chester A. Crocker, Fen Osler Hampson, and Pamela Aall, eds., *Managing Global Chaos: Sources of and Responses to International Conflict* (Washington, D.C.: U.S. Institute of Peace Press, 1996), pp. 445–462.

24. Christian Dietrich, "Power Struggles in the Diamond Fields," in Jakkie Cilliers and Christian Dietrich, eds., *Angola's War Economy: The Role of Oil and Diamonds* (Pretoria: Institute for Security Studies, 2000), pp. 173–194.

25. Jake H. Sherman, "Profit vs. Peace: The Clandestine Diamond Economy of Angola," *Journal of International Affairs* 53, no. 2 (Spring 2000): 699–719.

26. Reno, *Warlord Politics,* pp. 61–68; and Smillie, Gberie, and Hazleton, *Heart of the Matter,* pp. 54–60.

27. Fairhead, "Natural and Environmental Resources," pp. 154–159; and Peleman, "Mining for Serious Trouble."

28. Kaldor, *New and Old Wars;* and Mark Duffield, *Global Governance and the New Wars: The Merging of Security and Development* (London: Zed Books, 2001).

29. Harden, "Black Mud from Africa."

30. Global Witness, *All the President's Men: The Devastating Story of Oil and Banking in Angola's Privatised War,* March 2002, p. 3, available online at www.globalwitness.org./campaigns/oil/downloads/all_the_presidents_men.pdf (accessed September 18, 2002).

31. Ken Silverstein, "Privatizing War: How Affairs of State Are Outsourced to Corporations Beyond Public Control," *The Nation,* July 28, 1997; William Reno, "The Real (War) Economy of Angola," in Cilliers and Dietrich, *Angola's War Economy,* pp. 219–236; and Global Witness, *All the President's Men.*

32. Mark Duffield, "Globalization and War Economies: Promoting Order or the Return of History?" *Fletcher Forum of World Affairs* 23, no. 2 (Fall 1999): 21–38.

33. David Keen, "War and Peace: What's the Difference?" in Adebajo and Sriram, *Managing Armed Conflicts,* p. 19.

34. See, for example, Michael Barnett, *Eyewitness to a Genocide: The United Nations and Rwanda* (Ithaca, N.Y.: Cornell University Press, 2002).

35. David Shearer, "Aiding or Abetting? Humanitarian Aid and Its Economic Role in Civil War," in Berdal and Malone, *Greed and Grievance,* pp. 189–203.

36. David Cortright and George A. Lopez with Richard W. Conroy, "Sierra Leone: The Failure of Regional and International Sanctions," in David Cortright and George A. Lopez, *The Sanctions Decade: Assessing UN Strategies in the 1990s* (Boulder: Lynne Rienner, 2000).

37. BBC, "Angola Gripped by Mass Starvation," July 9, 2002, available online at http://news.bbc.co.uk/1/hi/world/africa/2117049.stm (accessed September 18, 2002).

38. I. William Zartman, "Mediating Conflicts of Need, Greed, and Creed," *Orbis* 44, no. 2 (Spring 2000): 255–266.

39. Lomé Peace Agreement, Articles VII and IX, reprinted in John L. Hirsch, *Sierra Leone: Diamonds and the Struggle for Democracy* (Boulder: Lynne Rienner, 2001), pp. 135–157.

40. Paul Hare, *Angola's Last Best Chance for Peace: An Insider's Account of the Peace Process* (Washington, D.C.: U.S. Institute of Peace Press, 1998), pp. 124–126.

41. United Nations, "Report of the Panel on United Nations Peace Operations," A/55/305-S/2000/809, August 21, 2000, para. 25.

42. For example, Ian Fisher, Norimitsu Onishi, Rachel Swarns, Blaine Harden, and Alan Cowell, "Many Armies Ravage Rich Land in the 'First World War' of Africa," *New York Times,* February 6, 2000.

43. United Nations, "Report of the Panel of Experts on the Illegal Exploitation of Natural Resources and Other Forms of Wealth of the Democratic Republic of Congo," S/2001/357, April 12, 2001.

44. International Crisis Group, "Disarmament in the Congo: Investing in Conflict Prevention," June 12, 2001, available online at www.crisisweb.org/

projects/showreport.cfm?reportid=312 (accessed September 18, 2002).

45. Cortright and Lopez, *Sanctions Decade,* tab. 11.1, pp. 205–207.

46. United Nations, "Report of the Panel of Experts on the Illegal Exploitation of Natural Resources," para. 15(a).

47. This resolution was subsequently amended in October 2000 to exempt those diamonds processed through a new governmental certification scheme.

48. United Nations, "Report of the Panel of Experts Appointed Pursuant to Security Council Resolution 1306 (2000), Paragraph 19, in Relation to Sierra Leone," S/2000/1195, December 20, 2000, para. 78.

49. David Cortright and George A. Lopez with Linda Gerber, *Sanctions and the Search for Security: Challenges to UN Action* (Boulder: Lynne Rienner, 2002), pp. 77–89, 184–186.

50. United Nations, "Report of the Panel of Experts on Violations of Security Council Sanctions Against UNITA," S/2000/203, March 10, 2000.

51. Ibid.

3

Oil, Drugs, and Diamonds: The Varying Roles of Natural Resources in Civil War

Michael L. Ross

According to several recent studies, when states rely more heavily on the export of natural resources, they are more likely to suffer from civil war. But are all types of commercially valuable natural resources—including oil, hard-rock minerals, gemstones, timber, agricultural commodities, and illegal drugs—equally likely to lead to civil war? Do different types of resources have different effects on conflict?

This chapter is a modest effort to describe how different types of resources have influenced recent conflicts, as well as to develop hypotheses that can be tested in future studies. It begins by showing that of all major types of natural resources, diamonds and drugs are most strongly associated with the civil wars that occurred between 1990 and 2000. The second section offers seven hypotheses about how three characteristics of natural resources—their lootability, their obstructability, and their legality—are likely to influence civil wars. The hypotheses are illustrated by evidence from fifteen recent conflicts in which natural resources played some role (documented in Table 3.1). The chapter concludes with a discussion of the implications of these hypotheses for different types of natural resources.

This chapter advances four main arguments. First, resources have sharply different effects in separatist conflicts compared to nonseparatist conflicts. Second, the impact of a particular resource largely depends on whether or not it is "lootable"—that is, whether it can be easily appropriated by individuals or small groups of unskilled workers. Third, lootable resources—such as diamonds and drugs—are more likely to ignite nonseparatist conflicts, which once begun are harder to resolve; but they pose little danger of igniting separatist conflicts. Finally, unlootable resources—like oil, natural gas, and deep-shaft minerals—tend to produce separatist conflicts, but seldom influence nonseparatist conflicts. In sum, lootable resources negatively affect nonseparatist conflicts, and unlootable resources negatively affect separatist conflicts.

This chapter illustrates but does not test these arguments, and the hypotheses that undergird them. The hypotheses were derived from the fifteen case studies. To determine whether they are valid beyond these scenarios—and hence have predictive and not just descriptive value—they should be tested with a different data set.

Civil Wars Among Resource-Rich States

There is good evidence that resources and civil wars are causally linked.[1] Several studies have found a strong statistical correlation between a state's reliance on the export of natural resources, and either the likelihood it will suffer from civil war,[2] or alternatively, the duration of a civil war once commenced.[3]

There is also good evidence at the case-study level that natural resources have contributed to the onset, duration, and intensity of many civil wars. An earlier study by Michael Ross, drawing on case studies of thirteen conflicts between 1994 and 2000, confirms this conclusion, and also finds that natural resources tend to influence separatist conflicts differently than they influence nonseparatist conflicts, further distinguished by the lootability of a resource.[4] But are all natural resources equally at fault? Are some types of resources more likely than others to generate, or lengthen, civil conflict?

One way to address these questions is to observe a sample of civil wars in which resources played some role, and take note of what types of resources were involved. Table 3.1 summarizes information about twelve civil wars, plus three low-level conflicts, that occurred between 1994 and 2001 and have been causally linked to the exploitation of natural resources in case studies.[5] The resources most frequently linked to civil conflict are diamonds and other gemstones (seven conflicts, all of them civil wars); oil and natural gas (seven conflicts, six of them civil wars); illicit drugs (five conflicts, all of them civil wars); copper or gold (four conflicts, two of them civil wars); and timber (three conflicts, all of them civil wars). Legal agricultural crops played a role in two conflicts (both civil wars), although in each case other natural resources played larger roles.

While this type of analysis has some value, it is unsatisfying in at least two ways. First, some types of natural resources are more common than others; this alone might explain why there are more civil wars in states that produce oil (which is a relatively common resource) than in

Table 3.1 Civil Conflicts Linked to Resource Wealth, 1994–2001

	Duration	Type	Resources
Afghanistan	1978–2001	Lootable	Gems, opium
Angola (UNITA)	1975–	Both	Oil, diamonds
Angola (Cabinda)[a]	1975–	Unlootable	Oil
Burma	1949–	Lootable	Timber, gems, opium
Cambodia	1978–1997	Lootable	Timber, gems
Colombia	1984–	Both	Oil, opium, coca
Congo Republic	1997	Unlootable	Oil
Democratic Republic of Congo	1996–1998	Both	Copper, coltan, diamonds, gold, cobalt, coffee
Indonesia (Aceh)	1975–	Unlootable	Natural gas
Indonesia (West Papua)[a]	1969–	Unlootable	Copper, gold
Liberia	1989–1996	Lootable[b]	Timber, diamonds, iron, palm oil, cocoa, coffee, marijuana, rubber, gold
Papua New Guinea[a]	1988–	Unlootable	Copper, gold
Peru	1980–1995	Lootable	Coca
Sierra Leone	1991–2000	Lootable	Diamonds
Sudan	1983–	Unlootable	Oil

Source: Figures on conflict duration taken from Paul Collier and Anke Hoeffler, "Greed and Grievance in Civil War," Policy Research Working Paper no. 2355 (Washington, D.C.: World Bank, 2001).
    Notes: Italic denotes separatist conflict.
    a. Conflict did not generate 1,000 battle deaths in any twelve-month period.
    b. Since the resources in Liberia's conflict were overwhelmingly lootable, I classify it as "lootable" rather than "both."

states that produce copper (which is a less common resource). What we would like to know is whether civil wars occur at anomalously high rates among the producers of a given commodity. For example, do civil wars occur more frequently among oil producers than among nonproducers, more frequently among copper producers than among nonproducers? Second, there may be subtle causal links between civil wars and natural resources that are difficult to observe in case studies; for this reason some conflicts may have been wrongly excluded from Table 3.1.

One simple way to address these problems is to observe whether civil wars occur at different rates among states that are highly dependent, moderately dependent, or minimally dependent on the export or production of a given resource. If civil wars occur at above-average rates among states that are highly dependent on a given resource, it would imply that the resource is tied to the occurrence of conflict.[6]

Table 3.2 shows a simple tabulation of civil war rates between 1990 and 2000, by level of resource dependence. Resources are divided into four categories, as used by the World Bank: oil, gas, and other fuel-based minerals; nonfuel minerals, excluding gemstones; food-based agricultural exports; and nonfood agricultural exports, including timber but excluding illegal drugs.[7] The cross-tabulations show the civil war rates among countries that ranked in the top, middle, or bottom third of all states in the ratio of resource exports to gross domestic product (GDP) in the midpoint year of 1995.[8] Between 1990 and 2000, 32 out of 161 countries surveyed had civil wars; this means that for any random country, there is an approximately 20 percent chance that it suffered a civil war at some point in the 1990s.[9] As Table 3.2 shows, civil wars occurred at slightly lower rates among states that were highly dependent on resource exports in all four categories.[10]

One reason why there is no obvious correlation in this table between resource dependence and civil war rates is that other factors—most important, income per capita—are not controlled for. A second reason is that these standard four categories exclude (or in the case of timber, fail to isolate) several types of resources that have been most visibly linked to conflict in the media: diamonds, timber, and illicit drugs. To address the first shortcoming, Table 3.3 adjusts the figures in Table 3.2 by dividing the ratio of resource exports to GDP by each

Table 3.2 Civil War Rates 1990–2000, by 1995 Ratios of Resource Exports to GDP

	Oil and Gas	Minerals[a]	Food Crops	Nonfood Crops
Top Third	.146	.122	.133	.100
Middle Third	.208	.146	.166	.100
Bottom Third	.188	.195	.133	.233

Sources: For civil war occurrences, Paul Collier and Anke Hoeffler, "Greed and Grievance in Civil War," Policy Research Working Paper no. 2355 (Washington, D.C.: World Bank, 2001). All other data taken from World Bank, *World Development Indicators 2001* (Washington, D.C.: World Bank, 2001), CD-ROM.
Note: a. Nonfuel minerals, not including gemstones.

Table 3.3 Civil War Rates 1990–2000, Adjusted for GDP per Capita

	Oil and Gas	Minerals[a]	Food Crops	Nonfood Crops
Top Third	.207	.172	.241	.207
Middle Third	.166	.133	.166	.166
Bottom Third	.100	.138	.033	.067

Sources: For civil war occurrences, Paul Collier and Anke Hoeffler, "Greed and Grievance in Civil War," Policy Research Working Paper no. 2355 (Washington, D.C.: World Bank, 2001). All other data taken from World Bank, *World Development Indicators 2001* (Washington, D.C.: World Bank, 2001), CD-ROM.
Note: a. Nonfuel minerals, not including gemstones.

country's income per capita, producing a figure that simultaneously reflects both resource dependence and per capita wealth. In this table, resource-dependent countries are at a notably higher risk of civil war. There is no obvious difference among types of resource dependence, as all seem to make conflicts more likely once per capita income has been accounted for.[11]

Tables 3.4, 3.5, and 3.6 address the second shortcoming. Table 3.4 shows the civil war rates among timber-producing states, measured in four different ways—each representing an effort to determine whether timber production or export is in some way correlated with the incidence of conflict. The first column of numbers divides states by the quantity of commercial timber (i.e., industrial roundwood) they produced from both natural forests and plantations in 1995. Thus these data may suggest whether conflict became more likely when more commercial timber was harvested. Of course, other things influence the amount of timber produced, such as the size of the country: the United States and Russia cut more timber than Gabon or Honduras, but this reflects in part their greater size. Hence the second column, timber per capita, divides states by the volume of timber they produced per capita. Once again, states that are more timber-intensive do not seem to face a higher risk of civil war; in fact, they appear to face a lower risk.

Perhaps, however, civil war becomes more likely as states grow more dependent on the export of unprocessed timber. The third column in Table 3.4 divides states by the value of their unprocessed timber exports as a ratio of their GDP—making these data comparable to the figures in Table 3.2.[12] As in Table 3.2, there is no obvious correlation between a country's reliance on the commodity and the likelihood that it suffered a civil war in the 1990s. Finally, the fourth column adjusts the figures in the third column by dividing them by GDP per capita, to

Table 3.4 Civil War Rates 1990–2000, by 1995 Timber Production and Exports

	Timber Production	Timber per capita	Timber Exports per GDP	Adjusted for GDP per capita
Top Third	.116	.047	.111	.194
Middle Third	.250	.273	.243	.189
Bottom Third	.250	.318	.270	.243

Sources: For civil war occurrences, Paul Collier and Anke Hoeffler, "Greed and Grievance in Civil War," Policy Research Working Paper no. 2355 (Washington, D.C.: World Bank, 2001). For timber production and export figures, Food and Agriculture Administration Statistics Database (FAOSTAT), http://apps.fao.org/. For GDP figures (measured in purchasing power parity), World Bank, *World Development Indicators 2001* (Washington, D.C.: World Bank, 2001), CD-ROM.

account for the influence of income on civil war. Even here, however, there is no evidence to suggest that greater timber dependence is associated with higher rates of conflict. This appears to contradict accounts like those of Michael Klare, who suggests that timber production or export is linked to civil conflict.[13]

Table 3.5 shows civil war rates by production of three other commodities that are commonly faulted for "fueling" civil wars: diamonds, coca, and opium. The first column lists the civil war rates among diamond producers and nonproducers, with the second column distinguishing the production of alluvial diamonds—that is, diamonds that can be extracted from riverbeds and alluvial plains, typically at a minimal cost. Although the numbers are small, the civil war rate among diamond producers (five wars in eighteen states) is anomalously high—and among the producers of alluvial diamonds (four wars in eight states), it is exceptionally high.

The third column of Table 3.5 compares the civil war rates among coca and opium producers with rates among nonproducers.[14] I combine opium and coca producers for several reasons: they are an overlapping group of countries; the production of these drugs is highly similar in land use, transportability, and value per weight; and it is easier to make inferences about larger categories of states than about smaller categories. The civil war rate is much higher among the drug-producing states than among nonproducers.

Finally, Table 3.6 records the civil war rates among states that, according to Interpol, were primary producers, secondary producers, or nonproducers of cannabis—a drug that is more widely grown, is less penalized against, and has a much lower value-to-weight ratio than coca or opium products.[15] Although the civil war rate is higher among primary producers than among secondary producers, this finding appears somewhat fragile statistically, because nonproducers have a higher civil

Table 3.5 Civil War Rates 1990–2000, by 1995 Diamond and Drug Production

	Diamonds	Alluvial Diamonds	Opium and Coca
Producers	.278 (5/18)	.500 (4/8)	.444 (4/9)
Nonproducers	.188 (27/143)	.183 (28/153)	.184 (28/152)

Sources: For civil war occurrences, Paul Collier and Anke Hoeffler, "Greed and Grievance in Civil War," Policy Research Working Paper no. 2355 (Washington, D.C.: World Bank, 2001). For diamond production, Ronald F. Balazik, "Industrial Diamonds" (Washington D.C.: U.S. Geological Survey, 1998). For opium and coca production, UN Office for Drug Control and Crime Prevention, "World Drug Report, 2000" (New York: Oxford University Press, 2000).

Table 3.6 Civil War Rates 1990–2000, by Cannabis Production

Primary Source Countries	.300 (3/10)
Secondary Source Countries	.132 (9/68)
All Other Countries	.241 (20/83)

Sources: For civil war occurrences, Paul Collier and Anke Hoeffler, "Greed and Grievance in Civil War," Policy Research Working Paper no. 2355 (Washington, DC: World Bank, 2001). For cannabis production, UN Office for Drug Control and Crime Prevention, "World Drug Report, 2000" (New York: Oxford University Press, 2000).

war rate than secondary producers, and because dropping just a single civil war from the category of primary producers would no longer create an anomalously high rate.

The analysis in this section is exceedingly simple in statistical terms, and has several important limitations: it only considers civil wars that occurred in the 1990s, not before; it is purely cross-sectional, and does not include a time-series dimension; it does not properly control for other factors that influence civil war rates; it compares civil war rates among the top, middle, and bottom thirds of countries rather than examining the continuous effect of resource dependence on civil war risks; and it compares decade-long civil war rates to levels of resource dependence in 1995, the year for which the greatest quantity of data are available.

Despite these limitations, the data suggest three things. First, there is no obvious difference in the civil war rates among states dependent on the four general categories of natural resources. Second, higher rates of timber production and export do not appear to be linked to higher rates of civil wars. Finally, there is a strong association between civil war and both the production of diamonds—especially alluvial diamonds—and the production of drugs, especially coca and opium. What accounts for this pattern?

Few prior studies have addressed this question. An important exception is Philippe Le Billon, who makes two key distinctions: between those that are proximate to a national capital (and hence easier for governments to capture) and those that are distant (and hence easier for rebels to hold); and between "point-source" resources, which are concentrated in a small area (and therefore more easily controlled by a single group), and diffuse resources, which are scattered over a larger area (and hence harder for any single group to capture).[16] These two categories, Le Billon suggests, yield a fourfold typology of conflict: point-source resources near the capital create violent incentives to control the state, and hence produce coups d'état; point-source resources far from the capital produce secession movements; diffuse resources near the capital lead to rebellions and rioting; and diffuse resources far from the capital lead to "warlordism," areas of de facto sovereignty with economies built around the resource itself. The Le Billon study provides an important precedent for the analysis below.

Seven Hypotheses on Resources and Conflict

This section develops seven hypotheses about the ways that natural resources tend to influence civil wars. It suggests that the role played by any natural resource depends largely on its lootability, and to a lesser extent on its obstructability and its legality.

A resource's lootability is the ease with which it can be extracted and transported by individuals or small teams of unskilled workers.[17] Drugs, alluvial gemstones, agricultural products, and timber are relatively lootable; deep-shaft minerals and gemstones, oil, and natural gas are relatively unlootable.

A resource is obstructable if its transportation can be easily blocked by a small number of individuals with few weapons; it is relatively unobstructable if it can only be blocked with many soldiers and heavy equipment. A resource's obstructability is in part a function of its physical characteristics. Resources that have a high value-to-weight ratio, such as gemstones, coca, and opium, are usually transported by air and are difficult to obstruct, since they can be flown out of remote areas. Resources with a lower value-to-weight ratio that must be transported by truck or train—like minerals and timber—are moderately obstructable, if they must cross long distances. Resources that are transported in liquid form and travel long distances through above-ground pipelines (e.g., oil and natural gas) are highly obstructable, since pipelines are continuously vulnerable to disruption along their entire length. A resource's location also helps determine its obstructability: if an oil field is in a remote, landlocked location, it is highly obstructable; if it is located near a port or offshore, it is relatively unobstructable.

Finally, most resources can be legally traded on international markets; drugs—coca, opium, cannabis, and their derivatives—are the main types of illegal natural resources.[18] Figure 3.1 categorizes most types of resources according to these criteria, which yield seven hypotheses about the social and political consequences of resource extraction, summarized in Table 3.7.

Figure 3.1 Natural Resources, by Lootability, Obstructability, and Legality

	Lootable	Unlootable
Highly Obstructable	—	Onshore, remote oil and gas
Moderately Obstructable	Agricultural products Timber	Deep-shaft minerals
Unobstructable	**Coca** **Opium** Alluvial gems	Deep-shaft gems Offshore oil and gas

Note: **Bold** denotes illegal resources.

Table 3.7 Hypotheses on Resources and Civil War

1. The more lootable a resource is, the more likely it is to benefit local peoples and the poor.
2. The more unlootable a resource is, the more likely it will lead to separatist conflicts.
3. The more lootable a resource is, the more likely it is to benefit a rebel group; the more unlootable it is, the more likely it is to benefit the government.
4. The more lootable the resource, the more likely it is to create discipline problems inside the army that controls it.
5. The more lootable the resource, the more likely it is to prolong nonseparatist conflicts.
6. If a resource is obstructable, it is more likely to increase the duration and intensity of conflicts.
7. If the resource is illegal, it is more likely to benefit the rebels—unless the government is willing to endure international sanctions.

Hypothesis 1: The more lootable a resource is, the more likely it is to benefit local peoples and the poor.

This first hypothesis does not directly address the issues of conflict, but it provides the basis for the other hypotheses that do. The extraction of highly lootable resources relies more heavily on the use of unskilled labor; the extraction of unlootable resources relies more heavily on skilled labor and capital. Hence lootable resources are more likely to generate income for local communities, and for unskilled workers—for example, the poor. Unlootable resources are more likely to produce revenues for skilled workers, for those who provide the requisite capital, and for the government. In developing countries, where skilled labor and capital tend to be scarce, these factors are more likely to come from outside the region—possibly from other countries.

If true, this hypothesis implies that the extraction of lootable resources such as alluvial gems, drugs, timber, and agricultural products is more likely to have a popular local constituency than is the extraction of unlootable resources such as oil, gas, and deep-shaft minerals. This also means that efforts to stop the flow of lootable resources are more likely to face opposition from local communities, and to harm low- and moderate-income sectors of the economy.[19]

Hypothesis 2: The more unlootable a resource is, the more likely it will lead to separatist conflicts.

This hypothesis follows directly from the previous one. If a resource is highly lootable, it is more likely to generate direct benefits for the poor, and to benefit local peoples; if it is relatively unlootable, it is more likely to generate revenues for skilled workers (who are less likely to originate from the region), the extraction firm, and the government— and hence to produce grievances about the distribution of resource wealth. This has important consequences for separatist conflicts, which in resource-rich areas are commonly incited by grievances over the distribution of resource revenue.

Figure 3.2 divides the six separatist conflicts from Table 3.1 into those involving lootable resources and those involving unlootable resources. The nine nonseparatist conflicts from Table 3.1 are similarly divided for comparison. Of the six separatist conflicts, five feature unlootable resources: the Cabinda conflict in Angola (over oil); the Aceh conflict (over natural gas) and the West Papua (Irian Jaya) conflict in Indonesia (over copper and gold); the Bougainville conflict in Papua New Guinea (over copper); and the conflict in Sudan (over oil).[20] In each of these five cases, grievances over the distribution of resource wealth have helped spark or exacerbate the conflict. Just one separatist conflict features lootable resources: Burma, where rebel groups have used opium and gemstones to fund themselves, but the production of those goods has not in itself caused separatist grievances.

Hypothesis 3: The more lootable a resource is, the more likely it is to benefit a rebel group; the more unlootable it is, the more likely it is to benefit the government.

If a resource is highly lootable, whichever party controls the surrounding territory can use it for funding. But if it is unlootable, it is more likely to benefit the government, since the government is more able to credibly provide the security guarantees necessary to attract and maintain the requisite skilled labor and capital. Both sides in a conflict can benefit from controlling an area that produces alluvial diamonds or drugs, but only the government is likely to benefit from controlling an area that produces oil or copper.

Figure 3.2 Lootability and Separatism

	Separatist	Nonseparatist
Lootable	Burma	Afghanistan Angola (UNITA)[a] Cambodia Colombia[a] DRC[a] Liberia Peru Sierra Leone
Unlootable	Angola (Cabinda) Indonesia (Aceh) Indonesia (West Papua) Papua New Guinea Sudan	Angola (UNITA)[a] Colombia[a] Congo Republic DRC[a]

Note: a. Conflict entails both lootable and unlootable resources.

Skeptics may point out that a rebel army still profits from gaining control of an unlootable resource, since this action will deny resource revenues to the government. This is true, but an unlootable resource will still be of less value to the rebels than a lootable resource. Imagine that a rebel army captures from the government an unlootable resource. The net change in the government's revenue from this event is the amount of annual revenue lost in exploiting this resource, plus the amount of annual revenue gained by the rebels, which is zero since they cannot extract the resource. Now imagine that the rebel army captures a lootable resource from the government, which produces the same revenue as the unlootable resource above. In this case, the loss to the government's revenue is doubled, since the rebels can now exploit the resource. Hence lootable resources should be more valuable than unlootable resources to the rebels; unlootable resources should be more valuable than lootable resources to the government.

Figure 3.3 shows that the cases in Table 3.1 are consistent with this pattern.[21] In all ten conflicts over lootable resources, resource revenues flowed to either the rebels exclusively, or to both sides. In the eight cases with unlootable resources, revenues went exclusively to the government in four cases, to both sides in four cases, and to the rebels exclusively in none. Of the four conflicts in which unlootable resources produced revenues for both sides, in two cases (Colombia and Sudan) it was because long oil pipelines made the resource obstructable, and hence susceptible to holdups (see Hypothesis 6).

It is also notable that in the three conflicts with both lootable and unlootable resources—Angola (UNITA), Colombia, and the Democratic

Figure 3.3 Which Side Earns Revenues from Resource Wealth?

	Rebels	Government	Both Sides
Lootable	Afghanistan (gems) Cambodia Liberia Peru DRC[a]	—	Afghanistan (opium) Angola (gems) Burma Colombia (drugs) Sierra Leone DRC
Unlootable	—	Angola (oil) Angola-Cabinda Indonesia-Aceh Indonesia–W. Papua	Colombia (oil) Congo Republic Sudan DRC[b]

Notes: a. Including coltan, gold, coffee, and timber.
b. Including cobalt and kimberlite diamonds.

Republic of Congo—in two cases (Angola and the Democratic Republic of Congo), the government has continuously controlled the unlootable resources, while the rebels have periodically controlled the lootable resources. In the third case (Colombia), the leftist guerrillas as well as the right-wing paramilitaries have raised money from both resources.

Hypothesis 4: The more lootable the resource, the more likely it is to create discipline problems inside the army that controls it.

If a resource is unlootable—such as oil or natural gas—then it will most likely help fund the military of the side that controls it through a centralized process. Unlootable resources must be managed by large firms or state-owned enterprises, which will generate revenues for the government; these in turn will be appropriated to military forces through some type of budgetary mechanism. This centralized process should help give commanding officers fiscal tools to help them maintain control over lower-ranking officers and soldiers.

If a resource is lootable, however, it is less likely to generate funds for the government. It also creates opportunities for soldiers of all ranks to earn money by extracting or transporting the resources themselves, or extorting money from others who do.[22] The result is likely to be a reduced level of discipline and central control in the armed forces of the party that controls the resource.

There is only sporadic data on discipline problems within government and rebel forces. It is noteworthy, however, that of the fifteen cases in this sample, there were five cases in which a breakdown of military cohesion was so severe that some units defected to the other side, or did battle with each other. Four cases involved lootable resources: Cambodia (among the rebels), the Democratic Republic of Congo (among the rebels), Liberia (among the rebels), and Sierra Leone (on the government side). The fifth case, Sudan (among the rebels), involved oil, an obstructable resource.

Hypothesis 5: The more lootable the resource, the more likely it is to prolong nonseparatist conflicts.

There are three rationales behind this hypothesis. The first is based on Hypothesis 3. When resource revenue flows to the rebels, it is likely to prolong a conflict, since the rebels are typically the weaker party, and without this funding they are more likely to be forced to the negotiating table or extinguished. Conversely, if resource revenue accrues to the government, it is likely to shorten a conflict by bringing about a quicker victory or settlement—provided that the government is the stronger party.[23] If both parties carry out resource looting, the net effect should be to lengthen the conflict, since combat is likely to continue as long as the weaker party does not run out of money. Hence unlootable resources are more likely to shorten a war, by strengthening the stronger side; lootable resources are more likely to lengthen a war, by strengthening the weaker side, or both sides. The second rationale is based on Hypothesis 4. Discipline problems—which should be more strongly associated with lootable resources—are also likely to lengthen conflicts by making it harder for commanding officers to impose the terms of a settlement on their own forces.[24] There is also a third possibility: that wartime resource exploitation will become so profitable for rebels that they prefer war to peace. Again, this is more likely if resources are lootable—and hence can generate profits for rebels—than if they are unlootable.

This hypothesis only applies to nonseparatist conflicts. As James Fearon points out, separatist and nonseparatist conflicts appear to have substantially different characteristics: separatist conflicts tend to last longer, and often continue even when the separatist movement is at an overwhelming financial disadvantage.[25] This may be because separatist movements can often sustain themselves indefinitely in a territory dominated by members of their own ethnic group, where government forces are considered alien.

This is a difficult hypothesis to investigate empirically, in part because so many of the conflicts in this sample are ongoing—meaning that we do not know much about their ultimate duration. One way to examine the hypothesis is to put this problem aside and compare the duration of nonseparatist conflicts over lootable resources to those over unlootable resources. Table 3.8 shows this comparison. The only non-separatist conflict with unlootable resources—the 1997 war in the Congo Republic, which lasted just four months—is also the briefest conflict.

This hypothesis can also be examined indirectly by determining whether any of these three causal processes—resource exploitation by the weaker side, discipline problems that impede a settlement, and resource profiteering that impedes a settlement—have occurred in the fifteen cases. While this will not tell us if these conflicts have actually been lengthened by resources, it can tell us if any of the three processes, which I argue are likely to lengthen the conflicts, have occurred.

Table 3.9 codes the fifteen conflicts according to whether or not the three processes have occurred. Since three conflicts include both loot-able and unlootable resources, these conflicts are each listed twice, and the effects of each type of resource are coded independently. I included both the separatist and nonseparatist conflicts in this table to provide additional data on the incidence of these three processes, even though the hypothesis only applies to nonseparatist conflicts.

Table 3.9 shows that resource revenues went to the weak side in nine out of nine conflicts over lootable resources, but in only five of nine conflicts over unlootable resources. In two of these five cases (Angola and the Democratic Republic of Congo), the unlootable resource still bene-fited the government (Hypothesis 3), but at junctures when the govern-ment was the weaker party. In two other cases (Colombia and Sudan), the weak side profited from an unlootable resource (oil) due to its obstructability.

Major discipline problems were observed in five of the nine con-flicts over lootable resources, but in none of the conflicts over unlootable

Table 3.8 Duration of Nonseparatist Conflicts

	Type	Period	Duration (years)
Afghanistan	Lootable	1978–2001	23
Cambodia	Lootable	1978–1997	19
Peru	Lootable	1980–1995	15
Sierra Leone	Lootable	1991–2000	9
Liberia	Lootable	1989–1996	7
Angola (UNITA)	Both	1975–	26+
Colombia	Both	1984–	17+
Democratic Republic of Congo	Both	1996–	5+
Congo Republic	Unlootable	1997	<1

Table 3.9 Resources and Duration of Conflict

	Weak Fund	Discipline	Incentive
Lootable Resources			
Afghanistan (opium, gems)	Yes	No	No
Angola-UNITA (gems)	Yes	No	No
Burma (gems, opium)	Yes	No	Yes[a]
Cambodia (gems, timber)	Yes	Yes[a]	No
Colombia (coca)	Yes	Yes	No
Democratic Republic of Congo			
(gems, coltan, gold)	Yes	Yes	Yes
Liberia (gems, etc.)	Yes	Yes	Yes
Peru (coca)	Yes	No	No
Sierra Leone (gems)	Yes	Yes	No
Unlootable Resources			
Angola-UNITA (oil)	Yes	No	No
Angola-Cabinda (oil)	No	No	No
Colombia (oil)	Yes	No	No
Congo Republic (oil)	Yes	No	Yes[a]
Democratic Republic of Congo			
(cobalt, copper)	Yes	No	Yes
Indonesia–Aceh (gas)	No	No	No
Indonesia–W. Papua (copper)	No	No	No
Papua New Guinea (copper)	No	No	No
Sudan (oil)	Yes	No	No

Notes: Italic denotes separatist conflicts. The conflicts are coded "yes" for weak fund if the weaker side received revenues from the extraction, transport, or sale of resources, and "no" otherwise; "yes" for discipline if the presence of resources created substantial discipline problems within the military force that controlled it, and "no" otherwise; and "yes" for incentive if the resource created an economic incentive for one side or the other that undermined a proposed peace agreement. Note that in two cases, Burma and the Congo Republic, the resource appeared to create an economic incentive in favor of a peace settlement; and in the case of Cambodia, the discipline problems created by the resources led to a quicker end to the conflict.

a. Made the conflict shorter.

resources.[26] The evidence is somewhat harder to interpret regarding the third process. Resources appeared to create an economic incentive that undermined peace treaties in Liberia and the Democratic Republic of Congo.[27] In the former case, the resources were lootable; in the latter, they were both lootable and unlootable. In two other cases, Burma and the Congo Republic, resource wealth appeared to create incentives that hastened a settlement.[28] It is difficult to draw any general conclusions about this final dynamic.

In short, there is indirect evidence that both lootable and unlootable resources may trigger at least two processes that prolong conflicts, and that—as Hypothesis 5 suggests—lootable resources tend to trigger these processes more frequently than unlootable resources.

Hypothesis 6: If a resource is obstructable, it is more likely to increase the duration and intensity of conflicts.

There are two reasons why this may be so. First, obstructable resources are subject to holdups, a tactic that benefits a weaker party in its campaign against a stronger opponent, and hence will tend to lengthen a conflict. The most easily obstructed resource, oil, has been a factor in five of the fifteen conflicts in the sample. In three cases the oil has been offshore and hence impervious to holdups (Angola-Cabinda, Angola-UNITA, and the Congo Republic); but in the other two cases (Colombia and Sudan), rebels have bombed pipelines to extort money from the government or oil firms, and to disrupt the government's revenues.[29]

In Colombia, for example, the country's oil must be transported to the coast from the unstable interior through two exceptionally long pipelines.[30] In 2000 the pipelines were bombed ninety-eight times. Colombia's rebel groups have used these attacks to extort an estimated U.S.$140 million annually; this windfall has enabled one group, the National Liberation Army (ELN), to grow from fewer than 40 members to at least 3,000.[31]

Obstructable resources can also have a second effect: a government may anticipate that its resources will be subject to holdups by aggrieved local peoples, and decide to act preemptively by using terror and repression against them. Here we might not witness a full-blown civil war—if the repression is "successful" in the government's eyes—but nonetheless have a large number of resource-related casualties. Such preemptive campaigns have occurred in the Indonesian province of Aceh, where a natural gas facility was threatened by a proseparatist movement; and even more lethally in Sudan.

Sudan has witnessed both holdups by the rebel group and preemptive repression by the government. Sudan's oil reserves are located in the country's south, a region with long-standing separatist aspirations. The north's efforts to gain access to the south's oil have been a major source of grievance, which has been evident in both the rhetoric and the actions of the Sudan People's Liberation Army (SPLA): it has issued complaints that the north is stealing the south's resources, and between 1983 and 1999 it repeatedly demanded that work cease on a pipeline that would take oil from wells in the south to a refinery in the north. It also periodically attacked the workers and equipment associated with pipeline construction. These attacks helped the SPLA to fund itself by extorting money from Western oil firms that wished to protect their equipment.[32]

To counter the rebels, the government has tried to forcibly create a cordon sanitaire around the pipeline, and to clear whole populations from the oil fields. Clearances in the upper Nile region began in 1980, halted in the mid-1980s when oil development temporarily ceased, then commenced anew in the late 1990s when oil development resumed. Since early 1999 the government has used summary executions, rape, ground attacks, helicopter gunships, and high-altitude bombing to force tens of thousands of people from their homes in the oil regions. It has also razed houses, destroyed crops, and looted livestock to prevent people from returning. Although foreign observers have often been prevented from entering the affected areas, the pattern of displacements has been documented by both a special rapporteur for the UN Commission on Human Rights and several nongovernmental organizations.[33]

Hypothesis 7: If the resource is illegal, it is more likely to benefit the rebels—unless the government is willing to endure international sanctions.

There are strong international sanctions against the production of illegal natural resources—for example, coca, opium, and cannabis; these sanctions are more effective against states than against nonstate entities, like rebel movements. If illegal substances are cultivated in a country suffering a civil war, it will be hard for the government's forces to profit from their presence, since they are likely to be subjected to international sanctions; a rebel group should be less responsive to international sanctions and hence should be more likely to seek funding from drug sales. This should not hold true, however, for governments that are willing to endure international sanctions, and pursue autarkic economic policies.

There are just four drug-producing states in the sample, which makes it difficult to know if this is a valid generalization. Table 3.10 lists these states, along with the side that benefited from the drug trade. In one case (Peru), only the rebels systematically raised money from the drug trade. In the other cases, both sides earned money from drugs—in two cases (Afghanistan and Burma) because the government was willing to endure international sanctions, and in the third case (Colombia) because drug revenues were collected by paramilitary forces, which were allied with the government but sufficiently independent from it (at least nominally) to allow the government to avoid international sanctions.

Implications and Conclusions

The aim of this chapter is to help determine whether some types of natural resources are more closely tied to civil wars than others, and if so,

Table 3.10 Which Side Profits from Illegal Drugs?

	Substance	Beneficiary
Afghanistan	Opium	Both
Burma	Opium	Both
Colombia	Coca, opium	Both
Peru	Coca	Rebels

why. The first section, using simple cross-tabulations, showed that alluvial diamonds and illegal drugs appear to be more strongly linked to civil war than other resources; that timber is not associated with civil war; and that other categories of natural resources are about equally tied to civil wars. The second section used evidence from fifteen recent civil wars to develop hypotheses about why this pattern may hold. I argued that three qualities of any natural resource—most important, its susceptibility to low-cost extraction, or "looting"—tend to influence the incidence and duration of civil wars. The data also suggested that different types of resources have different consequences for separatist wars than for nonseparatist wars. Below I describe the implications of these seven hypotheses for both unlootable and lootable resources.

Unlootable Resources

Unlootable resources include oil, natural gas, and all types of deep-shaft minerals.[34] The seven hypotheses have both positive and negative implications for states with unlootable resources; in general, the good news concerns nonseparatist conflicts and the bad news concerns separatist conflicts.

The good news is that unlootable resources should make nonseparatist conflicts briefer, because they tend to be of greater benefit to the government. If the government is the stronger party—which is true in most of the fifteen cases presented here—this should hasten the end of the conflict by bringing about a quicker government victory. On the other hand, if the government is the weaker party, but still receives revenues from unlootable resources—as in the case of Angola in 1993–1994, and in the Democratic Republic of Congo in 1997–1998—it may prolong the conflict by averting the government's defeat.

The bad news about unlootable resources is that they are more likely than lootable resources to cause separatist conflicts; moreover, separatist conflicts tend to last longer than nonseparatist conflicts. Five separatist conflicts in this sample were in part caused by grievances over the distribution of resource wealth; such grievances appear more likely to arise over unlootable resources than over lootable resources. In cases where the resource is obstructable—in particular, when it must travel through a long, above-ground pipeline—it creates a further class of problems, by presenting rebel groups with an unceasing flow of extortion opportunities.

These two dangers—that unlootable resources will be a source of grievance (in separatist conflicts), or a source of finance (if they are obstructable)—are depicted in Figure 3.4. The upper-right quadrant contains nonseparatist conflicts with an obstructable resource; in this cell, natural resources should be a source of rebel finance (because they are obstructable) but not a source of rebel grievance (because they are not separatist conflicts). The Colombia case fits this description closely.

The lower-left quadrant contains cases where the resource cannot be used for finance (since it is relatively unobstructable) but where it is a source of grievance (since it is found in a province with separatist aspirations). Each of the four cases in this cell are persistent, long-running conflicts in which violence has been minimal—generally producing fewer than 100 deaths per year. This pattern is consistent with a conflict over a long-standing grievance (the perceived maldistribution of resource revenues), in which the separatist group does not have a major source of finance, and hence is unable to fight a war that produces a large number of casualties.

The conflict in the Indonesian province of West Papua (formerly Irian Jaya) provides an illustration. Indonesia invaded the former Dutch colony in 1962, and later annexed it; a small proindependence army, the Organisasi Papua Merdeka (OPM), has been active since around 1965. In the early 1970s a U.S. firm, Freeport-McMoran, began to operate a major copper mine on the southern part of the island; since then, the mine has been a further source of grievance for the island's indigenous

Figure 3.4 Conflicts Involving Unlootable Resources

	Separatist ($\rightarrow$ grievance)	Nonseparatist ($\rightarrow$ no grievance)
Obstructable ($\rightarrow$ finance)	Sudan	Colombia[a]
Unobstructable ($\rightarrow$ no finance)	Indonesia (Aceh) Indonesia (W. Papua) Papua New Guinea Angola (Cabinda)	Angola (UNITA)[a] Congo Republic DRC[a]

Note: a. Has both lootable and unlootable resources.

population. The mine has intermittently been the target of OPM attacks. Proseparatist propaganda, including that generated by the OPM, argues that West Papua's resource wealth is wrongfully appropriated by the central government, and that Papuans would be wealthier if the province were independent. The government's military operations around the mine site, in turn, have led to human rights violations and have further heightened anti-Indonesia sentiment. There is no indication, however, that the OPM has used resource looting or extortion around the mine site to fund itself. Moreover, resource wealth has helped the stronger side in the conflict—the Indonesian military—not the OPM, which remains small and ill equipped. The OPM has perhaps several hundred "hard-core" members, and several dozen firearms—mostly old and rusted weapons from World War II. The conflict generates fewer than 100 casualties a year.

The upper-left quadrant of Figure 3.4 contains the most troubled category of conflicts: separatist conflicts over obstructable resources, in which an unlootable resource becomes both a source of grievance and a source of finance. There is, fortunately, just one state from the sample that fits into this cell: Sudan.

The lower-right quadrant includes states with unlootable, unobstructable resources engaged in nonseparatist conflicts. These three cases—Angola (UNITA), the Congo Republic, and the Democratic Republic of Congo—feature conflicts in which the resource is neither a source of grievance nor a source of finance via extortion. Two of these conflicts (Angola and the Democratic Republic of Congo) have both lootable and unlootable resources, and it has largely been their lootable resources that have made these conflicts long and bloody. The only case that has unlootable, unobstructable resources exclusively—the Congo Republic—was an unusual conflict, in that the opposition group received funding from a foreign oil firm and expected an imminent takeover of the government. After a four-month war, financed in part by this payment, the opposition group was proven right.

Lootable Resources

Alluvial gemstones and agricultural crops, including drugs, are all lootable resources. Diamonds and drugs were strongly associated with civil conflict in the 1990s, and are commonly viewed as the most troublesome resources. But this chapter suggests that there is another side to these commodities: they also tend to produce more widespread benefits for local peoples, and the poor, than do unlootable resources. The seven hypotheses have positive and negative implications for countries with lootable resources. In this case, the positive implications are for separatist conflicts, the negative for nonseparatist conflicts.

The good news is that lootable resources do not seem to generate separatist conflicts. Since lootable resources produce more revenues for unskilled workers, and for local peoples, they also seem to generate fewer grievances. There are six separatist conflicts in the sample. Five entail grievances over unlootable resources (see Figure 3.2).

The bad news about lootable resources is that they appear to prolong nonseparatist conflicts, due to two factors: their tendency to benefit rebel groups, and their tendency to cause discipline problems in the army that exploits them. These two effects have helped produce long, chaotic civil wars in eight of the fifteen cases in the sample: Afghanistan, Angola, Cambodia, Colombia, the Democratic Republic of Congo, Liberia, Peru, and Sierra Leone. If the resource is also illegal, this makes it even more likely to favor the rebel side.

For these reasons, lootable resources appear to create more complicated civil wars, with greater fragmentation and shifting alliances among the armies that control the resource. They may also be harder to resolve, due to this fragmentation, and because the widespread benefits they produce may make sanctions harder to implement and more costly for poor and local peoples.

In short, this study suggests that some resources are more dangerous to exploit than others; and that different resources are associated with different types of conflicts: unlootable resources are more likely to produce separatist conflicts, and lootable resources are more likely to produce nonseparatist conflicts. These patterns appear to hold true for the fifteen conflicts in the sample; to know whether they are true for a larger set of conflicts, they would have to be subjected to further testing, especially with a different data set. Still, they may hint at the complicated and contradictory effects that a country's natural resource endowment may have organized violence occuring inside its own borders.

* * *

Appendix 3.1 Diamond and Drug Producers, 1995

Diamond producers: **Angola,** Australia, Botswana, Brazil, Central African Republic, China, **Democratic Republic of Congo,** Côte d'Ivoire, Ghana, Guinea, **Liberia,** Namibia, **Russia, Sierra Leone,** South Africa, Venezuela, Zimbabwe.

Alluvial diamond producers: **Angola,** Brazil, Central African Republic, **Democratic Republic of Congo,** Côte d'Ivoire, Ghana, **Liberia, Sierra Leone.**

Opium producers: **Afghanistan, Burma, Colombia,** Laos, Mexico, Pakistan, Vietnam.

Coca producers: Bolivia, **Colombia, Peru.**

Cannabis producers: **Afghanistan, Cambodia, Colombia,** Jamaica, Morocco, Mexico, Nigeria, Pakistan, South Africa, Thailand.

Sources: Ronald F. Balazik, "Industrial Diamonds" (Washington, D.C.: U.S. Geological Survey, 1998); UN Office for Drug Control and Crime Prevention (UNOCCP), "World Drug Report, 2000" (New York: Oxford University Press, 2000).
Note: **Bold** denotes countries that experienced civil wars in the 1990s.

Notes

I am grateful to Karen Ballentine, Philippe Le Billon, and Jake Sherman for comments on an earlier draft.

1. Like most scholars, I define civil wars as conflicts that occur within the recognized boundaries of a single state; involve combat between the state and at least one organized rebel force; and result in at least 1,000 deaths during a single calendar year. I use the database assembled by Paul Collier and Anke Hoeffler to determine when civil wars have occurred. See Paul Collier and Anke Hoeffler, "Greed and Grievance in Civil War," Policy Research Working Paper no. 2355 (Washington, D.C.: World Bank, 2001).

2. Paul Collier and Anke Hoeffler, "On the Economic Causes of Civil War," *Oxford Economic Papers* 50, no. 4 (October 1998): 563–573; Collier and Hoeffler, "Greed and Grievance"; Indra de Soysa, "Natural Resources and Civil War: Shrinking Pie or Honey Pot?" paper presented at the International Studies Association, Los Angeles, March 2000; and Ibrahim Elbadawi and Nicholas Sambanis, "How Much War Will We See? Estimating the Prevalence of Civil War in 161 Countries, 1960–1999," *Journal of Conflict Resolution* 46, no. 2 (June 2002): 307–334.

3. James D. Fearon, "Why Do Some Civil Wars Last So Much Longer Than Others?" paper presented at the World Bank–UC Irvine conference on "Civil Wars and Post-Conflict Transition," Irvine, Calif., May 18, 2001.

4. Michael L. Ross, "How Does Natural Resource Wealth Influence Civil War? Evidence from 13 Case Studies," paper presented at the World Bank–UC Irvine conference on "Civil Wars and Post-Conflict Transition," Irvine, Calif., May 18, 2001.

5. Ibid.

6. Collier and Hoeffler suggest that the relationship between resource dependence and civil wars is curvilinear, so that the danger of civil war peaks when resource dependence reaches a relatively high level, but declines at the

very highest levels. Other scholars estimate the relationship between resource dependence and civil war to be linear. Both estimates would predict a higher civil war rate among the top one-third of resource-dependent states than among the middle and bottom thirds. Collier and Hoeffler, "Greed and Grievance."

7. World Bank, *World Development Indicators 2001* (Washington, D.C.: World Bank, 2001), CD-ROM.

8. I chose 1995 because it is the year for which the greatest quantity of data are available, by far. By comparing 1995 levels of resource dependence to decade-long civil war rates, I am increasing the danger of endogeneity—that is, that causation may be running in both directions. On the problem of endogeneity in assessing the relationship between natural resources and civil conflict, see Ross, "How Does Natural Resource Wealth Influence Civil War?"

9. Collier and Hoeffler, "Greed and Grievance." Of these 161 states, 15 failed to produce any data on their export of natural resources, leaving a sample of 146 states with 29 civil wars for Table 3.2. The rate of civil wars in this smaller sample, however, is identical to the rate in the larger sample: 19.9 percent.

10. I use the period 1990–2000 because it is easier to use in analyzing more recent conflicts. The end of the Cold War may have produced an unusually large number of resource-related wars during this decade, since it may have forced combatants in some developing countries (such as Cambodia, Afghanistan, and Angola) to replace funding from superpowers with funding from natural resource exploitation. See David Keen, *The Economic Functions of Violence in Civil Wars* (Oxford: Oxford University Press for the International Institute for Strategic Studies, 1998).

11. Collier and Hoeffler find that oil is somewhat more closely tied to conflict than mining and agricultural products—although their database does not appear to include diamonds or drugs. Collier and Hoeffler, "Greed and Grievance."

12. Note that the first and second columns measure the quantity of timber harvested, while the third and fourth measure the value of timber exports, as a fraction of GDP.

13. Michael Klare, *Resource Wars: The New Landscape of Global Conflict* (New York: Metropolitan Books, 2001).

14. I define "nonproducers" as states that produced five or fewer tons of opium and coca.

15. "Primary producers" are the main sources of internationally traded cannabis, while "secondary producers" export lesser amounts.

16. Philippe Le Billon, "The Political Ecology of War: Natural Resources and Armed Conflicts," *Political Geography* 20, no. 5 (June 2001): 561–584.

17. I am borrowing the concept of lootability from Collier and Hoeffler, "Greed and Grievance," and Le Billon, "Political Ecology of War," although the definition is my own.

18. There is also an illegal international trade in endangered species and their products; I have found only one instance of their sale by military forces. See Ros Reeve and Stephen Ellis, "An Insider's Account of the South African Security Forces' Role in the Ivory Trade," *Journal of Contemporary African Studies* 13, no. 2 (July 1995): 227–244.

19. I am grateful to Karen Ballentine for pointing out this implication.

20. Other prominent examples from earlier decades are the Biafra rebellion in Nigeria, and the Katanga rebellions in the Democratic Republic of Congo.

21. Note that for conflicts in which both lootable and unlootable resources

mattered (Angola, Colombia, and the Democratic Republic of Congo), I have listed separately which party generated money from which resource.

22. Le Billon makes a similar point. Le Billon, "Political Ecology of War."

23. An important assumption is that conflicts will tend to last longer when the two sides have more equal resources. This assumption is supported by evidence from interstate conflicts. D. Scott Bennett, and Alan C. Stam III, "The Duration of Interstate Wars, 1816–1985," *American Political Science Review* 90, no. 2 (June 1996): 239–257.

24. Fearon, "Why Do Some Civil Wars Last So Much Longer Than Others?"; and Ross, "How Does Natural Resource Wealth Influence Civil War?"

25. Fearon, "Why Do Some Civil Wars Last So Much Longer Than Others?"

26. Note, however, that in the case of Cambodia, these discipline problems led to an earlier end to the conflict when a rebel faction defected to the government side in order to retain its access to timber and gems.

27. Stephen Ellis, *The Mask of Anarchy: The Destruction of Liberia and the Religious Dimension of an African Civil War* (New York: New York University Press, 1999); UN Panel of Experts, "Report of the Panel of Experts on the Illegal Exploitation of Natural Resources and Other Forms of Wealth of the Democratic Republic of Congo," S/2001/357, UN Security Council, April 12, 2001.

28. Bertil Lintner, *Burma in Revolt* (Bangkok: Silkworm Press, 1999).

29. Obstructable resources are similar to lootable resources, since small bands of unskilled troops can use them to generate revenues.

30. One pipeline, operated by BP Amoco, is 444 miles long; the other, operated by Occidental Petroleum, is 485 miles long.

31. Thad Dunning and Leslie Wirpsa, "Andean Gulf? The Political Economy of Oil and Violence in Colombia," paper presented at the University of California, Davis, conference on "The Wars in Colombia," May 17–19, 2001, mimeo.

32. Edgar O'Ballance, *Sudan, Civil War, and Terrorism, 1956–1999* (New York: St. Martin's Press, 2000); and G. Norman, *Sudan in Crisis* (Gainesville: University Press of Florida, 1999).

33. UN Commission on Human Rights, "Situation of Human Rights in the Sudan," draft report, 57th sess., E/CN.4/2001/L.11/Add.3, April 21, 2001; and Christian Aid, *The Scorched Earth: Oil and War in Sudan,* 2001, www.christian-aid.org.uk/indepth/0103suda/sudanoil.htm (accessed September 1, 2001). It is important to acknowledge that the Sudanese civil war does not conform to simple "separatist," "Muslim versus non-Muslim," or "north-south" descriptions. Often these divisions have been blurred: the northern Muslim government has sometimes made alliances with non-Muslim Dinka or Nuer militias in the south, while the rebels have sometimes been allied with northern Muslim groups that have fallen out of favor with the government. According to a report by Amnesty International, "during the last few years, more people have lost their lives in inter-factional fighting amongst Southerners than in armed encounters with government forces." Amnesty International, "Oil in Sudan: Deteriorating Human Rights," Report no. AFR 54/01/00ERR, May 3, 2000, p. 3.

34. This includes diamonds that are deposited far underground—often called kimberlite diamonds.

PART 2

Case Studies

4

The Colombian Conflict: Political and Economic Dimensions

Alexandra Guáqueta

UNLIKE MANY OTHER CONFLICTS THAT HAD THEIR ORIGIN IN THE COLD WAR era and wound down with the end of superpower confrontation, the Colombian civil war experienced unprecedented intensification in the 1990s. Except for the rise of illegal right-wing paramilitary groups, the broad political dynamics of the conflict remain largely unchanged. Left-wing guerrillas, such as the Fuerzas Armadas Revolucionarias de Colombia (FARC) and the Ejercito de Liberación Nacional (ELN), and the state continue to be locked in a violent contest focused on determining who exercises political power, redressing historically rooted socioeconomic grievances of marginalized classes, and competing ideas on the type of political and economic system Colombia should have.[1] Guerrillas want a socialist welfare system and the redistribution of wealth. Rightwing illegal paramilitary groups, which appeared in the early 1980s under the aegis of the Autodefensas Unidas de Colombia (AUC), want to eliminate the guerrilla threat and retain the political and economic status quo. Meanwhile, the weakened Colombian democratic state has sought to fend off both threats by steadily increasing military expenditure and courting increased U.S. military and counternarcotics assistance.

This said, certain dynamics of the forty-year conflict have changed perceptibly since 1996. Globalization, economic recession, and expanded access to international flows of funds and weapons have all fueled the escalation of the conflict, the growth in the number of armed combatants, and the spread of conflict to previously unaffected areas of the country. These events have also led to the unprecedented internationalization of the conflict, both in terms of spillover effects to neighboring countries and in terms of direct international involvement.

Since 1982, successive efforts to resolve the conflict through negotiations have foundered. The failure in February 2002 of the almost four-year-long peace initiative led by former president Andrés Pastrana was especially frustrating, since the political conditions seemed more favorable to a peaceful resolution to the conflict than in previous years. To induce the guerrillas to demobilize and enter peace talks, Pastrana conceded a 41,000-square-kilometer demilitarized zone and "safe haven" to the FARC. Dozens of U.S., European, and local nongovernmental organizations (NGOs) working to foster a culture of peace sprang up throughout the territory, while the UN and "Groups of Friends" offered their good offices in mediating the conflict. Yet the FARC and the ELN only continued to escalate their attacks.

The stubbornness of the conflict has prompted some policymakers and academics to reexamine the nature of the conflict and the factors that drive it. This has focused attention on crucial economic dimensions of the war that have been ignored or downplayed by traditional analyses. All three sides in the conflict have ample financial resources to continue fighting. The FARC and the ELN rely on revenues derived from the extortion and kidnapping of both local and foreign individuals and companies, and the FARC is notorious for its increasing involvement in the international narcotics trade. The right-wing paramilitaries have been even more closely linked to the production and trafficking of narcotics, with drug revenues constituting the main source of financing for their campaign against the guerrillas. The Colombian state has received steadily increasing amounts of economic and military aid from the United States to fight drug trafficking and, more recently, to defend against guerrilla attacks on the Caño-Limón oil pipeline. Given these facts, it is not surprising that some policymakers and analysts have come to question whether the combatants have "lost their way," transforming the conflict from a largely ideological and political dispute to an economically driven war in which opportunity for combatant self-enrichment has become paramount. Some emerging theories on the economic dimensions of civil war are inclined to support this position.

While conceding that these economic factors have altered and complicated the dynamics of the conflict, this analysis shows that, for the most part, the Colombian civil war continues to be politically and ideologically driven at its core. Examining the Colombian situation through the lens of the emerging economic theories of conflict, however, highlights the importance of economic factors to both the intensity and the duration of the civil war, while also drawing attention to the role of a range of economic actors—from companies involved in natural resource extraction, insurance, and private security, to global arms manufacturers and brokers, to local and international drug smugglers, to rural coca and poppy growers with few alternative livelihoods who derive benefit from the economy of war and whose behavior contributes to its continuation. In so doing, this analysis seeks to shed light not only on the contemporary predicament of Colombia, but also on key academic and policy debates on the nature of resources that fuel conflicts and on the interplay between the economic and political incentives that shape the behavior of the main actors involved. The chapter concludes with an assessment of possible policy responses to both the political and the economic dimensions of the conflict.

Background and Current Trends
Within the Colombian Conflict

The FARC emerged in 1964 as a remnant of *la violencia* (1948–1957)—the violent irregular confrontation, predominantly in small towns and rural areas, between civilian supporters of the Liberal and Conservative Parties. When party leaders in Bogotá signed a peace agreement, radical Liberals splintered off from the mainstream party, took refuge outside Bogotá, and joined members of the Communist Party to form a Marxist rebel group. Adapting Soviet Marxism and the Cold War struggle to the local political and social context of *la violencia* and inequitable land distribution, the FARC aimed to break the tight hierarchical socioeconomic structure of Colombian society and construct a socialist one in its place. The agreement between Liberals and Conservatives to alternate the presidency under four-year terms during 1958–1976, the Frente Nacional, further restricted the participation of advocates of socialist and communist political ideologies. The Colombian government and its security forces, seen as proxies of U.S. hegemony, became the FARC's enemy.

The ELN emerged in 1962 with a core group of twenty members, mostly university students attracted by the Cuban Revolution model and influenced by liberation theology. Like the FARC, they based their struggle on political and social grievances and were rural-based. Neither group advocated separatism or had ethnic affiliations.

The civil war between the guerrillas and the state was in reality a rather contained confrontation until 1992, and peace negotiations were the norm.[2] The guerrilla groups received little financial support from external actors, such as Cuba or the Soviet Union, but they looked to Fidel Castro and the Soviet regime for political and ideological endorsement. During their first years of existence, these groups were smaller in size than they are today and tended to recruit supporters in lowly populated areas that lacked state presence, far away from the urban centers where 60–75 percent of the population lived. Military battles were usually of a low intensity and frequency. Civilian policymakers in Bogotá, who ran a centralist administration, perceived the guerrillas as a distant and manageable threat to the country's continuous economic development and stable administrative and political institutions. The state was aware that guerrilla groups had gained tacit and at times overt support among the urban poor. Although they were not directly involved in or affected by the fighting, the urban poor sympathized with the basic ideas of redistributing economic and political power, but believed that differences could be resolved through negotiation.

A combination of political culture, pragmatism, and the general awareness in Colombia of the insufficiency of its political and economic institutions led the state to undertake peace negotiations with the insurgents. President Belisario Betancur (1982–1986) launched the first major initiative in 1982. By then, taxing coca production and extorting oil companies were emerging as promising means of guerrilla fundraising. FARC and ELN leaders believed they could expand their membership and thereby increase their demands in future negotiations. As a result of the relative strength of the guerrilla movement, Betancur obtained an imperfect cease-fire in which only 10 percent of FARC members demobilized. Both sides learned important lessons in the 1980s, which continue to influence their behavior. In particular, the guerrillas learned that demobilizing was unsafe. The political arm of the FARC, the Unión Patriótica, which was formed by communists and demobilized members, was gradually exterminated through internal vendettas and selected assassinations by paramilitary and corrupt military officers. Security forces, in contrast, saw how the guerrillas exploited the cease-fire in order to arm and continue to recruit and train. Despite these misgivings, however, Betancur's successor, Virgilio Barco (1986–1990), renewed peace offers and prepared the ground for the demobilization of other Colombian rebel groups, including the Movimiento 19 de Abril (M-19), the Ejército Popular Revolucionario (EPR), Quintín Lame, and the Corriente de Renovación Socialista. The demobilization took place after President César Gaviria (1990–1994) was elected in 1990 and launched the watershed 1991 National Constituent Assembly, which introduced substantial reforms to accommodate the guerrillas' political demands and improve participatory and representative democracy at the local level. Yet neither the FARC nor the ELN gave up their struggle. Instead, both groups continued growing at a steady pace. Confrontations with the Colombian security forces and attacks against police garrisons increased.

Political violence increased with the spread of right-wing paramilitarism. Small groups of 50 to 100 men began mushrooming in the countryside to provide peasant self-protection or to defend farmers and landowners from guerrilla kidnapping and extortion. Some of these landowners had originally amassed their wealth through the drug trade.[3] Well-funded paramilitaries soon turned to offensive vigilantism.

The August 30, 1996, attack by the FARC against the Colombian Armed Forces base at Las Delicias in Putumayo, which led a wave of twenty-five assaults against military bases and police stations all over Colombia on August 30–31, and the consolidation of the AUC in 1997 were unequivocal signs that Colombia's political violence had entered a new phase. Ideology, deep-rooted socioeconomic grievances, and motivations of political power had ignited the Colombian conflict, but the continuous stream of money and weapons helped to transform it into a full-scale civil war. The administration of Ernesto Samper was unable to counter the emboldened combatants or offer a new peace process because it lacked legitimacy and was overwhelmed by other mounting political and economic crises, which acted as catalysts for the escalation of the conflict since 1996. These crises included the long and damning political turmoil unleashed when it was revealed that the Cali cartel had paid U.S.$6 million into Samper's presidential campaign in 1994; the resulting U.S. diplomatic war against Samper—which never achieved his ouster but weakened his government; and the rapid and unprecedented slowdown of the economy, including rising unemployment.

Since then, the war has experienced several trends. First, the number of combatants, illegal and legal, has increased. Over the past two decades the FARC progressively expanded its fronts from twenty-seven in 1984, to sixty in 1992, to eighty in 2000,[4] involving approximately 15,000–18,000 members.[5] Since 1996, the FARC has also changed its structure, forming, in addition to the fronts, at least four mobile blocks totaling 800 members. The ELN grew from 70 members in the 1960s,[6] to 800 in the mid-1980s, to as many as 5,000 in 1996,[7] before suffering heavy losses against the Colombian Armed Forces and the paramilitaries since 2000. It is speculated that the weakened ELN now has 3,000 men. The Colombian Armed Forces began a recruiting and training campaign in 1998. Regular recruits increased from 57,041 to 83,068 in 2002, professional soldiers from 22,891 to 55,071, while high school graduate recruits decreased from 36,000 to 3,000.[8]

Second, combat has spread. Villages and cities that were formerly peaceful have suffered violent attacks. Paramilitaries, in particular, spread swiftly from their initial strongholds in Córdoba, Urabá, and

César. They have entered municipalities in Antioquia, oil-rich Arauca, coca-rich Putumayo, and Valle. They have also encircled part of the FARC's former demilitarized zone in Meta. The FARC has increased its urban cells and since 2001 has launched a spate of bomb attacks to terrorize urban inhabitants, hoping to weaken state authority. It has also attacked vital infrastructure like water supply centers, electricity towers, and phone transmission towers.[9] The ELN, after peaking in terms of military strength and territorial domain in 1998, encountered severe attacks from the paramilitaries and is now more likely to demobilize or be absorbed by the FARC. The escalation of military and political competition among larger and better-equipped armed groups has increased war-related casualties, made the massacres more frequent and brutal, displaced larger numbers of innocent civilians, and increased kidnapping.[10]

Third, amid the human security crisis, the political space for neutrality has diminished. Both in the cities and in the countryside, Colombians have become increasingly polarized, siding out of fear, opportunism, or conviction with either the guerrillas, the paramilitaries, or the security forces. The AUC has developed a base of social and political influence. The urban middle class, targeted by guerrilla kidnappings, began sympathizing with the paramilitary cause. In smaller rural towns, inhabitants have turned to paramilitary leaders to resolve personal disputes related to property, debts, and political rivalry, which de facto has turned them into a quasi-legitimate authority. In the past, left-wing guerrillas had occupied this role, but lost popular support due to their terrorist methods. Under the AUC, the paramilitaries that were once regarded as narco-funded criminals have become a politically recognized force, eligible for both participation in peace negotiations and amnesty.

Fourth, conflict-related crime has risen as combatants resort to participation in the drug trade, extortion, kidnapping, money laundering, the illegal exploitation of minerals, and common theft to buy weapons and train combatants. However, in contrast to many internal conflicts elsewhere in the developing world, systematic pillaging and plundering has not occurred.

Fifth, the Colombian conflict has become internationalized. Since 1999, war has spilled over into neighboring countries in several ways: through temporary refugees fleeing from cross-fire or selective killings by armed groups; through the permanent migration by those in danger of being kidnapped or seeking safer homes; through the short-term use of border zones by state security forces conducting operations against nonstate actors; through the establishment of guerrilla camps in border areas; through criminal fundraising by illegal combatants using extortion and kidnapping in neighboring countries; and through the greater

integration of inhabitants from the border zones and of regional criminal networks into the war economy via contraband, arms trafficking,
and drug trafficking. For some neighboring countries, these spillovers
have posed urgent security threats.

Finally, departing from the historical pattern of prudent and limited
engagement in Colombia, the United States has steadily become more
involved in the conflict through technical and military assistance to the
Colombian security forces, mainly to carry out counternarcotics operations, but also to mount selected counterinsurgency operations such as
those undertaken to protect oil pipelines. Above all, the United States
has become the major international influence shaping Colombia's conflict resolution strategies. Also unprecedented is the level of international media reporting, NGO activism, and international diplomatic
involvement at high political levels. In 1998, Colombia and the United
Nations agreed to appoint Jan Egeland as a Special Adviser of the
Secretary-General to Colombia. In 1999, "Groups of Friends" joined the
separate peace processes with the ELN and the FARC.[11]

The International Drug Market, Transnational Crime, and the Growth of Illegal Armed Groups

Both the guerrillas and the paramilitaries benefited from the progressive
growth of illegal drug production and smuggling in Colombia. Their
participation in the highly profitable international illegal drug industry
has strengthened their respective military capacities and determined
their choices for territorial expansion. From 1970 to 2000, Colombia
went from being a minor marijuana producer and exporter to the
world's largest cocaine exporter since 1982, an important source of
heroin since 1996, and the world's largest coca leaf producer since
1997. Drug cultivation grew apace with the escalation of conflict. Both
accelerated in 1996, at which time Colombia had 67,200 harvestable
hectares of coca leaf—nearly double what it had in 1990—and 32 percent of the total world cultivation. In 2000 the figure skyrocketed to
136,200 hectares, 74 percent of total world cultivation. This occurred
despite the intensification of aerial and manual eradication efforts by
U.S.-funded Colombian antinarcotics police.

Several factors prompted this transformation in the illegal drug
market. The success of antidrug policies in Bolivia and Peru in the mid-
1990s resulted in a drop in the amount of coca base, essential for the
production of cocaine, supplied to Colombia, and opened a new market
opportunity for domestic producers. The air interdiction operations of

1995–1998 carried out to break the Peru-Colombia air bridge depressed the earnings from coca leaf cultivation in Peru, at least until 1999, and acted as a temporary disincentive for cultivation. In Bolivia the reduction of coca base resulted from forced manual eradication campaigns from 1992 to 1997. Given the constant high levels of global drug demand, cultivation needed to be relocated. New fields sprung up in Colombia, where conditions were favorable. Colombia had entrepreneurial drug traffickers with access to global markets, capital, and the experience to replace supply, diversify production, and maintain profits by initiating farmers into the cultivation of coca and poppy through distribution of seeds and credit. This was facilitated by a needy agrarian work force. The Colombian agricultural crisis that began in the early 1990s had left many peasants and rural workers destitute and therefore eager to turn to profitable coca leaf and poppy crops. The crisis was partly related to mistakes in the government's economic liberalization policies and exposure to competition by foreign-subsidized agricultural products. Rural violence had also affected legal agricultural development and work opportunities for peasants, and squatters had become increasingly scarce.[12] Illegal armed groups controlled vast and isolated rural areas where coca leaf could be grown without much state interference. The guerrillas and the paramilitaries also had the capability and the incentive to facilitate the emergence of new fields and laboratories. In short, war facilitated the massive relocation of coca and poppy cultivation in Colombia.

The FARC and the Illegal Drug Trade

At its 1982 and 1984 conventions, the FARC made it their policy to raise funds by taxing coca production. As the conflict escalated, however, its involvement in the illegal drug industry expanded, especially after 1996. In the 1980s the FARC taxed peasants who harvested coca leaf as well as middlemen who bought base and paste to be further processed. Occasionally the FARC provided surveillance for owners of laboratories and airstrips located in its areas of influence. With the escalation of conflict, the FARC expanded the radius within which it carried out these activities. It also began to acquire plots, process coca leaf into cocaine, and develop contacts of its own with regional mafia networks, such as the Mexican Tijuana cartel, which has access to global consumer markets. The April 2001 capture of the Brazilian drug baron Fernandiño while he was meeting with the FARC in Colombia was a key indication of this evolution. The FARC's refusal in 1998–2001 to admit international verification of the 41,000-square-kilometer demilitarized zone was instrumental to its ability to profit from the drug business and led Colombian authorities to further question the "true" aims and good faith of the group during the peace negotiations. It is estimated that the guerrillas' drug trade–related revenues were U.S.$3.2 billion from 1991 to 1999, and that yields in the late 1990s averaged U.S.$1.5 million a day—48 percent of their total income.[13]

To be sure, the level of participation by the guerrillas in the illegal drug trade is a controversial topic that has serious political repercussions for the prospects for a negotiated resolution to the conflict. Those in favor of a negotiated peace are inclined to overlook the criminal behavior of the nonstate armed groups. In contrast, the guerrillas' drug-processing and drug-trafficking activities have made it easier for hardline opponents to characterize them as mere criminal traffickers, thereby stiffening their unwillingness to accord any legitimacy to the guerrillas or to seek compromise with the FARC and the ELN on outstanding political and economic disputes. Likewise, peace efforts have been complicated by U.S. requests for extradition of guerrillas and paramilitaries on drug-trafficking charges. While extradition is based on 1997 Colombian antidrug legislation and related commitments to the United States, extradition requests were formulated only since the breakdown of peace talks in 2002 and the classification of the FARC, the ELN, and the AUC as international terrorist groups. Aside from the diplomatic problems this policy has posed for the Colombian authorities, U.S. extradition requests add to a growing tendency to treat insurgency as a criminal rather than a political phenomenon, to be resolved by criminal prosecution rather than peace talks.

The Paramilitaries and the Illegal Drug Trade

In March 2001, Carlos Castaño, the political leader of the Autodefensas de Córdoba y Urabá (ACU) and of the AUC, publicly admitted the AUC's involvement in the drug trade to finance its operations.[14] Paramilitary connections to drug trafficking have a long history, however. Indeed, one of the first right-wing proactive antiguerrilla organizations, Muerte a Secuestradores (MAS), or "Death to Kidnappers," was established in 1982 by wealthy Medellín drug traffickers and landowners.[15]

The connection between paramilitarism and drug trafficking was consolidated when paramilitary forces filled the vacuum in domestic and international smuggling activities left by the successful dismantling of the Medellín cartel in 1993 and the Cali cartel in 1995.[16] Since then the paramilitaries' drug business has become vertically integrated throughout the chain of production, from control over crops to international distribution.

Since 1996 the paramilitaries have sought to disrupt and take over the guerrillas' economic base, half of which is tied to drugs. The AUC has extended beyond its traditional strongholds in the departments of Magdalena, Córdoba, and Sucre, reaching coca-rich areas such as Putumayo. It gains the support and sympathy of the local population by offering to charge lower taxes and pay better rates than the FARC. Once they penetrate an area, the paramilitaries start up their own crops and displace farmers and peasants. This process of "cleansing" territories from guerrilla influence and gaining control over the coca market is invariably violent. The level of violence, however, decreases once paramilitaries obtain full control of a zone. The drug business earns the paramilitaries approximately 70 percent of their income, though estimates vary on the net amount (from U.S.$20 million to U.S.$200 million per year).[17] Voluntary contributions are less significant in financial terms, though not in political terms. Landholders pay extremely low sums—the equivalent of U.S.$5–$10 per hectare according to the yield capacity of the land and the type of agricultural activity they engage in—but these payments are enough to bind them to the paramilitaries: by paying, landowners become both economic supporters and de facto political guarantors of the paramilitary cause.[18]

Illegal Armed Groups and the Global Market

Globalization has helped illegal armed groups on all sides to translate drug money into military strength. Both the FARC and the AUC manage their finances using modern investment strategies and financial institutions outside Colombia.[19] The FARC, for instance, has fixed-term deposit investments in Panamanian banks. Part of the money is deposited directly in Panama after being collected in the demilitarized zone and part is transferred electronically from bank accounts in Colombia.[20] In 2001 the AUC used the Barnett Bank of Miami to make transactions that were camouflaged by legal businesses in Colombia and the United States, most of the latter based in Miami.[21] To conduct these transactions, paramilitaries co-opted members of the Colombian diaspora in the United States, some of whom are a product of conflict itself.[22]

Both the guerrillas and the paramilitaries purchase weapons and training services through international criminal networks. They have taken advantage of the large numbers of weapons available from the Central American war of the 1980s,[23] as well as the arms markets outside Latin America. New and old weapons flow from places as diverse as Bulgaria, Russia, Ukraine, Jordan, China, Israel, and the United States. Very often transactions involve corrupt government officials who issue and approve export licenses and end-use certificates and arrange for safe transportation to Colombia, as well as unscrupulous arms brokers.[24] The FARC reportedly also contracted foreign technical training from the Irish Republican Army (IRA) on the use of sophisticated explosives.[25]

Reassessing the Relation Between Oil and Conflict in Colombia

Natural resource extraction, especially in the oil and mining sectors, has been frequently linked to human rights abuse and environmental despoliation by repressive and corrupt states. In Angola, Sudan, Burma, Indonesia, and to a lesser extent Nigeria, natural resource extraction has also been identified as a major if indirect contributor to armed conflict. In some cases, lucrative revenues from concessions to multinational oil companies are used to finance government campaigns against nonstate armed groups. In others, conflict is exacerbated by crude efforts to secure oil and mineral production, including the forcible displacement of civilian communities from areas of extraction and the contracting by oil companies of unscrupulous or corrupt security forces. Because oil and mineral extraction is a capital-intensive enterprise, requiring sovereign guarantees against financial risk, it accrues to the benefit of state combatants. Oil windfalls are rarely associated with rebel profiteering, which is why the connection between oil and conflict in Colombia is somewhat atypical.[26]

The ELN was militarily defeated in 1973 but reemerged in the 1980s as it learned to exploit Colombia's oil boom.[27] In 1984, oil composed 20.46 percent of Colombia's exports. By 1990 this increased to 48.09 percent and by 1996 to 67.12 percent, or nearly 4 percent of Colombia's gross domestic product (GDP).[28] For the ELN, the oil boom offered new and lucrative opportunities for obstruction and extortion.[29] Bomb attacks on oil pipelines placed economic and security burdens on the state, while also generating jobs for ELN supporters, who would be hired to carry out reconstruction. These attacks also maintained the credibility of the ELN as anti-imperialist and anticapitalist, a political agenda that resonated with many Colombians who felt that multinational companies and the United States were exploiting Colombia's resources to their own advantage. The ELN also profited from oil extraction by extending its established practice of kidnapping for ransom from wealthy farmers and cattle ranchers to foreign oil workers and executives. Here the returns on kidnapping were perversely encouraged by corporate practices of insuring employees against kidnapping, a cost that was largely borne by insurance companies. But efforts to avoid this trap proved to be highly problematic. In 1984 the ELN kidnapped several employees of Mannesmann Anlagenbau A.G., a German engineering firm subcontracted by Occidental Petroleum, and the state-owned oil company Ecopetrol to build the Caño-Limón oil pipeline. To forestall further kidnappings, Mannesmann concluded a deal with the ELN that involved a onetime payment (reportedly U.S.$2–$10 million, but far less than the U.S. $300 million penalty Mannesmann was contractually bound to pay Occidental in the event of delayed construction), as well as an agreement to hire ELN supporters for community works, all in exchange for uninterrupted operations.[30] This payment helped to finance the ELN for several years, permitting it to recruit men and purchase weapons. The ELN also gained popularity by influencing the content and level of private-sector-funded community projects.[31]

More pervasively, the ELN found other ways to use oil resources as a source of funding. When oil came on stream in 1986, Colombian policymakers and legislators introduced a series of measures to distribute oil rents according to regional economic development plans and to avoid common problems generated by oil windfalls, such as central government corruption and grievances caused by perceived inequities in revenue distribution. Originally the central government agreed to transfer 12 percent of its 20 percent share of royalty revenues to less developed departments, while Ecopetrol and Occidental kept 40 percent each. Both companies still had to pay taxes, which contributed to further transfers to the state and the oil-rich regions. The 1991 and 1994 reforms to oil legislation and the process of administrative decentralization were undertaken to promote the transparent, equitable, and efficient use of revenue. To avoid central the government corruption and promote economic development outside the traditional urban centers, larger amounts of money were allocated to the oil-producing zones. To avoid local corruption, the 1991 constitution incorporated clauses with general guidelines on the allocation of oil and other mineral royalties. The 1994 National Law of Royalties contained detailed if confusing specifications for distributing oil revenues among health, education, and infrastructure. Additional provisions sought to avoid "Dutch disease" by applying lessons from Colombia's successful management of coffee earnings in the past.[32] These arrangements began to enlarge local coffers. In Arauca, where the ELN operated, oil revenue made up approximately 70 percent of the budget and the sparsely populated municipalities became some of the richest per capita in Colombia. Backed by the use of force, the ELN exploited oil royalties once the money reached local public budgets. The ELN did so in part by backing its candidates in local elections for positions where they could directly influence decisions on the spending of oil money. The ELN also sought to influence civil society organizations active in local politics, such as the Juntas de Acción Comunal. Violence and intimidation were often employed to influence the outcomes of elections and policy decisions, and thus the ELN had an important advantage over traditional politicians. As the oil zones were far from the central government, they lacked efficient policing, military surveillance, and justice administration. Ironically, then, well-intentioned, decentralized revenue-management schemes and democratization, which introduced the local election of mayors and town councils in 1986, unwittingly contributed to expose oil rents to guerrilla manipulation in the context of fragile and inexperienced local administrations.[33]

Following the ELN's successful model in Arauca, the FARC soon arrived in Casanare, a nearby oil-rich region, to reproduce the game of oil extortion and political influence. Over time the guerrillas became more adept at isolating traditional politicians through violence. Since 1988 the FARC and the ELN have been competing against each other for influence in the region,[34] yet the escalation of conflict in the 1990s has exacerbated competition over oil rents and over the support of labor unions and community groups in Arauca. In 2001 alone the FARC and the ELN staged 170 attacks against the Caño-Limón oil pipeline. The FARC's motivation was to effectively cut the flow of royalties to Arauca, which were benefiting the ELN. Kidnappings of employees of oil and engineering companies also increased. British Petroleum, one of the largest foreign investors in Colombia since 1987, stopped insuring its employees against kidnapping, not only because paying ransom became illegal under Colombian law, but also because it had proven self-defeating. Despite a warning by the Colombian government in 2001 to oil companies to desist providing kidnapping insurance, which is an illegal transfer of funds to insurgents, not all corporations have adopted the same policy.[35] In 2001, insurance companies were routinely paying up to U.S.$1 million per victim, thereby continuing the incentive for further kidnappings and extortion.

As Colombian security forces have been unable to fend off attacks from rebels, the security risks facing companies are genuine. However, as companies try to manage these risks, they have also increased their indirect involvement in the conflict by hiring private security firms for their protection and making direct payment into national and local security budgets to have police or military troops guard their infrastructure.[36] Although there is no systematic participation of oil corporations in armed conflict, they often fail to monitor the behavior of private security forces in their employ or end up associated with army and police officers who violate human rights.[37] In the absence of adequate preventive measures by corporations seeking to ensure the security of their operations and personnel, there is a continuing danger of companies inadvertently contributing to the conflict through their reliance on unaccountable security services and perhaps becoming more directly complicit in the strife.

Several other developments may deepen the involvement of corporations in the conflict. Colombian policymakers are now seeking new ways to finance defense expenditure. In 2001 the Pastrana administration proposed a bill authorizing private donations specifically for defense purposes. More recently the newly elected Alvaro Uribe administration has proposed issuing compulsory security bonds to be bought by private corporations and high-income individuals, a measure that was used in 1997 and 1998.[38] Depending on the formula, raising funds in this manner may lead to the semiprivatization of state security. It may also generate conflicts of interest, since security forces would have an incentive to serve the largest donors. Another development is the request by the U.S. executive to Congress in 2002 for $98 million in foreign military financing for counterinsurgency assistance to protect oil infrastructure in Colombia from rebel attacks. This request reflects the interconnection between corporate interests, U.S. domestic politics, and U.S. foreign policy objectives. U.S. oil companies have lobbied Congress and the president to increase military aid to Colombia, influencing not only the contours of U.S. policy in the Colombian conflict, but also Colombia's own security policy. This adds to the complexity of incentives at play in the Colombian war and may complicate the peace process, since one of the aims of insurgency groups is the reform of Colombia's energy policy specifically as regards the terms of foreign exploration and extraction. Meanwhile the Pastrana administration improved the conditions for foreign oil and energy companies from a 50-50 to a 70-30 share in order to stem the decline in foreign direct investment.[39]

Other Resources, Other Actors:
U.S. Aid and the Colombian Armed Forces

Foreign aid and credit are two primary sources of financing for Colombia's security forces, the only legal combatants in the conflict. As the largest foreign donor of military aid and counternarcotics assistance, the United States is the most important external actor shaping the agenda and incentives of the Colombian government, the police, and the military. While U.S. involvement in Colombia is not new, the nature and scope have changed fundamentally since 1997. To help the Colombian government's counterinsurgency efforts, U.S. policymakers have designed a complex array of policies focused on strengthening Colombia's security forces and reducing the illegal armed groups' access to drug revenues through heavily militarized interdiction and crop eradication. Whether this strategy can help achieve peace—and at what human and economic cost—is a subject of intense debate. So far, the current range of policies have spurred improvements in the strategic planning and human rights record of the security forces; nevertheless, U.S. policy and increased military aid have neither reduced the drug trade nor driven the armed groups to demobilize, let alone resulted in the outright military defeat of the armed groups.

The United States began giving Colombia assistance to fight drug trafficking in 1971. After several years of testing antidrug strategies, U.S. and Colombian policymakers concluded that success in the war against drugs depended on more funds, greater logistical support from the militaries of Colombia and the United States, the inclusion of an economic development component, and the strengthening of Colombian law enforcement and the judiciary. Accordingly, U.S. projects in Colombia expanded with President George H. W. Bush's comprehensive 1989 Andean Strategy initiative, President Virgilio Barco's 1990 Special Cooperation Plan, and the February 1990 Cartagena Summit Agreements. This expansion did not create a full militarization of drug control nor did it result in the deployment of U.S. troops, as is often misportrayed in academic writing.[40]

Despite all the policy improvements, drug control cooperation ultimately failed to stop the expansion of drug cultivation and trafficking in Colombia, but it did set a precedent for further U.S. involvement in the Colombian conflict. The United States progressively increased its presence in Colombia through long-term antidrug law enforcement programs, while the annual decertification process increased U.S. involvement in Colombian domestic politics.[41] U.S. policy toward Colombia began to change in 1997, when Samper tried to deter U.S. decertification and political pressure by claiming that sanctions would only weaken the government's attempts to counteract the growing "narco-guerrilla" threat, thereby threatening both national *and* international security. Among U.S. policymakers, the idea that the design of drug policy toward Colombia had to take into account worsening security conditions was gaining acceptance. In fiscal year 1997, Congress approved $66.6 million in military aid to Colombia—nearly double that of each of the previous three years. In fiscal year 1998, counternarcotics and military aid increased to $119.6 million and included the creation of the first of three U.S.-trained counternarcotics battalions equipped to fight drug traffickers as well as insurgency, provided there was "credible evidence" of guerrilla involvement in illegal drug-related activities. In this way, U.S. support for counterinsurgency was introduced through the "back door" of counternarcotics.[42] The United States also provided a $500 million grant to the Colombian alternative development program PLANTE, aimed at luring peasants away from coca crops and winning their "hearts and minds."

U.S. involvement in the Colombian conflict and the peace process was formally sealed in 1999 with Plan Colombia, a key turning point in the history of U.S.-Colombian relations. President Andrés Pastrana, elected in August 1998 with the mandate to reach peace and smooth relations with the United States, developed a $7.5 billion peace plan based on $4.5 billion in foreign aid.[43] After intense hearings and debates in Washington, Congress approved a $1.3 billion two-year supplemental aid package for Plan Colombia, approximately 75 percent of which was allocated to the security forces, in addition to regular appropriations, and the remainder to governance and economic development.[44] In 2001 and 2002 the George W. Bush administration, maintaining the U.S. commitment to Plan Colombia, formulated the Andean Regional Initiative (ARI), an $882.29 million package of economic and counternarcotics assistance not only for Colombia, but also for Bolivia, Brazil, Ecuador, Peru, and Venezuela to maintain the region's commitment to prohibition and guarantee the support of these countries for U.S. policies in Colombia.[45]

The emphasis of the ARI on military aid directly affects the Colombian government's own approach to the peace process. Those who believe that the guerrillas have, in essence, valid grievances, argue that the confrontational approach of the ARI will intensify and lengthen the fighting, resulting in heavy civilian casualties and internal displacement, and prevent long-needed socioeconomic reforms in the country. [46] Those who view the armed groups as an exclusively military threat, unconnected to the socioeconomic system, would prefer that U.S. policy toward Colombia set counterinsurgency as its first priority.[47]

Inevitably, the examination of these issues raises questions about political and economic interests within the United States and Colombia that influence U.S. policy. The U.S. military industry, U.S. security consultants, and Colombian contractors, all of which make profits in the context of the Colombian conflict, represent significant interest groups.[48] To what extent these interests prevent the formulation of a different U.S. policy—one more responsive to Colombia's economic recession, more effective at inducing a quicker demobilization of combatants, and less costly for rural inhabitants in Colombia—is a matter of continuing controversy.

In regional and historical comparative perspectives, U.S. political and economic involvement in Colombia contradicts what appeared to be a post–Cold War trend around the globe: the political and financial disengagement of the superpowers from civil wars and a corresponding increase in the involvement of combatants in alternate fundraising activities, frequently criminal. Rather, U.S. involvement in Colombia has increased at the same time that the guerrilla groups have increased the illegal self-financing activities in which they were already engaged. In Colombia the Marxist guerrillas never received significant funding from the Soviet Union or Cuba, which is why their search for local money began early on. Similarly, the Colombian Armed Forces—despite enjoying historically special relations with their U.S. counterparts, received only modest backing to fight the guerrillas, while the paramilitaries never received the support accorded to groups like the "Contras" in the Central American wars of the 1980s. One possible conclusion is that limited U.S. presence in Colombia helped to contain the size of the conflict in the past, whereas now U.S. policy feeds its escalation by altering the incentives of legal and illegal combatants. Ironically, the U.S.-backed counternarcotics policy may have added economic and political value to the already profitable coca and poppy crops, consequently adding to the incentives of armed groups to keep up the production of drugs. Some members of the guerrilla and paramilitary groups calculate that they stand to increase their bargaining power in a potential peace negotiation by participating in drug production, because eliminating drugs is what they believe the United States really cares about. A different possible conclusion is that greater U.S. counternarcotics assistance can alter the military balance in favor of the Colombian government, because the more stringent that antidrug law enforcement measures are, the greater the chances that the costs of continued involvement in the drug business by illegal combatants will become prohibitive.[49]

Economic Dimensions of the Colombian Conflict: Analysis and Policy Implications

Contemporary Debates over Natural Resources and the Colombian Conflict

The emerging literature on war economies argues that natural resources play a pivotal role in many civil wars of the post–Cold War era. But how and why exactly is a matter of discussion.[50] Paul Collier and Anke Hoeffler argue that dependency on primary commodities exports increases the risk of conflict in a country, largely because natural resource revenue gives insurgents the opportunity to finance rebellion through looting.[51] At a first glance, this "economic viability" hypothesis fits the Colombian conflict well, since coca leaf and poppy, both primary commodities (albeit illegal), make up to 45 percent of the insurgents' income and 70 percent of the AUC's income. Although contests over coca and poppy were not at the heart of the onset of the Colombian conflict, they have undoubtedly lengthened and intensified the war. Collier and Hoeffler, however, arrived at their conclusion on natural resources and conflict without ever incorporating illegal commodities into their statistics, which leaves the reader to wonder: What exactly is the connection between Colombia's other natural resources and war versus that between drugs and war?

In Colombia there is a direct correlation between the progressive growth of the guerrillas, the emergence and growth of the paramilitaries, and the escalation of conflict on the one hand, and the increasing cultivation of illegal drug raw material on the other. As Figure 4.1 demonstrates, both drug cultivation and the number of combatants expanded slowly from 1981 to 1996, then faster since 1996. This strong association between the production of illegal drugs and war has been

Figure 4.1   Illegal Armed Group Membership vs. Illegal Drug Cultivation

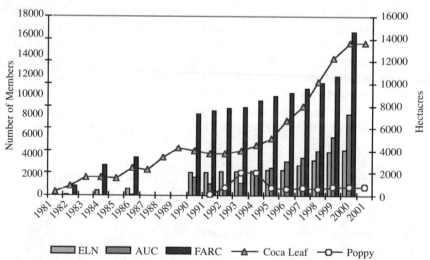

Sources: Information on armed groups from the Dirección de Justicia y Seguridad, Departamento Nacional de Planeación, Bogotá, Colombia, July 2002. Information on illegal drug cultivation from U.S. State Department, *2001 International Narcotics Control Strategy Report* (Washington, D.C.: U.S. Department of State, 2002).

manifested elsewhere, including Afghanistan, Burma, Lebanon, and Peru. Drugs have special features and connections to war. Like diamonds and timber, they are "lootable," that is, easily "extracted and transported by individuals or small teams of unskilled workers."[52] But drugs are also illegal and in high demand in a globally integrated market. Drug revenues are of foreign origin; ultimately, it is the drug addicts and recreational users mainly in the United States and Europe who finance guerrillas and paramilitaries. This makes coca and poppy cultivation atypically profitable and the market difficult to control. Illegality also precludes states from taxing drugs, which would presumably see a reduction in their value if they were legal. A more complex relation to war is the negative effect of drug trafficking on the state and its governance capability. In Colombia, drug trafficking has eroded institutions in three ways: via corruption, via the diversion of resources that otherwise could have been used for counterinsurgency and economic development to counternarcotics operations and the dismantling of cartels, and via the direction of government human resources to the drug issue, to the neglect of other important policy areas.

Among legal natural resources, oil has been singled out in the literature on the political economy of civil wars for having a "distinct effect" on the risk of conflict.[53] Oil revenue usually accrues to the state, often providing an incentive for corruption, which distorts the allocation of revenue and feeds political and social grievances. Grievances caused by the production of oil are also related to the violation of human rights by state security forces protecting oil infrastructure, the displacement of local communities, and negative environmental effects. Oil, like natural gas and minerals, but unlike coca and poppy, is geographically bound, which is why disputes over oil rent may feed the cause of separatist movements.[54] As illustrated above, neither of these developments figure prominently in Colombia; it is not a large oil producer by international standards and the principal grievances of insurgents are not directly related to oil.[55] Rather, guerrillas' quarrels with oil production have more to do with leftist ideology, that is, the belief that all foreign private-sector companies are agents of exploitative capitalism, that revenue-sharing agreements with these companies are heavily skewed against Colombia, and that Colombia should nationalize the extraction of natural resources.[56] Ultimately, oil rent is related to the war in Colombia not only because it is "obstructable" by rebel groups, as Michael Ross argues in Chapter 3 of this volume, but also because rebels can capture oil royalties after they have entered local coffers by intimidating and bribing local authorities, as well as kidnapping oil company executives and employees. However, oil has also become increasingly important for the Colombian economy. It constitutes a growing percentage of Colombia's exports, and oil companies are its top foreign investors. This is due mostly to the shrinking of other economic sectors and the plummeting of foreign investments amid economic recession and war, which may lead the Colombian state to become more dependent on oil revenues and may lead oil production to become further politicized.

The connection between oil and conflict in Colombia brings to light one of the fundamental relationships between natural resources and war: their lootability.[57] In Colombia, all natural resources have become directly or indirectly lootable. Equally relevant to the economy of this war is the extortion of coal-mining operations, the illegal exploitation of emeralds and gold, the theft of cattle and extortion of cattle ranchers, and the extortion of farmers in general and of private-sector companies producing legal crops, such as bananas or oil palms. All economic activities undertaken in rural areas outside the reach of security authorities are at the mercy of extortion or theft. Manufactured goods have also become extortable or lootable, especially when they require transportation along roads with little surveillance.[58] The extreme levels of extortion and kidnapping in Colombia are only partially tied to natural resource extraction (see Figure 4.2). The guerrillas have "systematized" kidnapping, targeting not just well-off entrepreneurs, but also the middle class in an indiscriminate way. Annual abductions in Colombia (by combatants and by common criminals combined) surpassed 1,000 in 1990, rose to more than 2,000 cases in 1998, and reached 3,706 in 2000—the highest rate in the world. Insurgents have developed the *pesca milagrosa* ("miracle fishing") modality of random massive kidnappings, with ransom fees ranging between U.S.$50,000 and U.S.$200,000. This underscores the urgency of formulating policies that focus on extortion and kidnapping.[59]

Economic Opportunities for War and Their Influence on Combatants' Aims

Favorable economic opportunities allow all combatants, whether motivated by profit or conviction, to continue fighting. Thus, depriving combatants of finances may be one way to stop violence. Nevertheless, conflict resolution, peace implementation, and reconstruction in any particular setting still must be formulated according to the character and motivation of the combatants involved in order to influence both their short- and long-term behavior.[60] Contemporary debate on the economic aspects of civil wars has focused on the types and functions of economic activities engaged in by combatants. There is a deep controversy

Figure 4.2 Income Distribution of Illegal Armed Groups

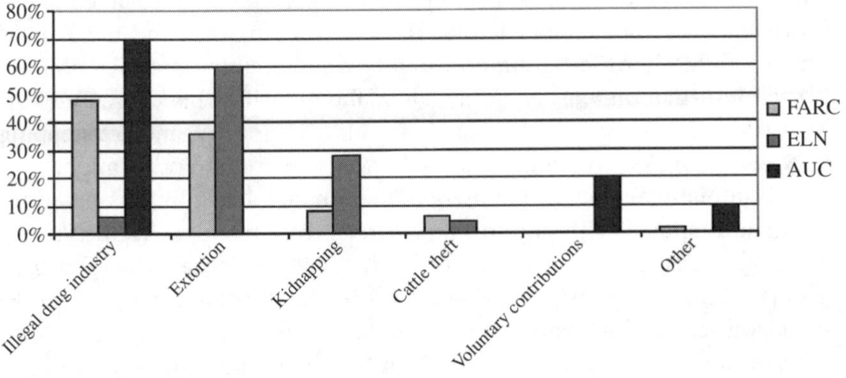

Source: Estimates by Alfredo Rangel, "Parasites and Predators: Guerrillas and the Insurrection Economy of Colombia," *Journal of International Affairs* 53, no. 2 (2000): 577–601, based on reports by the Comité Interinstitucional de la Lucha Contra las Finanzas de la Subversión, Bogotá.

over what are the "real" motivations and ultimate aims of combatants: Are they greedy profit-seekers or, specific to rebels, do they have legitimate grievances? The dispute is not just academic; it has profound policy implications. In the context of Colombia, it influences decisions on whether to launch a full military offensive against illegal armed groups or lure them into demobilization by addressing their grievances; on how much to concede and acknowledge in peace negotiations; on whether fundamental economic reforms (including redistribution of land and wealth) must take place; and finally on whether all combatants (paramilitaries and guerrillas) should receive amnesty. Choosing a course of action depends upon the answers to several fundamental questions: Has profit-making replaced ideology for Colombia's guerrillas? Are paramilitaries but drug traffickers in political disguise? Are Colombia's security forces accomplices of the paramilitaries or are they exploiting the war only to benefit from increases in defense expenditures?

Complicating such questions even further is the fact that combatants' preferences are not static. Originally, the guerrillas' aims were to redress political and socioeconomic exclusion and form a socialist state. However, it is possible that, with "institutionalization" of the guerrillas' criminal fundraising activities, rent-seeking may have become their raison d'être. It is also possible that the fast rate of recruitment since 1996 may have prevented the armed groups from fully socializing new recruits into their ideological cause, changing the identity of the groups from within and from the bottom up. Yet based on the lack of adequate empirical evidence about combatants' ultimate political and economic aims, it is not clear whether these changes in preference have taken place. Moreover, it is not clear whether the Colombian state and the United States would alter their counterinsurgency and counternarcotics policies if such information was available, since the guerrillas have been unwilling to demobilize, are building up their military capacity, and are stepping up violent attacks, which are mostly hurting the civilian population.

Systematic and extended involvement in criminal fundraising activities and disputes with paramilitary forces over resource-rich territory suggest that accruing wealth is a priority for Colombia's illegal armed groups. Although most of the guerrilla leadership continue to hold to their political visions and goals of fundamentally transforming Colombia's political and economic institutions, maintaining reliable sources of revenue has clearly influenced their military strategies and tactical decisions, including the timing of demobilization. For the guerrilla groups, economic strength determines military strength and therefore their expected gains at the negotiating table.

The fractioning of the AUC, which began in early 2002, more clearly demonstrates the possible contradiction between economic and political aims. The historical connections of the AUC to the drug trade and the rapid growth of its members have caused factions to break away from the AUC's control and instead use their networks and capabilities to pursue economic self-interest through drug trafficking, theft, kidnappings, extortions, and violent appropriations of land. This behavior runs counter to Castaño's attempts to gain political legitimacy for the paramilitaries, which would require that they clean up their image and disengage from criminal activities, in particular kidnapping and drug trafficking, which tend to be condemned by the Colombian public and the state.[61]

In general, noneconomic factors have been as important as economic factors in shaping the contours of the Colombian war. The perception by guerrilla groups of their economic strength vis-à-vis state combatants and of the willingness and ability of Colombian authorities to honor a potential amnesty have influenced their calculations on whether or not to demobilize. The guerrillas' skepticism about the ability of the central government to ensure protection if they were to demobilize are well grounded. As the killing of demobilized FARC members in 1984 demonstrated, Bogotá has often lacked sufficient control over police and military on the ground to prevent vendetta-related killings of former guerrillas. At the international level, transnational litigation and U.S. extradition requests may legally and politically challenge formal peace agreements. Similar political calculations appear to be preoccupying those paramilitaries that have not made economic self-interest their main goal. Their demobilization depends on the international political context and whether or not the United States decides to ask for their extradition.

There are two final issues tied to the continuing policy and academic debates on the Colombian war: whether or not illegal combatants' grievances are legitimate, and if they are, when and how to address these grievances through a peace process. The guerrillas have historically claimed that they are fighting against the systematic political and socioeconomic exclusion of the majority of the population in Colombia by a small urban elite. As mentioned in the beginning of this chapter, civilian authorities largely acknowledged these claims and progressively introduced political reforms to increase participatory democracy and worked to improve Colombia's economic development. They also have been willing to reach important compromises at peace negotiations.[62] Today the Colombian political system is formally open to democratic contest. Claims of political discrimination, therefore, are viewed as largely invalid. Conversely, there has been no academic, policy, or societal consensus in Colombia on whether socioeconomic grievances, as invoked by illegal combatants, were ever legitimate. Socioeconomic indicators in Colombia have improved substantially, especially in the 1960s and 1970s, compared to the first half of the century. There was sustained economic growth even throughout the so-called Latin American lost decade of the 1980s, when recession and debt crises hit the major economies of the hemisphere. At this time, it was often argued that insurgents' claims were unsubstantiated, because Colombia was doing well compared to other countries in the region.

Economic facts have changed, however, and there has been a stark deterioration over the past six years, as war and economic recession conflate. Inequality has worsened during the past decades, reversing the improvements of the 1960s and 1970s. In 1999 more than half of Colombians lived in poverty—a return to 1988 levels, despite 20 percent decline in the number of people living in poverty between 1978 and 1995. Since 1996 there has been a decline in macroeconomic performance and a doubling in unemployment, reaching approximately 20 percent in 2001.[63] Colombia's income inequality is considered "extreme" when compared internationally (though not in comparison to other Latin American countries).[64] Recent massive forced displacement and drug traffickers' investments in land since the 1980s have had a negative impact on land distribution and former agrarian reform policies. Furthermore, war has generated a profound humanitarian crisis: Colombia has 1.5–2 million internally displaced persons, and conflict-related civilian casualties reach more than 4,000 per year. Whether and when to address which grievances therefore remain critical political and tactical questions in the context of peacemaking. Short- and long-term policies aiming to reduce the combat capability of the illegal armed groups will have to be combined with emergency attention to civilians affected by war and with long-term economic development policies that meaningfully address pervasive inequalities in landholding and income.

Conclusion

As this chapter demonstrates, the political economy of the Colombian conflict has undergone a significant transformation over the last fifteen years. During this time, the national economy has faltered, while access to local and global markets has provided combatants with new economic opportunities and sources of revenue. The FARC and the ELN have became increasingly engaged in narcotics production and trafficking, extortion, and kidnapping. The paramilitaries have forayed vigorously into international drug trafficking, but have also received local voluntary contributions. Meanwhile, the state, largely dependent on tax revenues, has received increasing assistance from the U.S. military since 2000 to fight drug trafficking and, as of 2002, counterinsurgency and paramilitarism. With these changes, both the intensity of the conflict and the challenges for resolving it have increased.

From the perspective of Colombia's illegal armed groups, the expansion of economic activities has not only provided new sources of revenue; it has also enabled them to recruit new members and to expand the territory under their military and economic control. Consequently, illegal combatants' perceptions of their relative military strength is directly related to their economic power. Indeed, their pursuit of economic resources has influenced their strategic behavior and their respective dispositions toward continuing or resolving the conflict; as their economic power grew during the 1990s, the illegal armed groups have developed a powerful incentive to defect from peace talks. Economic strength appears to have bought them both time and confidence. The apparent logic of their current behavior is that the longer they wait, the stronger they will be militarily and the better will be their bargaining position and ability to secure concessions from the government in future negotiations.

The profitability of the economic activities in which Colombia's illegal armed groups have engaged has allowed a more rapid recruitment of new combatants. While this has strengthened respective armed groups as a whole, it has also increased the power and influence of certain units within the armed groups. In the long term, this combination of profit and power may be detrimental, as it risks undermining the coherence of these groups' command structures and their political agendas. In the case of the left-wing guerrilla groups, this political agenda has remained largely intact. It is possible, however, that a spoiler situation may arise in which the political leadership of a guerrilla group enters into negotiations with the Colombian government (and ideally the AUC) based on political objectives, but splinter factions within the group defect in order to continue their coercive economic activities.

As the profitability of economic enterprises undertaken by illegal armed groups continues, it likely will have an increasingly negative effect on the incentive structure of some elements within these groups. This not only complicates the prospects of these groups negotiating an end to the war by increasing the likelihood of spoilers, but also, as criminality increases, influences how policymakers view the legitimacy of the armed groups and therefore influences their preferred policy responses. Increased criminality by factions or units within left-wing guerrilla groups may undermine the legitimacy of the political grievances of the groups as a whole, may simultaneously strengthen the legitimacy of the paramilitaries, and may push policymakers in Bogotá to pursue more hard-line military solutions to the conflict rather than seek negotiated settlement. Within the AUC, historical connections to the drug trade and rapid growth in membership have already caused increased splintering, as factions use their networks and capabilities to pursue economic self-interest through criminal activities. This is undermining the legitimacy the paramilitaries have gained in response to the expanding threat of insurgency.

Increased criminality by certain factions within both the guerrilla and the paramilitary groups poses a dilemma for policymakers. Whether policymakers regard the grievances and political claims of the guerrillas and paramilitaries as legitimate influences their determination of whether the desired outcome is the military defeat of the illegal armed groups or the resolution of the conflict through peaceful negotiation. At present, Colombia's civilian leaders, seeking to avoid the short-term political costs of all-out war, continue to maintain an open door to negotiations with the guerrillas, at times restraining military action against them that would undermine this position.

To be successful, any package of policies aimed at reducing violence and ultimately stopping the conflict in Colombia must provide an incentive for demobilization. Even though the goal of most Colombian guerrillas is not self-enrichment, their economic strength has informed their decision not to demobilize. Amid the expectation of ongoing gains in resources, both the guerrillas and the paramilitaries have toughened their positions regarding the terms of potential peace talks. Yet the peace process to date has failed to address this economic dimension of the conflict. Weakening the economic base of the illegal armed groups by restricting their activities, increasing their transaction costs, and reducing their profitability is a possible means of inducing a reappraisal of their current cost-benefit analysis.

The ability of illegal armed groups to engage in illegal economic activities or to use legal operations to their advantage is in part a function of the opportunity structure that makes such activities feasible. State policies should therefore focus on undermining the three main economic activities engaged in by the illegal armed groups: drug trafficking, extortion, and kidnapping. At the national level, this entails three broad dimensions: first, identifying and criminalizing those economic transactions not already prohibited by national and international law; second, strengthening the law enforcement and judicial capabilities of Colombian authorities in order to improve policing as both a deterrent and a complement to military strategies; and third, improving military strategy through better coordination with alternative eradication programs, strict enforcement of the prohibition on military-paramilitary ties, and zero tolerance for human rights violations against civilians. At the international level, greater cooperation between states is needed to shut down the networks through which illicit financial transactions and conflict-related commodities flow.

Combating the illegal drug trade has been a core policy of the Colombian state since 1986. Colombia should draw from this experience to reframe drug control strategies in the context of overall military strategy and the goal of conflict resolution. Here, Colombian authorities, as well as international policymakers, face two challenges. First, drug control policies to date have failed to reduce the size of the global and local drug markets and the area of raw-material cultivation. Crop eradication efforts have only caused the relocation of coca-growing areas and their related "violence pockets." Together with poorly implemented alternative development programs, eradication has exacerbated grievances in rural areas. Second, Colombian drug control policies, supported by the supply-side control orientation of the United States, have been designed to eradicate cultivation and interdict shipment, rather than as a means of reducing combatants' economic and military power. In other words, drug control policies have been designed with an emphasis on criminalization. Given the link between illegal drugs and conflict in Colombia, drug control policies must be adjusted to complement and reinforce the goals of conflict resolution. More careful consideration is needed by the Colombian authorities of the incentives for involvement in narcotics production and trafficking. Narcotics are a principal source of funding for both insurgency *and* counterinsurgency—therefore, control strategies must also address underlying motivations for insurgency and counterinsurgency. This includes not only the political and security issues underpinning support for the guerrillas and paramilitaries, but also the short-term macroeconomic conditions and long-term economic marginalization driving peasants to cultivate coca as a source of livelihood. However, the design of more comprehensive drug control strategies is complicated by the abiding reluctance of Colombian authorities regarding the legitimacy of illegal groups' claims, as well as political and financial pressure from the United States.

Extortion and kidnapping, the predominant modes of financing for the FARC and the ELN, are a second area where the control agenda needs refinement. Domestic antikidnapping laws were passed in 1991 and 1993 to prohibit the payment of ransoms and the support of external negotiators. The laws were subsequently criticized for being overly severe, and several of their principal articles were challenged in court. Although the laws remain in effect, their enforcement has been problematic from inception, and the payment of ransoms is effectively tolerated. Although a lack of sufficient Colombian judicial authority is partly to blame, it is uncertain whether the enforcement of stricter laws would prevent ransom payments. The policing apparatus against kidnapping and extortion was improved in 1996 with the creation of enforcement units, such as the Unified Action Group for Personal Freedom and Anti-Extortion (GAULA), but has suffered a loss of autonomy since its inception.[65] Some policymakers believe that the best way to combat kidnapping is through national-level peace negotiations. Yet agreements between the government and the guerrillas, secured in the context of peace accords, over the application of international humanitarian law with regard to kidnapping have not only been broken by the guerrillas, but have also undermined the credibility of international humanitarian law, as the agreements imply that it can be waived by combatants when they deem necessary or expedient. Several attempts have been made to establish funds to provide secure income for the rebel groups during the negotiations in exchange for a cessation of kidnapping. However, as there has been no serious commitment by the FARC and the ELN to the peace process, this gesture has served to further fund the conflict, rather than provide an incentive for negotiation and demobilization. Since the mass abduction of 150 persons at La Maria church on May 30, 1999, there have been voluntary movements for a "no-payment" civilian resistance, but their transformation into a national-level measure—a necessary step if the rebel groups are to be denied revenue—is unlikely given the high costs borne at the individual level. As kidnapping is covered by international humanitarian law (specifically Article 3 common to the 1949 Geneva Conventions and the 1977 Protocol II), the International Criminal Court may provide a possible new avenue for the prosecution of members of rebel groups who engage in kidnapping, but given enforcement problems it remains to be seen whether this will prove an effective deterrent.[66]

Finally, the theft of gasoline and crude petroleum provides a lucrative source of revenue to the paramilitaries, while the guerrilla groups profit from extortion of oil companies and kidnapping of their personnel. Under the Uribe administration, new strategies are being advanced to reduce these links, including instructing the Colombian Armed Forces to focus specifically on key petroleum and energy infrastructure areas, tailoring of military operations to the specifics of the sites themselves, and initiating criminal proceedings against those responsible for pipeline bombings and corruption related to oil royalties. These efforts should be supported by requirements for greater transparency of royalty payments made by oil companies to the government, public education campaigns to instruct local communities on the responsible use of royalties for local development, and the promotion of "accountability pacts" between civil society and local authorities. Greater partnership between state institutions, NGOs, and state-owned and international oil companies would facilitate these remedial activities.

Prior to the development of strategies to reduce the flow of money and weapons to illegal armed groups, Colombian policymakers must determine whether the overall goal is military defeat or inclusion in a political process. At present, all nonstate combatant groups in Colombia are illegal. If the objective is inclusion, then legal provisions must be made to provide amnesty to members of armed groups and to redesignate the groups from outlawed terrorist organizations to legitimate participants in the political process. These considerations, however, must be reconciled with the need to hold accountable those responsible for violations of humanitarian law and human rights.

It is assumed by Colombian policymakers that the end of the war should result in the consolidation of state control over all national territory. Yet the legitimacy of the state is questioned not only by the guerrillas, but also by large sectors of the population—particularly in rural areas—who have been subject to forced displacement, human rights violations, and loss of property at the hands of state security forces. Many people are sympathetic to the view that the distribution of political and economic power in Colombia is highly inequitable. For these reasons, a military victory over Colombia's illegal armed groups may remove the immediate threat posed to state sovereignty and national security, but alone is incapable of restoring state legitimacy, let alone addressing the underlying structural causes of conflict. Expanding political participation and economic opportunity to marginalized sectors of the population is a long-term goal and, given contradictory views on the legitimacy of combatants' grievances, a politically difficult one. Yet without a concerted effort to examine the validity of these claims and to redress these grievances in the context of the ongoing armed conflict, sustained peace will remain elusive.

Notes

I am grateful to Cesar Caballero, Jeremy McDermott, Jan Egeland, Nazih Richani, Ricardo Rocha, Gustavo Salazar, Javier Torres, and Sergio Uribe for their contributions, and to those who agreed to off-the-record interviews during field research in Colombia conducted in September 2001. The views expressed are solely those of the author and do not reflect the views of Occidental Petroleum Colombia.

1. This chapter focuses on the FARC and the ELN. Most other left-wing guerrilla groups, including the nationalist urban-based Movimiento 19 de Abril (M-19) and other minor groups demobilized in the peace processes of 1990–1991.

2. During the 1980s, Colombian policymakers viewed common criminality and terrorism by drug traffickers (or "narco-violence") as a more serious problem than the guerrilla insurgency.

3. Alejandro Reyes, "La expansión territorial del narcotráfico," in Bruce Bagley and Juan G. Tokatlian, comps., *Economía y política del narcotráfico* (Bogotá: Ediciones Uniandes CEI and CEREC, 1990), pp. 117–139.

4. Data from Alfredo Rangel and the Colombian military as quoted by Nazih Richani, *Systems of Violence: The Political Economy of War and Peace in Colombia* (Albany: State University of New York Press, 2002), pp. 76, 87.

5. Data obtained in July 2002 from the Dirección de Justicia y Seguridad, Departamento Nacional de Planeación.

6. Data from Alfredo Rangel and the Colombian military as quoted by Richani, *Systems of Violence*, pp. 76, 87.

7. Data obtained in July 2002 from the Dirección de Justicia y Seguridad, Departamento Nacional de Planeación.

8. Ibid. The Uribe administration (2002–2006) in August 2002 added 15,000 peasant recruits to operate as part-time armed soldiers.

9. See for example, Alfredo Rangel, "La toma de Neiva," *El Tiempo,* August 3, 2001; "Cae red urbana de las FARC en Bucaramanga," *El Tiempo,* November 8, 2001; and "El barazo urbano de Tirofijo," *Cambio 16,* February 4–11, 2002.

10. See "Indicadores sobre la situación de derechos humanos y el derecho internacional humanitario en Colombia: Resultados de la política de derechos

humanos y DIH," *Informe presentado a la CIDH* (Bogotá: Observatario de los Derechos Humanos en Colombia, Vicepresidencia de la República, February 2002), available online at www.derechoshumanos.gov.co (accessed July 2002).

11. The Comisión de Facilitación Internacional, which supported the peace process with the FARC in 2001, included Canada, Cuba, France, Italy, Mexico, Norway, Spain, Sweden, Switzerland, and Venezuela. It started out in 1999 with fewer members and was called the Grupo de Apoyo. The Comisión de Facilitación Civil, which engaged in the peace process with the ELN, included Canada, Cuba, France, Japan, Germany, Portugal, Norway, Spain, Sweden, and Switzerland.

12. The recent plummeting of international coffee prices is driving Colombian coffee growers and seasonal pickers to cultivate poppy. There are differing views on whether the agricultural crisis, as distinct from the dynamics of the violence and war, can account for the expansion of illegal crops, especially in the coffee-growing regions. See Observatorio del Programa Presidencial de Derechos Humanos y Derecho Internacional Humanitario, Vicepresidencia de la República, *Panorama Actual del Viejo Caldas* (Bogotá: October 2001); and "Colombian Coffee Growers Start Growing Poppies," *Financial Times,* October 25, 2001.

13. The accumulated figure is cited in Pax Christi, *The Kidnap Industry in Colombia: Our Business* (December 2001), available online at www.paxchristi.nl/coloeng.html (accessed February 2002), based on the statistics by the Departamento Nacional de Planeación. The recent daily average is cited in Alfredo Rangel, "Parasites and Predators: Guerrillas and the Insurrection Economy of Colombia," *Journal of International Affairs* 53, no. 2 (2000): 577, based on the 1998 and 1999 reports by the Comité Interinstitucional de la Lucha Contra las Finanzas de la Guerrilla. For quantitative estimates of the drug economy in Colombia, see Ricardo Rocha, "La economía colombiana y la producción de drogas ilícitas: Tras 25 años de inserción," United Nations Development Programme, 1999, mimeo.

14. Urgenet Digital, interview with Carlos Castaño, March 16, 2001, via the AUC's website, www.colombialibre.org/reportajes/urgente_digital.htm (accessed November 2001).

15. Anna Carrigan, "The Career of Carlos Castaño: A Marriage of Drugs and Politics," *Crimes of War Magazine,* August 2001, available online at www.crimesofwar.org/colombia-mag/career.html (accessed November 2001).

16. See, for example, "El hombre de la Sierra," *El Tiempo,* October 25, 2001.

17. Pax Christi, *Kidnap Industry in Colombia.*

18. Author interviews, Magdalena, Colombia, September 2000.

19. Rangel speculates that more than 80 percent of guerrilla income is not spent immediately, but laundered and invested in the formal domestic and global economy. Rangel, "Parasites and Predators," p. 595.

20. "Capturado cerebro financiero de las FARC," *El Tiempo,* November 4, 2001. International Monetary Fund director Michael Camdesus estimated in 1998 that international money laundering represented between 2 and 5 percent of global GDP (or U.S.$800 billion to U.S.$2 trillion per year). William Wechsler, "Follow the Money," *Foreign Affairs* 80, no. 4, (July–August 2001): 40–57.

21. "El 8000 de los paras," *El Tiempo,* October 21, 2001.

22. Approximately 1.1 million Colombians have left since 1996. Michael W. Collier and Eduardo Gamarra, "The Colombian Diaspora in South Florida," Latin American and Caribbean Center Working Paper no. 1, Miami, Florida International University, May 2001; and "Prosperous Colombians Fleeing, Many to the U.S.," *Financial Times,* April 10, 2001.

23. See Michael Klare and David Andersen, *A Scourge of Guns: The Diffusion of Small Arms and Light Weapons in Latin America* (Washington, D.C.: Federation of American Scientists, 1996), pp. 27–40.

24. See, for example, "Arms Dealer Implicates Peru Spy Chief in Smuggling Ring," *Los Angeles Times,* November 1, 2000; "Panama culpa a policía nicaraguense de tráfico de armas a Colombia," *El Tiempo,* May 2, 2002; and Ana Carrigan, "The Career of Carlos Castaño: A Marriage of Drugs and Politics," *Crimes of War Magazine,* August 2001, available online at www.crimesofwar. org/colombia-mag/career.html (accessed July 2002).

25. "La oleada de violencia de las FARC lleva la firma de la guerrilla irlandesa," *El Nuevo Herald,* February 8, 2002. In this article, Gustavo Guillén attributes the FARC's wave of attacks against energy towers since January 2002 to the teachings of IRA experts apprehended in Colombia in August 2001.

26. Helge Ole Bergesen, Torleif Haugland, and Leiv Lunde, "Petro-States: Predatory or Developmental?" *CEPLMP Internet Journal* 7, no. 120a (August 2000), available online at www.dundee.ac.uk/cepmlp/journal/welcome.htm (accessed February 2002); and Philip Swanson, *Fuelling Conflict: The Oil Industry and Armed Conflict,* Fafo Report no. 378 (The Economies of Conflict: Private Sector Activity in Armed Conflict project), March 2002.

27. Since 1998, however, the ELN has lost hundreds of men and territorial influence in battles against the AUC and the state security forces.

28. In the meantime, coffee went from being 84.08 percent of exports in the boom year 1974, to an average of 45 percent until 1986, and declined after the break of the coffee pact in 1986, reaching 21.38 percent of exports in 1999 and a historical low of 13.75 percent in 2001. Departamento Nacional de Planeación, available online at www.dnp.gov.co/archivosweb/direccion_ desarrollo_empresarial/indicadores/comercio_externo/xtra.xls (accessed October 2002).

29. In 1998 authorities estimated that extortions accounted for 60 percent of the ELN's income, kidnapping of nationals and foreigners 28 percent, drug-trade taxes 4 percent, and cattle theft the remainder. Rangel, "Parasites and Predators," based on the 1998 report by the Comité Interinstitucional de la Lucha Contra las Finanzas de la Guerrilla.

30. *Platt's Oilgram News,* October 13, 1988, p. 3; and *Financial Times Information,* Latin American Energy Alert, August 5, 1999.

31. Ignacio Gómez and Peter Schumacher, *La última misión de Werner Mauss* (Bogotá: Planeta, 1998).

32. Dutch disease refers to the deindustrialization of a nation's economy that occurs when the discovery of a natural resource raises the value of that nation's currency, making manufactured goods less competitive with those of other nations and thus increasing imports and decreasing exports.

33. Ironically, the policy of oil and engineering companies to forge closer relations with the local communities, as a mechanism to foster good relations

with the local people and prevent social conflict, reinforces the companies' complex relation with the guerrillas.

34. Andrés Peñate, "Arauca: Politics and Oil in a Colombian Province," M.Phil. thesis in Latin American Studies, University of Oxford, 1991.

35. In the late 1990s, oil companies alone were paying approximately U.S.$40 million per year in extortion, Comité Interinstitucional de la Lucha Contra las Finanzas de la Subversión, Informe 1997, cited in Rangel, "Parasites and Predators," p. 589, n. 20.

36. Human Rights Watch, "Colombia: Human Rights Concerns Raised by the Security Arrangements of Transnational Oil Companies," April 1998, available online at www.hrw.org/advocacy/corporations/colombia/oilpat.htm (accessed June 2002).

37. See, for example, "BP Denies Arms Dealings," *BBC News,* October 17, 1998; and "Occidental Petroleum's Cozy Relationship with Colombian Military Turns Fatal," *Drillbits and Tailings,* June 30, 2001.

38. "Se abren paso bonos obligatorios para financiar funcionamiento de Fuerzas Armadas durante 2003," *El Tiempo,* July 21, 2002.

39. In 2000 alone, Ecopetrol awarded thirteen new exploration and production contracts.

40. See, for instance, Juan G. Tokatlian, *Drogas, dilemas y dogmas. Estados Unidos y la narcocriminalidad organizada en Colombia* (Bogotá: Tercer Mundo Editores and CEI, 1995); and Juan G. Tokatlian, "Seguridad y drogas: Una cruzada militar prohibicionista," in Francisco Leal and Juan G. Tokatlian, comps., *Orden mundial y seguridad: Nuevos desafíos para Colombia y América Latina* (Bogotá: TME, IEPRI, and SID, 1994), pp. 77–117.

41. In 1986 the U.S. Congress introduced legislation requiring the executive branch to certify on a yearly basis the extent to which countries receiving drug control assistance had cooperated with the United States in the war against drugs. Expansion of the cooperation indicators beyond eradication of illegal crops has led to further U.S. involvement in foreign state institutions and political processes. With respect to the case of Colombia, see Alexandra Guáqueta, *Change and Continuity in U.S.-Colombian Relations, 1970-1998,* D.Phil. thesis in International Relations, University of Oxford, 2002, chap. 4.

42. Selective military participation for discrete missions had taken place in Colombia since it joined the war against drugs in 1970. The wave of narco-terrorism (terrorist attacks perpetrated by drug traffickers) from 1988 to 1992 led Colombians to involve military special forces in interdiction missions.

43. For a discussion on the several versions of Plan Colombia, see Adam Isaacson, "Colombia's Human Security Crisis," Disarmament Forum, 2002.

44. There are different sources on U.S. aid, which don't always coincide. I have used K. Larry Storrs and Nina Serafino, *Andean Regional Initiative [ARI]: FY2002 Assistance for Colombia and Neighbors, Congressional Research Service [CRS] Report for Congress* (Washington, D.C.: CRS, February 14, 2002), pp. 5–6, 12–17.

45. Ibid., pp. 32–33.

46. See Human Rights Watch, *The "Sixth Division": Military-Paramilitary Ties and U.S. Policy in Colombia* (New York: Human Rights Watch, 2001). In 2002 the same Foreign Operations bill that authorized U.S. assistance to protect Colombia's oil infrastructure required that the Colombian Armed Forces com-

bat paramilitary groups. See Bill H.R.5410 of the 107th Congress. Despite resentment by Colombian officials, some sectors of the U.S. government have developed legal mechanisms to avoid contributing to human rights violations in Colombia. The post–September 11, 2001, war on terrorism, however, has sent a mixed message: "accidental" human rights violations are permitted when combating terrorism.

47. The "Peruvian Fujimori model" has been often alluded to as the course to follow: concentrating intelligence and military assets to dismantle insurgent groups, as opposed to chasing peasant coca growers; stopping unpopular eradication efforts so as to prevent disgruntled peasants from swelling the ranks of guerrillas; and using armed legal paramilitary self-defense organizations to protect local communities.

48. Libardo Sarmiento Anzola, *El Plan Colombia y la economía política de la guerra civil;* and "A Government by the People, for the Military-Industrial Complex," *Los Angeles Times,* September 27, 2000.

49. "Un nuevo rumbo," press release by AUCC leader Carlos Castaño, July 14, 2002, available online at http://colombia-libre.org/colombialibre/comunicados. asp?id=275 (accessed July, 2002).

50. Different arguments can be found in Paul Collier and Anke Hoeffler, "Greed and Grievance in Civil War," World Bank Policy Research Working Paper no. 2355 (Washington, D.C.: World Bank, 2001); James Fearon, "Why Do Some Civil Wars Last So Much Longer Than Others?" paper presented at the "Civil Wars and Post-Conflict Transitions Workshop" by the World Bank and the University of California, Irvine, May 2001; David Keen, *The Economic Functions of Violence in Civil Wars,* Adelphi Paper no. 320 (Oxford: Oxford University Press for the International Institute for Strategic Studies, 1998); Michael Klare, "The New Geography of Conflict," *Foreign Affairs* 80, no. 3 (May/June 2001): 49-61; and Chapter 3 by Michael Ross in this volume.

51. Paul Collier and Anke Hoeffler, "Greed and Grievance in Civil War."

52. See Chapter 3 by Michael Ross in this volume.

53. Collier and Hoeffler, "Greed and Grievance," p. 12.

54. See Chapter 3 by Michael Ross in this volume.

55. The dispute between the U'wa tribe and Occidental Petroleum over the Gibraltar exploration field is the only case in which an oil company operating in Colombia was involved with serious social grievances due to potential massive displacement. After the U'was threatened collective suicide because the field was located on their sacred land, and amid the prospects of low revenues from that field, Occidental decided to withdraw from the project in 2002.

56. From 1970 to 1999, revenue-sharing agreements gave 50 percent to the investing company and 50 percent to Ecopetrol, Colombia's state oil company; this distribution changed in 2000 to 70 percent and 30 percent, in favor of the investor.

57. In contrast to Ross, who in Chapter 3 of this volume classifies oil as "unlootable" and "obstructable," I argue that with excessive extortion, supported by the unpunished use of force, the meaning of lootability used by Ross loses strength or sense, since just about anything is lootable when faced with a gun to your head. Likewise, when something is highly obstructable it becomes lootable. Ross acknowledges this: "Obstructable resources are similar to lootable resources, since small bands of unskilled troops can use them to generate revenues."

58. Gasoline, for instance, has become a war commodity. The 1,170-kilometer gasoline pipeline has been repeatedly perforated by paramilitaries, who install valves for siphoning off gasoline. "El otro cartel," *Semana,* no. 1049, June 6, 2002, available online at http://www.semana.com/archivo/articulos View.jsp?id=22052 (accessed November 19, 2002).

59. Mark Taylor has developed concepts such as "militarized transactions," "anarchic exploitation," and "criminalized transactions," which promise to be useful in synthesizing existing knowledge on economic activities and civil wars and pointing the direction for future policy development. See Mark Taylor, "Emerging Conclusions. Economies of Conflict: Private Sector Activity in Armed Conflict," Fafo Institute, March 2002.

60. See Jeremy Weinstein, "The Structure of Rebel Organizations: Implications for Post-Conflict Reconstruction," Conflict Prevention and Reconstruction Unit Dissemination Notes no. 4, Washington, D.C., June 2002, p. 4.

61. "Se descarta la unificación de los paramilitares," *El Tiempo,* July 28, 2002.

62. The 1991 constitutional reform, an integral part of the peace negotiations with the M-19 and other minor groups, introduced key articles on the decentralization of political and economic decisionmaking as well as progressive overarching norms on human and socioeconomic rights.

63. United Nations Development Programme (UNDP), *Human Development Report 2001: Poverty Reduction and Governance* (New York: UNDP, 2001).

64. Ibid. According to the Human Development Report, five out of seven inequality indicators show an acceleration in 1995–1999, which coincides with the economic slump and the escalation of war.

65. Pax Christi, *Kidnap Industry in Colombia.*

66. Ibid.

5

Nepal: Economic Drivers of the Maoist Insurgency

JOHN BRAY, LEIV LUNDE, AND S. MANSOOB MURSHED

THE COMMUNIST PARTY OF NEPAL–MAOIST (CPN-M) LAUNCHED ITS "PEO-ple's war" in the midwestern region of Nepal in February 1996.[1] By 2002 it had established a presence in almost all the country's seventy-five districts as well as in Kathmandu, the national capital. According to official figures, a total of 7,073 people had been killed by October 2002; more than 4,000 of these casualties had taken place in the previous year.[2] Neither the government nor the guerrillas has any realistic prospect of winning an outright military victory in the foreseeable future. Although both sides have referred to the need for dialogue, there is little sign of a serious move to address the underlying causes of the insurgency or bring about a peace settlement. Nepal's Maoist insurgency has turned into an enduring national crisis, threatening its political stability and economic development.

Nepal differs from the other case studies discussed in this volume in that it is not rich in natural resources. However, economic drivers and social inequalities have played a key role in the inception and expansion of the conflict, and may potentially play a key role in its resolution. Moreover, economic opportunities created by the war could conceivably shift combatants' incentives to carry on with fighting rather than pursue peace.

In Nepal, as in other cases, international players exercise an important—though far from decisive—influence on future outcomes. In particular, the Kathmandu government draws heavily on international donors for development aid, and draws increasingly on military assistance. External assistance is most likely to be effective if it is based on a detailed understanding of the causes of the insurgency.

This chapter seeks to contribute to this understanding through an analysis of the economic and social factors underlying the Maoist insurgency. It begins with an overview of the conflict and the Maoists' military and economic strategy. The second section focuses on the social and economic causes of the insurgency, placing the analysis within the current debate on "greed" or "opportunity" versus "grievance" as the causal factor of civil war and assessing the applicability of this analytical approach to Nepal's Maoist insurgency.[3] The third section examines the costs of war to both the Maoists and the government and the incentives for both sides to maintain or change their current strategies. Based on an assessment of the political, economic, and security outlook, the chapter concludes with policy implications for both the Nepali government and international donors.

The Maoist Campaign

The CPN-M was founded in 1995 by Pushpa Kamal Dahal—better known as "Comrade Prachanda"—and Baburam Bhattarai, the party's chief ideologue. The political justification for the new party was the need for a "complete democratic revolution" in Nepal. Four years earlier, Nepal had introduced multiparty democracy, but the CPN-M argued that this earlier revolution was incomplete because the state was still dominated by the same class and high-caste interests as before. The CPN-M believed that it would be impossible to achieve wholesale reform within the existing political system: the only alternative was armed struggle. The party launched its guerrilla campaign early the following year.

Although the CPN-M is relatively new, it draws on a long history of radical left-wing activism both in Nepal and in neighboring India. Nepal's first communist party was founded in 1946. The country's communist movement has since split and partially reunited several times. The mainstream Communist Party of Nepal—the United Marxist-Leninist (UML) Party—operates within the country's legal political framework. It was able to form a minority government at the national level for nine months in 1994 and 1995 and more recently has served as the main opposition party to successive administrations of the Nepali Congress (NC) Party. It hoped to win the national elections that were planned for November 2002, which were subsequently postponed. The rhetoric of armed struggle upon which the CPN-M draws is also far from unfamiliar in Nepal: there had been earlier if short-lived examples of armed militancy in the southeastern portion of the country, as well as in the neighboring Indian states of Bihar and West Bengal.

Military Strategy and Expansion of the Insurgency

In 2000–2001, Prachanda spelled out the so-called Prachanda Path, which combines the Chinese model of people's war in rural areas with the Russian model of general insurrection in towns. Mao Zedong's strategy of "protracted people's war" comes in three phases: a strategic defensive, followed by a strategic balance/stalemate, and finally a strategic offensive. Nepal's Maoists believe that they are currently moving from the strategic defensive to the strategic balance stage, and may soon advance to the strategic offensive. Their aim is to establish interim revolutionary governments in the countryside and to gradually expand the areas under their control while at the same time fomenting unrest in urban areas. In the revolution's final stages, rural guerrillas will join forces with their urban counterparts to bring down the state.

The Maoists launched their insurgency with a series of attacks on police posts in Rolpa and the neighboring midwestern districts of Gorkha, Jajarkot, Rukum, and Salyan. From the Maoists' point of view, the midwestern region has several advantages: its rugged, forested hills make ideal guerrilla terrain and there is ready access across the lightly guarded border to India. Moreover, as will be discussed in the next section, a background of rural poverty makes it relatively easy to gather willing recruits. The comparative remoteness of the midwestern region has a further advantage in that it initially allowed the Kathmandu political elite to dismiss the insurgency as a local problem of no particular importance. By the time the government began to take the insurgency seriously in the late 1990s, it was already becoming well entrenched. Even so, the authorities continued to treat the rebellion as a police matter, rather than as a major security threat that would require calling in the Royal Nepal Army (RNA).

In June 2001, Crown Prince Dipendra murdered his father, King Birendra, together with most of the members of his immediate family, and then committed suicide. Birendra's brother, Gyanendra, acceded to the throne in his place. While the crown prince's motivation remains uncertain, the palace massacre was not linked to the insurgency. However, it added to a sense of national crisis. The Maoists subsequently claimed that the late king had had a degree of sympathy for the movement, at least to the extent that he had refrained from deploying the army, and that his murder was part of a high-level conspiracy by hard-liners.

In July 2001, Nepali Congress prime minister Sher Bahadur Deuba agreed to an interim cease-fire with the Maoists. Over the subsequent four months there were three rounds of negotiations between the government and the insurgents. The Maoists' main demands were the formation of a new interim government, the abolition of the monarchy, and the introduction of a new constitution. The negotiations took place in public, a factor that made it difficult to achieve significant progress. In retrospect, it is uncertain whether the Maoists were genuinely committed to the talks. On November 24, 2001, the Maoists demonstrated their rejection of the talks by attacking an army outpost in Dang, killing eleven soldiers and nine policemen. A similar incident took place in Solokhumbhu the following day.

Following these attacks, the government declared a national emergency on November 26 and, for the first time, mobilized the full involvement of the army in counterinsurgency operations. Earlier, the army had implied that it could defeat the insurgents quickly. The reality proved different, and there were a series of successful Maoist attacks on the security forces—notably in Accham in February 2002, when seventy-six policemen and fifty-seven soldiers were killed. Poor intelligence and limited access to equipment such as helicopters have hampered the army's counterinsurgency operations. Meanwhile, in Kathmandu and other towns the Maoists have organized a series of strikes (*bandhs*) lasting from one to five days at a time. Shopkeepers and small tradesmen have been forced to comply with the *bandhs* out of fear of violent retaliation.

The insurgency has been marked by a high degree of brutality on both sides, giving rise to concerns about human rights abuses.[4] The Maoists are accused of using unarmed civilians as "human shields" to protect them from gunfire and of recruiting child combatants. On the government side, observers question how many of the casualties reported as "Maoists" in official figures truly belonged to the guerrilla movement and how many have been ordinary civilians caught up in the fighting.[5]

Political and Economic Goals and Strategy

The CPN-M has no formal manifesto, but it has outlined its economic program in a series of policy statements and ad hoc announcements. At the insurgency's outset in 1996, it issued its *Forty Demands,* which summarized its political and socioeconomic objectives. In 1998, Bhattarai issued a booklet titled *The Politico-Economic Rationale of People's War in Nepal,* according to which the party's goal is to "usher in vibrant, self-reliant, independent, balanced and planned economic development in the country primarily through a radical land reform programme based on the policy of 'land to the tiller' and national industrialisation."[6]

The primary objective of the CPN-M is to bring about a revolution in agriculture, and it has highlighted issues of landlessness and poverty both as a matter of political conviction and to build up popular support. The Maoists do not plan to introduce full socialism at the outset. Instead, the people's democracy will strike a balance between private, joint, and collective ownership. The state will own large industry while private individuals will continue to own small and medium-sized industries.

The CPN-M's political analysis is primarily based on class, in accordance with its Maoist ideology, but the conflict also has ethnic and caste overtones. Nepal's highly diverse society is dominated by the elite Bahun-Chetri-Newari peoples centered on the Kathmandu valley.[7] The Maoists have proved skilled in exploiting discontent among less privileged ethnic groups such as the Magars of midwestern Nepal—for example, by drawing on and adapting Magar folk culture in the CPN-M's propaganda initiatives.

The Maoists have attacked both political and economic targets in a manner that is broadly consistent with their ideological framework. In the early stages of the "people's war," they focused on the police. By late 2002 they had attacked hundreds of police outposts nationwide. Since the army joined the war in November 2001, the Maoists have launched a series of well-coordinated raids on army garrisons, notably in Dang, Accham, and Rolpa districts. Some of these raids have involved hundreds of combatants on both sides. For example, in early September 2002, large-scale Maoist assaults on security forces' positions in Bhiman (Sindkhuli district) and Sandhikharka (Arghakanchi district) resulted in more than 200 government casualties.

Through their selection of political targets, the Maoists aim to destroy the grassroots manifestations of the current political system and to prepare the way for their own district-level people's government. By November 2001 they had announced twenty-three such district administrations. By May 2002 the Maoists had destroyed more than 1,000 Village Development Committee (VDC) offices nationwide.

The Maoists have conducted regular attacks on land registration offices and, consistent with the party's plans for wholesale land reform, have destroyed existing documentation. They plan to confiscate land that is owned by feudal and bourgeois landowners and to redistribute it to landless and poor farmers. All existing land deeds and loan arrangements will be declared void and new papers will be issued after investigation by local people's governments. The Kamaiya (bonded labor) system, addressed in greater detail below, will be abolished along with other feudal practices.

The same basic rationale of total societal reform applies to their destruction of economic targets. Offices of the government-owned Agricultural Development Bank, and to a lesser extent of the Grameen Bank, have been subject to attack. By mid-May 2002 the Maoists had destroyed 132 Agricultural Development Bank branches nationwide. They claim that borrowers will have no need to repay loans once their records have been destroyed. In some areas, the Maoists are reported to have set up their own alternative lending institutions, but these do not appear to be well developed.

The Maoists plan to take over key industrial sectors, with an emphasis on vital products such as clothing, shoes, tools, and paper. Cooperatives will be encouraged in small and cottage industries. Bhattarai argues that Indian companies, many of which often operate as subsidiaries of large multinationals, are among the main agents of international capitalism. As such, he singles them out for particular condemnation. Item six of the CPN-M's *Forty Demands* states: "The domination of foreign capital in Nepali industries, business and finance should be stopped."

In 2000 and 2001, suspected Maoists bombed a series of factories owned by, among other companies, Coca-Cola, Colgate Palmolive, Surya Tobacco (partly owned by British American Tobacco [BAT]), and Nepal Lever (a subsidiary of Unilever). As noted above, Bhattarai had specifically denounced multinational companies, especially those operating in the country through their Indian subsidiaries. In 2001 the Maoists also singled out Nepali liquor companies for sabotage attacks, arguing that their product was socially undesirable—an argument that appears to have a degree of popular sympathy, while indirectly hitting at one of the government's major revenue sources. Similarly, they have denounced overcharging in private schools, which are run as commercial enterprises.

Since November 2001, and particularly since March 2002, the Maoists have attacked the transport, communications, and electricity infrastructures. Targets attacked in the first six months of 2002 included fourteen airport towers, leading to the closure of six airports and twelve electricity projects, including the Jhimruk, Andhikola, and Modi power plants. They have sabotaged two districts' drinking-water supplies and staged a series of attacks on telecommunications towers.

These attacks appear to be inconsistent with the Maoists' avowed objective of helping poor people, but they are broadly consistent with the Maoist policy of attacking government targets to undermine the credibility of Kathmandu's development policies. Some of the targets, such as airports, have military applications. However, at least initially, the attacks have not amounted to a wholesale Maoist assault on the nation's economic infrastructure: the Maoists are capable of inflicting much greater damage—for example, through more systematic attacks on electricity transmission towers or a sustained attempt to cut north-south communications between Kathmandu and India.

The Maoists' approach to nongovernmental organizations (NGOs) and development agencies has been ambivalent.[8] Generally, the CPN-M is critical of NGOs; item nine of the *Forty Demands* states: "The invasion of colonial and imperial elements in the name of NGOs and international non-governmental organizations [INGOs] should be stopped." Similarly, the *Politico-Economic Rationale* calls for a halt to the "entry of imperialist capital" through NGOs and INGOs. Maoist rhetoric frequently highlights the perceived corruption of development agencies drawing on foreign aid.

In practice, the Maoists are most likely to be hostile to development projects that might have military implications, such as road construction. By contrast, they may tolerate projects that are conducted transparently and bring clear benefits to the poor.[9] It appears that the Maoists do not have one consistent policy toward NGOs and development assistance. Local commanders appear to have some leeway and sometimes bow to pressure from the general public in the areas that they control. However, there are signs that the Maoists have recently become more hostile to development assistance and NGOs, in conjunction with the conflict's general escalation. The Maoists also carry out limited development work—for example, by imposing their own version of land reform, or running local schools in the areas where their influence is strongest. These projects are intended to support their claim to be acting in the interests of the poor. In practice, their capacity to implement substantive development is limited by the demands and distractions of the conflict.

International Connections

The Maoists draw their name and their ideological inspiration from revolutionary China. However, there is no evidence of formal links with the People's Republic. On the contrary, Chinese government representatives explicitly disavow any connection with the CPN-M and dismiss any analogies with their own country's revolutionary struggle.

The party's most important international connections are across the border in India, where ideological sympathizers have provided sanctuary and material assistance. Indian groups who are believed to have established links with the CPN-M include the Maoist Coordination Centre (MCC) in Bihar and the People's War Group (PWG) in Andhra Pradesh.

The Indian government points out that it has difficulty in containing even its own radical leftists and therefore can scarcely be blamed if small numbers of underground Nepali activists are able to operate within its borders. Many Nepalis nevertheless believe that New Delhi could do more to crack down on CPN-M militants in India. Perhaps alarmed by the expansion of the insurgency, the Indian government now appears to be responding. In July 2002 the Indian authorities banned the Akhil Bharatiya Nepali Ekta Samaj (All India Nepali Unity Society) for suspected links with the CPN-M. India also made several offers of military assistance to Kathmandu in the course of 2002.

Both foreign counterinsurgency experts and the Maoists themselves have drawn analogies between their movement and Peru's Sendero Luminoso (Shining Path) because of its radicalism and its high-altitude origins. Nepali Maoists have expressed solidarity with Sendero Luminoso via the websites of the London-based Revolutionary Internationalist Movement (RIM). However, despite intermittent rumors to the contrary, there is no evidence of more substantive links between the two groups.

Opportunity and Grievance in Nepal

The government of Nepal is unlikely to withstand the Maoist challenge unless it addresses the deeper causes of the insurgency. This raises the question of what motivates the belligerents: opportunity or grievance?

In recent years, prompted by continued economic underdevelopment and political instability, policymakers and scholars have started paying more attention to the economic causes of internal conflict. Analysis of the political economy of civil wars has focused on improving understanding of how the economic interests of competing factions influence their behavior during conflict and their incentives for conflict resolution. However, the literature is divided over the relative importance of two causal factors in the incidence of civil wars: "grievance," the pursuit of redress for perceived injustice over the way in which a social group is treated, and "greed" or "opportunity," which is shaped by the availability of capturable resources for rebellion, geographically dispersed populations, terrain favorable to the evasion by insurgents of government forces, such as dense forests or mountainous regions, and a relatively large population of unemployed youth with limited opportunities for education, from which to draw recruits.[10]

According to the proponents of the opportunity theories of civil war, grievance- or motive-based explanations do not provide an adequate explanation for rebellion. According to Paul Collier and Anke

Hoeffler, opportunity is largely defined by economic resources—access to finance through predation of civilians, extortion of natural resources, diversion of diaspora remittances, and contributions from hostile governments determine whether rebellion is economically viable, and therefore, whether it will occur.[11] Discussion of economic opportunity as a cause of conflict has arisen mainly in the context of natural resource endowment, an abundance of which, at least for some commodities, appears to increase the risk of a country falling into violent conflict.[12] Indeed, according to Collier and Hoeffler, primary commodity dependence is the single most significant risk factor.[13]

In resource abundant states, revenues generated from this endowment often have perverse developmental effects; in states with capturable resource rents, such as oil, diamonds, or drugs, these revenue streams can lead to high levels of corruption, unaccountable government, the breakdown of institutions for nonviolent conflict resolution, and inequitable distribution of public goods. It is in this context that poverty and grievances also play a part in fueling war.[14]

The inequality that frequently arises from this process is horizontal—that is, between heterogeneous social groups based on geography, ethnicity, religion, or class.[15] This must be distinguished from vertical inequality, which is usually a measurement of private income distribution across a relatively homogeneous community. Some of the salient aspects of horizontal inequality include the following:

Asset inequality. Land inequality and the limited poverty reduction associated with economic growth in highly unequal societies provide fertile ground for insurrection, particularly when the dispossessed belong to separate and distinct groups drawn along caste, ethnic, or religious lines.

Unequal access to public employment. Discrimination in the allocation of public employment is particularly resented in societies in which it represents the principal avenue for personal advance.

Unequal access to public services and overtaxation. Discrimination in access to public services and public-sector jobs may generate grievances and potentially lead to insurrection.

Economic mismanagement. The risk of civil war is greater in low-income developing countries where poverty is endemic and poor human development indicators abound. Societies characterized by poor governance and widespread corruption are also more prone to conflict. The same holds for absence of economic opportunities.[16]

Most contemporary civil wars in developing countries have an ethnic dimension, in part because ethnicity resolves the collective action problem of mobilizing groups to fight one another.[17] If there is a shared perception of well-defined grievances among members of the ethnic group, then it is easier to recruit support from within the group. Significantly, horizontal inequality of assets, employment opportunities, or access to public services can serve this function.

In practice, opportunity and grievance are inextricably intertwined. A conflict's duration is clearly related to combatant groups' ability to sustain financing of the war effort, especially, but not exclusively, for rebels.[18] Empirical evidence suggests that very few conflicts are motivated solely by opportunity.[19] Nevertheless, conflicts may at times gain an acquisitive character as the once marginalized are tempted by the opportunities for profit-making that can be derived from the continuation of fighting. Meanwhile, civil war fueled by the desire to capture resource rents can foment grievances among civilians as lives and livelihoods are lost during combat. Generally, the longer a conflict, the greater the price of peace in terms of the concessions that need to be made. Evidence from a cross section of conflict countries demonstrates that it takes several attempts at peacemaking, as well as many failed peace agreements, before lasting peace emerges.[20] This suggests that belligerent parties are generally unwilling to fully commit to peace agreements. As Tony Addison and S. Mansoob Murshed point out, one reason for this reluctance may be because of a desire to continue deriving rents and revenues that arise in the context of war.[21]

Application of Horizontal Equality to the Case of Nepal

Unlike in Angola, Indonesia, or Colombia, Nepal has few capturable resources that would make rebellion either viable or attractive. Rather, the circumstances in Nepal point to grievances as the major catalyst for conflict: the marginal elements of society have not prospered as much as the elite, and the gap between them appears to be getting wider. In Nepal, social divisions are often expressed in caste or ethnic terms, which frequently overlap. The less privileged ethnic groups in the hills and the Terai tend to be classified among the lower castes, and these are the communities where support for the Maoists has proved strongest.

According to the 2001 UN Human Development Index (HDI), Nepal ranks 129th out of 162 countries assessed, falling within the category of "low human development." Nepal made progress in development between 1996 and 2000; the national HDI improved from 0.325 to 0.466.[22] However, purchasing power parity (PPP)—gross domestic product (GDP) per capita or income per head—worsened for the far-western and midwestern regions between 1996 and 1999. These regions, which constitute the focal point of contemporary Maoist armed struggle in Nepal, have not benefited from the rest of the economy's recent growth. This is prima facie evidence of worsening horizontal inequality.

The picture is even more startling when considering districtwide data for 1996—the year in which the current insurgency commenced. Midwestern districts such as Rolpa, Jajarkot, and Salyan obtained 25 percent, 19 percent, and 17 percent respectively of Kathmandu's average income. In the far-western district of Achham, the average income was only 24 percent of Kathmandu's in 1996. Accompanying the per capita income differentials are wide gaps in HDIs. For example, the regional HDIs for Rolpa, Jajarkot, and Salyan were only 45 percent, 44 percent, and 35 percent respectively of the Kathmandu level in 1996. In Achham, the HDI for 1996 was only 39 percent of that of Kathmandu.[23]

These indicators are evidence of severe horizontal inequality vis-à-vis the capital in areas that can be described as the major flash points of the Maoist insurgency. If we correlate the intensity of conflict (measured by the number of deaths in each district) against regional HDIs, we find that the negative correlation between HDI and the intensity of conflict is –0.29, which suggests that grievance and horizontal inequality play a vital role in determining the intensity of the insurrection.[24] The correlation between landlessness or marginal landholding and the intensity of the rebellion is higher, at 0.43, pointing to land issues and associated malpractices as an even more significant factor in determining the insurgency's depth.

Official figures on the country's pattern of landholding show that the percentage of large holdings (greater than four hectares) has declined following land reform and land ceiling acts.[25] However, the percentage of medium-sized holdings (one to four hectares) shows an upward trend, at least in terms of the acreage covered by such holdings. This implies avoidance of land ceiling legislation by parceling off ownership to relatives, subverting the intention of reform. More important, the 2001 census reports that about 1.2 million households (approximately 25 percent of Nepali households) are landless.

This means that approximately 1 million out of 6 million agricultural laborers in Nepal are totally landless. Under the modern Kamaiya system, common in five midwestern and far-western districts, indebted landless laborers are forced to render labor services in lieu of debt servicing. Affecting predominantly ethnic Tharus, the Kamaiya system creates dependence of laborers on their employers for work and credit. Loans by employers, or *sauki,* to laborers force them into debt bondage, as their wages are insufficient to pay back the loans.[26] Although the government officially outlawed Kamaiya on July 17, 2000, necessary administrative and legal mechanisms for ensuring the release of bonded laborers are still absent. This institutional failure, and the inhuman cycle of debt and deprivation that it involves, is very much part of the wider institutional breakdown that has fueled the conflict.[27] In the past, land given to the Kamaiyas under official land redistribution schemes has eventually returned to the hands of the erstwhile landlords, with the Kamaiyas again falling into debt owing to their inability to generate enough income from their temporary land tenure rights. Along with the Kamaiya system, landlessness and the unfair practices connected with it are at the center of the rural unrest that fuels the insurgency.[28]

All societies exhibit inequality, but in Nepal socioeconomic inequality is divided along ethnic, geographic, and caste lines. The upper castes (Bahun, Chetri, Newar) constitute 37.1 percent of the population according to the 1991 census, yet their human development indicators can be about 50 percent greater than the hill ethnic, Terai ethnic, and occupational caste groups.[29] Income per capita among the hill ethnic groups is about 55 percent of the Newaris' average.

Not surprisingly, the upper castes dominate the civil service, and their representation is vastly in excess of their population share.[30] Bahun, Chetri, and Newar domination of the upper levels of the civil service was even more entrenched in 2000 than in 1989, when Nepal was under the monarch's direct rule. This reflects endemic educational inequality along caste lines. In 1992, about 87 percent of graduates came from the higher castes.[31] The lack of employment opportunities for ethnic peoples at the level of central civil service, combined with landlessness and the debt trap, greatly reduces their opportunities for peaceful employment, making the alternative—armed rebellion—a less unattractive option. This could be seen as in line with Collier's claim that unemployment creates opportunities for rebellion because the income foregone by becoming a rebel is atypically low.[32] However, this explanation is insufficient, because the support base for the Maoists comes not from all unemployed groups, but only from those who belong to discriminated ethnic minorities.

A Failure of Democracy?
The Breakdown of the Social Contract and Institutions

The catalog of potential grievances presented above pertains to the risk of war. But not all societies with characteristics contributing to the risk of conflict, even those at high risk, descend into open warfare. For that to occur there must be a failure of the institutions of conflict management—for example, the judiciary. This is what Addison and Murshed refer to as the breakdown of the social contract.[33]

Theories abound as to what prevents robust institutions from emerging or causes them to weaken and fail.[34] In certain countries, mismanagement and corruption may at times lead to a predatory state, in which public and private assets are transferred to elites at the expense of the rest of the population. This prevents balancing civil institutions, especially related to property rights and the rule of law, from taking root. Such societies also tend to depress the middle-class share of income in favor of elites. Unlike in middle-class-dominated societies, publicly financed human capital formation and infrastructural development are ignored, which depresses growth prospects and increases the risk of conflict. This is especially true for natural resource–rich states, but may also be the case for states in transition.

Håvard Hegre, Tanja Ellingsen, Scott Gates, and Nils Gleditsch have demonstrated that the likelihood of civil conflict is lowest in both established, well-functioning democracies and perfect autocracies.[35] It is at some intermediate or transitory stage between autocracy and democracy that the risk of internal conflict is greatest. In this context, Nepal's current security crisis is all the more poignant because it follows a period of political reform.

Multiparty democracy was introduced in Nepal only in 1991, following a long history of feudalism. In 1990 the so-called People's Movement, or Jana Andolan, staged a series of popular protests in Kathmandu. These led to the collapse of the previous panchayat system of government, which was dominated by the monarchy, and the establishment of multiparty democracy. Under the former system, which banned political parties, four tiers of panchayat—historically, councils of elders based on caste groups—were established at the village, district, zonal, and national levels. Members of the zonal-level councils, with professional and class organizations, indirectly elected the National Panchayat, or Rashtriya Panchayat, but 20 percent of its 134 members were nominated directly by the king. Under the 1991 constitution, the king remained the head of state and the focus of national unity but—at least in principle—was less involved in day-to-day political decisionmaking.

Democratic reform raised expectations but failed to deliver in many crucial areas. In practice, the performance of successive Nepali democratic governments has been disappointing. The recent history of the Nepali Congress and the UML has been marked by constant factional infighting, a pattern that has persisted despite the country's security crisis. This has distracted political leaders from more substantive policymaking. Corruption, too, has been a constant problem.[36] Many Nepalis—not just those on the left—have questioned the extent to which the political parties are truly representative, particularly of the poorer, rural sections of the population.

Events in 2002 were not encouraging. In May, Prime Minister Shah Bahadur Deuba dissolved parliament and called elections for the following November. Deuba's Nepali Congress Party responded by expelling him from its ranks. The Maoists made clear that they would disrupt the electoral process, and by early October the viability of the elections was in doubt. Deuba went to King Gyanendra to ask for emergency measures to postpone the polls for a year. The king reacted by sacking Deuba for "incompetence" and invoked Article 127 of the constitution to assume executive powers himself. He subsequently appointed Lokendra Bahadur Chand from the promonarchy Rastriya Prajatantra Party (RPP) to serve as an interim prime minister, pending elections—the date of which had yet to specified by early November 2002. Political infighting flared up again following Deuba's dismissal.

These events do not mean that democracy in Nepal is irredeemable. Arguably, the present constitutional monarchy needs more time to mature. The question is whether it can reform quickly enough, and establish sufficient credibility to withstand the challenge from the far left before the insurgency escalates still further.

The Costs of War and Incentives for Peace

There can be no doubt of the costs of Nepal's conflict to individual citizens: some 7,000 lives have been lost, while hundreds of thousands of civilians have been forced to leave their homes and move to safer areas in Nepal or abroad. The war has disrupted agriculture and damaged the country's few industries. Large sections of the country live in fear either of the Maoists or of the security forces—or of both at the same time.

However, in assessing the prospects for peace, the key question is not so much the costs to the community as a whole as the cost-benefit calculations made by key decisionmakers on either side. What is the cost of continuing the war? What sacrifices must be made for peace? What are the personal incentives for seeking peace? Here the balance sheet is much less certain. Grievance-based motivations for the civil war may gradually change if the conflict is allowed to continue. Key actors on the government side may benefit from kickbacks and defense contracts. On the Maoist side, rebel leaders could become accustomed to living off the profits of revolutionary "taxation" and economic crime, both leading sources of income. Alternatively, if the war becomes protracted, a breakdown in discipline could lead to the fragmentation of the insurgency in which local commanders pursue their own economic self-interest. This section assesses the costs of the war to both the Maoists and the government and outlines the incentives both sides have—or do not have—to change their approaches to the conflict.

The Maoists

Expenditure. The information available on the Maoists' expenses suggests that the movement probably needs less than 5 billion rupees annually to sustain its current level of activity. Estimates of the total number of CPN-M cadres vary widely, but a plausible figure would be 7,000–10,000. In addition, there is a part-time Maoist militia, many of whose members are press-ganged into fighting. The consensus opinion is that the militia members have been unpaid, whereas the hard-core cadres receive a monthly salary in addition to food and shelter. Estimates of the salary range between 150 and 4,000–6,000 rupees a month.[37] The food supply seems to be covered locally through extortion and contributions in kind. Cadres operating underground in the towns will naturally incur greater expenses in food and lodging than their rural counterparts. The Maoists mainly rely on captured arms and ammunition. These are thought to be supplemented by purchases on the northern-Indian underground arms market.

Sources of finance. The Maoists' ability to conduct an effective campaign depends on their ability to raise cash and other resources. Currently, their main sources of financing derive from taxing the local population, remittances from Nepali workers abroad, extortion of private businesses and individuals inside Nepal, theft, and possibly investment in local businesses. However, unlike guerrilla groups in Burma and Colombia, there is no evidence of Maoist involvement in the international drug trade or similar international crime networks. It is impossible to obtain accurate figures on the level of financing raised by the CPN-M today. However, based on scattered (and necessarily speculative) information, our assessment is that the Maoists raised somewhere between 3 billion and 5 billion rupees during 2001 and that, at the end of the cease-fire, they may have accumulated reserves of 2 billion to 3 billion rupees. When compared to their estimated expenditures, this implies that thus far the CNP-M has had sufficient resources to underwrite its insurgency.

Maoists often demand benefits in kind—including food and shelter—from the more affluent peasantry in the areas under their control. The degree and extent of this "taxation" is likely to vary both with the availability of other sources of finance and the intensity of fighting.

There are increasing signs that the Maoists are also starting to extort from the poorer segments of the population.

Remittances from Nepali workers abroad are a second important source of income. There are some 6 million Nepali workers in India and thousands more in other regions from the Middle East to the United States. Conservative estimates of overseas remittances to Nepal amount to 10–15 percent of GDP, and they could be as high as a quarter of GDP.[38] Accurate figures are impossible to obtain because most of this money circulates through informal channels. However, it is likely that a proportion of the remittances falls into Maoist hands as a form of "tax" either in Nepal or abroad. For example, in Hong Kong, a small Maoist cell reportedly demands "donations" from richer members of the 20,000-strong local Nepali community.[39] According to one source interviewed in Kathmandu in April 2002, remittances account for as much as 50–60 percent of the Maoists' total income.

Demands for "donations" from private companies and individuals is a well-established Maoist practice in Kathmandu and other urban areas.[40] The amount of money raised in this way likely totals hundreds of millions of rupees. The Maoists utilized the cease-fire in 2001 to intensify urban extortion. Similarly, there have been several reports of trekkers facing extortion demands when passing through areas that the Maoists influence or control. For example, in October 2002 members of a Slovenian expedition reported that suspected Maoists had demanded climbing fees of around 25,000 rupees per head, similar to the amounts paid to the government. In other cases, the amounts demanded have been much smaller, more in the region of 4,000–5,000 rupees.

Finally, robbery provides a major source of income. By May 2002 the Maoists had attacked a total of 132 branches of the Agricultural Development Bank, 17 branches of the Rastriya Banjiya Bank, and 13 branches of Nepal Bank Ltd. The same pattern has continued since.[41] Total estimates of cash and gold stolen from banks range from 400 million rupees to 800 million rupees.[42]

There are unconfirmed reports that Maoist leaders have invested funds in local businesses. A hospital and a local transport company in the Terai (lowland Nepal) have both been mentioned in this regard. These are, however, unlikely to become a major source of the insurgents' income.

The recent state of emergency and the army's entry into the conflict have made it more difficult for the communist insurgents to operate effectively. This has undermined the credibility of their threats to businesses and individuals in areas that fall outside their control. Subsequently, the amounts raised from extortion appear to have fallen in urban areas, although demands certainly continue. Furthermore, the migration from rural areas and the general decline in the economy have likely eroded parts of the Maoists' "tax base." Taken together, the observable increase in the incidence of bank robberies, rural banditry, and extortion of the poor suggests that the Maoists may be running low on funds. It is not known if this is the case for the movement as a whole or only locally, as the transport of funds has been disrupted by the government's counterinsurgency campaign.

Organizational incentives for change. One of the greatest challenges facing the Maoists is the task of maintaining internal discipline during a people's war that, by their own definition, is expected to be "protracted." To date, the CPN-M has maintained a disciplined political and military command structure. However, several recent developments suggest that discipline may yet be strained.

The army's counterinsurgency campaign is the first and most obvious pressure on the Maoists. In particular, the army has disrupted the movement's communication network. A detailed analysis of recent military developments is outside the scope of this chapter, but it is clear that the Maoists are facing greater military pressure than previously, particularly in Rolpa and its neighboring midwestern districts. As a result, Maoist commanders may be tempted to stage diversionary attacks on major economic targets elsewhere in an attempt to press the government to enter peace talks. This might be part of the reason for the recent escalation in fighting.

Second, the Maoists have compounded their own communications problems: their attacks on the mainstream road and telecommunications infrastructures have made it more difficult for all sides—rebels as well as government forces—to send messages to their troops across the country.

Third, there are the inherent problems of overexpansion, especially in the east of the country, where the movement has made alliances with existing local groups rather than building up its own organizations from scratch. These allies may be less willing to submit to central discipline than the CPN-M's original hard-core cadres.

Fourth, increasing military and financial pressures facing the CPN-M may compel individual commanders to act increasingly on their own initiative without necessarily waiting for orders from the central command. So far, discipline appears to be holding, but it will be more difficult to retain the loyalty of local commanders if the movement is unable to provide the resources that they need, or if there is no early prospect of victory. If military and financial pressures grow, the CPN-M may begin to fragment. A breakdown of central, ideologically motivated discipline would increase the risk of purely criminal attacks prompted by the desire for personal gain rather than political motives.

Individual incentives. Various political and economic incentives motivate individual cadres. Regular CPN-M members are understood to receive monthly wages, in addition to other benefits, but reports of the scale of their allowances vary. In any case, there are other incentives to continue fighting, notably the power and personal prestige that comes from warfare as well as the fear of retribution if they defect. Once cadres have taken up arms, there is no easy way back to civilian life.

Official sources have claimed that Maoist leaders—particularly those living abroad—have been living comfortable lives at the expense of their less favored compatriots.[43] So far, the evidence to support such claims is limited. At least for the time being, it is unlikely that the desire for personal enrichment plays a major role in the motivations of Maoist decisionmakers at the national level.

Meanwhile, the general breakdown of law and order that has ensued from the conflict has provided opportunities for other illegal activities such as timber-smuggling and poaching in national parks. There have been several reported cases of freelance robbers and extortionists claiming to be Maoists to scare their victims, and this pattern is likely to become more commonplace. Maoist cadres do not appear to have engaged in criminal activity for personal gain to any extent, but this could change if the movement fragments.

The Government

Costs to the national economy.[44] The conflict has had a direct and largely negative impact on the livelihood of millions of people, particularly in rural areas. Killing, extortion, confiscation, forced recruitment, and infrastructure destruction have created a climate of fear and have resulted in outmigration, decreased agricultural production, and a general fall in living standards. Approximately 300,000 people are reported to have migrated to Kathmandu and the surrounding areas since 2000, and an unknown number have moved to other towns as well as abroad to India.[45]

Recent figures show a marked decline in Nepal's economic growth rates: the Central Bureau of Statistics reports that the country registered a GDP growth rate of –0.61 percent in fiscal year 2001–2002.[46] This compares with an average annual growth rate of 4.8 percent in the three preceding years. The Maoist insurgency is by no means the only cause of this decline, but it is by far the most important. Rough estimates indicate that the costs of the insurgency amount to around 8–10 percent of GDP.[47] Infrastructure damage and the fact that the economy is working well below its full potential account for these costs. *Bandhs*—strikes—are claimed to have cost approximately 4 percent of GDP in the last fiscal year. Decreasing business confidence and falling tourism revenues are threatening to become a significant drain on the economy.

Nepalese businesspeople are acutely conscious of the commercial losses that the insurgency is inflicting. There has been some dialogue between business leaders and Maoist representatives, both on issues affecting individual companies, such as extortion demands, and on wider sectoral issues, but there is little sign of an emerging "business for peace" lobby.

Current projections indicate that the economy can bear the insurgency for several more years. Our analysis suggests that the government can continue its military campaign at the current level until 2004 without provoking a major financial crisis. However, this prognosis is dependent upon two factors: first, whether the Maoists retain the capability to inflict deeper and far more serious damage on the transport, communications, and energy infrastructures, and second, whether the government will have to further reduce the development budget to boost military expenditure. An escalation in the conflict resulting in infrastructure breakdown and significant shifts from socioeconomic to security spending would quickly create a major threat to the country's economic sustainability.

Fiscal decisions will become more difficult as the conflict continues. The national budget for 2002–2003 is showing the first signs of strains, with projected revenue lower than the expected recurrent spending, almost 25 percent of which has been allotted to defense and security. The government is likely to increase its budget deficit by 50–100 percent, which risks undermining fundamental economic stability. Likewise, the financial sector is already coming under increasing strain due to growing numbers of conflict-related nonperforming loans. It remains to be seen how foreign donors will react to a protracted conflict.

Incentives for change. The government's overall approach to the Maoist insurgency appears to be reactive. It is not in the interests of any of the key players to encourage the conflict's continuation. However, deep-seated systemic obstacles, including political patronage, impede much-needed political reform.

The need to maintain fragile patronage relationships is a major disincentive to political and economic reform. Without far-reaching changes, it will be difficult to address the insurgency's causes. Kathmandu-based political intrigue will continue to divert decisionmakers' attentions away from the substantive measures needed to address the deeper causes of the insurgency. The lack of a clear political strategy means that the government is more likely to fall back on military action for remedy.

Corrupt elements within the ruling elite will seek to make the most of new opportunities arising from the armed conflict. These include the increased potential for kickbacks from military procurement and the misuse of special funds that have been set up to compensate victims of the insurgency. Furthermore, party divisions and the prospect of elections—when and if these eventually take place—will increase the likelihood of leaders diverting funds to finance political patronage. However, these gains are likely to be more than offset by lost opportunities for political patronage following the reallocation of development funds to the security budget. While patronage politics is a major obstacle to reform, the "war economy" has yet to reach the extent where decisionmakers will oppose peace moves as a means of protecting their personal gains.

Military dynamics. As of November 2002, the army has been fully engaged with the insurgency for only a year, and thus it remains at a relatively early stage in its adaptation to the demands of guerrilla warfare. One informant with high-level military connections observed that the army views its task as forcing the Maoists to the negotiating table rather than seeking an outright military victory. As the insurgency continues, military and civilian casualties will mount, leading to increased political polarization. The army may be less willing to countenance negotiations with an organization that is responsible for the loss of many soldiers' lives. Meanwhile, the army will demand, and most likely receive, larger defense budgets. It will be reluctant to accept reduced defense spending when, and if peace, returns.

Outlook and Policy Implications

As of November 2002, the Maoist movement is deeply entrenched. It is unrealistic to imagine that the movement can be eliminated in the near future. At best it may be possible to contain and gradually erode the insurgency over a period of several years. This will require a combination of military operations with strategic political and economic initiatives to address the insurgency's root causes.

The primary responsibility for defeating the insurgency rests with the Nepali government. The first requirement is resolute political leadership.

The king's assumption of executive powers in early October 2002 resulted in a redrawing of Nepal's political map, at least temporarily. The attention of political leaders has been focused on how to respond to the new constitutional situation and whether the king's action was within the spirit and the letter of the constitution. Their immediate question seemed to be what alliances and defections might be necessary to help them reacquire to power. Whatever pattern of political leadership eventually emerges in Kathmandu, it must be hoped that the government concentrates on long-term strategic initiatives rather than short-term party political advantage.

One key question will be the extent to which formal dialogue with the CPN-M is feasible or desirable. The Deuba administration was bruised by the failure of the 2001 peace talks and subsequently dismissed any prospect of future dialogue, unless the Maoists first laid down their weapons. In retrospect, the manner in which the 2001 talks were conducted—in particular the fact that they were held in public—was scarcely conducive to effective negotiations. Clearly, a different approach will be needed in any future negotiations. However, it is questionable whether the Maoists are genuinely interested in dialogue—except for short-term tactical purposes—at a time when they may still feel that they have the political advantage and when the costs of running the insurgency remain sustainable.

The immediate focus of the Nepali government is likely to remain on military operations to contain the insurgency. However, counterinsurgency is not without its drawbacks. The government will not be able to secure the trust and practical support of its citizens (including, for example, the provision of intelligence information) unless they feel secure. In this context, reports of human rights abuses by government forces are highly damaging. Official initiatives to investigate and establish accountability for such abuses will form an essential part of any effective counterinsurgency initiative.[48] At the same time, it will be important to strengthen community-based NGOs and independent media that can play a watchdog role within Nepal.

Military operations are, at best, only part of the solution. The root causes of the Maoist problem include deep-seated social inequalities and the perception that the Kathmandu government is not truly representative, particularly of the less-privileged castes and hill peoples. The CPN-M has been adept at exploiting these economic and political grievances. To defeat the insurgency, the government will need a combination of short-term initiatives ("quick hits") to achieve immediate results and longer-term projects whose benefits may not become apparent for several years. It is in this arena that international assistance may prove most beneficial.

The overriding objective for bilateral donors and other international actors must be the reduction and eventual elimination of poverty. In some instances, short-term military objectives may be at odds with development priorities. For example, the security forces are currently restricting the import of supplies to the areas worst-affected by the insurgency in the hope of denying resources to the Maoists, depriving those most in need of the benefits of assistance and exacerbating grievances underlying the conflict. Yet increased aid may also increase the resources that are available to the guerrillas through "revolutionary taxes." This contradiction may be inevitable. The precise means of resolving it will depend on local circumstances, but in the longer term there will be little chance of defeating the insurgency without demonstrated economic development.

Effective land reform is a priority and may be an area where donors can help—for example, by supporting arrangements for compensating people who have lost some of their land or who are landless. An associated issue is the need to reduce the debt burden of landless agricultural workers: local and international NGOs may be able to help develop income-generating skills—for example, through the promotion of small-scale local tourism or craft projects.

In the medium term, increased devolution to local governments is highly desirable, provided that security conditions permit them to operate safely. International donors may be able to assist by providing financial support and expertise to local administrations, drawing from the experience of other developing countries.

One of the benefits of increased devolution is—or should be—greater accountability, although this is a need at all levels of government in Nepal. It is essential that the authorities work hard to reduce corruption. A significant positive development in 2002 was the introduction of new laws to strengthen the investigative and prosecuting powers of the Commission for the Investigation of Abuse of Authority (CIAA). Shortly after the new laws came into force in August, the CIAA launched overnight raids on the homes of twenty-two revenue and customs officials.

International donors retain considerable leverage in Kathmandu. Currently, international aid amounts to 5–6 percent of GDP, consisting of 25–39 percent of total government expenditure.[49] Traditionally, aid has financed more than 50 percent of the country's development budget. The international community, therefore, needs to decide how best to exercise the influence this implies without undermining the legitimacy of the Nepali government—and, indirectly, lending credence to the Maoist claim that the present regime is a tool of international imperialism.

In the worst-case scenario, continued policy failures in Kathmandu will facilitate an escalation of the insurgency. A very high-level conflict could lead to mass migration from the most conflict-affected areas in the hills to lowland areas in the Terai. Food insecurity could produce a complex humanitarian crisis. Large parts of the country would be effectively cut off from development assistance. In the remainder, the emphasis of aid agencies would shift from development to emergency humanitarian assistance. At a national level, the issue of external military assistance—while highly controversial—would inevitably come to the fore. An outright communist takeover on the pattern of Beijing in 1949 or Saigon in 1975 remains highly unlikely. The alternative is not so much a future People's Republic of Nepal as spiraling fragmentation and chaos. In this scenario, the present government or its successors would likely retain control over the Kathmandu valley, but its authority over the rest of the country would be minimal. Nepal would become a "failed state," with damaging consequences for regional stability, particularly in India. This worst-case scenario is still avoidable, but only if concerted action is undertaken now to address the underlying social and economic grievances that have helped create the Maoist insurgency in the first place.

Notes

This chapter is based upon an earlier report, *Economic Aspects of the Insurgency in Nepal* (report no. 57/02), prepared by the ECON Centre for Economic Analysis (Norway) on behalf of the UK Department for International Development (DFID) (Oslo: ECON Centre for Economic Analysis, August 2002). It draws on research conducted in Nepal in April and May 2002, and was reviewed in November 2002 to take account of more recent developments. All three authors took part in the initial ECON study, and gratefully acknowledge the DFID's permission to publish their findings, as well as the contributions of their fellow team members. Leiv Lunde and Audun Gleinsvik of ECON had the overall responsibility for putting together the initial study in close cooperation with John Bray of Control Risks. Mansoob Murshed of the Institute of Social Studies (ISS) made the major input to the section on the causes of the conflict. In Nepal, Binod Bhattarai was particularly helpful in sharing his close understanding of the Maoists: the sections on Maoist strategy draw heavily on his insights as well as the work of fellow independent consultant Sudhir Sharma. Govind Aggarwal from Tribhuvan University shared his economic expertise. Chris Jackson from DFID/Nepal and Malcolm Smart from DFID/London provided inspiration and detailed comment throughout. The views expressed in this chapter are the authors' and do not necessarily reflect official DFID policy.

1. Nepal is divided into five development zones: eastern, central, western, midwestern, and far-western.

2. "7,073 Nepalis Killed During Insurgency," *Kathmandu Post,* October 31, 2002.

3. Paul Collier and Anke Hoeffler, "Greed and Grievance in Civil War," World Bank Policy Research Working Paper no. 2355 (Washington, D.C.: World Bank, 2001).

4. Amnesty International, *Nepal: A Spiralling Human Rights Crisis,* Amnesty Index ASA 31/1016/2002, London, 2002.

5. Ibid. See also K. N. Dixit, "Insurgents and Innocents," *Himal Magazine* (Kathmandu), June 2002.

6. Baburam Bhattarai, "Politico-Economic Rationale of People's War in Nepal," 1998, available online at www.humanrights.de/n/nepal/politics/010298_pol_eco.htm (accessed November 26, 2002).

7. In traditional Indian Hinduism there are five castes: Brahmins, Kashtriyas, Vaishyas, Sudras, and outcastes (untouchables or Dalits). The first two correspond to the upper strata of society. In Nepal they are known as Bahun and Chetri respectively, to which the Newari group is added to form the upper-caste group. Nepal also has its untouchable or Dalit group, who are frequently referred to as the "occupational" castes.

8. This point is discussed in detail in a separate report commissioned by the DFID: Emery Brusset and Raghav Raj Regmi, "Conflict and Development in Nepal," May 2002.

9. Ibid., p. 22.

10. For examples of these types of arguments, see Paul Collier and Anke Hoeffler, "Greed and Grievance in Civil War"; James Fearon and David Laitin, "Ethnicity, Insurgency, and Civil War," paper presented at the Annual Meeting of the American Political Science Association, San Francisco, Calif., August 30–September 2, 2001.

11. Collier and Hoeffler, "Greed and Grievance in Civil War," pp. 3–4.

12. See ibid.; Indra de Soysa, "Natural Resources and Civil War: Shrinking Pie or Honey Pot?" paper presented at the International Studies Association, Los Angeles, March 2000; and Michael Ross, "How Do Natural Resources Influence Civil Wars?" University of California Los Angeles, Department of Political Science, 2001, mimeo.

13. Paul Collier, " Economic Causes of Civil Conflict and Their Implications for Policy," in Chester A. Crocker, Fen Osler Hampson, and Pamela Aall, eds., *Turbulent Peace: The Challenges of Managing International Conflict* (Washington, D.C.: U.S. Institute of Peace Press, 2001), p. 147.

14. See Tony Addison and S. Mansoob Murshed, "Credibility and Reputation in Peace Making," *Journal of Peace Research* 39, no. 4 (July 2002): 487–501.

15. Frances Stewart, "Crisis Prevention: Tackling Horizontal Inequalities," *Oxford Development Studies* 28, no. 3 (October 2000): 245–262.

16. Ibid.

17. See, for example, Russell Harden, *One for All: The Logic of Group Conflict* (Princeton: Princeton University Press, 1995); and Michael Hechter, *Principles of Group Solidarity,* California Series on Social Change and Political Economy no. 11 (Berkeley: University of California–Berkeley, August 1988).

18. See Tony Addison, Philippe Le Billon, and S. Mansoob Murshed, "Finance in Conflict and Reconstruction," *Journal of International Development* 13, no. 7 (October 2001): 951–964.

19. Francis Stewart, "The Root Causes of Humanitarian Emergencies," in Wayne E. Nafzinger, Francis Stewart, and Raimo Väyrynen, eds., *War, Hunger, and Displacement: The Origins of Humanitarian Emergencies,* vol. 1 (Oxford: Oxford University Press, 2000), pp. 1–41.

20. Barbara F. Walter, *Committing to Peace: The Successful Settlement of Civil Wars* (Princeton: Princeton University Press, 2001), pp. 5–7.

21. Addison and Murshed, "Credibility and Reputation in Peace Making," p. 488.

22. UN Development Programme (UNDP), *Human Development Report 2001: Poverty Reduction and Governance* (New York: UNDP, 2001). The HDI is an average of three indices ranking national or regional standard of living (measured by GDP per capita, or purchasing power parity), life expectancy at birth, and adult literacy and gross enrollment in primary, secondary, and tertiary education. It measures performance against an ideal level, or goalpost, yielding a value between 0 and 1. See UNDP, *Human Development Report 2002,* technical note 1, "Calculating the Human Development Index," available online at http://hdr.undp.org/reports/global/2002/en/pdf/backtwo.pdf (accessed November 27, 2002).

23. All regional and district HDI figures from UNDP, *Nepal Human Development Report* (Kathmandu: UNDP, 1998), pp. 263–266.

24. Data based on UNDP, *Nepal Human Development Report 2001,* p. 131.

25. Central Bureau of Statistics, cited in Arjun K. Karki, "The Politics of Poverty and Movements from Below in Nepal," Ph.D. diss., University of East Anglia, UK, 2001, p. 127.

26. See ibid.

27. The outlawing of Kamaiya, which affected 70,000–110,000 members of the Tharu community in five districts, has led to the eviction and voluntary departure of nearly 10,000 families, many of whose livelihoods remain insecure. UN Subcommission on the Promotion and Protection of Human Rights, "The Enslavement of Dalit and Indigenous Communities in India, Nepal, and Pakistan Through Debt Bondage," February 2001, www.antislavery.org/homepage/resources/goonesekere.pdf (accessed November 27, 2002).

28. See Karki, "Politics of Poverty."

29. UNDP, *Nepal Human Development Report 2001.*

30. See Harka Gurung, *Nepal Social Demography and Expressions* (Kathmandu: New Era, 1998).

31. Ibid.

32. Collier and Hoeffler, "Greed and Grievance in Civil War," p. 4.

33. See Tony Addison and S. Mansoob Murshed, *From Conflict to Reconstruction: Reviving the Social Contract,* UNU/WIDER Discussion Paper no. 48 (Helsinki: UNU/WIDER, 2001).

34. For a survey, see S. Mansoob Murshed, "On Natural Resource Abundance and Underdevelopment," Background Paper, *World Development Report 2003* (Washington, D.C.: World Bank, 2002).

35. Håvard Hegre, Tanja Ellingsen, Scott Gates, and Nils Petter Gleditsch, "Towards a Democratic Civil Peace? Democracy, Civil Change, and Civil War, 1816–1992," *American Political Science Review* 95, no. 1 (March 2001): 17–33.

36. The poor state of governance and the institutionalization of corruption since 1990 are well documented in 2001 UNDP and Enabling State Programme

(ESP) reports—UNDP, *Nepal Human Development Report 2001* (Kathmandu: UNDP, 2001), ESP, *Pro-Poor Governance Assessment in Nepal* (Kathmandu: Polyimage, 2001)—as well as the draft interim Poverty Reduction Strategy Paper (PRSP) prepared by the International Monetary Fund and World Bank for public consultation in February 2002—National Planning Commission, Concept Paper on Poverty Reduction Strategy Paper/10th Plan, Singhadurbar, Kathmandu, February 2002.

37. These estimates are based on interviews in Nepal in April–May 2002.

38. David Seddon, Jagannath Adhikari, and Ganesh Gurung, *Foreign Labour Migration and the Remittance Economy of Nepal,* Overseas Development Group (Norwich, UK: University of East Anglia, 2000).

39. Bertil Lintner, "Maoist Moneybags," *Far Eastern Economic Review,* October 24, 2002.

40. Interviews with businesspeople in Kathmandu and Nepalganj, April–May 2002.

41. "Maoists Robbed Rs330 Million from Banks," *Kathmandu Post,* May 12, 2002.

42. Interviews in Kathmandu, April–May 2002.

43. See, for example, "Maoist Leader Found Stashing Away Rs. 5.6m," *Kathmandu Post,* July 22, 2002.

44. See the ECON study for more details of the financial impact of the insurgency.

45. Interviews in Kathmandu and Nepalganj, April–May 2002. The figure of 300,000 migrants to Kathmandu was widely attributed to the city's mayor.

46. "GDP Crashes to All Time Low in Two Decades," *Kathmandu Post,* December 11, 2002.

47. See the ECON study for more details.

48. "RNA Is Looking Into Human Rights Abuses," *Kathmandu Post,* November 1, 2002.

49. Calculations based on figures from International Monetary Fund, *Nepal: Staff Report for the Article IV Consultation,* August 19, 2002, table 1, p. 29, www.imf.org/external/pubs/ft/scr/2002/cr02205.pdf (accessed on January 7, 2003); and OECD Development Aid Committee, *2002 Development Cooperation Report Statistical Annex,* table 25, available online at www.oecd.org/en/document/0,,en-document-notheme-2-no-1-2674-0,00.html (accessed January 7, 2003).

6

The Bougainville Conflict: Political and Economic Agendas

Anthony J. Regan

Bougainville, in Papua New Guinea (PNG), provides perhaps the only case in the world where a single large and highly profitable mining venture operated by a multinational corporation has been both at the center of a violent separatist conflict (1988–1997) and was also forced to close by that conflict—perhaps permanently. Those initiating violence against Bougainville Copper Ltd. (BCL) in November 1988 were not doing so in support of secession or an end to mining. However, throughout both the subsequent conflict and the remarkably successful peace process to date, both secession and the future of mining have remained issues of central importance. The following analysis of the political economy of the origins, development, and aftermath of that conflict seeks to evaluate several propositions concerning the importance of political and economic agendas in the onset and persistence of civil wars, particularly the claimed relationship between natural resource abundance and the risk of armed conflict.[1]

Current debates on the causes of armed conflict focus in part on whether the main determinant of rebellions and civil wars is "greed" (the pursuit of profit) or "grievance" (the redress of injustice).[2] Earlier research by Paul Collier and Anke Hoeffler identified the pursuit of economic interests as a major causal factor in both the origins of wars and their persistence.[3] Their more recent work de-emphasizes motive-based explanations and instead now focuses on the opportunity for rebellion.[4] In both variants, however, their analysis focuses on the ways in which war can be profitable for at least some of the parties via their capture of either "lootable" resources or trade networks.

Michael Ross, on the other hand, suggests that separating the causal role of political and economic factors is very difficult, as the two are often empirically interrelated. He notes a range of possible initial causes

of conflict arising from natural resources—looting, predation, or grievance, with grievances commonly related to the inequitable distribution
of resource revenues.[5] In a study of fifteen cases, Ross finds that "unlootable" resources, such as deep-shaft mines and oil fields, are especially likely to generate separatist conflicts.[6] He argues that grievances
about real or perceived inequitable revenue distribution—the accrual of
resource revenues to the extraction firm, to skilled workers, and to the
government rather than to local people or the poor—can lead to armed
conflict.[7]

The Bougainville case does not support the pattern posited by Collier and Hoeffler. Although grievances about distribution of mine revenue were central to the origins of the conflict, the conflict was not primarily about rebel access to the wealth of the mine, nor did that wealth
provide the funding needed to make the rebellion more viable and
thereby contribute to its persistence. Rather, as the following analysis
will show, this was a conflict in which economic, political, and other
agendas were mutually reinforcing. Consistent with Ross's analysis,
local grievances about the impact of mining operations and the way that
its revenues were allocated fed into a long-standing sense of cultural and
political exclusion felt by Bougainvilleans, precipitating armed rebellion.
Less certain is the extent to which a desire to capture mining revenues
for the benefit of Bougainvilleans fueled separatism, as those supporting independence from PNG have been divided from the start on the
social desirability of mining, whatever its economic costs and benefits.

Bougainville and PNG in the Colonial Period

At 1,000 kilometers east of the mainland national capital, Port Moresby,
Bougainville is the most remote of PNG's nineteen provinces. Composed of a group of islands—the two largest of which are Bougainville
and Buka—the region is geographically, culturally, and linguistically
part of the Solomon Islands chain. Bougainville's integration into PNG
is relatively recent; it became part of PNG rather than the Solomon
Islands in one of the "accidents" of late-nineteenth-century colonial
map-drawing.[8] Its relations with successive colonial authorities, most
recently the Australian-administered Territory of Papua and New
Guinea (1946–1975), have often been troubled. In short, the later conflicts over the mine tended to amplify preexisting grievances arising
from the accumulated impacts of colonial rule.

Despite the profound intrusions of colonialism and postcolonial development, precolonial social structures, within which small landholding

clan lineages are dominant, have shown a high degree of resilience. Most of Bougainville's population of 200,000 rely on subsistence agriculture in isolated rural communities—a fact that accounts for both their high level of de facto autonomy from the state and their continued cultural and linguistic diversity.[9] While much of what occurred in colonial Bougainville was similar to developments elsewhere in PNG and the Solomon Islands, some aspects of Bougainville's short experience of colonial rule were unusually traumatic. In particular, four related aspects contributed to the formation of deep underlying resentments: the violence with which colonial rule was imposed and administered; the unalloyed racism of Australian rule; the alienation of traditional land for plantations under processes and terms little understood by the Bougainvillean "sellers," for whom landownership was central to economic and social relations; and the persistent failure of successive colonial administrations to make effective provisions for Bougainville's economic development.[10]

During the colonial period, the relatively powerless Bougainvilleans, like other colonized peoples, struggled to come to terms with the new world being forced upon them. Seeking to retain the autonomy of their communities and their traditional way of life, the Bougainvilleans adopted various forms of resistance to colonial rule. Other resistance movements emerged after World War II, after the repeated failure of colonial administrators to honor promises to improve economic conditions.[11] These sometimes violent protests led colonial administrators to concede more resources for various local development projects.[12] As James Griffin notes, from this cycle of neglect, protest, and concession, "the moral for Bougainville was that Port Moresby would only respond when its authority was challenged."[13]

There was continuity between these earlier forms of resistance and support for Bougainville separation from PNG, which came to the fore in the early 1970s. The separatist movement was ethnonationalist, based on a sense of pan-Bougainvillean identity distinct from the rest of PNG, the chief marker of which was the dark skin color of the Bougainvilleans.[14] Although commentary on Bougainville frequently presents Bougainvilleans as a people united in resisting colonialism, the mine, and the PNG administration, in fact the situation with respect to both resistance and separatism varied considerably in different parts of Bougainville, reflecting in part differences in language, culture, length and intensity of colonial contact, and economic status.[15] Separatist support has generally been less in Buka and the north of the main island of Bougainville, the areas with earliest colonial contact and consequential advantages in terms of education and access to economic opportunities.

Moreover, within the separatist movement there were competing visions of Bougainville's future and the role of mining. Alongside modernizers who envisioned an independent and economically developed Bougainville were groups such as the Me'ekamui Pontoku Onoring or Fifty Toea Movement, led by Damien Dameng, the most persistent of a number of traditionalist anticolonial movements that emerged from the late 1950s to defend customary social and economic relations against the corrosive effects of the outside world. From the 1960s, Dameng's opposition extended to the Panguna copper mine, and to mining generally, which was seen as destroying traditional landholdings, the very basis of social relations.[16] To date, these competing visions have not been reconciled.

Overview of Mine-Related Grievances

The Panguna copper mine, one of the world's largest copper and gold mines, was operated in Bougainville from 1972 to 1989 by Bougainville Copper Ltd., a subsidiary of Conzinc Riotinto Australia (CRA) Ltd., now Rio Tinto Ltd. (RTL). This was the first major industrial mining project in PNG and its single most important economic asset.[17] The mine was a major contributor to PNG's gross domestic product (GDP) and government revenue. From 1972 to 1989, it contributed 16 percent of PNG's internally generated income and 44 percent of its exports.[18] Mining revenues were deemed essential to the improved economic viability of PNG as a newly independent state.

The original imposition of the copper mine by the colonial regime for the benefit of the rest of PNG was widely resented in Bougainville. This resentment was reinforced by a range of issues specific to the impact of mining operations as well as to the agreements on revenue-sharing that underpinned them.[19] Throughout, the two major sources of grievance were PNG's insensitivity to concerns of local communities by the mine's two main shareholders, the PNG government and BCL, and inadequate economic compensation and revenue shares from the mine for local landowners, affected communities, and Bougainville as a whole.

Concerns about the community and environmental impacts of mining first surfaced in the mid-1960s, when the project was still in its developmental and exploratory stage, and grew as operations began in 1972. From the outset, the PNG government's policy was that all subsurface minerals were owned by the state and that mining was being undertaken to benefit PNG as a whole. This clashed with traditional understandings and practices of property-holding. Bougainville's landowners believed that their property rights extended to subsurface minerals. They were also concerned with the destructive effects of the mining operation upon agrarian subsistence farming and landholding patterns.

These concerns were not unjustified. Leases for the mine and related purposes, including access roads, tailings, and waste dumps, cut across the heart of Bougainville, about 50 kilometers from coast to coast, covering 13,047 hectares or 1.5 percent of Bougainville territory. Only one-third of that land was actually utilized for mining-related purposes. Mining operations had massive impacts on both the local communities in the immediate vicinity and also the wider community, including the forced relocation of villages, which affected several hundred people; the destruction of gardens and cash crops; the destruction of land through huge open-pit extraction; environmental damage from huge tonnages of mine waste (overburden and tailings left by crushing of the low-grade ore), which were dumped into surrounding rivers; and the influx of large numbers of outsiders, who were increasingly resented as unwanted competitors for land and economic opportunities as well as a threat to traditional mores and culture.[20]

Mining and its impacts were part of wider social and economic changes that significantly affected Bougainville, placing great stresses on the previously small-scale and highly egalitarian social structures of Bougainville. These structures had been based on principles of reciprocity and balance. Order was maintained by constant reciprocal exchanges of goods primarily directed toward maintaining balance, but also tending to encourage egalitarian distribution of goods. Increasing population and expanding allocations of land to individually owned cash-crop plantations combined with the impacts of mining contributed to increasing inequality, undermining the balance within and between social groups and exacerbating localized tensions and conflicts.

Given the deep attachments Bougainvilleans have to the land, the impact of the mine on landholding has been a particular source of grievance.[21] Traditionally, land belongs to numerous small, local matrilineal clan lineages and the right to exploit it is shared by clan members. Ownership of land can be transferred away from a lineage by custom, but only in limited circumstances, such as in the process of mortuary practices. The concept of leasing to outsiders for extensive periods for purposes involving destruction of land are not encompassed by landownership rules. Given increased population pressures, a lineage who lost or alienated their lands had very little likelihood of gaining land elsewhere. This pattern of ownership was undermined by the compensation deals that were offered to landholders in the affected lease areas, which provided for distribution of compensation payments through nominated male representatives of the matrilineal clans. In addition to the intraclan disputes that this method caused, compensation deals provoked intragenerational disputes about fairness, as younger landowners, who had not been adults when the original land survey was undertaken in the 1960s, tended to receive smaller shares. In this way, the main dispute between Bougainville and the PNG government over control of natural resources generated secondary intracommunal conflicts.[22] In the late 1980s, these secondary disputes in turn provided the spark for a wider ethnonationalist rebellion against PNG.

The revenue-sharing agreements between the PNG government and Bougainville Copper Ltd., the operator of the mine, constituted the second major source of grievance. There were two such agreements, one in 1967 and another in 1974.[23] The first, the Bougainville Copper Agreement (BCA), was negotiated by Australian colonial officials at a time when independence still seemed many years away. While the agreement set royalties to the Australian administration of 1.25 percent of the export value of ore concentrate produced, it also ensured BCL controlling shares (54 percent) and provided it with a three-year tax holiday, following which the tax rate would be 50 percent, rather than the normal rate of 25 percent. The agreement also provided for BCL to build most of the infrastructure—port, roads, housing, and the like—for the mine. The Australian administration granted these generous terms because they not only met BCL's concerns by rapidly discharging its debt, but also ensured high returns to the government in the approach to, and aftermath of, independence. Unusually, the agreement also gave the administration a 20 percent equity option in BCL at par once the feasibility of the mine was established, an option the administration took up, and one that gave government a seat on the board of BCL. Government shareholding was proposed by CRA "in order to commit the [colonial] government to the project."[24]

On the eve of independence, the new PNG-led government renegotiated the terms of the 1967 agreement, which seemed to the new government far too generous to the company. BCL was extremely profitable in the first eighteen months of operations (1972–1973), due to both the tax holiday and the unprecedentedly high copper prices. The new agreement was directed mainly at revising the tax regime: the three-year tax holiday would end in January 1974 rather than April 1, 1975; a high marginal rate of tax ("additional profits tax") was to apply when taxable income exceeded a threshold (related to return on investment); and various other exemptions and accelerated depreciation allowances were ended.

The outcome was widely applauded as a victory for PNG,[25] but as Donald Denoon notes, "in retrospect BCL was lucky: the government's move gave it a sense of ownership of the project."[26] As a shareholder, the PNG government received significant dividends revenue over the succeeding years. From total earnings of 4.4 billion kina, the mine generated 1.754 billion kina in total revenues in its seventeen years of operation.[27] With over two-thirds of mine revenue going to interests in PNG (the majority to the central government), BCL could be assured that there would be no further major challenge to its mining operations from the PNG government.

Significantly, although Bougainville's concerns were a factor in the 1974 renegotiation of the original agreement, Bougainville as a whole was not a party to these revenue-sharing agreements, nor were local interests consulted in any effective way when either agreement was being negotiated. Initially, the prevailing view of the two main shareholders was that Bougainville as a whole would gain primarily as a consequence of local economic multiplying effects of the mining operation. Indeed, the mine generated 10,000 jobs in the construction phase, almost 4,000 long-term jobs once it began operating, as well as indirect jobs in service industries that sprang up around the mine.[28] While the figures varied from time to time, well under 50 percent of jobs were held by Bougainvilleans. In contrast to the benefits it held for BCL and the administration, the 1967 agreement contained no provision for Bougainville as a whole to receive a share of revenue that would be generated by the mine's operations.

As for the affected landholders, they were originally offered very limited rents and compensation, based on practice elsewhere applicable to land acquired for public purposes such as roads or schools.[29] A series of confrontations with landowners in the late 1960s led the administration to change its compensation policies. Affected landowners would now get 5 percent of the 1.25 percent royalty payable to the national government and much higher levels of land compensation and occupation fees than originally stipulated. Compensation covered a wide range of damages, including destruction to crops and rivers, as well as social inconvenience. While they reluctantly accepted the terms offered, the landholders increasingly came to view the size and the method of these payments as inadequate. Distribution of compensation among landowners caused growing problems and provoked resentment in a number of ways. First, there was general resentment that landowner compensation was mainly related to usage of land, with only a limited share of mine revenues offered to landowners. Second, the total amount of compensation and occupation fees paid to each landowner was seen as too little. Third, the compensation payments were seen as not meeting the changing needs of villagers; for example, as populations grew, relocation housing deteriorated. Fourth, as mentioned above, younger landowners, whose names had not been listed as members of lineages when land-ownership demarcation was undertaken in the late 1960s, tended to receive smaller shares. Finally, and more generally, unequal distribution of compensation among landholders and lack of payments to neighboring groups led to resentment among the have-nots as well as concern over the destructive effects of incipient class differences for a tradition-ally egalitarian society.[30]

It was not until 1974, and in the context of political confrontation over Bougainvillean demands for devolution of power, that the national government agreed to provide Bougainville as a whole with a share of the mining royalties initially payable to the national government. Compared to revenues allocated to the government and BCL, however, Bougainville received only a 5.63 percent share (4.27 percent to the provincial government—mostly royalties—and 1.36 percent to land-owners, through royalties, rents, and compensation), a fact that would prove an enduring and dangerous source of resentment.

General dissatisfaction continued, as reflected in a series of claims from the late 1970s onward for increased or new forms of compensation. When BCL was slow to respond to new demands put forcefully by a representative landowner organization—the Panguna Landowners Association (PLA), formed in 1979—landowners set up roadblocks and looted a supermarket in one of the two BCL mining towns. This resulted in the rapid negotiation of a new compensation agreement, mainly to the benefit of PLA members.

In general, the impacts of the massive social change associated with the mine were felt more strongly as time went on, especially those involving the influx of outsiders, who were increasingly seen as competing for land and economic opportunities, undermining culture, and causing crime. These resentments increased support for separatism and reflected an ethnonationalist view that if Bougainville's mineral wealth was to be exploited, then the benefits should flow to Bougainville, not to remote PNG, to which most felt little connection.

Separatism and Mining

Underlining the opportunities and challenges that decolonization would present Bougainville, the commencement of mining operations in late 1972 coincided with the establishment of the first PNG-led government, for which early independence from Australian tutelage was a primary goal. For Bougainvilleans, staking out both its future political status and a claim for greater shares of resources generated by the mine became issues of central importance in the period from 1972 to 1976. With independence achieved in 1975, however, the accumulated resentments that Bougainvilleans felt toward the colonial government were transferred to the new government in Port Moresby. This simplified the task of those seeking to mobilize Bougainvillean identity around their own separatist agenda.

Throughout the late 1960s and early 1970s there had been increasing calls for Bougainville's separation from PNG, a trend that reflected intensified resentments associated with the arrival of the mine and its intrusive operations.[31] But there was also significant opposition to secession—especially, but not only, in Buka and north Bougainville. With no clear consensus emerging, many outside Bougainville had assumed that secession was a dead issue.[32] The mine had begun operations without overt opposition, and after 1972 Bougainvillean members of the newly elected colonial legislature held significant positions in the national government in Port Moresby, including the effective leadership of a Constitutional Planning Committee (CPC). The CPC developed proposals for political devolution, partly in response to separatist sentiments expressed in Bougainville, which involved elected provincial governments enjoying some exclusive powers under entrenched constitutional arrangements.

It was the December 1972 "payback" killings by New Guinea Highland villagers of two senior Bougainvillean public servants, whose vehicle had struck a child in a road accident, that triggered overt demands for separation. For the first time, separation had widespread support in all areas of Bougainville. Public opinion against "red-skins" was inflamed, and within two months a committee of leaders from all over Bougainville was set up to negotiate the future status of Bougainville with PNG.[33]

The Bougainvillean leadership was certainly interested in secession, but many questioned its feasibility. Hence their initial bid was to press for a high level of political devolution with a share of mine revenue for Bougainville as a whole, backed by the threat of secession if these demands were not met. The PNG government eventually, if reluctantly, conceded to an interim provincial government, which began operating in January 1974. During the same year, agreement was reached on payment of 95 percent of mine royalties to the Bougainville Interim Provincial Government (BIPG). However, discussion of other funding arrangements for the new provincial government (levels of grants, sharing of tax powers) broke down in April 1975, and the BIPG assembly voted to secede.

A decision in July 1975 by the PNG government to remove provisions from the almost completed independence constitution, guaranteeing the devolution to provincial government was the last straw for Bougainville. A unilateral declaration of independence was made on September 1, 1975—just days before PNG's Independence Day, September 15. Despite some localized violence and destruction of government property in Bougainville that accompanied the declaration, there were no deaths or serious injuries. The Bougainville leadership, many of whom remained ambivalent about secession, also sought to avoid violence. The revenues generated by the mine were also seen as critical to the success of either independence or devolution, and so the leaders sought to ensure that the mine would continue to operate with as little disruption as possible. Aware that armed conflict could destroy the newly independent PNG, the central government was cautious and—in general—conciliatory. In the face of this, and finding no international support for secession, the Bougainvillean leadership abandoned their unilateral assertion of statehood and renewed negotiations on devolution.

The matter was settled in 1976 by a constitutional guarantee for decentralization that offered more autonomy to Bougainville than the original CPC proposals had envisaged, including more exclusive powers and taxes. The arrangements became the basis for a national system of nineteen provincial governments and resulted in the establishment of the North Solomon Provincial Government (NSPG)—the name chosen by the Bougainville government to emphasize its cultural links with the Solomon Islands. A more equitable share of revenues was at the heart of the agreement. The NSPG received confirmation of the previously agreed arrangements on royalties and grants for existing functions; powers over retail sales taxes—an important source of revenue given the high level of economic activity associated with the mine; and an annual grant to meet the costs of the activities it had taken over from the national government. In a sense, these concessions amounted to a return of a greater share of mining revenues from Port Moresby to Bougainville.

Some Bougainville leaders saw these arrangements as a long-term settlement, others as a starting point for later movement toward either increased devolution or outright separation. The issue of the share of BCL revenue received by the provincial government remained, however, a contentious issue.[34] BCL continued to be highly profitable, and the proportion of revenue payable to the national government was increasingly seen as unfair, especially as the NSPG developed policies and the capacity needed to invest these revenues in broad-based economic and social development.

The NSPG generally performed well, administering basic services (health, education, etc.) effectively and making good use of its considerable revenues (mainly from mine royalties and sales taxes) to develop infrastructure to promote economic development in rural areas.[35] While the Bougainville elite became gradually more confident of the benefits of remaining part of PNG—including political and bureaucratic positions, access to higher education, and enhanced business opportunities—the situation was more complex for the wider population. The attempted secession of 1975–1976 had focused attention on independence as a way to resolve Bougainville's social and economic problems. Initial high expectations that the NSPG would have powers and resources close to those of an independent state and the capacity to make policy on mining, environment, land, squatter issues, and crime were not met. As social and economic problems worsened during the 1980s, many ordinary people lost faith in devolution. While discussions of whether it would have been better to press ahead with secession in 1976 became more frequent, with the provincial leadership committed to devolution, it seemed that there was little likelihood of secession again becoming a major issue.

Origins of Armed Conflict, 1988–1997

From the mid-1980s, the long-festering grievances of marginalized younger landowners resurfaced, fed by a number of tensions related to mining as well as to other mounting socioeconomic problems.[36] These tensions contributed to a growing sense of crisis in Bougainville in the middle to late 1980s. The NSPG clearly felt the pressure and responded by developing new policies to deal with problems associated with crime and squatters, land distribution patterns, and unemployed youth. It also began exploring ways to strengthen traditional authority, in response to increasing concerns about the way that modern development was seen to be eroding customary social formations. While there was growing awareness of social problems, there was little, if any, concern among any of the authorities that major social disruption was approaching.[37]

From the mid-1980s, Francis Ona and other leaders of a group of younger landowners began to challenge the leadership of the Panguna Landowners Association, whose members they claimed were benefiting unfairly from the mine and had failed to represent all landowner interests. From late 1987, the young landowners sought to take control of the PLA. By early 1988, they had also secured the support of disgruntled semi-skilled Bougainvillean mine workers, as well as Damien Dameng's Me'ekamui Pontoku Onoring, the prominent traditionalist opponents of mining.[38] Known as the "New PLA," they made a series of escalating demands against BCL, including a huge monetary compensation for environmental and other impacts of mining operations, a 50 percent share of mine revenue to the landowners and the NSPG, and the transfer of ownership of BCL to the people of Bougainville within five years. The government responded by setting up an independent inquiry. While critical of some aspects of BCL's operations, its report largely dismissed the landowners' claims about environmental damage.[39]

In November 1988 the New PLA and its allies responded by attacking BCL buildings and destroying the power supply to the mine. While no coherent account has yet been provided by those involved in the violence against BCL in November and December 1988, it appears to have been prompted by the frustration of the younger generation of landowners at the failure of the PLA, BCL, and the national government to redress their demands for a more equitable share of mine revenues, for both landowners and Bougainville as a whole, and for environmental protection and compensation. No doubt, past experience of the concessions that could be achieved by violent challenges to authority provided an incentive to violence. Most likely, those involved in the attacks on the mine intended them as a tactic to squeeze further concessions from the authorities and BCL.

The authorities, however, did not play according to script. Instead of concessions, they sought to restore what they viewed as a serious breach in law and order by deploying mobile squads of riot police. This forceful response was in stark contrast to the national government's measured reaction to Bougainville's unilateral declaration of independence of 1975. Two factors may account for the change. First, at this stage, the rebellion remained highly localized and the unprepared Bougainville leadership sided with the national government against the rebels. Second, unlike the unrest of 1975, these attacks were directed squarely at the mine, threatening the very mainstay of the national economy.

With the benefit of hindsight, it is clear that the riot-squad deployment was a disastrous move. Trained mainly to deal with intercommunal fighting in the Highlands of PNG, the riot squads employed their standard tactic of using violence to intimidate communities into ending their conflicts. In Bougainville, police reprisals were directed indiscriminately at communities in and around the mine lease areas. This action had little direct impact on the small but growing groups of "militants" supporting Francis Ona, but provoked outrage and further violence among the general populace, many of whom until then had little reason to support Ona's nascent movement.[40]

Within weeks of being deployed, the almost entirely non-Bougainvillean riot squads became seen as the enemy by many. There was rapid mobilization behind Ona, who emerged as the central leader of a diverse coalition of actors and interests, which eventually adopted the name Bougainville Revolutionary Army (BRA). Composed of small, armed units based in and supported by local communities, the BRA was never a hierarchical and tightly organized body. Units retained a high degree of autonomy, but would often cooperate in particular operations, employing guerrilla tactics that the PNG forces had not been trained to counter.

In this way, both the attacks and the reprisals they elicited touched off simmering tensions and acted as the catalyst for mobilization of a wider ethnonationalist rebellion, in which secession came to be seen as a panacea for a wide range of accumulated social and economic ills. Initially, Ona's objective was to effect a redistribution of mine revenues. He soon found, however, that wide support was conditional on his embracing the goal of secession, and at least paying lip service to those committed to closure of the mine. From February 1989, he took up the secessionist cause and began to mobilize widespread support. As always, however, the picture in Bougainville was complex. There were people in all areas who opposed the rebellion. There were interrelated regional and nascent class interests in this opposition; as in the past, in Buka and parts of north Bougainville, and in more developed areas of the east coast, as well as among the emerging Bougainville elite who had benefited from mining and related businesses, there was considerable, if uneven, support for remaining part of PNG.

While some members of the national government ministry supported a hard line against the rebellion, others supported a negotiated settlement from the beginning and made strenuous efforts in that regard.[41] These included informal talks with Ona in December 1988, a major new mining benefits package offered in May 1989, peace ceremonies late in 1989, and a bipartisan committee to examine ways of resolving the conflict (although established in 1989, it did not report until 1992).[42] But all such efforts proved futile amid the continuing brutality of the security forces and the concomitant increase in support for Ona's movement.

As the conflict intensified in early 1989, the PNG security forces sought to keep the mine operating, but the security threat faced by its workers forced BCL to close operations in May 1989. Alarmed by the escalating violence and the secessionist threat, and concerned with restoring mine operations, the PNG government made a fateful decision to reinforce the overwhelmed riot police by deploying the PNG Defense Forces (PNGDF).[43] However, the PNGDF proved unable to quell the violence. On the contrary, once they started taking casualties, their behavior became worse than that of the riot squads, and appalling abuses of human rights occurred. However, other than appeals by the prime minister to the defense forces to protect the innocent and act in accordance with the law, nothing substantive was done to bring the security forces to account.[44]

As rebellion escalated into widespread ethnonationalist conflict, there was a change in the balance of views among the loose coalition of interests within the BRA and its allied groups on the subject of the future of mining operations. Initially, the attacks on the mine were not intended to close it, but to extract concessions, especially for landowners and local mine workers, but also for Bougainville more generally. Once the government made clear its intention to reopen the mine and deployed force to this end, however, the BRA leaders, including Ona, came to view mine closure as a tactic in the fight for secession. Repeated efforts on the part of Port Moresby and BCL to reopen the mine during and after 1989 were successfully thwarted by the BRA. For Ona, closure was expected to be temporary—the mine would later be the source of wealth for an independent Bougainville. However, other members of the coalition supporting secession favored permanent closure. These interests included some mine lease landowners, especially those who received limited compensation and those whose land was threatened with destruction by the ever increasing tailings dumps, as well as young men with "leveling" agendas—notably from areas with limited economic activities—who resented the apparent wealth of mine lease landowners. Closure was also supported by many who objected to the influx of outsiders into Bougainville, and also by Damien Dameng and leaders of movements similar to Me'ekamui Pontoku Onoring, who had always opposed the mine as eroding traditional ways and authority. Dameng's views resonated with many in the BRA and in the wider community. They proved influential in shaping the ideology of the BRA and later the Bougainville Interim Government (BIG), both of which remain ambivalent about the future of mining in Bougainville.

Conflict Transformation, 1990–1994

Unable to contain the escalating violence, the PNGDF was evacuated following a March 1990 cease-fire. In the months before and immediately after March, there was a mass exodus of the 15,000 to 20,000 non-Bougainvillean residents, as well as many Bougainvilleans, especially the elite and skilled workers.[45] All formal government authority lapsed after departure of the security forces. Surprised by the withdrawal and unprepared for rule, it took nearly two months for the BRA to establish the Bougainville Interim Government, with Ona as its president. One of its first acts was a unilateral declaration of independence in May 1990. The new government adopted a national program, influenced by the traditionalist ideology articulated by Dameng and others, based on communal self-sufficiency, restored egalitarianism, and a rejection of both outsiders and the modernizing influences of the outside world. While this led to the strengthening of the authority of traditional leaders in some areas and some impressive efforts at local self-help, the interim government proved unable to assert its authority throughout all areas of Bougainville.

What ensued in the early 1990s was a situation of semi-anarchy, which saw the emergence of multiple intra-Bougainvillean conflicts over power and resources. In particular, in those regions where there were significant interests opposed to secession, resistance to the BRA began to emerge. Resistance that had little to do with ideology and more with local disputes also developed in many areas. Armed groups developed in opposition to the BRA, often composed of BRA defectors who had been on the losing side of localized conflicts. Beginning with the island of Buka in September 1990, local leaders who opposed the interim government invited the return of the PNGDF, which reestablished authority and public services in "government-controlled areas." The PNGDF also strengthened local opposition to the interim government by gradually uniting disparate armed groups under the Bougainville Resistance Forces (BRF). From the early 1990s onward, the conflict intensified along both dimensions—between Bougainville and PNG and within Bougainville, and between the BRA and the BRF, backed by the PNGDF. Complicating matters further were ongoing skirmishes over localized disputes within and between local BRA and BRF elements.

From mid-1992 until 1994, the national government of Prime Minister Paias Wingti initiated a more aggressive policy toward the Bougainville Interim Government. Rather than achieve a decisive military defeat of the rebellion as hoped, this policy only exacerbated the conflict. When the Wingti government was replaced by that of Sir Julius Chan in August 1994, concerted peace efforts soon followed, notably through a major pan-Bougainville peace conference in October 1994. At the last minute senior BIG and BRA leaders refused to attend. Frustration over the lack of progress of the peace talks contributed to the emergence of new moderate leadership distinct from the interim government, the BRA, and the pronational local governments established in government-controlled areas in the early 1990s. The new leadership persuaded the national government to reestablish the provincial government (suspended in 1990) and set about seeking to build unity in Bougainville as a prelude to negotiations with the national government.

This resulted in pan-Bougainville talks in Australia in September and December 1995, which provided the foundations for reaching under-standings between the Bougainville factions. It was agreed that the talks would be resumed early in 1996.

However, an ambush by the PNG security forces of leaders of both the interim government and the BRA on their return from the December 1995 talks in Australia resulted in a further escalation of violence in 1996 and prevented a resumption of the talks. The new wave of confrontation resulted in the virtual defeat of the PNG security forces by the BRA, whose fighters also captured significant amounts of modern weaponry and ammunition in the process. These developments were important fac-tors in the decision by the Chan government from late 1996 to engage mercenaries through the UK-based firm Sandline under a U.S.$36 million contract directed at crushing the BRA and reopening the Panguna mine. However, tensions between the mercenaries and elements of the PNGDF resulted in the latter ousting the mercenaries in a move that precipitated a political crisis, forcing Chan to step aside as prime minister.[46]

Despite the promise of peace talks, the fighting continued. In 1996 there were 800 PNGDF soldiers and 150 riot police active in Bougain-ville. Although precise figures have never been available, it has been estimated that the BRA had 2,000 armed men, most of whom were home guards, providing security for villagers and refugee camps in BRA-controlled areas. Only a few hundred fought on the front lines of battle. The BRF, meanwhile, numbered approximately 1,500, including those providing civilian protection. The BRF was able to supplement homemade arms and vintage World War II arms with modern weapons supplied by the PNGDF.

The BRA, however, had a more difficult time gaining needed sup-plies to pursue its campaign, in large part due to a sea and naval block-ade on BRA-controlled areas that had been imposed by Port Moresby from mid-1990. During the first phase of the conflict, the BRA gained limited funding and supplies through the looting of the BCL mine as well as other captured government and commercial properties. These assets, however, were quickly exhausted, and the BRA was forced to rely on its own limited resources. Basic needs were met by the BRA's own communities, whose economy of subsistence agriculture enabled them a ready food supply. As its support base developed in 1989 and in the early 1990s, the BRA managed to improve methods for making homemade weapons and for reconditioning vintage World War II arms. Modern weapons were acquired opportunistically, through capture from defeated PNGDF soldiers and, in some cases, through purchases across enemy lines. Few weapons were purchased from outside Bougainville, despite a number of unsuccessful efforts to circumvent the PNG blockade. Likewise, very little financial support came from the Bougainvillean diaspora, although some largely humanitarian assistance was provided by sympathetic groups in the Solomons and Australia. That the BRA was able to sustain successive military victories against the combined forces of the PNGDF and the BRF, despite its loss of support in many areas, was largely the result of superior guerrilla tactics and a widespread base of support from the population in significant areas—support that flowed as much or more from the misguided strategy of successive PNG governments to crush the rebellion through indiscriminate force as from the ideological commitment of some to secession.

Peace Efforts, 1997–2002

As already noted, peace efforts were attempted at the earliest stages of the conflict and continued to be made at various points thereafter, at the initiative of both the national and Bougainvillean authorities, and in a number of instances with facilitation and mediation by governments in the region.[47] By the mid-1990s, several factors converged to make the conflict receptive to negotiated resolution. In essence, there was a growing unwillingness on all sides to bear the cost of continued conflict.[48]

By 1996 the conflict had taken a terrible human and material toll on Bougainvillean society. While the actual number of deaths and injuries is not known, approximately 500 PNG security force members and perhaps twice that number of BRA and BRF combatants were killed in action. Among the civilian population, the number of deaths directly attributable to the conflict is frequently placed at between 15,000 and 20,000. While this number is probably too high, several thousand civilian lives were probably lost, either directly, as a result of battles and extrajudicial executions committed by all combatant parties, or indirectly, as a result of the humanitarian crisis that was exacerbated by the nine-year-long blockade of BRA-controlled areas. Civilian suffering also took the form of forcible displacement, which by 1996 had created a population of internally displaced persons numbering 60,000. In absolute terms, these numbers may seem small in comparison to conflict elsewhere, but for a population of 200,000, it was a massive toll.

The material toll for Bougainville was also punishing. Other than subsistence agriculture, the conflict resulted in the cessation of all economic activity. An estimated 8,000–10,000 jobs related to mining and a similar number in the cocoa and copra sectors were lost. Almost all mining and mining-related infrastructure was destroyed, as were most government-supported health and educational facilities, and transportation infrastructure. There was also considerable damage to plantation infrastructure, as the lack of new investment in maintenance and plantings resulted in plummeting productivity. By 1996 these factors contributed to an increasing war-weariness among local leaders and communities, who supported their own efforts to end the cycles of local conflict between the BRA and the BRF.[49] This same war-weariness made the BRA receptive to renewed peace initiatives from Port Moresby, even though the BRA was by then in its strongest military position ever, following the virtual defeat of the PNG Defense Forces in 1996 and the abortive attempt of the Chan government to employ the Sandline mercenaries early in 1997.

On the PNG side, there was always significant opposition to the use of violence to resolve problems in Bougainville, as evidenced by efforts in 1990 and again in 1994 to find a peaceable settlement.[50] By 1994 the PNG economy was in serious trouble, and the costs of the conflict began to be seen as a serious drain on the economy, a view that was part of the reason for the Chan government's peace initiative that same year. For PNG, the loss of the revenue from the mine had the greatest economic impact, which was felt most acutely in the first two years after mine closure and which resulted in PNG's first structural adjustment package with the International Monetary Fund (IMF). Over time, the loss of the mine affected the PNG government's ability to maintain funding for social services while also financing security force operations, subsistence for the refugee camps, and other services related directly to the war. By the mid-1990s, pressure to reopen the mine, which had been a primary objective of PNG in continuing its military campaign, was less intense because other major resource extraction projects in gold mining and oil drilling came on line in other areas of PNG, and because of a growing recognition that resumption of copper mining in Bougainville might be neither practical nor economically feasible. Overall, the conflict contributed to the escalating economic and fiscal crisis faced by PNG from 1994,[51] not only in terms of direct cost, but also in terms of lost opportunities for foreign investment, the breakdown of budgetary discipline involved in the heavy and unbudgeted expenditures by the PNG security forces, and increasing difficulties with the World Bank and the IMF—which culminated in the suspension of structural adjustment program funding following the Sandline affair of 1997. Taken together, these developments opened the way to PNG's resumption of the pan-Bougainville talks in mid-1997.

While the peace process that produced the Bougainville Peace Agreement of August 2001 is generally regarded as beginning in July 1997, in fact it was in many respects a continuation of prior efforts to end the conflict. An understanding among leaders of most Bougainville factions on the need to end the conflict was reached in New Zealand, where the first 1997 talks were held. This cleared the way for officials from Bougainville and PNG to meet for a second set of talks in New Zealand in October 1997, where a truce was agreed. An unarmed regional Truce Monitoring Group, involving New Zealand, Fiji, Vanuatu, and Australia, was also agreed upon, and was deployed in December 1997.

Leadership talks in New Zealand in January 1998 resulted in the Lincoln Agreement.[52] It provided for an "irrevocable cease-fire," continuation of the regional monitoring force (now called the Peace Monitoring Group—PMG), establishment of a UN Observer Mission on Bougainville (UNOMB), and a program for a political settlement to begin in 1998. The cease-fire has held, and the PMG and the UNOMB monitoring missions have both operated well, creating a secure space within which groups previously highly suspicious of one another have been able to engage, build trust, and resolve differences.

The peace process was not without difficulty, however. It was opposed by Francis Ona, who for a time insisted that the unilateral declaration of independence of May 1990 had settled Bougainville's political status once and for all, despite the fact that no country had recognized it. However, early support for most elements of the BRA effectively marginalized Ona's influence. While he has continued to oppose the process and has remained a potential alternative leader should progress in the peace process falter, his views have had limited impact since 1998.

As a result of unforeseen difficulties in implementation of the Lincoln Agreement, negotiations for a political settlement did not commence until June 1999, and they continued for over two difficult years before producing the Bougainville Peace Agreement in August 2001.[53] The main focus was on a referendum and autonomy as an alternative to secession. The future of mining was not specifically on the agenda. However, it was understood on all sides that this would be a matter for Bougainville to decide, although PNG would reserve its right to a share of revenues should the mine be allowed to reopen. That understanding is reflected in the peace agreement, which includes three main elements:

- A constitutionally guaranteed referendum for Bougainvilleans on independence for Bougainville from PNG, deferred for a period of fifteen years.
- Constitutional arrangements for development of a high degree of autonomy for Bougainville in the interim, under which the arrangements with respect to powers and distribution of revenue in relation to future mining are provided.

- A complex, multistage plan for the disposal of weapons by former Bougainvillean combatants, various stages being tied to both withdrawal of the PNG security forces and the passing and coming into operation of the constitutional laws on referendum and autonomy.

As of late 2002, the implementation of the peace agreement was already well under way. Phased withdrawal of the PNG security forces is almost complete, and weapons disposal by the BRA and the BRF is proceeding well. The PNG parliament has met the stringent constitutional requirements for passing the constitutional laws needed to give effect to the peace agreement.[54] However, the full implementation of the provisions of those laws will depend on continuing progress in the implementation of the agreed weapons disposal process.

Prospects for Bougainville: Peace, Development, and Self-Government?

The prospects for peace and development in postconflict Bougainville and PNG in general will largely depend on how well the manifold tensions of social and economic modernization are managed. Given the devastating impact of the conflict on the economy and the livelihoods of Bougainvilleans, the main goal of the population and the leadership is rapid economic development, and ultimately fiscal self-reliance. While there are major differences from the situation in the 1980s, insofar as there are now no mining operations and revenues, similar socioeconomic dynamics may be in place, as many people struggle for access to a much smaller pool of economic resources, which could create new divisions and tensions. In today's postconflict situation, where resort to violence as a method of redressing grievances is still deeply ingrained, it might prove even more difficult to resolve these tensions than in the 1980s.

The Bougainville leadership hopes to develop new policies and institutions to manage these challenges in ways suitable to Bougainville. These include building institutions of government, including local administration, courts, and police according to traditional models of authority, as well as development strategies that seek to create wider economic opportunities. However, building new institutions is likely to involve considerable costs.

Under the autonomy arrangements of the Bougainville Peace Agreement, the costs of providing government services, at least to the level at which they are provided elsewhere in PNG, as well as the restoration of infrastructure, are to be met by the PNG government until Bougainville achieves fiscal self-reliance.[55] These arrangements largely leave Bougainville with the burden of the extra costs involved in establishing new institutions. Fiscal self-reliance based on the present agricultural subsistence economy, however, is unlikely in the near term, placing the onus back on PNG—or donors—to fund postconflict Bougainville's new autonomy. Indeed, part of the rationale underlying the PNG government's decision to concede to a deferred referendum on independence was the hope that, in the interim, the government would be able to convince Bougainville of the benefits of remaining within PNG.

Yet there are serious doubts about the ability of the PNG government to allocate significant new funding to Bougainville, even despite supportive donor states. If this is the case, without significant donor funding there is likely to be a considerable gap between Bougainvillean expectations of the benefits of autonomy and what can actually be provided. There is a danger that a situation rather like that of the 1980s will be repeated, in which much touted expectations are not met, social tensions rise, and early secession—perhaps again supported by violence—re-emerges as an attractive, albeit simplistic, answer to Bougainville's ills.

This highlights the critical role that mining can yet play in Bougainville's path to peace, development, and self-reliance. Given the lack of economic alternatives, Bougainville is unlikely to achieve self-reliance for many years without a return to mining in some form. As it stands, the immediate future of mining remains open to speculation, as in 2001, BCL announced its intention to exit Bougainville.[56] Given the extremely high startup costs, exacerbated by the extensive destruction of mine property during the conflict, investors will likely view Bougainville as a risky place to operate. With international patterns of mining investment moving away from the high-rainfall tropics, the prospect of attracting alternative investors seems unlikely at present.

In the postconflict period, Bougainvillean public opinion on mining remains divided. For those committed to a permanent closure of the mine, the status quo is a desired state of affairs. Many Bougainvilleans, however, would welcome renewed mining as a source of income, albeit with more participatory involvement of landowners, better environmental management, and more equitable distribution of revenue. In addition to those former rebel leaders who originally envisaged revenues from resumed mining as essential to political independence, some groups in other parts of Bougainville now argue that, as they suffered in a conflict that originated in the areas around the mine, the people of those areas owe a "blood debt" to the rest of Bougainville, which can best be met by a resumption of mining.[57]

While it leaves many questions about the future of mining unanswered, the peace agreement has introduced several differences with regard to legislation and revenue-sharing arrangements, which could prove important if mining were to resume. Bougainville will be able to impose many forms of taxes related to mining operations. Corporate taxation, however, will remain a national government power, as will customs duties and the value added tax on consumer goods and services. In this way, if mining were to resume and result in a revenue bonanza for Bougainville, it would nevertheless be required to contribute to PNG government revenues.

While the specific terms of revenue-sharing are subject to further negotiation, the state (including the national and provincial governments) and resource developers appear to have learned valuable lessons from the conflict. Most important, a more direct involvement of landowner communities in consultations about resource development and in the sharing of benefits from resource projects is seen as important to conflict prevention.

As Colin Filer has noted, the conception underlying PNG's immediate pre- and postindependence policy on resource rents was that, as the owner of the resources in question, the state appropriated the revenue for investment in pursuit of long-term economic growth, reduction in resource dependency, and equalization of development between different parts of PNG.[58] Landowners were compensated mainly for inconvenience. In large part influenced by the Bougainville conflict, the conception underlying policy since 1989 recognizes, at least tacitly, that landowners also have a legitimate claim to the mineral and forest resources found on or under their land—although the law still asserts state ownership. Negotiations around the Porgera gold mine in 1989, for example, produced a process to ensure that landowners are closely involved in negotiations prior to and during the development of extractive operations. While the national government remains responsible for negotiating the project agreement directly with the resource developer, the process involves a "development forum," a tripartite negotiating process in which the national government, the provincial government, and landowners negotiate the division of benefits between themselves.[59] Developers have also been more active in involving landowners in employment and business opportunities. This process and a set of principles about the distribution of benefits now apply to all mining and hydrocarbon projects in PNG.

This more participatory approach seems to provide a basis for reducing the likelihood of conflict between resource developers and the state, on the one hand, and landowners, on the other. However, in a country such as PNG, where small societies remain so autonomous and the state remains so weak, there are reasons for caution. First, landowners have also learned from Bougainville. The threat of "creating another Bougainville" is regularly heard in the context of disputes over natural resource extraction operations elsewhere in PNG. Further, the prospect of additional benefits to landowners and provincial governments under the new mining regime is contributing to other problems. Some arise from the activities of what Filer calls "secondary claimants," especially groups who claim that the wrong landowners have been compensated, contributing to localized conflicts in relation to some projects.[60] The revenues flowing to the Southern Highlands Provincial Government from the Kutubu oil project, for example, have contributed to several years of intense and destructive intergroup fighting.

Despite improved policies, then, revenue-sharing and compensation issues could again become a source of controversy if mining in Bougainville were to resume. Economic issues are also important in terms of the limited options available for economic development in Bougainville, and the stresses that these limitations are already beginning to cause. Dameng's vision of a Bougainville without mining continues to have wide appeal, but there are many who oppose it, and who want rapid economic development at any cost. These two distinct approaches to Bougainville's development, which were at the heart of the conflict, provide the potential for continuing tensions and renewed conflict, unless the government of Bougainville is extremely creative in its policies.

Assessing the Role of Economic Factors in the Bougainville Conflict

As this study has shown, economic factors connected to natural resource abundance in Bougainville were deeply implicated in the origins of the conflict. A close contextual analysis, however, suggests that theories of conflict based on a dichotomy of greed and grievance stand in need of qualification.

First, the economic factors that precipitated the Bougainville conflict cannot accurately be captured by the concept of "greed." It might be argued that the younger landholders and disgruntled mine workers who initiated the rebellion were motivated by a desire to reap larger personal benefits from the mine. If the mine had continued operating, presumably new revenue-sharing arrangements would have been to their direct benefit. However, at no point did their positions or their behavior suggest a unique agenda of self-enrichment. Consistently, they fought for more equitable compensation, both for marginalized land-owners and for Bougainville as a whole. In other words, the key issue for Ona was more equitable revenue redistribution, or socioeconomic justice.

Likewise, neither the rebels nor the cause for which they were fighting profited from the mine during the conflict. To use Collier and Hoeffler's terminology, natural resource abundance did not provide an "opportunity for rebellion" by serving as a source of funding for the rebels that would add to the feasibility of rebellion. Aside from some looting of mine-related properties at the outset, the copper mine was effectively an "unlootable" resource; without the capital and skill of BCL, the rebels could not keep the mine going, let alone derive revenue from it. While securing better economic concessions from the mine may have made rebellion an attractive option at the outset, mining wealth did not contribute to the persistence of the conflict in any significant way.

Bougainville did possess a large number of undereducated young males with limited economic opportunities, a factor that, in the context of abundant natural resources, Collier and Hoeffler cite as an indicator of risk of greed-driven conflict, insofar as the lack of other opportunities reduces the costs foregone to would-be rebels. In a context where alternative sources of rural incomes were shrinking due to the PNG government's hard-currency strategy and falling cocoa prices, mining revenues were subject to increased claims by Bougainville's economically marginalized groups. While this combination of factors certainly enlarged the risk of conflict for Bougainville, the data do not necessarily support Collier and Hoeffler's greed-based explanation. The effect of exclusion and impoverishment of Bougainvilleans—who received limited economic benefits from the considerable revenues of the mine—was as much an increased sense of grievance as it was an increased opportunity for rebellion.

Accordingly, Bougainville also demonstrates that there is no place for a standard set of policy responses when violent conflict involving natural resources does occur. One major policy implication of greed-driven explanations is that conflict would be mitigated or ended by reducing rebel access to sources of revenue associated with lucrative natural resources. Doing so would undercut both the means and the ostensible motive for rebel groups to continue fighting. In the Bougainville case, however, the rebel groups were denied access to resources, de facto by the closure of the mine and de jure by the PNG government's imposition of a naval blockade in rebel-held areas. Yet this did little to shorten the conflict or to enhance rebel dispositions for a negotiated solution.

As for the relationship between "unlootable" natural resources and separatism, the situation at the outset of the Bougainville conflict is consistent with Ross's analysis; the grievances of local people—both landowners and semi-skilled mine workers—to receive a "just" share of the mine revenue triggered the acts of violence that precipitated the conflict. But if grievances about actual or perceived inequities in the distribution of revenue from an "unlootable" resource contribute to *separatist* conflicts, then one would expect the separatists to seek to maintain the resource so as to be able to exploit it if separation is achieved. What is perhaps unusual when Bougainville is compared to other cases is the additional set of rebel agendas supporting permanent mine closure, the most important being Damien Dameng's Me'ekamui Pontoku Onoring. Dameng's program might be characterized as an economic agenda, but only in the loosest sense, as it was based on achieving a different model of economic development—a Bougainville society based on traditional social structures with an economy relying largely on subsistence and small-scale cash-crop agriculture, developing at its own pace. Again, this agenda was also inherently a political one, insofar as its main goal was a just society, appropriate to the needs of Bougainville, as envisioned by Dameng and his supporters.

This issue points to a methodological shortcoming of the "greed versus grievance" analysis. This analysis is largely based on attempts to understand group behavior in conflict situations on the basis of inferences about responses of rational actors to economic incentives and costs involved in the choice to engage in conflict. Rational actors faced with economic opportunities with low economic costs are expected to take advantage of them. But the "rationality" of the actors depicted by the theory is that of people with long involvement in the modern economy. The Bougainville case demonstrates a different sort of rationality, according to which actors outside the modern economy may pursue quite different goals. There is no doubt that Damien Dameng was a rational actor. Indeed, there are many parallels between the role he and his movement played and analysis by Patrick Chabal and Jean-Pascal Daloz of the apparent "retraditionalization" of Africa evident in the resurgence of ethnicity, witchcraft, and other cultural traits. Chabal and Daloz argue that these trends are not evidence of increasing backwardness—that is, irrationality—but rather of the development of Africa's own multifaceted path to modernization.[61]

For many Bougainvilleans, the aim of rebellion was not to harness the mine to a free and independent Bougainville but to have an independent Bougainville free of mining, as well as all other economic activities threatening traditional society. This highlights another pitfall in making too rigid a distinction between political and economic factors. Ross's analysis takes as given that, in cases such as Bougainville, it is economic grievances that drive separatism. Other studies of separatist movements, however, argue for the primacy of political claims based on ethnic identity. Still others suggest that these factors are not easily disaggregated; just as some separatist groups may invoke identity to mask self-serving economic motives, other groups "pursuing ethnic political purposes may put their demands in an economic form to gain wider legitimacy for them."[62] Political mobilization around Bougainville ethnic identity did not occur primarily because of grievances about unfair distribution of mine revenues. In fact, ethnonationalist mobilization predated the mine, while some mobilization aimed at its outright rejection. This suggests that much of the debate about distribution of revenue might in fact have been a way of enhancing the legitimacy of Bougainvillean ethnic separatist demands.

Overall, the "greed versus grievance" debate tends to focus on the economic agendas of rebel groups. But states and other entities with economic interests also play a role in conflict, especially where natural resources are concerned. In Bougainville these included both BCL and the PNG government—different parts of which had distinct interests. The lines dividing BCL and the state were blurred by the PNG equity stake in BCL and the dividends thereby derived. This blurring had its impact on Bougainvilleans, who tended to perceive the two as intimately connected. Both BCL and PNG had vested interests in maximizing their own returns from Bougainville mining, interests that dictated Bougainville's relatively small share of mining revenue. In this way, the PNG government and BCL contributed to the origins of the conflict. Indeed, it may well be the case that if the PNG government had been less eager to keep the mine operating in late 1988 and 1989, its response to the rebellion may not have been so brutal and the conflict may not have escalated as it did. If, as is likely, Ona and his group attacked the mine as part of an ambit claim for further concessions, and if, as seems certain, it was the state-sponsored violence directed at keeping the mine open that transformed the rebellion into wider conflict, then it is likely that had the state and BCL agreed to close down the mine while negotiations proceeded, the conflict may never have developed.

In this regard, the Bougainville case suggests a further qualification of the relationship between resource dependency and conflict risk postulated by Collier and Hoeffler. They find that where natural resource exports revenue exceed 32 percent of GDP, the risks of conflict decline, because governments are then likely to have sufficient revenue to build a military capacity strong enough to reduce the feasibility of rebellion.[63]

In PNG, revenue from mining, petroleum, agriculture, fisheries, and forestry as a percentage of GDP has been above 40 percent every year since the late 1970s.[64] There is no evidence, however, that the higher revenue proportion in PNG helped to avert or reduce violent conflict. The critical issue in the Bougainville case was the incapacity of the PNG government to utilize mining revenues effectively and fairly.

This is not to suggest that the PNG government or BCL were driven exclusively by economic greed. Government policy on mining revenues was, in principle, directed toward justice—investing in sustainable economic growth for the country as a whole and the equalization of development between parts of PNG. In retrospect, however, it is clear that PNG's policies failed to take sufficient account of landowner and wider interests in Bougainville, and so could not be sustained. As for BCL, the company put considerable effort into community relations. From the late 1970s onward it had enjoyed a good relationship with the NSPG, and generally was supportive of the NSPG's positions in relation to mining-related issues.[65] While its understanding of the situation it was operating in was limited, as evidenced by its failure to understand the extent of the complex tensions building in Bougainville in the 1980s, it was not alone in that regard, for neither did the NSPG nor the PNG government. When the conflict began, BCL initially welcomed the security forces for the protection it needed to continue its mining operations, and provided some material support. Despite some claims to the contrary,[66] there is as yet no credible evidence that BCL took any direct part in the operations against the BRA. The company also wisely did not attempt to play a mediating role in the conflict, although it did offer significant inputs to the joint PNG/NSPG proposals in mid-1989 for a major development package directed at resolving the conflict.

Conclusion

Based on the evidence from Bougainville, the conceptualization of economic factors that may contribute to conflict as "greed" and of political factors as "grievance" is an unhelpful, and indeed misleading, dichotomy. Economic factors can themselves give rise to legitimate political grievances. In the Bougainville case, political and economic factors are closely interwoven—at least they cannot be meaningfully separated. The main causes of the conflict were the specific and generalized grievances of many Bougainvilleans toward BCL and the PNG government over mining. While these grievances were very much economic in nature, they were also inherently political: for Bougainvilleans, the struggle over mining operations and revenues was part of a longer and larger ethnonational struggle to redress Bougainville's historically marginalized political status. Without an understanding of Bougainville's specific historical and cultural context, it would be difficult to understand the interplay of the various political and economic factors that operated to produce the outcomes that occurred.

The Bougainville case highlights the importance of the policies and capacities of the state and the resource developers, in both generating and preventing conflict in natural resource–dependent countries. The capacity of the state is critical in terms of its ability to develop coherent policies that reduce the risk of conflict occurring and to reduce conflict when it does occur. In settings such as PNG, where states with weak capacity and legitimacy confront strong but politically and economically marginalized societies, there is a likelihood that natural resource extraction will pose severe challenges for security and development. The safe and successful management of these challenges depends on finding ways by which outside actors, including resource developers, can help to strengthen and support legitimate and effective governance by state authorities. At the very least, much more attention needs to be paid to understanding the historical, cultural, and political context in which resource extraction activities occur; to assessing the likely political and other impacts these activities will have on local social, economic, and political relations; and to engaging both the national government and the local community in development projects that are consensual and mutually beneficial.

Notes

I am grateful for the comments provided on an early draft of this chapter by Tim Curtin, Harry Derkley, Sinclair Dinnen, David Hegarty, Ben Kerkvliet, Peter Larmour, and Bill Standish, and for advice on substantial revisions received from an anonymous reviewer and from Karen Ballentine.

1. See, for example, Mats Berdal and David M. Malone, eds., *Greed and Grievance: Economic Agendas in Civil Wars* (Boulder: Lynne Rienner, 2000); Paul Collier and Anke Hoeffler, "Greed and Grievance in Civil War," World Bank Policy Research Working Paper no. 2355 (Washington, D.C.: World Bank, 2001); Mary Kaldor, *New and Old Wars: Organized Violence in a Global Era* (Stanford: Stanford University Press, 1999); David Keen, *The Economic Functions of Violence in Civil Wars,* Adelphi Paper no. 320 (Oxford: Oxford University Press for the International Institute for Strategic Studies, 1998); and Michael Klare, *Resource Wars: The New Landscape of Global Conflict* (New York: Metropolitan Books, 2001).

2. Paul Collier and Anke Hoeffler, in a large-number study, find correlations between instances of rebellion and the access of rebels to funding and low

levels of foregone costs of rebellion for rebel fighters. They find that the risk of conflict occurring is highest for countries where primary commodity exports are relatively high, peak danger being when the value of such exports is 32 percent of GDP, after which risk declines. Concerning costs foregone, they find that low foregone earnings tend to increase the risk of conflict, with low rates of male secondary school enrollment, low per capita income, and falling growth rates all proxies for costs foregone. They are not clear, however, as to how low earnings facilitate conflict, accepting that there may be a grievance element involved. See Collier and Hoeffler, "Greed and Grievance in Civil War."

3. Paul Collier and Anke Hoeffler, "On the Economic Causes of Civil War," *Oxford Economic Papers* 50 (1998): 563–573; Paul Collier, "Doing Well Out of War," in Berdal and Malone, *Greed and Grievance,* pp. 91–111.

4. They focus on economic factors that provide opportunity for building a rebel organization—in particular, access of rebels to sources of funding and lack of other economic opportunities, which results in low levels of foregone costs for rebel fighters. See Collier and Hoeffler, "Greed and Grievance in Civil War."

5. See Michael Ross, "Natural Resources and Civil War: Evidence from Case Studies," paper prepared for the World Bank/University of California at Irvine workshop on "Civil Wars and Post-Conflict Transitions," Irvine, May 18–20, 2001.

6. That is, not able to be extracted and transported by individuals or small teams of unskilled workers. So drugs, alluvial gemstones, agricultural products, and timber are relatively "lootable," while deep-shaft minerals, oil, and natural gas are relatively "unlootable." See Chapter 3 by Michael Ross in this volume.

7. Ibid.

8. Yash Ghai and Anthony J. Regan, "Bougainville and the Dialectics of Ethnicity, Autonomy, and Separation," in Yash Ghai, ed., *Autonomy and Ethnicity: Negotiating Competing Claims in Multi-Ethnic States* (Cambridge: Cambridge University Press, 2000), pp. 242–265.

9. Ibid.; Eugene Ogan, "The Cultural Background to the Bougainville Crisis," *Journal de la Société des Océanistes* 92/93, nos. 1–2 (1991): 61–67; and John Terrell, *Pre-History in the Pacific Islands* (Cambridge: Cambridge University Press, 1986).

10. For more detailed discussions of these and many other aspects of colonialism in Bougainville, see Jill Nash, "Paternalism, Progress, Paranoia: Patrol Reports and Colonial History in South Bougainville," in Naomi McPherson, ed., *In Colonial New Guinea: Anthropological Perspectives* (Pittsburgh: University of Pittsburgh Press, 2001), pp. 111–124; Eugene Ogan, *Business and Cargo: Socio-Economic Change Among the Nasioi of Bougainville,* New Guinea Research Bulletin no. 44 (Canberra: Australian National University, 1972); Michael Oliver, *Black Islanders: A Personal Perspective of Bougainville, 1937–1991* (Melbourne: Hyland House, 1991); and Terence Wesley-Smith, "Development and Crisis in Bougainville: A Bibliographic Essay," *The Contemporary Pacific* 4, no. 2 (Fall 1992): 407–432.

11. During the twenty years following World War II, Bougainvilleans were deeply resentful about the racist treatment they received and about the failure of the administration to meet promises made during the war that their conditions would be improved—especially for those who supported the United States and Australia against the Japanese. For discussion of the impacts of World War

II, see Oliver, *Black Islanders;* and Hank Nelson, "Bougainville in World War II," paper presented to the conference on "Bougainville: Change and Identities, Division and Integration," organized by the State, Society, and Governance in Melanesia Project, Australian National University, Canberra, August 2000. I am grateful to Damien Dameng and James Tanis for information about continuing resentment in Bougainville concerning Australia's alleged failure to honor promises made in World War II.

12. See James Griffin, *Bougainville: A Challenge for the Churches,* Catholic Social Justice Series no. 26 (Sydney: Australian Catholic Social Justice Council, 1995), p. 11; Oliver, *Black Islanders,* pp. 86–89; and Max Rimoldi and Eleanor Rimoldi, *Hahalis and the Labour of Love: A Social Movement on Buka Island* (Oxford: Berg, 1992).

13. See Griffin, *Bougainville,* p. 11.

14. For more on the development of Bougainvillean identity and the process of its politicization, see Ghai and Regan, "Bougainville and the Dialectics of Ethnicity"; Jill Nash and Eugene Ogan, "The Red and the Black: Bougainvillean Perceptions of Other Papua New Guineans," *Pacific Studies* 13, no. 2 (March 1990): 1–17; and the works referred to in note 17.

15. See Ogan, "The Cultural Background"; and Nash, "Paternalism, Progress, Paranoia."

16. See Anthony J. Regan, "Bougainville: Beyond Survival," *Cultural Survival Quarterly* 26, no. 3 (2002): 20–24.

17. See John Connell, "Compensation and Conflict: The Bougainville Copper Mine, Papua New Guinea," in John Connell and Richard Howitt, eds., *Mining and Indigenous Peoples in Australasia* (Sydney: Sydney University Press, 1991), pp. 55–76; Herb Thompson, "The Economic Causes and Consequences of the Bougainville Crisis," *Resource Policy* 17, no. 1 (March 1991): 69–85; James Griffin and Melchior Togolo, "North Solomons Province, 1974–2000," in R. J. May and A. J. Regan, eds., *Political Decentralisation in a New State: The Experience of Provincial Government in Papua New Guinea* (Bathurst: Crawford House Press, 1997), p. 357.

18. Connell, "Compensation and Conflict," p. 55.

19. There is an extensive literature on the impact of the mine, including Richard Bedford, and Alexander Mamak, *Compensation for Development: The Bougainville Case,* Bougainville Special Publication no. 2 (Christchurch: University of Canterbury, Department of Geography, 1977); Donald Denoon, *Getting Under the Skin: The Bougainville Copper Agreement and the Creation of the Panguna Mine* (Melbourne: Melbourne University Press 2000); James Griffin, "Napidakoe Navitu," in R. J. May, ed., *Micronationalist Movements in Papua New Guinea,* Political and Social Change Monograph no. 1 (Canberra: Australian National University, 1982), pp. 113–138; Alexander Mamak and Richard Bedford, *Bougainvillean Nationalism: Aspects of Unity and Discord,* Bougainville Special Publication no. 1 (Christchurch: University of Canterbury, Department of Geography, 1974); Ogan, *Business and Cargo;* as well as the works cited in note 37. See also the bibliography in Terence Wesley-Smith, "Development and Crisis."

20. See John Connell, "Compensation and Conflict: The Bougainville Copper Mine, Papua New Guinea," in John Connell and Richard Howitt, eds., *Mining and Indigenous Peoples in Australasia* (Sydney: Sydney University Press,

1991), pp. 55–76; Herb Thompson, "The Economic Causes and Consequences of the Bougainville Crisis," *Resource Policy* 17, no. 1 (March 1991): 69–85; James Griffin and Melchior Togolo, "North Solomons Province, 1974–2000," in R. J. May and A. J. Regan, eds., *Political Decentralisation in a New State: The Experience of Provincial Government in Papua New Guinea* (Bathurst: Crawford House Press, 1997), p. 357.

21. See John Dove, Theodore Miriung, and Melchior Togolo, "Mining Bitterness," in Peter G. Sack, ed., *Problem of Choice: Land in Papua New Guinea's Future* (Canberra: Australian National University Press, 1974), pp. 181–189.

22. Information supplied to the author by numerous members of landowning lineages in the mine lease areas.

23. For more detail on the agreements, see Denoon, *Getting Under the Skin,* pp. 80–99, 186–192; Oliver, *Black Islanders,* pp. 134–135, 153–155; and Paul Quodling, *Bougainville: The Mine and the People* (Sydney: Centre for Independent Studies, 1991), pp. 23–28.

24. Denoon, *Getting Under the Skin,* p. 92.

25. See, for example, R. Garnaut, "The Framework of Economic Policy-Making," in J. Ballard, ed., *Policy Making in a New State: Papua New Guinea 1972–77* (St. Lucia: University of Queensland Press, 1981), pp. 193–210; and Raymond F. Mikesell, *Foreign Investment in Copper Mining: Case Studies of Mines in Peru and Papua New Guinea* (Baltimore: Johns Hopkins University Press, 1975).

26. Denoon, *Getting Under the Skin,* p. 192.

27. Quodling, *Bougainville,* p. 34. The average exchange rate for the PNG kina over the period in question was approximately U.S.$1.1.

28. Connell, "Compensation and Conflict," p. 55.

29. Approximately 4,500 Bougainvilleans lived in the mining lease areas in the late 1980s.

30. Of importance here were arrangements under a 1980 agreement with BCL under which compensation for social inconvenience went to a landowner entity that by the mid-1980s was widely believed to be largely benefiting members of a new elite, who were increasingly reviled by leaders of younger landowner groups. More generally, see Anthony J. Regan, "Causes and Course of the Bougainville Conflict," *Journal of Pacific History* 33, no. 3 (November 1988): 269–285.

31. See, for example, Griffin, "Napidakoe Navitu"; Denoon, *Getting Under the Skin,* pp. 171–181; Mamak and Bedford, *Bougainvillean Nationalism;* and Oliver, *Black Islanders,* pp. 178–191.

32. In fact, however, secession continued to be discussed at meetings in Bougainville in 1972.

33. Bougainvilleans tend to refer to the generally lighter-skinned people of other parts of PNG by the pejorative term "red-skins." See Ghai and Regan, "Bougainville and the Dialectics of Ethnicity"; and Nash and Ogan, "The Red and the Black."

34. Terence Wesley-Smith, "The Non-Review of the Bougainville Copper Agreement," in Matthew Spriggs and Donald Denoon, eds., *The Bougainville Crisis: 1991 Update* (Canberra: Australian National University in association with Crawford House Press, 1992), pp. 92–111.

35. Griffin and Togolo, "North Solomons Province."

36. These included rapid population increase and land pressure, reduced returns from cash crops, increased economic inequalities, heightened resentment against outsiders, labor disputes among the semi-skilled Bougainvillean mine workers, and the prospect of BCL extending its mining operations. See Regan, "Causes and Course."

37. For more on the issues concerning the origins and unfolding of the conflict touched upon in the following paragraphs, see Ron J. May and Matthew Spriggs, eds., *The Bougainville Crisis* (Bathurst: Crawford House Press, 1990); Regan, "Causes and Course"; Anthony J. Regan, "Why a Neutral Peace Monitoring Force? The Bougainville Conflict and the Peace Process," in Monica Wehner and Donald Denoon, eds., *Without a Gun: Australia's Experience of Monitoring Peace in Bougainville, 1997–2001* (Canberra: Pandanus Books, 2001), pp. 1–18; and Spriggs and Denoon, *The Bougainville Crisis: 1991 Update.*

38. In the Nasioi language of the people of central Bougainville (in whose area the Panguna mine site is situated), Me'ekamui Pontoku Onoring involves complex concepts loosely translatable as "government of the guardians of the sacred land." It was a movement led by Damien Dameng to restore traditional customary ways. When first initiated in 1959 during the colonial period, it opposed the colonial government and outside influences; by 1988 it became a key player in the coalition of Bougainvillean groups opposed to both the PNG government and the Panguna mine. For more on Dameng and Me'ekamui Pontoku Onoring, see Regan, "Bougainville: Beyond Survival." On formation of the "New PLA" and its relationship with Dameng, see Quodling, *Bougainville,* p. 58.

39. Applied Geology Associates, *Environmental Socio-Economic Public Health Review: Bougainville Copper Mine Panguna* (Wellington: Applied Geology Associates, 1989).

40. I am grateful to James Tanis for this insight.

41. See Oliver, *Black Islanders;* Griffin and Togolo, "North Solomons Province"; Peter Sohia, "Early Interventions," in Andy Carl and Lorraine Garasu, eds., *Weaving Consensus: The Papua New Guinea–Bougainville Peace Process,* Accord no. 12 (London: Conciliation Resources, 2002), pp. 16–23; and Anthony J. Regan, "The Bougainville Political Settlement and the Prospects for Sustainable Peace," *Pacific Economic Bulletin* 17, no. 1 (2002): 114–129.

42. John R. Kaputin, *Crisis in the North Solomons Province: Report of the Special Committee Appointed by the National Executive Council* (Port Moresby: Department of the Prime Minister, 1992).

43. Regan, "Causes and Course."

44. Oliver, *Black Islanders,* p. 217.

45. Regan, "Causes and Course"; and Regan, "Why a Neutral Peace Monitoring Force?"

46. For analysis of the Sandline affair, see Sinclair Dinnen, Roy May, and Anthony J. Regan, eds., *Challenging the State: The Sandline Affair in Papua New Guinea* (Canberra: Australian National University Press, 1997); Sean Dorney, *The Sandline Affair: Politics and Mercenaries and the Bougainville Crisis* (Sydney: ABC Books, 1998); and Mary-Louise O'Callaghan, *Enemies Within: Papua New Guinea, Australia, and the Sandline Crisis—The Inside Story* (Sydney: Doubleday, 1999).

47. See, for example, Bob Breen, *Giving Peace a Chance: Operation Lagoon, Bougainville 1994—A Case Study of Military Action and Diplomacy,* Canberra Papers on Strategy and Defence no. 142 (Canberra: Strategic and Defence Studies Centre, Australian National University, 2001).

48. For more concerning the origins and unfolding of the Bougainville peace process, see Rebecca Adams, ed., *Gudpela Nius Bilong Pis: Peace on Bougainville—Truce Monitoring Group* (Wellington: Victoria University Press, 2001); Monica Wehner and Donald Denoon, eds., *Without a Gun: Australia's Experience of Monitoring Peace in Bougainville, 1997–2001* (Canberra: Pandanus Books, 2001); Anthony J. Regan, "The Bougainville Political Settlement"; and Andy Carl and Lorraine Garasu, eds., *Weaving Consensus: The Papua New Guinea–Bougainville Peace Process,* Accord no. 12 (London: Conciliation Resources, 2002).

49. Communities were often responding to deep-rooted cultural imperatives vital to the small-scale stateless societies of Bougainville, imperatives directed to maintaining balance within and between societies through reciprocal exchanges, as well as peacemaking and reconciliation ceremonies when conflict disturbed balance.

50. Carl and Garasu, *Weaving Consensus;* and Regan, "Why a Neutral Peace Monitoring Force?"

51. Generally, see Tim Curtin, "Economic Development in Papua New Guinea, 1975–2000," in James Chin, ed., *Contemporary Papua New Guinea* (Port Moresby: University of Papua New Guinea Press, forthcoming 2003).

52. Lincoln Agreement on Peace, Security, and Development in Bougainville, January 23, 1998.

53. For more on the political settlement, see Regan, "The Bougainville Political Settlement"; and Carl and Garasu, *Weaving Consensus.*

54. Under the PNG constitution, two votes of at least two-thirds absolute majority, with the votes being separated by at least two months, were required. The votes were achieved on January 23 and March 27, 2002.

55. Under the agreement, Bougainville will be regarded as self-reliant once the amount of tax revenues generated by economic activities in the province exceeds the amount of the PNG government's grant to Bougainville to meet "recurrent" costs of providing government services.

56. Bougainville Copper Ltd., *Bougainville Copper Limited Annual Report 2000* (Melbourne: Bougainville Copper Ltd., 2001).

57. Statements to this effect have been made at a number of public meetings in Bougainville that I attended.

58. Colin Filer, "Resource Rents: Distribution and Sustainability," in Ila Temu, ed., *Papua New Guinea: A 20/20 Vision* (Canberra: National Centre for Development Studies, 1997), p. 222.

59. A "basic mining package" originating with the Porgera project provides for three main changes when compared to arrangements in Bougainville: (1) increased revenue for landowners, through receipt of 20 percent of the 1.25 percent royalty (up from a 5 percent share), with provincial governments receiving 80 percent of royalties (down from 95 percent); (2) increased revenue for the provincial government, through payment of a special grant valued at 1 percent of the value of production; and (3) potentially increased revenues for both provincial governments and landowners through rights to purchase part of state equity in the project in question on favorable terms. Ibid., pp. 240–241.

60. Ibid.

61. Patrick Chabal and Jean-Pascal Daloz, *Africa Works: Disorder as Political Instrument* (Oxford and Bloomington: International African Institute, James Currey, and Indiana University Press, 1999).

62. Peter Larmour, "The Politics of Race and Ethnicity: Theoretical Perspectives on Papua New Guinea," *Pacific Studies* 15, no. 2 (1992): 99, discussing the analysis of Anthony Smith, *The Ethnic Revival* (Cambridge: Cambridge University Press, 1981).

63. Collier and Hoeffler, "Greed and Grievance in Civil War."

64. Bank of PNG, *Money and Banking in Papua New Guinea* (Port Moresby: Bank of PNG, 1998); and Bank of PNG, *Quarterly Economic Bulletin,* June 2001 (Port Moresby: Bank of PNG, 2001). I am grateful to Tim Curtin for assisting me by locating and analyzing these data.

65. For example, in relation to the 1981 review of the mining agreement. See Wesley-Smith, "The Non-Review of the Bougainville Copper Agreement."

66. For example, in the claims made in a class action launched in 2000 in a U.S. court by some Bougainvilleans against BCL. See *Alexis Holyweek Sarei et al. v. Rio Tinto plc and Rio Tinto et al.,* U.S. District Court, Central District of California, Western Division, no. 00-11695 MMM AIJx.

7

Kosovo: The Political Economy of Conflict and Peacebuilding

ALEXANDROS YANNIS

AN EXAMINATION OF THE POLITICAL ECONOMY OF CIVIL WARS HAS RECENTLY emerged in international relations debates as a new analytical approach claiming to improve our understanding of internal conflicts and to identify more effective international responses. The political economy perspective offers a complementary role in the analysis of conflicts by shifting, to some degree, attention away from the traditional political analysis of conflicts to their seemingly neglected economic factors and dimensions. The underlying proposition, central to the recent "greed and grievance" debate, is that economic factors—such as the economic motivations and agendas of belligerents, whether rebels or governments—can in some cases be more important elements in the outbreak and evolution of an internal conflict than political or other factors, thus requiring an appropriate adjustment of policy responses.[1]

A major consideration in understanding domestic conflicts, and one that helps to better situate the political economy perspective, is that each war is the product of its own particular geopolitical, geographical, political, socioeconomic, and cultural context. All of these factors, including the socioeconomic ones, have historically been central elements in the analysis of conflicts. The post–Cold War interest in the political economy of conflict originated in the examination of conflicts in Sudan, Sierra Leone, Liberia, Angola, the Democratic Republic of Congo, and Cambodia, in which competition over natural resources appeared to be both a central element of conflict and principal barrier to peaceful settlement. In all these cases, the political economy approach claims to have discovered new ground in the analysis of internal conflicts. While this claim is questionable, the political economy perspective has indeed contributed to a renewed recognition of the need for a more holistic and comprehensive examination of the multifaceted process of complex emergencies and civil wars.

This chapter examines the political economy of the Kosovo conflict and the relevant international responses to the crisis, particularly in the context of the establishment of the international administration in the aftermath of the North Atlantic Treaty Organization (NATO) intervention in Kosovo. The objectives of this analysis are, first, to evaluate the relative importance of political and economic factors in the agendas of the local opponents and the evolution of the conflict in general; second, to assess the effectiveness of the international policies to tackle the challenges of the political economy of Kosovo, particularly during the ongoing phase of the international administration; and third, to identify appropriate approaches and instruments for future action in Kosovo, as well as in similar peace operations, so as to address more effectively economic and social dimensions of conflicts.

I argue here that the escalation of the Kosovo crisis in the 1990s from a long-standing political dispute into a full-blown violent conflict was a function of the destabilizing processes unleashed by the disintegration of the Socialist Federal Republic of Yugoslavia. The motivations of Kosovo Albanians were primarily to liberate themselves from the increasingly oppressive rule of Serbia and gain independence. The government of Serbia's policy was mainly driven by President Slobodan Milosevic's opportunistic manipulation of nationalism, and the Kosovo question in particular, in order to consolidate his power in Belgrade. The Kosovo crisis has not been a dispute over power or government but a conflict over territory driven by nationalism and ever multiplying political and historical grievances.

Socioeconomic underdevelopment and the realities of a virtual apartheid, especially massive unemployment and interethnic inequality, were important factors in reinforcing Kosovo Albanian grievances and in facilitating the escalation of the conflict—for example, by providing ample recruitment opportunities from the vast army of unemployed, frustrated, and disillusioned young men into the ranks of the Albanian rebels.[2] Moreover, the widespread informal economy that emerged in Kosovo in the 1990s in response to the political, economic, and social exclusion and oppression of the Albanians by Serbs, together with the effects of the lasting regional instability and economic decline, also played an important role in strengthening the Kosovo Albanian rebel movement. This well-established informal—and often criminal—economy and its close ties with political extremism were exacerbated by the NATO intervention. Indeed, increased criminalization of economic transactions and political relationships has caused significant problems for the efforts of the international administration to bring peace and stability in Kosovo. These problems include the continuing insecurity of the Serb minority in the new Kosovo and the capacity of Albanian rebels to export their militant campaign to southern Serbia and Macedonia in 2001. While a modicum of peace and stability has today been established, the relatively limited international success in tackling the informal and criminal economy in Kosovo and its ties with political extremism continues to pose a major challenge to international efforts to bring peace and stability to Kosovo and the Balkans.

Rehabilitation and reconciliation in Kosovo will require a sustained commitment by the international community. International intervention has been relatively successful in alleviating immediate humanitarian problems and bringing peace to Kosovo, but long-term stability remains elusive. The international community, in the form of the UN Interim Administration Mission in Kosovo (UNMIK) and the NATO-led Kosovo Force (KFOR), has proven less adept at addressing the conflict's underlying causes, let alone its legacies. Political and social divisions between rival groups not only remain, but also the informal and criminal economies these groups have created have strengthened political extremism, corrupting the political, social, and economic fabric of society. More robust international capacities for dealing with these issues are being developed, including more balanced approaches between the requirements of strengthening accountability and the need for rapidly and effectively tackling the problems of war-torn societies. There is still much to be done in this area in Kosovo, but the lessons learned hold out the potential for more durable peace both here and for future international action in similarly criminalized environments.

Background: The Disintegration of Yugoslavia and the Kosovo Conflict

The Kosovo conflict is an integral part of the crisis that engulfed the Balkans in the 1990s as the result of the dissolution of Yugoslavia, and cannot be properly understood outside this political, historical, and regional context.[3] While the Kosovo dispute predates this disintegration, its escalation from political tensions in the early 1990s to a full-blown conflict by 1998–1999 was due to the destabilization that attended the breakup of Yugoslavia. In fact, the crisis originated in both the inability and the unwillingness of the local actors and the failure of the international actors involved in the region to peacefully manage the challenges prompted by the geopolitical changes in the region after the end of the Cold War and, more specifically, the challenges of the process of the breakup of Yugoslavia.[4] The transformative effects of the disintegration of Yugoslavia on the societies and the entities that emerged out of its ashes were devastating. The spiraling territorial revisionism, compounded by exalted historical claims and unabated nationalistic fervor, that swept the lands and the peoples of Yugoslavia in the early 1990s was both a cause and a consequence of Yugoslavia's dissolution.

The underlying cause of these wars—adeptly exploited by the forces of nationalism and extremist political leaders—was the "legitimacy deficit" of the former Yugoslavia and of the state structures and polities that emerged from it. The breakup of Yugoslavia fractured the social contract and undermined the moderating forces that had kept a modicum of peaceful coexistence between the peoples who had lived together under the same roof for most of the twentieth century. Political opportunism by local leaders who manipulated nationalism and violence to advance their political agendas to achieve and maintain power moved into the vacuum created by the decomposing Yugoslavia. The violent conflicts that followed highlight the lesson that stability requires not only effective but also legitimate state structures and public authorities, particularly in multiethnic societies. This legitimacy deficit, which defied the means and skills of the international community to prevent conflict, generated enormous grievances that fed into spirals of instability, violence, destruction, and misery. The continuing instability in the region is essentially about the unfinished process of the dissolution of Yugoslavia, the political vacuum that was left behind, and the still questionable legitimacy of the makeup of Bosnia-Herzegovina, Yugoslavia, and Macedonia in the eyes of their constituent ethnic groups.

Kosovo is a territory of about 10,887 square kilometers with approximately 2 million inhabitants.[5] Although Kosovo Albanians compose an overwhelming majority demographically, Kosovo has been effectively under Serb rule throughout most of the twentieth century. Serbs consider Kosovo to be the birthplace of their nation, while Kosovo Albanians generally maintain that they have been unjustly denied their own national state in Kosovo since the fall of the Ottoman Empire.

There were three critical moments in the recent history of Kosovo that transformed the political dispute between Kosovo Albanians and Yugoslavia into an open liberation and secessionist war. The first was Belgrade's effective abrogation in 1989 of the autonomy status that Kosovo enjoyed under the 1974 constitution. This was largely prompted by the opportunistic exploitation by Slobodan Milosevic, then leader of both Yugoslavia and Serbia, of the widespread sentiment among Serbs that their situation in Kosovo was worsening, a sentiment that would lead to a decade of systematic Serbian discrimination, persecution, and oppression of Kosovo Albanians that swiftly turned Kosovo into a virtual apartheid state. In response to Belgrade's policies of systematic discrimination and exclusion, Kosovo Albanians established the shadow "Kosovo Republic," a parallel government under the leadership of Ibrahim Rugova.[6]

Second, the accessions of Slovenia, Croatia, Bosnia-Herzegovina, and Macedonia to independence in 1991–1992 effectively dissolved any political commitment to Yugoslavia that may have remained among Kosovo Albanians in the brief period since 1989, during which demands for the restoration of the former autonomy of Kosovo and, more precisely, for gaining republican status within the former Yugoslavia were still on the political agenda of Kosovo Albanians.[7]

Finally, the Dayton Peace Accords, which in 1995 settled the conflict in Bosnia-Herzegovina, had a major destabilizing effect on Kosovo. On the one hand, the Dayton Accords left the question of Kosovo's political future unresolved, thereby exacerbating the simmering frustrations of Kosovo Albanians. On the other hand, the accords acted as a major disincentive for the continued pursuit of peaceful political solutions; the Kosovo Albanians could not fail to observe that the underlying logic of the peace accords was largely the ratification on paper of the ethnoterritorial gains made on the ground by the use of force. Consequently, the Dayton Accords strengthened the political commitment of radical Albanians to the use of force. Popular support for the militant program of the Kosovo Liberation Army (KLA) increased at the expense of the moderate strategy of Ibrahim Rugova, whose policy was to achieve independence through the internationalization of the Kosovo conflict by the means of peaceful resistance and noncooperation with Belgrade.[8]

The KLA's resort to violent attacks against Serbian targets was the trigger for the ethnic cleansing campaign against Kosovo Albanians launched by Belgrade in early 1999 and during the NATO intervention in Yugoslavia in spring 1999. This campaign effectively severed all relations between Kosovo Albanians and Serbs. The meek international response to the Kosovo crisis throughout most of the 1990s placed in sharp relief the NATO military intervention that followed. For most of the decade, the international community generally treated the Kosovo dispute as an internal problem of Yugoslavia. This policy was largely driven by the fear that internationalizing the Kosovo crisis would strengthen the cause for the independence of Kosovo and fuel the irredentist tendencies for the unification under a wider Albanian state of all the Albanians in the Balkans, thus creating a dangerous precedent that could lead to further disintegration in the Balkans and the broader destabilization of southeastern Europe.[9] In order to secure Serb cooperation in settling the Bosnia-Herzegovina conflict, Dayton sidestepped the Kosovo dispute, with key international actors evidently hoping that a violent conflict would not explode in Kosovo. This expectation proved wrong. And in a spectacular turn of events, the international response against Yugoslavia hardened in 1998 and eventually led to the NATO bombardment in 1999.

The NATO intervention was not part of any comprehensive or common policy by the international actors involved in the former Yugoslavia, nor did it reflect any coherent regional approach. It was another ad hoc response to yet another crisis produced by the unfinished process of Yugoslavia's disintegration. NATO's turn to military intervention can be attributed to several factors. The end of the Cold War forced NATO to reassess its traditional collective security role—it had to find a new role or become irrelevant. But by altering the global (and European) balance of power, the end of the Cold War also created new opportunities for the United States and its key European allies to use military action in pursuit of their geopolitical goals, including resolving conflict in their neighborhood. Serbia's campaign against Kosovo risked spreading instability in the region and creating a refugee crisis, but as the Belgrade regime's intention of launching a major ethnic cleansing campaign in Kosovo became apparent at the beginning of 1999, the humanitarian impulses and guilt over the delayed action in Bosnia-Herzegovina that haunted Western policymakers and European public opinion also played an important role in support of military action. When the very credibility of NATO, particularly of the U.S. administration, was put at stake by Slobodan Milosevic's gamble of calling the bluff of the bombardment threats, there was little room left for NATO but to resort to force, even though no clear plan or strategy had been devised on how to resolve the Kosovo dispute once the bombardment was over.[10] Fortunately, the regional geopolitics were also favorable to military action, as Russian opposition to the NATO bombardment was limited mainly to rhetoric.

The Political Economy of the Kosovo Crisis in the 1990s

The Kosovo conflict was overwhelmingly an ethnoterritorial contest, but there can be no doubt that economic and social problems fed political extremism and contributed to the political impasses between Kosovo Albanians and the Serbian leadership. Historically, Kosovo has been the poorest province of the former Yugoslavia.[11] In the mid-1990s, Kosovo was still a largely agricultural society, with agricultural activities producing about one-third of gross domestic product (GDP) and generating about 60 percent of total employment. Industry, particularly the extraction of raw materials, accounted for one-third of GDP, with trade and commercial activities accounting for the remainder. In 1988, per capita productivity in Kosovo was 28 percent of that of the former Yugoslavia as a whole. Nonetheless, the position of Kosovo Albanians had steadily improved from the 1960s until 1989, under the political and social reforms undertaken by Josip Broz Tito, then leader of former Yugoslavia.[12] In fact, in the years just prior to the effective abrogation of Kosovo's autonomy by Belgrade in 1989, Kosovo briefly enjoyed a "golden epoch" with increasing employment opportunities for Kosovo Albanians in public enterprises, an improving record of performance by the civil administration, and steadily rising living standards.[13]

Belgrade's policy after 1989 not only interrupted this process but also led to a rapid deterioration of the economic and social situation in Kosovo, which disproportionately affected its Albanian majority. Moreover, by the beginning of the 1990s the economy of the former Yugoslavia was in freefall. Decades of communist mismanagement had left a legacy of unbalanced and inefficient industries, weak and highly corrupted institutions, and chronic hyperinflation.[14] The wars of secession of the former Yugoslavia, especially in Croatia and Bosnia-Herzegovina, resulted in further economic and social dislocations, including the rapid deterioration of standards of living and a massive destabilizing influx of Serb refugees from Croatia and Bosnia-Herzegovina to Serbia proper, many of whom were resettled in Kosovo. According to official statistics, between 1989 and 1994, GDP in Kosovo contracted by 50 percent, falling to less than U.S.$400 per capita by 1995.[15] Industry, mining, and infrastructure were particularly hard-hit by the political developments in the 1990s. Overwhelmingly under state and social ownership, industrial production declined sharply under stagnating investment and neglect.

The economic crisis was particularly severe with respect to jobs. Under the infamous "1990 Labor Act for Extraordinary Circumstances" and other discriminatory legislation against the Kosovo Albanian community, an estimated 145,000 ethnic Albanians were dismissed from civil administration, social services (education and health), and public economic enterprises.[16] Systematic discrimination and other violations of human rights aimed at excluding Kosovo Albanians from the economic and administrative life of Kosovo took a heavy toll. Unemployment, particularly among young Kosovo Albanians, skyrocketed. By one account, it reached as high as 70 percent in 1995.[17] The preexisting imbalance in public employment between Serbs and Kosovo Albanians widened further, creating additional strains on relations between the two communities.

The absence of real prospects for recovery and employment and the widening social inequalities between the two communities were perhaps the most ominous factors in the political economy of the ever escalating Kosovo crisis in the 1990s. Against this grim socioeconomic background, the political impasses created by Belgrade's nationalistic policy toward Kosovo weakened public support for the moderate Ibrahim Rugova—but by providing a growing pool of young, unemployed Kosovo Albanians, they proved highly conducive to the KLA's objective of attaining independence. By 1998–1999, this population was increasingly prepared to use force, either directly, by joining the KLA, or indirectly, by supporting its violent methods by other means.[18]

The collapse of the Albanian state in March 1997 was a critical watershed in the strengthening of the KLA. Its impact on the political economy of the conflict was twofold. First, Sali Berisha, Albania's president from 1992 to 1997 and an open supporter of Ibrahim Rugova, was chased out of power in Tirana, thereby depriving Rugova of a major source of political and financial assistance outside of Kosovo. Second, the descent of Albania into anarchy and the ensuing widespread looting of Albanian weapons stores provided the KLA with a large quantity of small arms, ammunition, and other military hardware, which became readily available across the border at very low prices.

The Growth of Informal and Criminal Economic Activity

Three factors resulted in the emergence of a sophisticated informal economy. First, the massive unemployment created by the 1990 Labor Act necessitated individuals to seek alternative sources of income; with few legitimate alternatives, informal and black-market trade was both attractive and in demand. Second, the comprehensive sanctions imposed on Yugoslavia by the international community had further worsened the region's economic problems.[19] The closure of the borders between Kosovo and Macedonia blocked a major route for direct trade and commercial activities and exacerbated the trade disruptions brought on by the conflicts in Croatia and Bosnia-Herzegovina. Third, the establishment of an effective parallel state by Kosovo Albanians was dependent upon informal sources of revenue for its day-to-day functioning, including a 3 percent income tax levied both locally and in the diaspora. The formation of the "Kosovo Republic" was not only a political tactic of noncooperation and peaceful resistance to the Serb rule. Dictated by the increasingly threatening realities on the ground, it was also—if not mostly—a survival strategy, providing social services, particularly in the health and education sectors.

The virtual collapse of the civil administration, combined with the extortionist policies of the Serb authorities, led to the inevitable "clandestinization" of much of the economic activity in Kosovo. The line between the informal economy and economic crime became increasingly blurred. "Taxation" for social policies in many instances merged with extortion for ambiguous purposes, while protection against Serb rule in some cases merged with various forms of racketeering. As the crisis escalated, revenues generated in both the informal and the criminal economies in Kosovo became a major source of financial support for the KLA.

By spring 1998, a significant portion of diaspora remittances—which accounted for about half of Kosovo's annual GDP and played a critical role in helping to offset the worst effects of declining living standards throughout the crisis—and other contributions to the parallel structures had been transformed into a well-functioning machinery in support of the military objectives of the KLA.[20] A small group of extremists drawn from the rural population managed through their violent methods to challenge Rugova, to seize control of economic networks, and—helped by the brutal reprisals of the Serbs—to gain wide support within the Albanian population.

The Clandestine Economy and Conflict

By 1998, the informal and criminal economy of Kosovo was largely fueling the spirals of violent conflict. The political and economic crises of the 1990s, as much as the protracted interethnic and secessionist conflict itself, eroded respect for formal institutions and rules, encouraged a well-entrenched informal and often criminal economy, and provided the means by which to create a profitable war economy for both the KLA and the Serbian government. Across the former Yugoslavia, smuggling in oil, arms, illegal drugs, people, stolen cars, cigarettes and other commodities, prostitution, corruption, counterfeiting, and asset and property seizure became basic features of the new economy, frequently through the involvement of senior government officials and organized criminal groups operating in the region and beyond.[21]

Given rampant economic opportunities, one might wonder whether "greed not grievance" is at the root of the Kosovo conflict. Kosovo does exhibit some of the economic factors identified by Paul Collier as associated with a high risk of civil war, including economic decline, a large proportion of unemployed men with scarce economic opportunities and for whom little is to be lost by engaging in conflict, and the availability of lootable or extortable resources to rebel groups, in this case the availability of diaspora remittances and of the informal economy to the KLA.[22]

There are numerous reports by Interpol, Europol, U.S. and European governments, and the Paris-based Observatoire Géopolitique des Drogues, as well as investigative journalism accounts detailing the alleged financial links between the KLA and the Albanian organized criminal groups, asserting that the KLA financed the purchase of weapons by trafficking heroin from Turkey and laundered the money through European Union financial institutions, and that this relationship was condoned by NATO forces reluctant to get involved in the growing crisis.[23] However, the exact nature and extent of the sources that were financing the KLA remain even today a question largely open to speculation, fueling negative stereotypes of Albanians in Western Europe as barons of the illegal trade in drugs, prostitution, and weapons smuggling. As Robert Hislope points out, "most leaders of the Albanian paramilitaries [were] simply men sorely aggrieved by the plight of Albanians in the southern Balkans and have taken up arms to pursue their national cause."[24] Moreover, while the KLA engaged in widespread criminal activities to finance its campaigns, there is no evidence that these economic interests led to a mutation of the political agendas of the KLA after its uprising had gained momentum and wide popular support in Kosovo.

In Kosovo, as elsewhere in the Balkans, conflict was the result of competing nationalisms and political grievances fed by mutual perceptions of ethnic discrimination and by actual political and economic exclusion. Poverty and unemployment alone do not provide an adequate explanation for the escalation from crisis to conflict, in part because the appeal of nationalism cut across all socioeconomic groups of both Kosovo Albanian and Serb communities. Belgrade's systematic discrimination against Kosovo Albanians instrumentalized nationalism to justify the use of force. This supports the assertion that horizontal, or intergroup, inequalities can be a principal motivation for armed conflict.[25] For the Kosovo Albanian leadership, independence is a historical claim whose cause was enhanced in the 1990s by the changed international and regional environment, which encouraged territorial revisionism in the pursuit of national self-determination. After 1989, the oppression of the Kosovo Albanian population at the hands of Milosevic's Serbia only enhanced the desire to fight for independence.

The commitment of young Albanians to join the KLA and die for the cause of an independent Kosovo proved to be a formidable psychological victory and a major source of strength for the KLA. As Tim Judah argues, by the time the NATO bombardment of Yugoslavia had started, it was becoming clear that "Kosovo may be sacred to the Serbs, but it is the Albanians who are going to fight and die for it."[26] Many, if not most, of the young volunteers were joining the KLA not for money but for the cause of independence. Indeed, a significant number of KLA recruits returned from the diaspora, leaving behind lucrative jobs and physical safety to take up arms for Kosovo.

There is also no evidence that Belgrade's military campaign in Kosovo was directly driven by economic self-interest, though economically it certainly benefited from the growth of criminality. In addition to its control of formal economic resources, already extensive due to socialized ownership of major industries, the Milosevic government captured significant informal markets and secured financial resources through a range of criminal activities, including extortion, bribery, and kickback schemes that provided off-budget funding for the Army of Yugoslavia (the Vojska Jugoslavije, or VJ), the Serbian Ministry of the Interior (Ministarstvo Unutrasnjih Poslova, or MUP), and other federal and Serbian state institutions until 2000.[27] Milosevic also nurtured ties with influential individuals in the Serb economic and political underworld such as Zeljko Raznatovic, widely known as Arkan, who made his name and some of his fortune through the involvement of his paramilitary group in the conflicts of Bosnia-Herzegovina, Croatia, and Kosovo.[28]

Kosovo presented no major economic opportunities for Serbia (nor was the promise of economic opportunities a factor in the decision of NATO to intervene). The province remains a largely agricultural and commercial society relying on regional trade, and its industrial sector, which includes chemical processing, is not an asset despite local public perceptions to the contrary. Although mining is the centerpiece of Kosovo's economy, its mines suffer from underinvestment and overexploitation under Belgrade's control. Changed world-market conditions and new technologies have further rendered Kosovo's extractive industries of raw materials largely obsolete, making industrial revival in this sector inadvisable.[29] Kosovo's major economic potential therefore remains in agriculture and trade, while its major economic comparative advantage today is its cheap labor.[30]

It is likely, however, that the ruling class in Belgrade indirectly exploited the Kosovo conflict for both political and economic purposes, particularly after the conflicts in Bosnia-Herzegovina and Croatia had ended. The perpetuation of the Kosovo conflict served both to sustain the benefits that Milosevic's circle derived from the war economy, particularly their control over informal markets, and to secure their hold on power, thereby protecting both their political and economic interests. However, the political objective of retaining power appears to have been the overriding force that subsumed all other economic agendas. Indeed, the escalation of the conflict in Kosovo was aimed not at serving the economic agendas of the political elite in Belgrade, but at the survival of the regime itself. Stoking Serbian nationalism and cracking down on Kosovo Albanian nationalism were important factors in the policymaking calculus of the Belgrade regime in the late 1990s.

Nationalism brought the Milosevic regime to power and it was through nationalism that the regime expected to maintain power. President Milosevic and his clique used Kosovo mainly as a political instrument to generate and sustain popular support, to facilitate the manipulation of state assets and institutions for their own political purposes, to justify persecution of their opponents, and to divert attention away from serious domestic political and economic problems. To the extent that their opportunistic political agendas of maintaining power would also serve their economic agendas of exploitation of the war economy, both for political objectives or for self-enrichment, there may have been a degree of overlap between political and economic agendas and an indirect link between economic considerations and the hardening of the Belgrade stance in Kosovo.

The Political Economy of Postconflict Kosovo

The legacies of war—including the damage wrought by the NATO intervention—pose significant challenges to the reconstruction and recovery of Kosovo. The 1999 conflict exacerbated existing economic and social hardship and resulted in further declines in living standards, as evidenced by higher poverty, inequality, and unemployment. Already by 1999, agricultural production had plummeted, industrial output had collapsed, and the administration and key institutions were at a standstill. The departure of Serb authorities and Serb experts who had monopolized key positions in utilities, industry, and administration left Kosovo with few skilled personnel available to help restart the economy when the international administration arrived.[31] The homes of approximately 750,000 people were damaged or destroyed, amounting to more than 30 percent of all housing units in Kosovo.[32] Infrastructure, particularly telecommunications, was also severely damaged. The social dislocation exacerbated by the massive flight of people in spring 1999 was particularly acute.

The Establishment and Challenges of International Administration

A new phase in the history of Kosovo began with UN Security Council Resolution 1244 of June 10, 1999, which led to the withdrawal from Kosovo of all Yugoslavian military, police, and paramilitary forces and their replacement by an international administration under UN auspices.[33] This presence, composed of a civil and a military component—respectively UNMIK and KFOR—assumed full interim responsibility for Kosovo.[34]

With the arrival of UNMIK and KFOR, Kosovo Albanians and Serbs experienced a dramatic reversal of fortunes as the local balance of ethnic power shifted in favor of the Albanians. New political dynamics for the settlement of the Kosovo dispute and for stability in the region emerged. At the same time, the international community became an integral part of the Kosovo crisis on the ground and UNMIK and KFOR plunged themselves into Kosovo for an indefinite period of time. In summer 1999 the continuing nationalist extremism of the Milosevic regime in Belgrade and the widespread revenge by Kosovo Albanians against Serbs and other non-Albanian communities in Kosovo, coupled with the total paralysis of economic and social life, did not inspire UNMIK and KFOR with particular optimism. Kosovo and the wider region seemed to be doomed to perpetual instability, conflict, and misery.

The problems for the international administration were numerous. The UN in Kosovo was not only called upon to undertake the unprecedented responsibility of assuming plenary authority over a territory, but also had no clear road map for Kosovo's final status. Resolution 1244 had not addressed the underlying causes of the conflict and had left Kosovo in limbo. Yet UNMIK's policy direction was to move on forcefully with the implementation of Resolution 1244 and to navigate skillfully between the Scylla of independence and the Charybdis of Yugoslav sovereignty.

The immediate tasks facing UNMIK were enormous. First, UNMIK had to establish a functioning interim civil administration, including the restoration of law and order. Second, it had to promote the establishment of substantial autonomy and self-government, including the holding of elections. Finally, it was mandated to facilitate a political process to determine Kosovo's future status. KFOR was asked to assist in this process mainly through the deterrence of new hostilities and the establishment of a secure environment throughout Kosovo. In order to provide the necessary instruments to fulfill its vast tasks, UNMIK was structured around four pillars—humanitarian assistance, civil administration, democratization and institution building, and reconstruction and economic development—for which, respectively, the UN High Commissioner for Refugees (UNHCR), the United Nations, the Organization for Security and Cooperation in Europe (OSCE), and the European Union were responsible.[35] Humanitarian assistance was phased out in June 2000 and replaced by a new pillar, police and justice, under the auspices of the UN. In reality, however, the tasks entrusted to the international administration surpassed the required capacity and experience of the UN and the other participating international organizations.

Establishing and preserving security in Kosovo was the utmost priority for the international administration. However, UNMIK and KFOR were neither operationally nor mentally prepared for the scale of violence that engulfed Kosovo following the departure of Yugoslav forces. Early responses to the widespread attacks by Kosovo Albanians against Serbs, Roma, and Albanians branded as Serb collaborators did not provide sufficient protection to forestall the massive departure of Serbs from Kosovo through summer 1999 and the drastic deterioration of the security situation for the remaining Serb population.[36] These attacks provided stark warnings of continued volatility. Not only was the conflict not over, but both sides were prepared to continue their struggle by other means, as illustrated by the violent division of Mitrovica.[37]

The Challenges of Reconstructing Kosovo

Given the urgent security challenges faced by the international administration, it is perhaps not surprising that other considerations, including economic reconstruction and development, were not initially top priorities. Indeed, despite the purported equivalence of its component pillars, daunting political and security problems dominated UNMIK's agenda until at least the general elections in November 2001.[38]

For its part, the European Union had little experience in undertaking the wide array of tasks—from ensuring the basic supply of water, electricity, and housing, to creating a viable public sector, establishing financial institutions, and promoting growth led by the private sector—for which it was responsible. Nor did it have at its immediate availability the expertise to devise and implement strategies to achieve these objectives. Indeed, it took the European Union, in cooperation with the World Bank, nearly five months to develop an initial strategy for UNMIK with clear goals and priorities for the recovery and reconstruction of Kosovo.

The problem with devising a strategy for reconstruction was not conceptualizing the long-term objectives for reviving the formal economy, nor identifying the short-term priorities. Rather, the challenge was how to deal with the informal and criminalized nature of the economy and with the parallel political authorities established by both Kosovo Albanians and Serbs in their respective areas of control as a result of the political and security vacuum left behind by the rapid withdrawal of Yugoslav forces and authorities and the delayed establishment of the international administration.

In the second half of 1999, an informal and often criminal economy was rapidly reemerging in Kosovo. Although there are no available or reliable data to capture the real extent and patterns of activity of the informal and criminal economy, in 2001 UNMIK reported that public revenue collection operated at 50 percent of its potential, attributing 80 percent of this shortfall to illegal activities by organized criminal groups. These losses are estimated to be hundreds of millions of euros.[39] Increasing criminality was particularly acute among the Kosovo Albanian population, where organized criminal groups suspected of ties to the KLA swiftly took over apartments, real estate, and formerly "socially owned" economic assets such as petrol stations, hotels, and other commercial premises and started using them for political activities as well as for revenue generation.[40] For example, the Pristina Grand Hotel—the five-star former headquarters of Serbian extremist forces during the war, including Arkan—was heavily invested in by former members of the KLA. Many formerly public enterprises have in effect undergone de facto privatization. Accompanying these changes, there has been a considerable expansion of the already large influence of criminal elements throughout Kosovo—petrol stations are the most vivid case in point. The newly created state-owned Kosova Petrol "amalgamated" the Kosovo assets of Beopetrol and YugoPetrol. Kosovo today still boasts an excessive number of petrol stations operating largely outside of any licensing control by the international administration. Although many are legitimate businesses, others serve as fronts for money-laundering operations. Petrol stations are one of the major mechanisms for money laundering because their high turnover of small cash denominations justifies the possession of large amounts of money and sizable cash deposits. Moreover, customs documentation on petrol imports are easily forged.[41]

The situation in the field of local administration has also proven problematic. Some self-appointed mayors and local political leaders swiftly established systems of "taxation" of the economic activities in their jurisdictions in order to expand their political and economic base. It is unknown, however, what happens to the revenue generated by these parallel structures, though it is certain that it is not being used to fund the public programs.[42] Prior to the establishment of UNMIK, the self-declared

Provisional Government of Kosovo (PGK), led by Hashim Thaci, challenged Rugova's "Kosovo Republic" and the informal economic institutions it controlled. The PGK not only established its own government at the municipal and ministerial level, but also took over the management of as many "socially owned" businesses as possible.[43] These patterns of political and economic control were firmly established by the time UNMIK arrived. According to the International Crisis Group, by mid-2000 not much had changed:

> Traders are also subject to requests for donations from unofficial structures, allegedly sometimes associated with past KLA members and/or criminal elements, which are not in the traders' best interests to ignore. . . . [T]here is considerable anecdotal evidence that the civilianised successor to the KLA, the Kosovo Protection Corps (KPC), supplements the slender funds provided by international organisations with donations raised locally, either directly or through the organisation "Friends of the KPC." Informal contacts suggest that sums of between DM 300 and DM 3,000 per business per month are collected by organisations connected with the former KLA.[44]

The result has been the widespread institutionalization of criminal economic activity through the usurpation of power and control of economic resources by self-appointed groups and individuals. This development has been damaging to the political process. Hard-liners and extremist forces among both Kosovo Albanians and Serbs took advantage of the power vacuum to establish effective political and economic control and forge strong allegiances among specific parts of their communities, thereby undermining the efforts of the international administration to establish its own authority and promote more moderate forces. For example, the influence of the international administration over the Serb-dominated part of northern Kosovo has remained tenuous, not least because the Serb parallel structures, with the support of Belgrade, have systematically defied and undermined the establishment and consolidation of the international civil administration. The challenge of establishing the authority of UNMIK throughout Kosovo became more difficult, as UNMIK had not only to establish itself but also to dislocate and replace the self-appointed authorities and their activities with legitimate and representative ones.

The challenges for UNMIK posed by the close connection of the Kosovo underworld's criminal economy and extremism in the region have not been confined to the province. The same network of Albanian and Kosovo Albanian criminal organizations that are alleged to have provided support to the KLA from the early 1990s onward have used the proceeds from their Europe-wide involvement in smuggling and drug running to export conflict and militancy to southern Serbia and Macedonia. Alternative justifications have included the need to keep the border areas permeable for illegal trade, to aspirations of a Greater Kosovo.[45] The failure of UNMIK to completely disarm the KLA, let alone integrate all former KLA combatants into the KPC, enabled the National Liberation Army in Macedonia and the Liberation Army of Presevo, Medvedja, and Bujanovac (UCPMB) in southern Serbia to draw on KLA military hardware, logistics networks, and personnel.[46]

These events stress the limitations of the co-option policy of the international administration vis-à-vis Kosovo Albanian radicals, manifested in the creation of the KPC and the thus far moderate persecution of criminals, as well as the failure to give an end to impunity. Yet once more, one should not overestimate the policing capabilities of the international community in a foreign terrain in which the population has a long and sophisticated tradition of clandestine activities and a widespread gun culture. The "zero casualties" policy adopted by many KFOR national contingents was not helpful in tackling criminality and extremism in Kosovo and its regional implications became clearer in the relatively successful cross-border movement of Albanian radicals during the rebel campaigns in southern Serbia and Macedonia in 2001.

The International Response to Reconstruction

The international response to the challenges of the formal political economy can claim a number of considerable successes. For example, UNMIK's humanitarian effort to assist the return of large numbers of displaced persons, particularly to meet the pressing needs for housing and food for the returning refugees, was quite successful. Also relatively successful was the campaign for business registration that started early in 2000, which has gradually resulted in the legalization of the activities of many enterprises and contributed to the normalization of the economy. The establishment and good functioning of the UNMIK customs service has also contributed significantly to generating revenue for the Kosovo budget. A rudimentary banking system has been established as well. International financial assistance—U.S.$1.7 billion since 1999—as well as the international presence itself have helped to provide jobs and to increase the income of the Kosovo population. At the end of 2000 the World Bank estimated an increase of over 60 percent from the preconflict level of per capita GDP.[47]

In any case, much of the successes should also be credited to local investment and initiatives particularly supported by the substantial diaspora remittances, which for the International Monetary Fund (IMF) account for 40 percent of annual GDP, while for other sources much more. In general, given the constraints of the political, legal, and security environment in Kosovo, including the persisting regional instability and the post–September 11, 2001, readjustment of priorities in global politics, the international policies to the challenges of the formal political economy of Kosovo inspire relative optimism. However, the international administration has also experienced some policy failures, including the virtual absence of an officially endorsed privatization policy due to the legal uncertainty over the final status of Kosovo, the absence of a comprehensive regional integration policy, and the serious continuing problems in the provision of utilities (electricity, water, etc.).

More seriously, the initial response to the problems of the new informal and criminal political economy of Kosovo was both slow and inadequate. This was the result of a combination of political choices and operational constraints. First, the international administration did not initially have the institutional capacity or technical expertise necessary to fight economic crimes. Yet even if the means had been available, the prevailing view at the time was that openly confronting the well-armed Kosovo Albanian criminal groups was inadvisable, even where the identity, location, and activities of leaders were known. A direct confrontation could have caused a dangerous diversion from the major tasks of building and preserving the peace and would likely have involved greater risks to the lives of KFOR soldiers and UNMIK police personnel than the contributing countries were prepared to accept. In any case, the cooperation of the local Kosovo Albanian population in an assertive international effort to confront these problems was far from guaranteed.

A policy of co-option and systematic engagement of the local political leadership in the political institutions of the international administration was therefore chosen. The cardinal success of this policy was the agreement in December 1999 between Kosovo Albanian leaders and UNMIK for the establishment of the Joint Interim Administrative Structure (JIAS).[48] This agreement ensured the representation of Kosovo Albanians in some of the key policymaking mechanisms of UNMIK and consolidated the cooperation between the international administration and the Kosovo Albanian population in the creation of a civil administration in Kosovo. In so doing, it reinforced the legitimacy of the international administration among the local population. The agreement also achieved what is increasingly becoming an accepted doctrine in complex peace operations: that the international administration establish good governance and ensure the accountability to the local population through their democratic representation and participation in the work of the international administration.[49] This agreement was critical because it provided the means to address the potentially destabilizing development of the existence of parallel governments competing with the international administration for power and legitimacy. Without this agreement, the international administration risked drifting into irrelevance.

The other critical step toward increasing local participation in governance was the adoption by UNMIK in August 2000 of the Regulation on Self-Government of Municipalities of Kosovo, which led to the municipal elections of October 28, 2000, and the adoption in May 2001 of the Regulation on the Constitutional Framework for Provisional Self-Government, which in turn led to the general elections of November 17, 2001. These were important steps in establishing the required framework and institutions for substantial autonomy in Kosovo and the beginning of the transfer of administrative responsibilities to the local population. These developments are also expected to help gradually normalize the political economy of Kosovo and to reform the remaining parallel structures, budgets, and activities of its informal economy. Other important but less significant decisions in dealing with the parallel structures and the informal economy in Kosovo were the introduction in summer 1999 of the deutschemark as additional official currency in Kosovo, the 1999 establishment of a legal framework on customs, excise duties, and sales tax,[50] and the replacement of the deutschemark with the euro, all of which increased the risk of exposing criminal transactions to law enforcement officials.

Finally, the demilitarization of the KLA and its transformation into the Kosovo Protection Corps in September 1999 was a major initiative to contain the parallel authorities of Kosovo Albanians and the informal and criminal economic activities that sustained them.[51] The KPC, modeled on the Sécurité Civile of France, was designed to establish a disciplined, uniformed, and multiethnic civilian emergency response service. The decision to transform rather than disband the KLA was seen as the best incentive for preventing KLA fighters from destabilizing the fragile peace in Kosovo.[52] However, this decision was controversial from the start, particularly among the Serbs and Russian policymakers. The mixed results of its implementation during the first year of the functioning of the KPC raised further questions about the wisdom of this policy. In particular, the KPC, which was supposed to provide only emergency assistance and community services, undertook law enforcement and defense duties contrary to its mandate.

The apparent involvement of some former KLA fighters in skirmishes in Macedonia during the conflict in 2001 illustrates both the limitations of this approach and the importance of further pursuing the policy of transformation of the KLA. The clashes, facilitated by former KLA members and their networks in supplying arms, men, and matériel to coethnics in Macedonia, very nearly brought that country to civil war. This was a direct consequence of the dilemmas faced by UNMIK's strategy of cooperation and of its failure to break up the KLA's economic networks. Moreover, it demonstrates the need for peace missions to address organized economic criminality of combatant and former combatant forces if peace is to be sustained.

The emergence of parallel structures of governance and economic activity was also a problem within the Serb community. During the first phase of the international administration, the structures established by local Serb supporters of the Milosevic regime proved more capable of assisting the local population than the international administration. This helped Serbian extremists to outflank moderate forces who were advocating a more constructive engagement of the Serb community with the international administration. The removal of Milosevic in 2000 may have substantially reduced the political antagonism between Serbs and the international administration in Kosovo, but it did not automatically lead to the dissolution of the parallel informal economy in Serb areas, particularly in the predominantly Serb northern part of Kosovo, where the grip of the international administration remains limited. Yet the participation of the Serbs in the general elections in November 2001 may signal an eventual incorporation of the Serb society and economy into the structures of the international administration and those of the provisional self-government in Kosovo.

Several specific failures weakened the credibility and effectiveness of the international administration, including the slow and bureaucratic deployment of the civil administration, the initial hesitant response to the anti-Serb violence, and the prominent failure in establishing a functioning judiciary. One reason why UNMIK and KFOR were slow in reacting to the violence against Serbs, as William O'Neill points out, was the difficulty in readjusting to the reality that just a few months before, Serbs had been the perpetrators rather than victims of such violence.[53] Moreover, the lack of a functioning judicial and law enforcement system throughout Kosovo exacerbated the impunity for the continued acts of violence and jeopardized the security situation throughout the province; the longer this reality prevailed, the more difficult became UNMIK's task of redressing it.

The pragmatic approach adopted by UNMIK—co-option and systematic engagement of the local political leadership—did much to preserve the peace and to promote the normalization of Kosovo, despite the abiding uncertainty over Kosovo's final status. Some observers, however, have argued that a more robust approach should have been adopted in response to the violence as well as to the parallel structures and illegal economic practices of Kosovo Albanians during the initial period of the deployment of the international administration.[54] According to proponents of this view, the liberation euphoria that dominated the Kosovo Albanian society upon the arrival of UNMIK and KFOR created a window of opportunity of about six months to a year that would have enabled the international administration to use more heavy-handed tactics to tackle the warlordism and economic opportunism fostered by the parallel institutions. It is argued that a package of emergency measures, including tough action comparable to martial law, should have been adopted in critical areas such as security, judiciary, administration, economy, and media in order to establish firm control over key functions of the Kosovo society and prevent the KLA from filling the economic and political vacuum left by the Serbian withdrawal, and should have ended impunity for abuses, including retributive violence against minorities, enforcement of the policy of "zero tolerance" for Serbs in ethnic Albanian areas, and the resulting displacement to Serbia proper.[55]

This raises serious concerns about the prospects for political stability in Kosovo and the region. Nonetheless, recent initiatives have begun to address this shortcoming.[56] New criminal codes were introduced in 2002 to replace the piecemeal legal framework of old Yugoslav and ad hoc UNMIK legislation. The new framework does recognize economic and financial crimes, including tax evasion, bribery, corruption, and money laundering, and provides the legislative tools to deal with them. In November 2001 the EU pillar of UNMIK established the Anti–Economic Crime Unit to help improve the capacity of the international administration to combat organized economic crime. Its stated strategy is twofold: in the short run, to develop new tools to deter and disrupt economic crime; and in the long run, to facilitate the development of a civil society, media, and private sector who are intolerant of the corruption on which criminals depend and which extremists exploit for their own political purposes. Additionally, an Organized Crime Intelligence Unit was established in January 2001 under UNMIK police control to recruit specialized law enforcement agents and to better coordinate policing across Kosovo. Finally, a canine unit was added to support UNMIK customs authorities and UN Civilian Police (CIVPOL) and KFOR border patrols. Effective enforcement, however, is threatened by the very same bribery and corruption these efforts seek to curtail—many UNMIK officers come from countries whose national law enforcement ranks are tainted by corruption. Furthermore, there is a concern that graduates from the new Kosovo Police Service (KPS) are closely linked to the KLA, and that the alternative recruits from the former police force are also corrupt.[57] Still, the efforts by UNMIK to establish a new civilian administration and judicial and legal system do provide an opportunity for building mechanisms from the ground up to prevent and crack down on corruption. The EU and World Bank have, of late, examined how government structures could be altered to reduce opportunities for corruption and economic crime.[58]

There is little knowledge about the sources of revenue of the key political parties, even though it is highly likely that much of their financing originates in the economic underworld of Kosovo, the wider region, and several European states. The possibility of extensive links between political parties and organized crime has far-reaching implications for efforts to normalize Kosovo politics and society. These links risk subordinating political and economic decisionmaking in Kosovo to the priorities of organized crime at the expense of the society at large. Entrenched criminality cannot, in the long term, lead to a sustainable economy, nor will the prospective gains that it does offer redress the decades of poverty and economic neglect brought about under the former Yugoslavia. Moreover, it has already been demonstrated in Kosovo, Macedonia, and southern Serbia that these forces represent a serious threat to state sovereignty and regional stability. It is possible that the relationship between the civil society, the media, and the private sector with the economic underworld may prove to be more complex and more fluid than expected, warranting sustained international engagement to build capacities for truly independent media and civil society organizations, to provide incentives and policies for integrating the informal economy into the formal one, and to develop effective criminal enforcement.

Finally, the question of the impact of the very presence of international administration on the Kosovo economy has inevitably been an integral part of the political economy of Kosovo. There are currently about 8,000 international civilians in Kosovo and around 40,000 military personnel. This in a land with a total population of 2 million people. UNMIK alone has a budget almost two times higher than that of Kosovo. The substantially different salary scales and the wide gaps in the purchasing power between the locals and internationals obviously are responsible for serious inflationary effects—for example, in the food and real estate markets. The long-term dependency of the economy on internationals is a major challenge to the policies of sustainability. Yet the diaspora remittances, which currently contribute mainly to the improvement of the living standards of the families in Kosovo, may serve in the future, when international operations are scaled down, as the needed safety nets to help address the declining economic activity no longer generated by the international presence.

The impact of the international presence on the economy has been particularly strong on the labor market. On the one hand, job opportunities offered by UNMIK, KFOR, and the numerous other agencies and nongovernmental organizations present in Kosovo have had a positive effect on creating employment in the immediate aftermath of the conflict. The positive short-term psychological impact of this development should not be underestimated, particularly in a society suffering from long-term high unemployment rates. On the other hand, this constitutes a serious distortion of the labor market, as it is not a sustainable response to the structural problems of the economy. This is because the salary scales of unskilled local workers such as drivers, secretaries, cleaners, and security guards who are employed by UNMIK, KFOR, and others, both in offices and for private purposes, have been far higher than both the salaries of the local market and the salaries provided by UNMIK in the public sector for teachers, doctors, and other skilled civil servants. In consequence, the much needed skilled workers with professional expertise have ended up being underutilized as drivers and security guards. The implications of low public-sector wages for corruption are also obvious.

Conclusion

Clearly, preventing the escalation of a political dispute into an open violent conflict must remain a key policy priority for the international community. The descent into open conflict not only widens political and ethnic divisions and disrupts social and economic activity, but also corrupts the very fabric of society, resulting in chronic weaknesses that require long-term and costly investment and efforts for effective rehabilitation. Rebuilding societal cohesion and rehabilitating traumatized societies is a very daunting and a very long-term task.

This examination of the political economy of the Kosovo crisis both before and after the NATO intervention and the challenges posed for postconflict peacebuilding offers a number of concrete policy lessons related to the role of military and civilian policing for future international action in similar environments. First is the need for higher international preparedness to deal with the political, social, and *economic* consequences of violent conflict. Establishing a functioning legal system should have been a top priority for UNMIK, but it was not. In fact, UNMIK had not foreseen the need for an emergency justice procedure—and when one was put in place, it immediately became ensnared in the question of which legal framework to apply. To effectively respond to challenges of providing adequate security and law enforcement posed by interethnic violence and the parallel political and economic structures in Kosovo from the outset, the international administration should have focused on ending impunity from the very beginning by improving its crime-prevention and policing capacities, as well as the judiciary and the prison systems. This was perhaps the most important lesson of the Kosovo experience—one later applied with success by the International Force in East Timor (INTERFET).[59]

Second, an enhanced capacity for criminal law enforcement and strengthened political commitment is required. Competent law enforcement personnel with expertise in combating economic and organized crime should be deployed; in addition, officers with more routine policing skills should be of sufficient numbers to visibly display authority. Where it is determined possible, establishing security and enforcing law and order should take a more robust approach, entailing greater political determination in the short term, to crack down on the emergence of shadow political structures and economic activities that can undermine the efficacy of international administration and donor assistance in the long term.

Third, although politically risky, major economic assets that are illegally usurped by de facto local authorities and other criminal elements should be seized—by force, if necessary—to send a clear signal of the international administration's commitment to law and order and good governance. Fourth, there should be tighter coordination between the military and the civilian components of peace missions. Finally, political, administrative, legal, and operational means for continued monitoring to ensure the prompt use of these assets by the population should also be in place to prevent such measures from becoming a self-defeating policy that endangers the very credibility of the international administration.

Yet conflict prevention instruments as well as robust conflict management approaches also need to strike the right balance between law enforcement and political exigency or between projecting efficiency and building accountability. Peace implementation should be careful not to deviate from the overriding policy direction of engaging the local population in the process of political, economic, and social reconstruction. For an effective long-term international involvement in the management of a crisis in another country, the interests of efficiency should always be balanced by the requirements for accountability.

Ultimately, any meaningful response to the political economy of this conflict cannot be addressed at the Kosovo level alone. The political economy of Kosovo is regional and any international response should have a regional character and scope. The need for the reinvigoration of the European Union–led Stability Pact and the strengthening of its ties with Kosovo become even more urgent priorities when one realizes the problems that have been encountered by the international administration in Kosovo in trying to address the problems of economic crime that have direct regional links. In fact, the reverse is also valid, as the political economy of Kosovo is a very important factor for the future political stability of the region.[60]

Notes

1. For the more radical view that greed seems more important than grievance as a general proposition, see Paul Collier, "Doing Well Out of War," in Mats Berdal and David Malone, eds., *Greed and Grievance: Economic Agendas in Civil Wars* (Boulder: Lynne Rienner, 2000), pp. 91–111.

2. This is consistent with Collier's finding that large numbers of unemployed men, faced with few other income-earning opportunities, may be more willing to join a rebellion and therefore increase the risk of armed conflict. Collier, "Doing Well Out of War," p. 94.

3. For a comprehensive analysis of the evolution of the Kosovo conflict, see Tim Judah, *Kosovo: War and Revenge* (New Haven, Conn.: Yale University Press, 2000).

4. For a comprehensive early account of the breakup of Yugoslavia along this direction, see Misha Glenny, *The Fall of Yugoslavia,* 2nd ed. (London: Penguin Books, 1993).

5. In the 1990s, about 80–90 percent of Kosovars were ethnic Albanians, 10–15 percent Serbs, and the rest from smaller ethnic groups. However, these percentages are highly disputed and thus are given here in a very approximate manner in order to provide in general terms a demographic picture of Kosovo.

6. For more on this, see Judah, *Kosovo,* pp. 61–98.

7. For a thorough presentation of the evolution of the debate over the constitutional status of Kosovo, see Marc Weller, "Resolving Self-Determination Conflicts Through Complex Power Sharing: The Case of Kosovo," draft paper prepared for the project on "Resolving Self-Determination Disputes Through Complex Power-Sharing Arrangements" of the Carnegie Corporation, the Centre of International Studies and the Lauterpacht Research Centre for International Law of Cambridge University, and the European Centre for Minority Issues.

8. Misha Glenny, *The Balkans 1804–1999: Nationalism, War, and the Great Powers* (London: Granta Books, 1999), p. 653.

9. For a comprehensive analysis of the views and policies of the key international actors involved in the Kosovo crisis before the NATO bombardment, see Richard Caplan, "Crisis in Kosovo," *International Affairs* 74, no. 4 (October 1998): 745–761.

10. For a comprehensive analysis of the numerous aspects of the Kosovo intervention, see Albrecht Schnabel and Ramesh Thakur, eds., *Kosovo and the Challenge of Humanitarian Intervention: Selective Indignation, Collective Action, and International Citizenship* (New York: UNU Press, 2000).

11. On the background of the Kosovo economy, see Riinvest, "Economic Activities and Democratic Development of Kosova," Research Report (Pristina: Riinvest, 1998); World Bank, *Kosovo: Economic and Social Reforms for Peace and Reconciliation,* no. 21784-KOS, February 1, 2001; and Gramoz Pashko, "Kosovo: Facing Dramatic Economic Crisis," in Thanos Veremis and Evangelos Kofos, eds., *Kosovo: Avoiding Another Balkan War* (Athens: Hellenic Foundation for European and Foreign Policy [ELIAMEP] and the University of Athens, 1998), pp. 329–355.

12. For a comprehensive picture of the history of Kosovo, see Noel Malcolm, *Kosovo: A Short History* (London: Macmillan, 1998).

13. World Bank, *Kosovo,* p. 9.

14. On the background of the economy of Yugoslavia, see World Bank, *The Road to Stability and Prosperity in South Eastern Europe: A Regional Strategy Paper,* March 1, 2000; and World Bank, *Federal Republic of Yugoslavia Breaking with the Past: The Path to Stability and Growth,* vol. 1, June 12, 2001.

15. World Bank, *Kosovo: Economic and Social Reforms for Peace and Reconciliation,* p. 2.

16. Lajos Hethy, "Employment and Workers' Protection in Kosovo," Report for the International Labour Organization (ILO), Geneva, October 1999, available online at www.ilo.org/public/english/region/eurpro/geneva/country/kosovo/mreps/employ.htm (accessed December 17, 2002).

17. Report of the European Commission/World Bank, *Toward Stability and Prosperity: A Program for Reconstruction and Recovery in Kosovo,* November 3, 1999, p. 6.

18. For a thorough analysis on the origin and evolution of the KLA, see Chris Hedges, "Kosovo's Next Masters," *Foreign Affairs* 78, no. 3 (May–June 1999): 24–42.

19. UN arms embargoes were imposed against all the republics, but general economic sanctions were imposed against only Serbia and Montenegro. R. T. Naylor, *Economic Warfare: Sanctions, Embargo Busting, and Their Human Cost* (Boston: Northeastern University Press, 1999), p. 337.

20. See, for example, International Crisis Group (ICG), *Kosovo: A Strategy for Economic Development,* ICG Balkans Report no. 123, December 19, 2001, p. 4.

21. Naylor, *Economic Warfare,* pp. 350–380.

22. Paul Collier and Anke Hoeffler, "Greed and Grievance in Civil War," Policy Research Working Paper no. 2355 (Washington, D.C.: World Bank Development Research Group, 2001), p. 11.

23. For example, see U.S. Senate Republican Policy Committee, "The Kosovo Liberation Army: Does Clinton Policy Support Group with Terror, Drug Ties?" March 31, 1999; Alain Debrousse, head of Observatoire Géopolitique des Drogues, Testimony Before the Canadian Senate Special Committee on Illegal Drugs, May 28, 2001, available online at www.parl.gc.ca/37/1/parlbus/commbus/senate/com-e/ille-e/03eva-e.htm?language=e&parl=&ses=

&comm_id= (accessed December 18, 2002); Roger Boyes and Eske Wright, "Drug Money Linked to Kosovo Rebels," *Times of London,* March 24, 1999; and Jerry Seper, "KLA Funding Tied to Heroin Profits," *Washington Times,* May 3, 1999, p. 1.

24. Robert Hislope, "The Calm Before the Storm? The Influence of Cross-Border Networks, Corruption, and Contraband on Macedonian Stability and Regional Security," paper prepared at the 2001 annual meeting of the American Political Science Association, San Francisco, Calif., p. 24.

25. Francis Stewart, "Horizontal Inequalities as a Source of Conflict," in Fen Osler Hampson and David M. Malone, eds., *From Reaction to Conflict Prevention: Opportunities for the UN System* (Boulder: Lynne Rienner, 2002), pp. 105–136.

26. Tim Judah, "Inside the KLA," *New York Review of Books,* May 12, 1999, p. 23.

27. International Criminal Tribunal for the Former Yugoslavia, "Prosecution's Submission of Amended Expert Report of Morten Torkildsen," *The Prosecutor v. Slobodan Miloševiœ,* Case no. IT-02-54-T, June 7, 2002.

28. While Arkan was involved in the Kosovo crisis, his direct involvement in Kosovo was limited. Malcolm, *Kosovo,* pp. 351–352.

29. On the economic potential of the Trepca mines, which are highly valued among Kosovo Albanians, see ICG, "Trepca: Making Sense of the Labyrinth," ICG Balkans Report no. 82, November 26, 1999.

30. For an overview of the economic situation and potential in Kosovo, see World Bank, *Kosovo.*

31. For a more detailed analysis of the consequences of the conflict on the economy of Kosovo, see European Commission/World Bank, *Toward Stability and Prosperity.*

32. USAID, "Serbia-Montenegro: Complex Emergency," available online at www.usaid.gov/hum_response/ofda/99annual/europe8_serbia.html (accessed December 18, 2002).

33. UN Security Council Resolution 1244, June 10, 1999, paras. 3, 5. For a detailed analysis of the politics of the establishment of the international administration in Kosovo, see Alexandros Yannis, *Kosovo Under International Administration: An Unfinished Conflict* (Geneva: Programme for Strategic and International Security Studies [PESI] and ELIAMEP, 2001); and Alexandros Yannis, "Kosovo Under International Administration," *Survival* (London) 43, no. 2 (Summer 2001): 31–48.

34. Regulation no. 1999/1 stipulated that "all legislative and executive authority with respect to Kosovo, including the administration of the judiciary, is vested in UNMIK and is exercised by the SRSG." UNMIK Regulation no. 1999/1, "On the Authority of the Interim Administration in Kosovo," sec. 1, art. 1, July 25, 1999.

35. Report of the UN Secretary-General Pursuant to Para. 10 of Security Council Resolution 1244 (1999), S/1999/672, June 12, 1999, sec. 2.

36. In the early days of the international administration's deployment in Kosovo, the attention of KFOR was almost exclusively focused on securing the withdrawal of the Yugoslav forces and the consolidation of control over the boundaries of Kosovo with Yugoslavia. UNMIK international police virtually did not exist for some time. Even a year after the arrival of the international

administration in Kosovo, the UNMIK police force, though by then almost fully operational, continued to experience shortages of international personnel and its deployment was still around 77 percent of the authorized strength. No specific plans existed for some time on how to protect the Serbs from the revengeful hostility of the Albanians, as the international community generally was taken by surprise, not expecting this turn of events nor such a scale of violence inside Kosovo. A very good early account of the dramatic security situation of Serbs and Roma in Kosovo in summer 1999 is provided by Human Rights Watch, "Federal Republic of Yugoslavia: Abuses Against Serbs and Roma in the New Kosovo," *Report Series* 11, no. 10 (D) (August 1999).

37. See "UNMIK's Kosovo Albatross: Tackling Division in Mitrovica," ICG Balkans Report no. 131 (Brussels: ICG, June 2002).

38. European Commission/World Bank, *Toward Stability and Prosperity*, was the first official strategy paper on economic reconstruction produced in support of UNMIK's efforts to establish an international administration in Kosovo.

39. UNMIK/EU Pillar Briefing Paper, *Kosovo Anti-Economic Crime Strategy*, November 2001.

40. ICG, *Kosovo*, pp. 4–5; and Laura Rozen, "Organised Crime Gangs Rule Kosovo," *Independent of London*, February 8, 1999.

41. Benjamin Beasley-Murray, "Kosovo: Mafia Crackdown," *Institute of War and Peace Reporting*, December 21, 2001, available online at www.iwpr. net/archive/bcr2/bcr2_20011221_1_eng.txt (accessed December 20, 2002).

42. ICG, *Kosovo*, p. 7.

43. Ibid., pp. 4–5, 12. In many cases, political and economic competition between Rugova's Democratic League of Kosovo (LDK) and Thaci's Democratic Party of Kosovo (PDK) resulted in a split management within a single company, each backing one of the two factions.

44. Ibid., p. 7.

45. Hislope, "The Calm Before the Storm?" pp. 23–25.

46. Ibid., p. 32.

47. Robert Corker, Dawn Rehm, and Kristina Kostial, *Kosovo: Macroeconomic Issues and Fiscal Sustainability* (Washington, D.C.: International Monetary Fund, 2001), p. 14.

48. UNMIK unofficial document, *Agreement for the Establishment of the Joint Interim Administrative Structure*, December 15, 1999; and UNMIK Regulation no. 2000/1, *On the Kosovo Joint Interim Administrative Structure*, January 14, 2000, which incorporated the agreement into the legal and institutional setup of Kosovo. The agreement stipulated that "current Kosovo structures, be they executive, legislative or judicial (such as the Provisional Government of Kosovo [led by Hashim Thaci] and the Presidency of the Republic of Kosovo [led by Ibrahim Rugova]), shall be transformed and progressively integrated, to the extent possible and in conformity with this agreement, into the Joint Interim Administrative Structure."

49. Michael Williams, "Introductory Paper: Ending Anarchy—International Rule and Reconstruction After Conflict," Twenty-First Century Trust, Cambridge, UK, October 5–13, 2000.

50. UNMIK Regulation no. 1999/4, *On the Currency Permitted to be Used in Kosovo*, September 2, 1999; and UNMIK Regulation no. 1999/3, *On the Establishment of the Customs and Other Related Services in Kosovo*, August 31, 1999.

51. UNMIK Regulation no. 1999/8, *On the Establishment of the Kosovo Corps,* September 20, 1999.

52. On the potential destabilizing role of the KLA in Kosovo, see Chris Hedges, "Kosovo's Next Masters"; on an assessment of the transformation of the KLA, see ICG, *What Happened to the KLA?* ICG Balkans Report no. 88, March 3, 2000.

53. William O'Neill, *Kosovo: An Unfinished Peace,* International Peace Academy Occasional Paper Series (Boulder: Lynne Rienner, 2002), p. 48.

54. For more about this debate, see David Rohde, "Kosovo Seething," *Foreign Affairs* 79, no. 3 (May–June 2000): 65–79.

55. See, for example, O'Neill, *Kosovo,* pp. 48, 75–76.

56. See, for example, "Report on the Planning and Assessment Mission on Corruption, Organised Crime, and Money Laundering in Kosovo (Pristina, February 1–4, 2000)," Council of Europe Economic Crime Division, Strasbourg, February 11, 2000.

57. Ibid., p. 4.

58. Beasley-Murray, "Kosovo."

59. O'Neill, *Kosovo,* p. 76.

60. On the close relationship between the Kosovo conflict and regional stability, see Report of the UN Secretary-General Kofi Annan, *On the Search for Self-Sustaining Stability in South-Eastern Europe,* June 2000; Bernard Kouchner, *A Stable Kosovo: Essential for Regional Stability,* unofficial UNMIK document, June 2000; and Karl Bildt, "The Balkans' Second Chance," *Foreign Affairs* 80, no. 1 (January–February 2001): 148–159.

8

Sri Lanka: Feeding the Tamil Tigers

ROHAN GUNARATNA

THE SUPPORT OF DIASPORA AND MIGRANT COMMUNITIES FOR ARMED CONFLICTS in their homeland is not a new phenomenon.[1] As the Irish, Armenian, and Palestinian cases suggest, external political, military, and economic support for political violence affects the capability of armed groups, and thereby the outcome of a given conflict.[2] However, since the end of the Cold War, the scale of support lent by such communities has increased.

This chapter seeks to identify the key factors and conditions that enable guerrilla and terrorist groups to develop external support and the role of diaspora and migrant communities therein.[3] Using Sri Lanka as a case study, it examines the nature, amount, and quality of economic support from diaspora and migrant communities developed by the Liberation Tigers of Tamil Eelam (LTTE) and its impact on the Sri Lankan conflict. The chapter begins by outlining key issues in the history of the conflict. It then examines the global dimensions of the Sri Lankan conflict and attempts to identify the patterns and strategies adopted by the LTTE to garner economic support from the Tamil diaspora and migrants. The chapter concludes by addressing some of the opportunities and challenges for international efforts to prevent diaspora networks from facilitating the perpetuation of violent conflict.

Historical Background of the Conflict

The genesis of the Sri Lankan conflict is deeply rooted in its 2,500-year history. The current phase can be characterized as a primarily ethnonationalist conflict emerging from the failure of the state to manage ethnic differences and colonial legacies peaceably and in conformity with democratic principles. Historically, the country has been divided by the majority Sinhalese (74 percent), inhabiting the southwest of the island, and the minority Tamils (12.5 percent), inhabiting the northeast, each of whom trace their ancestries to Indo-Aryan and Dravida settlers from northern and southern India respectively.[4] Self-perceptions generated from their distinct histories have prejudiced the fostering of a common Sri Lankan identity.[5]

Sri Lanka's experience of imperialism further impeded the establishment of sound interethnic relations. Colonized by the Portuguese in 1505 and the Dutch in 1658, Sri Lanka gained independence in 1948 after 150 years of British rule. However, colonialist policies disproportionately empowered the Tamils over the Sinhalese.[6] Successive post-1948 Sinhala majority governments have sought to rectify this imbalance and create ethnically proportionate opportunities in education and employment.[7] However, policies such as "Sinhala Only," which made Sinhala the sole official language, in addition to provisions in the 1972 constitution that recognized Buddhism (primarily Sinhala) as the sole state religion, and the removal of other safeguards for minorities were perceived by the Tamil minority as steps toward further interethnic imbalance. Indeed, the majoritarian rule and exclusivist ethnic policies of the successive Sinhala majority governments in the aftermath of independence crystallized the development of a separatist ideology among many Tamil leaders.

The LTTE—a politically motivated, armed substate actor—has been fighting for secession from the Sri Lankan state since the early 1970s. The LTTE has developed a range of robust military, political, informational, and economic capabilities that have made it one of the most sophisticated insurgent organizations in the world.[8] These capabilities are employed both in Sri Lanka and worldwide to advance the aims and objectives of the LTTE. As the principal goal of the LTTE has been to establish a monoethnic Tamil state in northeastern Sri Lanka, the primary mission of its international organization has been to support its domestic agenda. As such, the LTTE's international and domestic organizations have played functionally distinct roles. Unless faced with threats to the LTTE's survival, the LTTE's international organization has refrained from engaging in political violence outside Sri Lanka.

The current wave of political violence can be traced to the 1970s, when the nonviolent political struggle for an independent Tamil Eelam was replaced by armed struggle led primarily by the LTTE.[9] The Sri Lankan state faced two main difficulties in effectively preventing the terror tactics that became favored by the LTTE. First, the Sri Lankan troops, trained largely to perform ceremonial functions, were incapable of meeting the terrorist threat during the formative phase of the secessionist campaign. By the time the military had transformed itself into a professional fighting force, the separatist insurgents had acquired a mastery of the use of terror tactics to further their aims, and had gathered a robust base of popular support. Second, the Sri Lankan authorities could not exercise effective control over the northern peninsula, where the separatist movements operated, or over their bases established across the Palk Straits in Tamil Nadu.

The slaying of thirteen government soldiers in an ambush by the LTTE and government action sparked the ethnic riots of July 1983. In their aftermath, 125,000 Tamils living in the south left for the predominantly Tamil northern province, while the Sinhalese population—estimated at 5,000—left the Jaffna peninsula.[10] The geographic polarization between Tamils in the north and Sinhalese in the south facilitated both recruitment for the insurgency movement and the formation of increasingly exclusionary identities between the two groups. In the course of three decades, the conflict led to extensive social and economic damage—65,000 lives were lost and about 1 million people were displaced domestically and overseas. There was large-scale human rights abuse on both sides.[11]

Toward mid-1987, India realized that the Sri Lankan insurgency was having adverse implications for Indian security. About 3 percent of the 60 million Tamils in India supported twenty small Indian Tamil political and militant groups campaigning for Dravidasan, an independent Tamil state in India. Initially, Indian efforts were directed at arming and training the Sri Lankan Tamil groups. They then turned toward attempting to mediate the conflict between the government in Colombo and the LTTE and other Tamil groups. On May 29, 1987, India and Sri Lanka signed a peace accord devolving greater autonomy to the Tamils and preserving India's geopolitical and strategic interests in the region.[12] The accord entailed the deployment of 100,000 Indian troops to monitor a cease-fire between the Sri Lankan military and Tamil groups and disarm the insurgents.

After three months of uneasy peace, LTTE leader Velupillai Prabhakaran declared war on the Indian peacekeeping force.[13] It was only after this declaration that the Indian authorities began to crack down on LTTE bases in India. By that time the LTTE had developed an extraregional procurement capability by establishing oceanic staging posts in Twante, off Burma, and in Pukhet, off Thailand. After the LTTE assassinated Rajiv Gandhi, it shared military technology and imparted training to anti-Indian insurgent groups in Assam, Punjab, Nagaland, Mizoram, Kashmir, and Tamil Nadu, and established contact with Pakistan. In response, India proscribed the LTTE. Indian policy in Sri Lanka, combined with the expansion of the diaspora and migrant community beyond Tamil Nadu, provided the necessity and the means respectively for the LTTE to develop a network of support beyond Sri Lankan and Indian jurisdiction.

Global Dimensions of the Conflict: Patterns and Strategies of Diaspora Support

While there have been a variety of interrelated political, economic, and military forms of support for the separatist insurgent movement, this section will focus on the economic dimensions of support by the diaspora and migrant communities to the LTTE. It will do so first by examining the trends in migration that have created the conditions ripe for diaspora support; second, the major dimensions of their economic support; and third, the strategies and methods adopted by the LTTE to create and maintain support from the diaspora and migrant communities living abroad.

Patterns of Migration

Sri Lanka witnessed several waves of out-migration. The disposition of each wave toward the LTTE and its program was different. Therefore, the LTTE itself developed different strategies and mechanisms to tap into the resources of the polymorphous Tamil community.

For nearly a century, Sri Lankan Tamils, particularly from Jaffna, ventured out of their birthplace in search of new opportunities. The missionary-imparted English education in Jaffna enabled many Tamils to travel to Burma and to Malaysia (then the Federated Malay States) where they served the authorities, taking up administrative and clerical positions, particularly in the rail and postal services. This first wave of migration, immediately after independence, was not politicized into supporting secessionism in Sri Lanka. The second wave, from 1956 onward, resulted primarily from the enactment of the "Sinhala Only" policy of the newly independent Sri Lankan government. A few thousand English-educated Sri Lankans migrated and settled mostly in the United Kingdom, Australia, Canada, and the United States. The third wave was primarily composed of Tamils who had been victims of ethnic violence. On each occasion a few hundred Tamils left Sri Lanka, affected by the ethnic riots of 1956, 1958, 1961, 1977, 1979, and 1981. The worst riots, those of July 1983, rendered about 300,000 Tamils homeless. Ninety percent of the Tamil business holdings outside the northeast and the central hills were damaged.[14]

The fourth wave started when the state authorities began to actively target Tamil nationalist groups in the mid-1970s. This included members, supporters, and sympathizers of various political and insurgent groups, some of which were rivals of the LTTE but united in their opposition to the Sri Lankan government. In additon to LTTE cadres, at least 20,000 members of these rival groups migrated. Estimates suggest that 8,000 of these reside in Canada and 5,000 in the UK, and that most are seeking protection against the LTTE.[15] The fifth wave resulted from three distinct phases in the conflict: the period of the international peacekeeping force from July 1987 to March 1990; the Second Eelam War, from June 1990 to December 1994; and the Third Eelam War, from April 1994 to December 2001. Estimates suggest that 300,000 Tamils migrated during this fifth wave. Overall, by 2002, an estimated one-third of the three million Sri Lankan Tamils lived overseas.

Although these waves are classified as distinct, all followed the pattern of chain migration. The earlier migrations (the first and second waves) were driven primarily by economic considerations, and the later migrations (the third, fourth, and fifth waves) were driven primarily by security considerations. There was a marked difference between the attitude toward their homeland of the migrants of the first and second waves, and those of the others. The first wave encouraged, supported, and absorbed the second wave: these migrants did not wish to mingle with the massive waves of post-1983 refugees. The first and the second waves spoke English fluently and looked down upon other migrants who could not. The third and successive waves were politicized and radicalized, having lived through persecution by the majority community and the state and conditions of ward. They also served as bridgeheads for subsequent migrants. Extending support for subsequent refugees, migrants from the third wave formed the core of the organizations that embarked on a campaign to care for the new refugees and to collect funds to support armed separatist movements.[16] Such movements increasingly infiltrated overseas organizations.[17] After the LTTE banned rival Tamil groups, external support coalesced primarily around the LTTE.

The homeland conditions that triggered each migrant wave were the primary factor that shaped the level of support for the militant separatist agenda. However, not all the migrant waves supported the terrorist tactics often adopted by the LTTE, even among "victim migrants"—that is, those Tamils who had felt victimized by the Sinhala majority governments and those forced to flee because of the war. Migrants who belonged to the first, second and fourth waves tended not to support a violent agenda. The first and second waves were personally detached from the escalation of the conflict in Sri Lanka, were emotionally resistant to the secessionist appeal, and were more economically integrated and socially assimilated into the host society. A segment of the third wave supported the goal of secession and tended to support the LTTE and its terrorist activities. Although the fourth wave was largely anti-LTTE, most were Tamil nationalists and expressed displeasure at the Sri Lankan state. While concerned about the fate of their homeland, they did not support the LTTE.[18]

For all migrant waves, the diaspora and migrant relationship with the separatist movements in the homeland was the main factor that determined the nature of LTTE support. Critical in shaping the disposition of the diaspora migrant was the degree of personal experience with the conflict, and whether he/she had been a victim of the LTTE terror or state persecution. However, supporting the separatist movement was dangerous, and could mean the death of an immediate or extended family member. As a result, support for the LTTE was dependent both on the migrant condition as well as on the migrant perception vis-à-vis the LTTE movement and the Sri Lankan state.

Economic Dimensions of Diaspora Support

Diaspora and migrant communities provide several forms of support for the LTTE. The most significant source of support comes from community organizations. Other forms of diaspora support are also important for the survival of the LTTE movement. In addition to direct contributions, diasporans and migrants indirectly assist the LTTE in generating funds through individual contributions, illegal and quasi-legal ventures, the narcotics trade, and managing and supporting international and domestic investments, trade, and businesses.

Community organizations. Although Sri Lankan Tamils are dispersed across sixty countries, they live as diaspora communities in only twenty.[19] The largest diaspora communities are found in Canada, the United Kingdom, and India, which together account for half of the Tamil diaspora worldwide. Community organizations are an important mechanism to build external support for domestic agendas, and the LTTE-controlled Tamil community organizations are no exception. The primary purpose of these organizations has been twofold: first, to advance collective socioeconomic, cultural, religious, and political interests of Tamils; and second, to sustain their identity and traditional values amid host country pressures to adapt, integrate, and assimilate.[20] Both of these goals contribute to building and sustaining support for the LTTE.

Diaspora organizations use multiple mechanisms to mobilize support for political, religious, cultural, and socioeconomic interests, but the most effective has been to organize community cultural and social events and to provide social services. They facilitate the maintenance of support for the separatist insurgent movement by supporting the preservation of ethnic authenticity in the Tamil community residing abroad. Diaspora organizations encourage Tamils to live in Tamil neighborhoods. As a result, to a Sri Lankan, La Chapelle in Paris, Scarborough in Toronto, and East Ham in London appear like Westernized neighborhoods of Sri Lanka. Given the presence of Sri Lankan shops, colorful cinema advertisements, and Hindu temples, many refer to these neighborhoods as "mini Jaffnas." To reinforce the preservation of identity, diaspora organizations urge Sri Lankan Tamil parents to send their children to community schools, usually Asian schools. To preserve traditional Tamil values, diaspora organizations encourage all Tamil children to take Tamil classes and young women to attend traditional dance schools. Diaspora associations also organize and encourage Tamil children to attend community cultural and social events.

Reminiscent of their cultural practices and traditions in Sri Lanka, these events take the form of dance and drama, music and theater, art and literary festivals, religious and spiritual functions, cultural and social evenings, and recreational and leisure events. The diaspora community organizations generate political support for the LTTE by encouraging Tamil participation in rallies, seminars, and demonstrations in support of the LTTE. They generate economic support through the sale of tickets and goods and by soliciting donations and loans for the LTTE. To reinforce LTTE diaspora and migrant interaction, the LTTE-affiliated organizations provide services and incentives: social and economic assistance, housing, immigration assistance, legal aid, information, education, communication, finance transfers, and the like. The provision of services helps to create dependence among Tamil communities on diaspora organizations for cultural and social fulfillment as well as for basic needs and services, and enhances the opportunity for the LTTE to gain and maintain support.

The attempts to preserve the Tamil identity and values are important to the maintenance of support for the LTTE movement in particular. However, pressures to assimilate or integrate into host communities, reinforced by the breakdown of traditional values over generations and the fragmentation of Tamil communities, have the potential to threaten ongoing diaspora support.

Penetrating and gaining control of a migrant community that is already highly networked is relatively easy. As such, the LTTE has infiltrated several community organizations or established new organizations for the purpose of building support for its insurgency movement and the tactics of terrorism adopted to further it.[21] Although individual members of Tamil diaspora and migrant communities have performed multiple roles for the LTTE, their interaction has been largely focused on disseminating propaganda and raising funds. The LTTE has been able to perform these two functions effectively through LTTE-affiliated organizations.[22] To ensure the compliance of diaspora organizations, the LTTE has instilled the discipline and dedication of its domestic organization in its overseas network. Many diaspora organizations are centrally coordinated by the LTTE.[23] Although the LTTE has had a worldwide presence, its political and fundraising activity has been confined to two dozen countries in the Western Hemisphere and Australasia. The LTTE has operated in public offices in eleven countries under four fronts—the Tamil Coordinating Committee (TCC), the World Tamil Coordinating Committee (WTCC), the United Tamil Organization (UTO), and the Tamil Coordinating Group (TCG). The fifth front, the World Tamil Movement (WTM), primarily operating in Canada and Germany, had scaled down its operations after some of its activists were arrested for extortion.[24]

By politically consolidating its control over the Tamil diaspora and migrants through diaspora organizations, the LTTE has reaped significant economic benefits. The leading LTTE-affiliated organization that had raised funds worldwide is the Tamil Rehabilitation Organization (TRO), with headquarters located in Australia and field offices located in LTTE-controlled northeastern Sri Lanka. The TRO public overseas offices, active throughout North America, continental Europe, Africa, and Asia, number fifteen.[25] The TRO approach to fundraising has been to highlight the suffering of the Tamil public and its events have been a useful tool to garner emotional support. The TRO appeal for support has been convincing. Attending a TRO-organized cultural event, one migrant said, "We do not know the whereabouts of our displaced family in the recent military offensive, but we are donating our jewels to you, with the hope that our family too will benefit from the relief the TRO is providing."[26] While the TRO presented itself as a charity, not all of the funds collected went to the LTTE humanitarian wing—some were also used to procure weapons.[27]

In addition to collecting charitable contributions and fees for services provided to members of the Tamil diaspora and migrant communities, the LTTE-affiliated community organizations also benefited from direct government and nongovernmental organization (NGO) grants. Host governments routinely contribute grants to community groups to fulfill the cultural and social needs of migrant communities as well as to provide services and incentives. In Canada, several organizations, either controlled by or sympathetic to the LTTE have received several grants amounting to over $1 million Canadian dollars.[28] From provincial and federal grants and loans provided to develop the Tamil community, the LTTE established four newspapers—*Namnadu, Senthamarai, Ulahath Tamilar,* and *Makkal Kural.* In addition to government grants, the LTTE-affiliated organizations received several grants from NGOs. For instance, in France the TRO received the support of the Lions Club of Cergy.[29] Similarly, in France the TCC received both governmental and nongovernmental humanitarian, refugee, and welfare grants. In Germany, the LTTE-affiliated WTM received grants from the German government to provide informational, educational, legal, housing, immigration, financial, cultural, and other support services to Tamil refugees. In the UK, the LTTE-affiliated Tamil Community Housing Association (TCHA) and its precursor the Tamil Refugee Housing Association (TRHA) received grants from borough councils. Similarly, the LTTE-affiliated Medical Institute of Tamils (MIOT) received sponsorship of pharmaceutical companies, most notably Boehringer Ingelheim Ltd.[30]

Operating through diaspora organizations has had additional advantages for the LTTE, and for other opposition movements that adopt terror tactics as one among several means to achieve their desired ends. First, segments of the diaspora, mostly the professional class, may not wish to be openly identified with a movement associated with attacks on civilians because it could affect their standing as a government employee, their social status, and the like. Under the banner of a community organization, the LTTE was able to garner wider appeal. Second, host organizations, both private and public (especially charities and donor agencies), as well as individuals, will likely refrain from interacting with groups that have strong political or other ends, especially if these are contested. On the contrary, host country organizations will have little hesitation to interact with a diaspora organization that is promoting community interests, providing services and incentives, and caring for the needs of the community. Third, by operating under the banner of a community organization, an insurgent movement that adopts terror tactics can operate under the umbrella of the host government without implicating it directly in its plight, thereby decreasing the risk of being expelled. For instance, a meeting organized by the Midwest Tamil Sangam and the International Tamil Language Foundation, both front organizations of the LTTE, was attended by the president of the Holocaust Foundation—an unlikely participant had it been known that the event was sponsored by the Federation of Tamil Associations of North America, composed of about thirty diaspora organizations and an

LTTE umbrella organization.[31] Fourth, by operating under the banner of a community organization, it is easier to evade the attention of the host security and intelligence agencies. For instance, since the LTTE, proscribed in Malaysia, could not operate there, it instead established a TRO office in Kuala Lumpur.[32] Fifth, and related, operating through diaspora organizations makes it easier to evade the laws of the criminal justice system. The Tamil Eelam Society (TES), an LTTE front in Canada, "currently has a contract to provide services under the Immigrant Settlement and Adaptation Program (ISAP)" to new immigrants.[33] However, despite an audit, Canada failed to establish a link between the TES and the LTTE that would "stand up" in a Canadian court of law. Sixth, in a host country, a diaspora organization can exert electoral pressure in return for political patronage. A sympathetic parliamentarian in a host country will not wish to be identified as taking up the cause of a movement known to support terror tactics. On the contrary, a parliamentarian will be willing to take up government issues presented by a community organization that represents his or her ethnic constituents. Seventh, to test the response of a foreign government, a terrorist group can make inroads into a foreign country under the guise of an innocuous community organization. For instance, in Botswana, the LTTE established a presence by forming a TRO office in late 1995, allowing it to assess whether to operate there through overt or covert means. Eighth, a diaspora organization is ideal for obtaining messages of goodwill and support and for ensuring participation of prominent individuals in events supportive of the goals of the movement it supports. For instance, on June 27–28, 1996, President Nelson Mandela sent a message to the International Conference on Peace and Justice, held at the Edmund Barton Center, Canberra, Australia, and organized by the Australasian Federation of Sri Lankan Tamil Associations and the Australian Human Rights Foundation, two front organizations of the LTTE.[34] The conference statement, read by LTTE central committee member and international spokesman Lawrence Tilakar, incorporated Mandela's message into the LTTE's statement. This implied that Mandela endorsed the LTTE's position. As a result, diasporans and migrants have long held the misperception that Mandela is an LTTE supporter.

In conclusion, diaspora organizations have been a central means by which the LTTE has mobilized political and economic support for its radical separatist agenda. Diaspora organizations provided the medium for the LTTE to permeate diasporans and migrants with Tamil nationalist, secessionist, and pro-LTTE rhetoric. The key LTTE strategy aimed at enhancing control over Tamils overseas was to make them dependent on LTTE services and incentives for their basic needs and to provide social and cultural fulfillment. To dominate the political mainstream of overseas Tamils, the LTTE has understood the importance of gaining effective control over rival or opposition Tamil organizations. This has been achieved either by infiltrating them with LTTE cadres, through co-opting, or by intimidating key individuals in diaspora organizations, thereby gaining decisive influence over the political direction of these organizations and their members and redirecting them toward LTTE objectives.

Individual contributions. Voluntary and coerced contributions from individual members have formed the principal source of economic revenue for the LTTE's procurement of military equipment.[35] To finance a protracted military campaign, the LTTE has encouraged periodic and regular contributions to help ensure a steady flow of income over a longer period.[36] Until late 1996, the LTTE solicited £200 per year from each Sri Lankan Tamil family in London.[37] After early 1997, the LTTE adopted a new formula, soliciting one day's pay per working person per month. These monies were in addition to funds collected at LTTE-organized events or for emergency purposes. The LTTE also routinely approached businessmen for periodic donations.[38]

Other than the diasporans and migrants contributing significantly to the LTTE war budget, diaspora and migrant remittances also went to the Tamil communities in the homeland to ensure their well-being. These remittances enabled Sri Lankan Tamils to remain in the war zone, indirectly facilitating recruitment to the LTTE. Field research indicates that members of the radicalized segments of the diaspora and migrant communities that remitted funds to their immediate and extended families typically accompanied their contributions with exhortations of support for Tamil Eelam and the LTTE. As diaspora and migrant influence in the affairs of the territorials was considerable, these efforts had a degree of influence on the predisposition of Tamils in Sri Lanka toward the LTTE.

Quasi-legal and illegal ventures. Both directly and indirectly, the LTTE has profited from quasi-legal and illegal business ventures, the success of which has also been dependent on support from diaspora communities. In some ventures, the LTTE was directly involved, while in others the LTTE took a percentage from profits generated by others. Some segments of the diaspora and migrant community were vulnerable to crime: the LTTE exploited these criminal elements and profited from many of their activities.[39] The LTTE imported films from India to Europe and Canada for entertaining both the Sri Lankan and the Indian Tamil diaspora and migrant communities. Although it was operational on a smaller scale even earlier, the LTTE inroads into the film industry reached a high peak when former LTTE Jaffna commander Satasivam Krishnakumar, alias Kittu, was appointed head of the LTTE's international secretariat in London. The first successful film the LTTE invested in was *Talapathi.* Thereafter the LTTE invested in *VIP,* another Indian Tamil film.[40] Toward the mid-1990s, the LTTE augmented trading and investing in films by entering into the video, audio, and CD market.[41] The LTTE also established a series of video and CD parlors in Paris, including *looni,* selling Tamil videos and CDs. The LTTE duplication and sale of videos, audiocassettes, and CDs generated considerable revenue. Often, such quasi-legal activities have been well camouflaged and conducted by semi-autonomous groups.

The money collected from these ventures was used to acquire military hardware and dual-use technologies. For instance, in mid-1994, UK-based LTTE activist Narendran Ratnasabapathy used an LTTE front company, the Euro-Ukranian Consultancy Agency in Kharkov City, Ukraine, to procure high explosives from Rubezhnoa, a chemical plant in the Lugansk region, and detonators, primers, detonating cords, and tetryl from the Impulse weapons plant in the Soumy region.[42] Until the mid-1990s, the LTTE continued to use sympathizers to transact these international deals. Subsequently, the LTTE built an independent procurement organization employing its own cadres as procurement officers, with the objective of reducing their reliance on the sympathetic migrants for weapons procurement. Yet the limitations of operating its own clandestine military procurement wing meant that the LTTE continued to rely on the support of others in the diaspora and migrant communities.[43]

Diaspora-supported military assistance enabled the LTTE to build a military and dual-use technology capability as well as to acquire the specialized training needed for conducting a high-intensity campaign. As domestic procurement was rudimentary, it was sufficient only for waging a low-level guerrilla campaign. But international procurement of military and dual-use technologies enabled the LTTE to engage directly with Sri Lankan troops. Furthermore, the LTTE was able to compensate for the sudden loss of Indian state sponsorship in 1987, largely due to stepped-up diaspora and migrant military support. The procurement of standoff weapons including light assault weapons, surface-to-air missiles, and rocket-propelled grenades greatly enhanced the military performance of the group. Overall, external military support was critical for the LTTE to sustain a high-intensity guerrilla and semi-conventional military campaign against the Sri Lankan state.

Narcotics trade. Prior to 1990, the LTTE had been involved in the wholesale and retail trade in narcotics to augment its revenue. LTTE ships transported narcotics from Burma, Pakistan, and Turkey, all principal transit centers of heroin reaching the UK.[44] Although shipping movements were being recorded in the Lloyds shipping register, ships plying these routes were neither searched nor interdicted. Prior to 1990, several couriers engaged in trafficking retail quantities of heroin were apprehended. LTTE activist Cecil Sooriyakumar Daniel was arrested in the UK on September 17, 1984, for possessing 980 grams of heroin. As one report noted, in the eighteen months preceding August 1987, "at least 10 Tamils carrying heroin worth £4 million have been caught at Heathrow. Several more have been detected in transit, each çarrying three kilos and have been followed to their final destinations before being arrested."[45] In addition, there have been several narcotics-related violent incidents that confirm the role of the LTTE.[46] Although its involvement in the narcotics trade is widely known, the LTTE has denied complicity.

Supporting and managing investments. The LTTE has also lent funds to their supporters to invest in legitimate businesses—travel agencies, restaurants, grocery stores, printing presses, housing companies, film/video ventures, export-import firms, transport companies, money exchange and transfer agencies, and telephone communication services. LTTE activists have also obtained the franchise of a substantial number of gas stations—from which they are expected to pay the LTTE a monthly fee.[47] In the United Kingdom the LTTE has also invested funds in ethnic radio stations and in newspapers.[48] As Sri Lankan Tamils are largely an asylum community, the current level of corporate support from the diaspora has been modest. However, given the trends toward increased trade and commerce among the migrant generation, large-scale corporate support may be possible from the second generation.[49] The main impediment against second-generation support is their overwhelming lack of emotional attachment to the homeland, as well as the LTTE's project of an independent Tamil state.

In conclusion, economic support by the Tamil diaspora and migrant communities has enabled the LTTE to pursue a more direct and high-intensity campaign against the Sri Lankan state security forces. Sri Lankan and foreign intelligence agencies have estimated the LTTE's annual revenue to have reached U.S.$100 million, of which about U.S.$60 million is generated from overseas.[50] Of the U.S.$60 million, about 90 percent meets the LTTE's international military procurement budget and the balance is utilized for managing LTTE offices and events worldwide.[51] Before it reaches Sri Lanka, the bulk of international economic support is translated to military support. The total war budget of the LTTE—both international and domestic—is about 10 percent of the Sri Lankan defense budget.[52] Since the mid-1990s, the LTTE has generated over 50 percent of its international revenue from solicited grants, trade, investments, and businesses.[53]

Emerging funding trends suggest that the LTTE has been seeking to increase its investments in legitimate trade and business ventures. On the one hand, this has rendered the LTTE less dependent on diaspora and migrant contributions. On the other hand, to a certain extent, even LTTE-owned businesses have continued to rely on members of the diaspora to manage their investments and conduct business transactions.

Consolidating Diaspora Support: Strategies and Methods

Various strategies have been adopted by the LTTE over the years to build and maintain the economic support from diaspora and migrant communities required for the LTTE's campaign against the Sri Lankan state. Typically, LTTE strategies and methods have adopted a combination of direct and indirect forms of coercion.

To understand the economic relationship between the LTTE and overseas Tamils, it is important to first understand the economic relationship between the LTTE and Tamils in Sri Lanka. The LTTE adopted a routine system of "taxation" of Sri Lankan Tamils that was gauged to individual incomes. In addition, the LTTE requested every family in "Tamil Eelam" to donate a flat fee of 10,000 rupees (about U.S.$200, or the equivalent monthly salary of a university don) or two sovereigns of gold toward the LTTE's national security fund.[54] In 1991 and again in 1995, the LTTE solicited extra donations, after announcing that resources were required to provide "protection" to the Tamil people and to promote the goal of "liberating Tamil Eelam." In actuality, the LTTE's funds had dropped dramatically during the peace talks in 1990 and in 1994 at the same time as hostilities had resumed during that period. Collectors from the LTTE's finance department visited homes in LTTE-controlled areas, accompanied by LTTE cadres from the nearest camp bearing documents from the central registry, where records of every family contribution were stored.[55] Family incomes as well as their properties were preassessed. Those who could not pay were given extensions, while those who defaulted were punished. Typically, the head of a defaulting household was detained by the LTTE in the nearest camp, typically in a bunker, where he remained incarcerated until a member of the family or a friend paid the debt. The only persons exempted from payment were the families of serving cadres or martyrs of the LTTE.[56] This was in keeping with the unwritten LTTE law that every family should give a son or a daughter for the "liberation of the motherland." The receipt issued upon payment also served as a pass that allowed a person either to leave the LTTE-controlled northeast or to apply for a position in the "Tamil Eelam administration."[57] The LTTE depended on these sources of domestic revenue to meet immediate expenses, especially during the early stages of the conflict, when diaspora and migrant funds were not yet forthcoming.

To discourage out-migration, the LTTE required any family leaving the northeast to hand over their immobile properties to the LTTE. The LTTE pledged to administer and return their lands and homes upon their return. In addition, the families who owned businesses or properties, or who had a son or a daughter abroad, had to pay additional taxes. In 1990, families were required to pay 50,000 rupees for the first family member abroad and 25,000 rupees for each additional person resident overseas.[58] By 1995 these amounts had increased to 100,000 and 50,000 rupees respectively. The LTTE taxed all local trade and commercial businesses. The LTTE also taxed private passenger buses and lorries transporting food and other supplies to and from the northeast. The LTTE tax assessors would assess the profit and request payment. Failure to pay resulted in confiscation of goods, and detention and a fine incurred by the defaulter. Clandestinely, the LTTE also collected money from Tamil-owned businesses elsewhere in Sri Lanka, particularly in Colombo, where the Tamil business community, with origins from Jaffna, is wealthy and prosperous. Those with extended families or business and property interests in the northeast were the most susceptible to payment.

The ability of the LTTE to garner and ensure support for its movement in the northeast meant that most Tamils there accepted LTTE taxation with resignation. In light of the LTTE's brutal treatment of opponents, even those who opposed these methods nonetheless conformed to the dictates of the LTTE quasi-administration. In most instances, the notoriety of the LTTE for punishing dissent created a climate of fear and acquiescence among Tamil civilians, and rarely did the LTTE have to single out and reprimand an individual or a particular family to ensure payment. The LTTE also projected it as a sacred duty of the Tamil people to "honor those who had sacrificed their lives for Tamil Eelam and contribute to perpetuate their vision and struggle."[59] For sustained results, LTTE propaganda, in particular propaganda that justified its terrorist methods, was also an important mobilization strategy.

The same methods of ensuring political and economic support for the LTTE were applied in the Tamil diaspora and migrant communities. The LTTE frequently dispatched "punishment teams" from one country to another to discipline "recalcitrants."[60] As a result, among the Tamil diaspora and migrant communities, there is considerable fear that defiance, or even mild nonconformity, would trigger the revenge of the LTTE.[61] Because diaspora and migrant communities tend to maintain direct personal and familial links to the homeland, the risk of retribution and nonconformity to the LTTE is real—unless immediate and extended family members are perceived to be beyond the reach of the LTTE.

In addition, the LTTE has maintained computer databases with extensive personal information of potential supporters, including details of their family members both overseas and in the homeland.[62] Part of the duties of LTTE regional and area leaders has been to collect information on potential supporters before approaching them for funds. LTTE fund collectors have access to personal details of the Tamils living in their area. As such, a fund collector will avoid visiting homes of a hard-core supporter or member of a rival Tamil group. In other cases, the collector would typically engage in conversation, announce the purpose of his or her visit, distribute literature, collect the compulsory donation, gather further details on others who might wish to contribute, and depart. By developing and maintaining a set of databases, the LTTE overcame the fallout of operating "punishment teams."

The solicitation appeals of the LTTE collectors were credible and effective, because they were accompanied by a thinly veiled threat of punishment for noncompliance. As each fund collector made certain to demonstrate his/her knowledge of the identity, politics, and family affiliations of the target, potential supporters would be aware that the LTTE knew the details of his or her extended family in the LTTE-controlled or -dominated northeast. In this way, the LTTE routinely solicited monthly or annual contributions by promptly visiting homes on preannounced days, and by soliciting special contributions to mark occasions such as "Martyrs Day," the "Sea Tiger Special Fund," or "Black Tigers Day" every three months. Rarely was it necessary for the LTTE to remind the members of the diaspora and migrant communities that relatives in the homeland would not be pressured for contributions so long as they had "fulfilled their duty."[63]

Curbing Diaspora Support for Armed Conflict: The Opportunities and Challenges of International and State Response

The legal and political systems of Western liberal democracies are conducive to the establishment and growth of diaspora support networks. Because of the blurred distinction between such networks that are "benign" and those support mechanisms that fuel and perpetuate armed conflict, liberal democratic systems have few discrete tools to address the latter. More generally, there are few tools, and a distinct lack of political will despite the attacks in the United States on September 11, 2001, to address sources of terrorist and insurgent activity that are domestically harbored.

Legal

The legal systems in Western liberal democracies are typically designed to target criminal activity and punish responsible individuals, not organizations. However, even with regard to individuals, because the LTTE has a high capacity to replenish leadership and membership losses, it has been able to circumvent this problem. At the same time, when a host state takes a firm stand against individuals, diaspora and migrant segments may feel emboldened to diminish or end their support for a movement into which they have been co-opted. This is especially true where diaspora members can forego the threat of retaliation against his or her family and other interests in the homeland.

The strategies and mechanisms used by the LTTE to establish and maintain support abroad make it difficult for diasporans and migrants to support the efforts of host-state authorities to target the activities undertaken by the LTTE within the host state's jurisdiction. The legal mechanisms regarding asylum may be used to provide an incentive to enlist the support of asylum seekers in counterterrorism efforts. However, such support depends on the ability of host governments to provide protection for, and to ensure the future protection of, those openly and actively opposing groups like the LTTE. However, there are few effective legal mechanisms through which to do so.

Political

Integration and assimilation strategies of host states are an important way of addressing the vulnerability of diaspora and migrant communities infiltrated and manipulated by insurgent or terrorist groups. For instance, although some segments of the Tamil diaspora and migrants shared the political ideal of the LTTE, host-state policies have helped build up anti-LTTE opposition and resistance within the Tamil community.[64] In the UK, as Sri Lankan Tamils have wanted to remain in good standing with the host state, they have been conscious of not being associated with crime and not engaging in illegal activities. Second- or third-generation migrants are more likely to be "imbibed" with host values that tend to make them less susceptible to supporting an insurgent guerrilla movement, particularly one that is associated with terrorist acts. The Tamils who assisted the LTTE in high-risk military procurement and training operations were all first-generation migrants. Because they had directly experienced the conflict before migrating, they were more committed than subsequent generations.

Electoral cycles in liberal democracies also provide an opportunity to exploit the need for votes in host countries to the advantage of political movements seeking political ends elsewhere. Several radical insurgent groups, including the Kurdish Workers Party (PKK), Babbar Khalsa International (BKI), the LTTE, and Kashmiri groups, have been able to generate substantial political support within the host country by mobilizing their constituents and "trading" their bloc vote for official expressions of support. As party policies and vote counts narrow, politicians have become increasingly dependent on ethnic votes to make up the difference between victory and defeat. To this end, community organizations have regularly invited respectable host leaders to address diaspora and migrant gatherings. Association with the host country's political establishment has also helped terrorist and insurgent groups conceal their illegal and quasi-legal activity behind a veil of legitimacy.

Terrorism and Democracy Since September 11: What Preventive Role?

The terrorist attacks of September 11, 2001, and the subsequent "war on terrorism" have altered the level of diaspora support for the LTTE in ways that have impacted the dispositions of the LTTE leadership toward resolving the conflict through dialogue. The new determination of host states to target terrorist financing has significantly curtailed diaspora support for the LTTE—as for other proscribed terrorist groups—as the penalties for such activities have become prohibitive. In turn, both the reduction in diaspora support and the new strategic environment appear to have been major factors in the LTTE's reconsideration of the use of violence to achieve its political goals. Immediately after the events of September 11, the LTTE embarked on peace negotiations with the Sri Lankan government, which led to the first sustained ceasefire agreement since the conflict began. In the peace talks that have ensued, the LTTE has avowed to renounce terrorism as well as its insistence on an independent Tamil homeland, provided the Tamils are accorded substantial autonomy.

While there is reason for optimism, peace in Sri Lanka is not yet guaranteed. There can be little doubt that the LTTE's newfound commitment to nonviolence has been impelled by a strategic decision to avoid being targeted by the United States' war against terrorism and to evade the international media spotlight. Although progressing on other fronts, agreement between the LTTE and the Sri Lankan government on core constitutional and human rights issues remains elusive. Even more troubling, the LTTE has continued to recruit and train militants in Sri Lanka and procure arms and other supplies. Despite a series of warnings by foreign governments, including the U.S. State Department, the LTTE has continued to build its military capability. In March 2003, an LTTE ship laden with military matériel was destroyed by the Sri Lankan navy. In retaliation, the LTTE attacked a Chinese commercial vessel in the Sri Lankan waters killing its crew. In a similar vein, several international human rights organizations continue to appeal to the LTTE to refrain from recruiting child soldiers. Although the LTTE has claimed a commitment to a peaceful resolution of the conflict and a willingness to compromise its avowed goal of Tamil Eelam, it has maintained the capacity to renew its fight against the Sri Lankan government and the option of recovering, by military means, the island's northeast region.

The Western experience in the fight against terrorism in the aftermath of September 11, 2001, also provides insight into the ongoing degree of tolerance and duality of Western response against those movements supporting terrorist tactics at home and those that do so abroad.[65] Until recently British policy was typical: while proscribing domestic terrorist groups and separatist militants, British policy permitted foreign insurgent and terrorist groups to function in the UK, provided they did not violate domestic laws.[66] To ensure the security of Britain, the Special Branch and MI5 maintained surveillance on terrorist groups based in the UK, while only selectively sharing intelligence about the activities of foreign groups with friendly foreign counterparts. Although this provided some degree of deterrence, most UK-based groups evaded British surveillance. Overall, most host states have tended to follow this pattern: tolerating the presence and activity of foreign insurgent and terrorist groups unless these activities adversely affect domestic security and foreign policy interests.

The high degree of tolerance and self-interest of host countries, especially Western liberal democracies, has facilitated the growth of formidable international support structures for terrorist and insurgent groups. Host-state policies appear to be guided by the fear that if they target a terrorist group, the group will avenge the host action by establishing links with groups inimical to host-state interests. Host-state policies also appear to be shaped by a belief that by designating and proscribing groups as "terrorist," they will be driven underground, become more clandestine in operation, and hence become more difficult to monitor. However, such policies can offer security and insulate host-countries from insurgent and terrorist groups only in the short term.

Most foreign political movements that adopt terror as a weapon, including the LTTE, do not directly threaten the national security interests of their host countries. Therefore, most governments, especially liberal democracies, typically have turned a blind eye to the operation of foreign terrorist groups on their soil. Rhetorical proscription of their activity is moreover unlikely to seriously disrupt the support networks of terrorist groups. For instance, along with twenty other groups, the UK proscribed the LTTE as a terrorist group in March 2001 under the Terrorism Act of 2000. Yet the UK has not pursued a policy of actively detecting, prosecuting, or dismantling terrorists and their physical infrastructure. After September 11, 2001, Europe has been targeting only the infrastructure of Islamist terrorist groups, especially Al-Qaida and its associated and affiliate groups—not, for instance, those groups that continue to support LTTE terrorist activity and operate in the United States through multiple front, cover, and sympathetic organizations. Many Western governments have been focusing on Islamist groups and not on secular terrorist groups, rushing to draft legislation to empower their law enforcement, security, and intelligence agencies to act against terrorist groups. As Canada and Australia deemed it politically incorrect only to proscribe Islamist groups, they proscribed a number of secular groups, including the LTTE. Post–September 11, the European Union banned a number of groups but left the LTTE off of its list, not least as a result of the effective LTTE lobbying of continental European parliamentarians. Even if host governments and the wider international community were to target non-Islamist groups more consistently, ending all diaspora support for terrorist and guerrilla groups would remain a daunting challenge. Terrorist and guerrilla groups have either established or penetrated several local charities, some of which are engaged in genuine relief, rehabilitation, and other socioeconomic and educational activities. Regulating this area of terrorist financing without compromising humanitarian objectives has already proven difficult. Unlike most international charities, these local charities are not transparent or accountable to their donors. Unless international humanitarian organizations play an expanded role in providing assistance to civilians in wartorn situations, there will be significant humanitarian repercussions of disrupting aid to local charities.

Moreover, targeting domestically based groups that support terrorism is a technically and legally complex as well as an expensive and labor-intensive task. First, host governments will be fighting groups that are foreign and will likely have deficient historical and other expertise required to tailor a response according to the particular challenge. Second, host governments will fear retribution from these groups. Third, host governments will be targeting groups fighting governments that violate human rights. These impediments complicate the development of effective counterterrorism and counterinsurgency policies.

The post–September 11 policy response—to criminalize terrorist groups—will be effective only by criminalizing their front, cover, and sympathetic organizations. However, there are few discrete tools to address the role of diaspora and migrant organizations supporting groups linked to foreign terrorist and insurgent activity. One such tool is the development of secondary lists—that is, lists that continuously identify new organizations that are created to allow insurgent and terrorist groups to evade proscription and allow their continued functioning. This requires close monitoring of the very same activists who are likely to set up new or infiltrate existing community or other organizations. Likewise, close cooperation between target states and host security and intelligence agencies is essential for the host state to identify and act against the new front, cover, and sympathetic organizations created or infiltrated by terrorist groups.

Conclusion

This chapter has sought to identify the economic dimensions of diaspora support for the LTTE movement. It has argued in particular that community organizations established in host states as fronts for the LTTE play an important role in building and maintaining economic as well as other forms of support for the LTTE. Linked as that movement is to the adoption of terror tactics, and to associated attacks against civilians, to achieve its desired end of an independent Tamil Eelam state, diaspora support poses particular challenges for host states with an interest in curbing terrorism and preventing armed conflict. There are, however, few discrete policy tools available to such host states to address the economic sources of diaspora support for armed conflict and terrorism. This requires holistic thinking to manage the challenges, concertedly, of the economic dimensions of civil war.

Notes

1. Colin Clarke, Ceri Peach, and Steven Vertovec, eds., *South Asians Overseas: Migration and Ethnicity* (Cambridge: Cambridge University Press, 1990);

Giorgio Gomel, "Migration Toward Western Europe: Trends, Outlook, Policies," *International Spectator* 27, no. 2 (April–June 1992): 67–80; Guy Goodwin-Gill, "International Law and Human Rights, Trends Concerning International Migrants and Refugees," *International Migration Review* 23, no. 3 (Fall 1989): 526–546; Danièle Joly, *Refugees: Asylum in Europe?* (London: Minority Rights Group, 1992); Daniel Kubat, *The Politics of Migration Policies* (New York: Centre for Migration Studies, 1990); Gil Loescher and Laila Monahan, *Refugees and International Relations* (Oxford: Clarendon Press, 1989); Gil Loescher, *Refugee Movements and International Security,* Adelphi Paper no. 268 (Oxford: Oxford University Press for the International Institute of Strategic Studies, 1992); Vaughan Robinson, ed., *The International Refugee Crisis: British and Canadian Responses* (London: Macmillan, 1993); and *Problems and Prospects of Refugee Law* (Geneva: Graduate Institute of International Studies, May 1991).

2. Ibid.

3. For the purposes of this chapter, "guerrilla" warfare refers to opposition groups that target primarily military personnel, and "terrorist" warfare refers to opposition groups that target primarily civilians.

4. Of the Sri Lankan population, 7.4 percent are Muslims, concentrated in the east, and 5.6 percent are Plantation Tamils of Indian origin, concentrated in the central hills (1981 census).

5. The Sinhala point of view has been powerfully argued by Kingsley M. de Silva, *A History of Sri Lanka* (Berkeley: University of California Press, 1981), and the Tamil point of view by several Tamil scholars including A. Jeyaratuam Wilson, *The Break-Up of Sri Lanka: The Sinhalese-Tamil Conflict* (London: C. Hurst, 1988); S. J. Tambiah, *Sri Lanka: Ethnic Fratricide and the Dismantling of Democracy* (Chicago: University of Chicago Press, 1986); Dagmar Hellman-Rajanayagam, "The Politics of the Tamil's Past," in Jonathan Spencer, ed., *Sri Lanka: History and Roots of Conflict* (London: Routledge, 1990); and V. Rudrakumaran, *The Tamil's Quest for Statehood in the Context of the Birth of New States in the Former Soviet Union and Yugoslavia* (Camberley: International Federation of Tamils, 1991).

6. Kingsley M. de Silva, *Managing Ethnic Tensions in Multi-Ethnic Societies: Sri Lanka, 1880–1985* (Lanham, Md.: University Press of America, 1986); and Kingsley M.. de Silva, *A History of Sri Lanka* (Berkeley: University of California Press, 1981).

7. Ibid.

8. The LTTE employs a range of tools in support of its aims. Military: sabotage, political assassination, terrorism, guerrilla warfare, semiconventional warfare, and ethnic cleansing. Political: lobbying and campaigning; establishing front, cover, and sympathetic organizations; and networking with and infiltrating political parties, NGOs, charities, and community organizations around the world. Informational: network structures (coordination of operations), propaganda, psychological operations, and information infrastructure attack. Economic: economic infrastructure attack; economic warfare; manufacturing, trading, and investing; and organized crime.

9. Walter Schwarz, *The Tamils of Sri Lanka* (London: Minority Rights Group, 1975), p. 1.

10. Helena J. Whall, *Repatriation of Displaced Tamils: Voluntary or Mandatory? Victims of War in Sri Lanka* (London: Medical Institute of Tamils,

1995), p. 123. Although the 1981 census recorded 4,000 Sinhalese in the Jaffna peninsula, there were more Sinhalese with homes in the south but living in Jaffna. It is likely that this number would not have significantly increased by 1983.

11. Amnesty International and Human Rights Watch annual reports documented violations on both sides during the conflict.

12. Kingsley M. de Silva and R. J. May, eds., *Internationalization of Ethnic Conflict* (London: Pinter Publishers, 1991); and Kingsley M. de Silva and S. W. R. de A. Samarasinghe, eds., *Peace Accords and Ethnic Conflict* (London, New York: Pinter, 1993).

13. Even under overwhelming military pressure, Prabhakaran was unwilling to compromise his position. At a subsequent commemoration meeting of its elite suicide cadres, the Black Tigers, Prabhakaran displayed his fervent commitment to establishing Tamil Eelam by stating that if he compromised the goal of Tamil Eelam, his life too could be taken. Unlike the bulk of the terrorist groups that developed from a political organization, the LTTE was an armed group from its inception. Very often the core thinking of such groups remains unaltered, constraining their transition from militancy to politics.

14. Author interview, Dr. Kumar Rupesinghe, secretary general, International Alert, London, July 1998.

15. Author interviews, The estimate for Canada is from the Canadian Security and Intelligence Services, July 1998. The UK estimates are based on interviews with UK representatives of Tamil groups, July 1998.

16. With a few exceptions, migrants of the 1950s also formed diaspora organizations, but because they wanted to be recognized as leaders in their communities. Their organizations either did not survive or their leadership was replaced by more committed post-1983 leaders to the nationalist cause. Pre-1983 migrants contributed toward the cause politically but not economically—they led, addressed, or marched in processions, but were not sufficiently motivated financially to donate their hard-earned money.

17. In France, the Tamil Coordinating Committee (TCC) was infiltrated by the LTTE, which took over the control of the organization. Today, the LTTE's premier front organization in France is the TCC. Author interview with Illango Nadarajah, alias Rajan, LTTE representative for France, August 1997. He said, "The TCC board decided in 1983 to support the LTTE."

18. Author interview, LRRE fund collector, London, July 1998.

19. They are Canada, the United States, Australia, New Zealand, Papua New Guinea, Fiji, South Africa, Zambia, Nigeria, the United Kingdom, Italy, France, Germany, Switzerland, Denmark, Norway, Sweden, Malaysia, Singapore, and India. Except the United Kingdom, where the Sri Lankan Tamils traditionally prefer to reside, India was geographically the closest country to Sri Lanka, and Canada's open-door policy welcomed Sri Lankan migrants.

20. "Tamil Pages 1999," *British Tamil Directory,* London, 1999; "Ulahatamilar (World Tamil) Business Directory, 1999–April 2000," *World Tamil Movement,* Scarborough, 1999; "East-West Connections, 1998," *Business Directory,* Ontario, 1998; and author telephone interview with a member of the Organization for Eelam Refugee Relief (OFERR), Madras, India, January 1997.

21. The term "LTTE-affiliated" is used to denote diaspora organizations controlled by the LTTE.

22. The LTTE's public offices are located in Palermo, Italy; Zurich,

Switzerland; Gummerabach, Germany; London, UK; Oslo, Norway; Herning, Denmark; The Hague, the Netherlands; New York, United States; Paris, France, Spanga, Sweden; and Victoria, Australia.

23. The LTTE's international secretariat, in London, coordinates international political activity. The head of the secretariat, Manoharan, appointed in April 1997, is Paris-based.

24. *Kalatheli* (LTTE newspaper), London, September 10, 1997, p. 16. *Kalatheli* refrained from listing the WTM, and especially any references to the WTM's Canadian office, after the arrest of its head, Suresh, who was also the head of the LTTE in Canada.

25. *Kalatheli,* London, August 17, 1997, p. 10.

26. Author interview with Subramaium Shanmugathasan, alias Shan, head of the TRO, Switzerland, July 26, 1997.

27. Author interview with Brian Watters, former MI6 station chief, Colombo, December 1996.

28. Such organizations include: the WTM, the Federation of Associations of Canadian Tamils (FACT), and especially the Tamil Eelam Society of Canada (TES). Author interviews with Royal Canadian Mounted Police Force and Canadian Security and Intelligence Service officials, Toronto, Montreal, and Ottawa, September 1999. The WTM and FACT are listed as LTTE fronts in Canada by the U.S. State Department's counterterrorism office.

29. In May 1997, the Organisation pour la Reinsertion des Tamouls (Organization for the Reintegration of Tamils) organized a festival with the participation of the Lions Club in Cergy Pontoise, France.

30. In May 1997 the LTTE in London organized a TCHA public event by invitation. Speakers from the Sri Lankan Tamil community praised the borough councils that supported their housing efforts. For MIOT sponsorship, see the quarterly publication *MIOT News,* April 1996, p. 12.

31. The meeting was held at the Nordic Hills Resort, Chicago, on June 1, 1997. During the meeting, the president of the foundation stated that "Sri Lankan war and genocide against Tamils is the best-kept secret in recent times."

32. TRO in Malaysia, *Hot Spring,* London, August 1997, p. 6.

33. ISAP facilitates the "adaptation, settlement and integration of newcomers to Canada so that they may become participating members of Canadian society as quickly as possible, through bridging services of an economic and social nature." The Tamil Eelam Society, conforming to ISAP contractual requirements, registered as a nonprofit organization at the community level to deliver direct, essential services to new arrivals, including reception, orientation, translation and interpretation, referral to community resources, paraprofessional counseling, general information, and employment-related services such as job placement. "ISAP Contracts Delivering Settlement and Integration Services," Canadian Department of Citizenship and Immigration, 1996, p. 1.

34. President Mandela's message, *Hot Spring,* London, July 1996, p. 5: "Peace, reconciliation, and development are the most difficult challenges for our troubled world today. It is my profound belief that every effort to stop conflict, wars, and human misery must be applauded and supported. It is our fervent wish and hope that the efforts of organisations such as the Australian Human Rights Foundation and all other endeavours to bring peace and climate for negotiated solution to the conflict in Sri Lanka, will achieve this goal. May

I wish your conference every success in creating a constructive and inclusive dialogue among all role players in order to create a climate where negotiations can thrive and the search for meaningful reconciliation enhanced."

35. Author interview with K. Balasekeran, the LTTE's UK officer in charge from 1983 to 1984, London, August 1999.

36. LTTE leader Velupillai Prabhakaran stated: "Every person from Tamil Eelam, who lives abroad, is a citizen of that country. It is their sacred duty to recover the land of Tamil Eelam. We regard all those who live outside Tamil Eelam and make their contribution as friends of the liberation of the Tamil land." "There Is an Appeal by Vellupillai Prabhakaran Himself," *LTTE*, London, September 1997, p. x.

37. The LTTE "tax" was dependent on the country. But on average, Sri Lankan Tamils living in affluent countries paid about Sterling £200 per year, except Switzerland, where the LTTE taxed the diaspora heavily.

38. In July 1997, LTTE members visited the Tamil shops in London and requested £1,000 per business in donations.

39. Illango Nadarajah, LTTE officer in charge in France, said: "When a contribution is made to the LTTE, we have no right to ask how the money was made." Author interview, Paris, August 1997.

40. The LTTE reportedly made £80,000 from *Talapathi,* in which Rajinikanth, the leading actor in Tamil Nadu, starred. With *VIP,* it is projected that the LTTE will make £20,000 in the UK. A well-received film will be screened in one theater from Thursday to Sunday. In a cinema hall of 800 seats, a ticket will be sold at £10.

41. On that occasion the last film the LTTE contracted was *Talapathi* ("The General").

42. For details on Ukrainian consignment and UK procurement, see "LTTE Arms Smuggling and Procurement Activities," confidential, Sri Lankan Ministry of Defense, 1997, pp. 10–11. See Criminal Investigations Department interrogation report on Satasivam Maheswaran, 1994. On narcotics, see "LTTE Involvement in International Narcotics Trafficking," annex A, confidential, Sri Lankan Ministry of Defense, March 7, 1996; Jas Gawronski, "Report on the Situation in Sri Lanka," European Parliament, Brussels, 1994, p. 8; and Bertil Lintner, "The Drug Trade in Southeast Asia," *Jane's Intelligence Review,* London, 1995 p. 18. On ship captains, see "LTTE International Links, Classification," confidential, Sri Lankan Ministry of Defense, 1992, p. 6.

43. Within the LTTE organization, especially in the military procurement wing, only a handful could read, write, and speak English. Author interview with N. Seevaratnam, first international accountant of the LTTE from 1983 to 1990, London, October 1999.

44. "Sri Lankan couriers have established close contacts with drug dealers and criminal syndicates in Paris, Rome and Amsterdam and have become involved with Indians, Pakistanis, Iranians and Nigerians, all of whom have proved to be significant heroin trafficking nationalities. Majority of Sri Lankan couriers were in possession of false and adapted passports with forged visa endorsements. They also carry separatist political propaganda. It is expected that Sri Lankan and other couriers move in a large quantity of heroin from India and Pakistan to Western Europe." See "Extract from the Country File Sri Lanka, Narcotics," *INTERPOL* Report, February 10, 1986.

45. Mazher Mahmood, "Inside the Tamil Tigers' Drug Racket," *Sunday*

Times, UK, August 30, 1987, p. 1.

46. "Man Has Fingers Cut Off in Revenge Attack," *Enfield Advertiser Series,* April 16, 1997, p. 14. A punishment team, believed to be from the LTTE, cut four fingers of a Tamil courier who failed to hand over the heroin package to them in London.

47. Author interview with Brian Watters, former MI6 station chief, Sri Lanka, December 1996.

48. The International Broadcasting Corporation in Vauxhall, engaged in worldwide dissemination of LTTE and pro-LTTE news, was an LTTE front.

49. In Canada, the premier LTTE front organization, the World Tamil Movement, annually publishes a commerce and business directory with over 1,000 businesses. Both in Canada and in the UK, commercial companies publish similar directories of Tamil businesses. The LTTE is actively soliciting contributions from these businesses.

50. "Socioeconomic Cost of the Sri Lankan Conflict, London," *International Alert,* 1997, p. 3. The budget is not a comprehensive estimate: the LTTE's income from trafficking narcotics and human smuggling has not been estimated by any agency since 1990.

51. Author interviews, Sri Lankan Directorate of Foreign Intelligence, October 2001.

52. The Sri Lankan defense budget is about U.S.$1 billion per year. Estimate is for 2002.

53. "LTTE Organisation in the UK," Sri Lankan Ministry of Defense, 1999, p. 8.

54. 10,000 rupees is equivalent to £200. This amounts to five months' living expenses of an average Sri Lankan family in the peninsula.

55. The LTTE maintained careful records of each family, including their political affiliation and details of relatives overseas.

56. In the LTTE the families of the martyrs enjoy a privileged status—they are called the *maha vira,* or the "great hero" families. Even at public functions there are special seats reserved for these families, who are treated with greater respect.

57. The exceptions were those who had the potential for joining the LTTE. Exceptions were also allowed in extreme cases, either if the family had influence in the LTTE or if the family could make payments.

58. Author interview, LTTE fund collector, July 1998.

59. Author interview, LTTE fund collector, London, June 1997.

60. Ibid.

61. Despite many such rumors, the LTTE has not targeted parents or children of families who do not follow its dictates. The maximum punishment the LTTE has meted out to families perceived to be anti-LTTE has been to ask them to leave the northeast. This has been done to prevent the buildup of an anti-LTTE bridgehead.

62. For instance, the LTTE database in Canada even lists a diasporan's past and current political affiliation. The information also details where the immediate family and extended family live, professional expertise and skills, and even the manner in which the diasporan could assist the LTTE. Author telephone interview with Father Joe Chandrakanthan, LTTE theoretician based in Montreal, July 1997.

63. "Report on LTTE Structure in Switzerland," Ministry of Defense, Sri

Lanka, 1998, p. 7. Murali appealed at a public meeting to the Tamil diaspora in Zurich on July 26, 1997: "Contribute generously so that we [the LTTE] will not have to ask for money from those in the homeland."

64. Author interviews with Tamil diaspora, London, September 2001.

65. See David Bonner, "The United Kingdom's Response to Terrorism," in Alex P. Schmid and Ronald D. Crelinsten, eds., *Western Responses to Terrorism* (London: Frank Cass, 1993), pp. 171–205. The duality of the Western response stems from the argument that earning the wrath of a foreign terrorist group is detrimental to the self-political and security interests of a state.

66. Author interview with Andrew Lennard, head of the UK Ministry of Defense's South Asia Division, September 1997.

9

Burma:
Lessons from the Cease-Fires

JAKE SHERMAN

RECENT SCHOLARSHIP ON CIVIL WARS, NOTABLY THOSE IN SIERRA LEONE, Angola, and the Democratic Republic of Congo (DRC), has emphasized the economic dimensions of conflict.[1] This approach seeks to understand conflict by examining the functions of violence and identifying its beneficiaries,[2] and notes the relationship between natural resources and cycles of competition and conflict over access to and distribution of the economic proceeds of resource exploitation. War has been identified as frequently being or developing into "an alternative system of profit and power" that favors certain groups at the expense of others. In many of these conflicts, violence has been used to control trade, seize land, exploit labor, extract benefits from humanitarian aid, and ensure continued access to economic privileges and assets. For particular groups, sustaining war and evading peace may be an effective way to pursue economic goals. As David Keen has noted, "Part of the function of war may be that it offers a more promising environment for the pursuit of aims that are also prominent in peacetime. . . . [K]eeping a war going may assist in the achievement of these aims, and prolonging a war may be a higher priority than winning it."[3]

Theoretically, however, the same logic that posits that the pursuit of economic self-interest leads to conflict also supports the obverse: economic self-interest can also move combatants to cease hostilities. While observers have noted several isolated instances where nominal combatants have colluded in exploiting lucrative natural resources rather than continue fighting, most often, competition over resources has been viewed as a cause or driver of conflict.[4] To date, there has been little sustained analysis of the way that economic self-interest may contribute to conflict reduction. This chapter seeks to fill this research gap by analyzing the cease-fire agreements between ethnic minority armed groups and the government of Burma.

Since independence, successive governments in Burma have faced active armed rebellion by no fewer than thirty insurgent groups, representing a diverse range of ethnic, political, ideological, economic, and geographically based causes. In many respects, Burma resembles other cases of incomplete state formation, in which peripheral communities have successfully resisted the imposition of central authority. In terms of the sheer number of insurgencies and their persistence, however, Burma may be unique among states of its size and level of development.

Throughout the decades-long conflict, both insurgent groups and government forces have taken advantage of state weakness and engaged in black-market trading in opium, the exploitation of natural resources and other commodities, as well as the taxation of this illicit trade to finance their military pursuits.[5] Yet in a little over a decade since the State Law and Order Restoration Council (SLORC) initiated a policy of seeking cease-fires with ethnic minority armed opposition groups, some twenty insurgent groups have abandoned armed violence against the Burmese regime. Significantly, not all ethnic minority armed groups have been offered cease-fires on the same terms, nor have all groups accepted them. In some cases, however, the cease-fires have lasted more than ten years.

Significantly, these cease-fire arrangements do not adhere to the established pattern of ethnic conflict resolution, wherein ethnic insurgent groups relinquish armed struggle in exchange for grants of local political, cultural, or economic autonomy. In Burma, the terms of cease-fire are not—nor are they portrayed as—agreements on local autonomy, nor have they led to permanent settlements. The government has recognized the right of some cease-fire groups to remain armed and to control territory, but has deferred formal delineation of political rights for minority groups to future constitutional negotiations.

One aspect of what has made the cease-fire agreements both attractive and relatively durable is the economic benefits that they have yielded to key elites on both sides. These benefits are not simply a function of the increased security that has ensued from the cessation of hostilities. In some cases, they have been accompanied by discrete side deals, ranging from the state's acquiescence to the illicit economic activities of ethnic armed groups, to state grants of timber and mineral concessions, to partnerships between state officials and insurgent leaders in lucrative business ventures. For the state, these arrangements have worked to co-opt former opponents, thereby enabling it to consolidate its control in peripheral areas. While economic interests are not the only factor that has influenced this outcome, in many cases they are a significant one. By examining select cease-fire arrangements, this analysis seeks to identify the extent to which economic incentives have led to conflict reduction relative to other political, ideological, strategic, and humanitarian factors, as well as the conditions under which they have done so. The discussion then turns to an appraisal of the trade-offs these bargains have entailed and their implications for a just and sustainable peace. In most cases, they have yielded "negative peace"— characterized by the absence of hostilities—rather than a comprehensive and durable settlement.[6] As long as underlying political and ethnic grievances remain unaddressed, Burma remains vulnerable to renewed cycles of armed conflict.

A Historical Perspective on Conflict in Burma

Burma has experienced continuous civil war of varying intensity since gaining independence in 1948. At present, one can identify two major conflict dynamics within Burma, one prodemocracy and predominantly nonviolent, the other pro–ethnic autonomy and armed.[7] The first, well known to the outside world, is the political standoff between the military government and prodemocracy activists, principally the National League for Democracy (NLD), which won the 1990 multiparty elections, and ethnic minority political organizations represented by the United Nationalities League for Democracy (UNLD). Although the modern prodemocracy movement poses the greatest threat to the government's long-term grip on power, it is not militarized in the manner of the second, and more long-standing, conflict dynamic between, on the one hand, the military government and certain ethnic minority armed groups with which it is informally allied, and on the other hand, opposition armed ethnic minority groups.

These ethnic conflicts are symptomatic of Burma's incomplete state-building process. The government of Burma has never exercised complete administrative control over the country as a whole, particularly the peripheral hill tract territories dominated by ethnic minority groups. Historically, control of the hill tracts by the central Burmese kingdoms was "largely nominal and usually exercised more through feudatory relations than territorial conquest and assimilation."[8] Instead of direct rule, traditional leaders in these areas formally recognized the central government and paid an annual tribute in exchange for autonomy. The absence of real state authority in the ethnic minority areas fostered a sense of independence among local leaders, but at the expense of political integration and economic development. British colonial rule, which administered the "Frontier Areas" separately from "Ministerial Burma," further cultivated a sense of independence among the leaders of ethnic minority states. By the time of Burma's independence from colonial rule, several ethnic minority movements, unsatisfied with their place within a "unified state," were already mobilizing to defend their own "independence."[9]

Since independence, Burma's successive governments have sought to unify the country by consolidating control over the frontier areas, but have faced insurgencies from nearly every ethnic group and political persuasion.[10] Given this history of violent confrontation, it is perhaps not surprising that ethnic diversity and recognition of the rights of ethnic minority peoples are regarded as a threat to state security and stability by the Burman-dominated military government.[11] Consequently, the 16 million ethnic minorities of Burma's approximately 52 million people have endured systematic political exclusion, military repression, and economic underdevelopment in excess of the conditions faced by the Burman majority.[12]

Under the 1947 Panglong Agreement, representatives from the Shan, Chin, and Kachin ethnic groups agreed to a federation with the Burman-dominated central government. Central to the agreement was its fifth clause, which in principle recognized the "full autonomy in internal administration for the Frontier Areas."[13] Additionally, the Shan and Karenni states were granted a right of secession after ten years. In practice, the agreement relegated the border states to "semi-autonomous satellites" of the central Burman state.[14] No other ethnic minority groups were present as delegates in Panglong, nor were they granted a right of secession.[15] During the brief period of postindependence parliamentary democracy, tensions between ethnic minorities and the central government flared.

These conflicts characterized not only a decade of abortive parliamentary rule, but also the era of military rule that has succeeded it. By 1949 the postindependence government faced armed uprisings by communists seeking its overthrow; Karen and other armed ethnic minority groups seeking autonomy, independence, or the reconfiguration of colonial administrative boundaries; and finally, an invasion by Kuomintang (KMT) forces driven into Shan state from China. Relations between ethnic minority groups and the government continued to deteriorate, as ethnic nationalist groups declared their own governments and ethnic minority regiments within the Burmese army defected. Insurgencies broke out in Shan and Kachin states in 1959–1961. These were particularly significant because, unlike other armed ethnic minority groups at the time, the Shan and Kachin had participated in the Panglong Agreement and until then had remained loyal to the Union of Burma.[16]

General Ne Win, the head of Burma's army, established a "military caretaker" government from 1958 to 1960.[17] Following a brief return to parliamentary government—marked by the failure to create a truly multiparty democracy—Ne Win led a second coup in 1962 to counter a proposed power-sharing arrangement between the minority states and the Burman majority areas, which would have granted greater self-governance for each.

The repressive policies of the new military government provoked greater armed resistance from the ethnic insurgents. The "Four Cuts" counterinsurgency policy, designed to defeat armed groups by cutting off their supplies of food, sources of funding, recruits, and intelligence, was introduced in the late 1960s. In practice, the policy targeted the support base of opposition armed groups through the forced relocation, forced labor, and other systematic abuses of basic human rights of civilian populations. Nonetheless, armed opposition continued, such that by the late 1970s, 20–30 percent of the country, including significant portions of the hill territory at the country's borders, was controlled by one or another of over a dozen armed opposition groups. In response, the government systematically restricted basic freedoms and sealed off the country from international trade and outside contact.

In March 1988, antigovernment protests, fueled by cumulative frustrations with the government felt throughout the country, broke out in Rangoon. By August, prodemocracy protests spread throughout Burma's major population centers, with millions of people taking part. In September 1988 the Burma Socialist Program Party (BSPP) government, which ended with Ne Win's resignation in July 1988, was replaced by the SLORC under General Saw Muang. The new government forcibly put down the demonstrations. Dissident students fled to border areas, forming armed resistance groups and linking up with ethnic insurgents in movements such as the All Burma Students Democratic Front (ABSDF) and the Democratic Alliance of Burma (DAB).

The SLORC justified its repressive military rule by maintaining that it was an interim government and, pending the restoration of law and order, would hold multiparty elections. More than two years after assuming power, the SLORC yielded to domestic and international pressure and staged a relatively open multiparty parliamentary election on May 27, 1990. The army-backed National Unity Party (NUP) expected to win easily, owing to political intimidation and a large propaganda campaign against the communists and the "enemies of national unity." It grossly underestimated public opinion. Candidates from Aung San

Suu Kyi's NLD party delivered a crushing defeat, winning 392 of the 485 seats. A coalition of ethnic parties under the UNLD won 67 seats, 23 of which went to the Shan Nationalities League for Democracy, making it the second largest seat-winner after the NLD. The NUP won only 10 seats nationwide. The SLORC quickly backpedaled, claiming that elections had produced the basis for a "constituent assembly" for drafting a new constitution, rather than a parliament, and refused to honor the election results. Once again, the government deployed security forces to enforce martial law and arrest prodemocracy protesters. The government continues to maintain that it is a transitional government, pending the completion of a new constitution. However, the national convention for drawing up the new constitution, established after the 1990 elections, has been suspended since 1996.

Cease-Fire Deals: The SLORC's Gamble Pays Off

Until the SLORC's takeover in 1988, the Tatmadaw (the Burmese armed forces) principally dealt with the ethnic insurgents through outright military assault, counterinsurgency, occupation, and pacification. After 1988 the government adopted a joint strategy of supplementing the Four Cuts counterinsurgency strategy, aimed at compelling local communities to press insurgent groups to seek cease-fires, with political and economic incentives aimed at co-opting these groups' leaderships.[18]

These cease-fire arrangements and the economic interests that underlie them on both sides are central to understanding what is happening in Burma today. As Martin Smith notes,

> As the 1990s drew on, the very existence of such co-operative schemes involving former battlefield foes decisively changed the military and political balance in much of the country. . . . Moreover, by vigorously entering the economic field, the Tatmadaw was to have far more success in seizing the local initiative from armed opposition groups than it had ever had in 26 years of fighting.[19]

The cease-fires initiated by the SLORC and the State Peace and Development Council (SPDC), which succeeded it in November 1997, had their genesis in the spring of 1989, when ethnic minority rank-and-file members of the Communist Party Burma (CPB) rebelled against the predominantly ethnic Chinese CPB leadership. The mutinies spread throughout the CPB's 15,000 troops, splitting the force along ethnic lines into five regional factions: the 12,000-strong United Wa State Party/Army (UWSA), the 2,000-strong (Kokang) Myanmar National

Democratic Alliance Army (MNDAA), and three smaller groups in Shan and Kachin states. The CPB leadership initially blamed the mutinies on local ethnic commanders who benefited from the opium trade and who opposed CPB attempts to rid the party of its connection to the trade. In truth, the defections were triggered by multiple political, economic, and nationalist grievances—not least of which were the war-weariness and frustration experienced by the minorities, who felt they were being used as cannon fodder by the CPB leadership.

Already facing unrest in the cities, the government feared the possibility of an alliance between the former CPB forces, particularly the UWSA and the MNDAA, and the National Democratic Front (NDF)[20] and the DAB,[21] as well as the possibility that the armed groups would arm the thousands of political activists who fled Rangoon in August 1988.[22] To forestall these threats, the SLORC offered cease-fires to the UWSA and the MNDAA. In exchange for promises not to arm the student activists or attack government forces, the UWSA and the MNDAA were given the freedom to pursue any economic activities they chose.

First and foremost, these arrangements were intended as military truces, rather than peace agreements or political settlements. But they proved to be a useful model for dealing with ethnic insurgencies elsewhere in Burma, where counterinsurgency alone was no longer a viable strategy. Following the success of the first cease-fires, armed groups within the NDF came under intense pressure to reach accord with the government. Within minority communities, who had suffered in great numbers from the Four Cuts campaign, support for cease-fires grew among the rank-and-file fighters and their commanders. Among the remaining armed groups, a division emerged between those that supported cease-fires, including the Shan State Army (SSA)/Shan State Progress Party (SSPP) and the Pa-O National Organization (PNO), which signed cease-fire agreements in 1991, and those that remained committed to armed conflict, including the Karen National Union (KNU) and the Kachin Independence Organization (KIO). After the KIO agreed to a cease-fire in February 1994, many other groups rapidly followed suit.[23] Indeed, the majority of armed ethnic minority groups have since accepted cease-fires in exchange for the right to maintain their weapons and control their base territory pending agreement on a new constitution. These cease-fires were backed by promises of economic development through the "Master Plan for the Development of Border Areas and National Races," launched in 1989 and upgraded to a ministry in 1994, and the "allocation" of business interests by the government. Taken together, they indicated an acknowledgment on the part of the government of the importance of economic grievances in fueling ethnic minority rebellion and of redressing them as a means of "national reconsolidation." While these prospects were welcomed in minority areas, both the design of the economic development plan and its objectives were also viewed with skepticism.

Although many within the SLORC worried that the cease-fire process would further jeopardize state security, the gamble paid off.[24] Under the cease-fire policy, the area of Burma under effective state control has steadily increased as the government moves into "liberated zones." The cease-fires have proved to be effective for the government's "divide and conquer" strategy. Within various ethnic minority armed groups, they have provoked the defection of splinter groups to the side of the government.[25] Among groups, the government policy of preventing contact between different cease-fire groups has worked to exacerbate rivalries among them. In this manner, the government has largely succeeded in removing its primary security threats—first, an effective alliance of the ethnic armies, and second, the more threatening possibility of a union between the ethnic minority armies and the majority Burman opposition.

Cease-Fires and Changing Fortunes: Black Markets and Economic Opportunities

During the insurgencies of the 1950s, Burma's armed groups were able to "live off the land" with the support of local communities. By the 1960s, however, a burgeoning black-market trade—fueled by macroeconomic mismanagement and nationwide shortages of essential commodities—enabled these armed groups to increasingly self-finance the procurement of arms and ammunition. The lack of centralized state control over Burma's remote and porous border areas facilitated the extension of regional informal and black-market economies into Thailand, China, and India. Most of those who have engaged in black-market trade have been involved in relatively low-level income-generating commerce intended to supplement meager incomes derived by near subsistence-level production.

Until the early 1990s, many armed groups also had received financial and material support from—or maintained and controlled trade with—Thailand and China. With the introduction of the cease-fire policy by the SLORC and changing geopolitics in Southeast Asia, these external sources of support began to dry up, increasing the reliance of Burma's armed groups on revenue derived from black-market smuggling and illicit trade.

Gaining control over illicit economic activity became essential to the very survival of ethnic minority insurgent groups. In the border areas, they imposed taxation of black-market trade and direct control over the valuable natural resources within these territories. In Kachin and Karenni states, these resources included gems, minerals, and timber; in Karen state, teak, cattle, and luxury consumer goods; in Arakan, rice and medicine; and for many armed groups in Shan state, narcotics.[26] Through the 1990s, at least ten different groups effectively ran the local economies of the territories under their control.[27]

The SLORC has moved to shut down this cross-border trade in two ways: through continued military assaults in non–cease-fire areas, and through the legalization of cross-border trade with Thailand, China, and India in cease-fire areas. Through the cease-fires, the military has gained access to every border in Burma, giving it control of the border checkpoints. Consequently, the majority of non–cease-fire insurgent groups have lost the ability to control and tax cross-border trade, while those cease-fire groups that retain these powers do so at the leave of the government. Most groups are also now unable to obtain resupplies of major military equipment or to counter increased military pressure. In cease-fire areas, the Tatmadaw has been leveraging away control of natural resources from ethnic minority organizations, which receive fewer and fewer of the benefits of exploitation as local Tatmadaw commanders are given rights over mineral resources and receive the majority share in joint ventures with military-run holding companies and outside contractors.

As the leaders of the ethnic armed groups have reaped economic windfalls in logging, mining, and narcotics, often to the exclusion of others within their organizations and the local communities they claim to represent, the preservation of these economic opportunities has provided the military with a powerful negotiating tool. The SLORC, and subsequently the SPDC, have made it materially beneficial for the leadership of certain armed groups to give up their struggle against the government—or to split from and turn against their former compatriots—provided they observe the terms of cease-fire.

The following three case studies briefly examine economic relationships between the SPDC and cease-fire groups in Kachin, Karen, and Shan states. In the first two instances, timber has been a prominent source of financing for insurgency and, following the cease-fires, lucrative business ventures. In the latter case, the principal resource is illegal drugs. There has been an increase in rapacious timber harvesting and illicit production in areas controlled by certain ethnic minority armed groups since their signing of cease-fire agreements. Evidence suggests that, in some cases, business deals were concluded between the government and many of these insurgent groups at the time of the cease-fire agreements. The salience of economic incentives for these groups appears to be increasing. In the case of the Democratic Karen Buddhist Army (DKBA), economic activity has eroded the command structure. Increased economic interest in the cease-fires also implies a widening of the gap between ethnic minority organizations, or at the very least their leaders, and those they represent, in effect undermining their legitimacy. For the DKBA and the UWSA, support for the cease-fires may be contingent upon their continuing profitability, though only in the latter case has the cease-fire strengthened the position of an armed group vis-à-vis the government.

Kachin State

In Kachin state,[28] the Kachin Defense Army (KDA), New Democratic Army, Kachin (NDAK), and KIO cease-fires have resulted in greatly increased exploitation of natural resources, above all timber.[29] Much of this exploitation occurs in concession areas taken over by SLORC/SPDC forces and then contracted to Chinese businesses. However, the leaders of cease-fire groups have also "prioritis[ed] business for themselves through the extraction of natural resources,"[30] negotiating timber concessions with the SPDC, though it remains unclear whether there is any formal arrangement to share profits. Control of logging concessions by the KIO—particularly large-scale projects—could not occur without the consent of the SPDC. Indeed, it is believed that a recently initiated logging project in the north of Kachin state is being carried out jointly by the KIO and under the auspices of the "Border Areas Development Program." In addition to allotting themselves personal concessions, which are then sold to Chinese companies,[31] leaders of the cease-fire groups also benefit from revenues derived from taxation of the timber trade. The proceeds from the concessions go to the leadership of the KIO and regional military commanders but are not redistributed to ordinary Kachin.[32] As timber-fueled corruption has penetrated the KIO, its relations with local communities have become more strained. Overall, logging has had a detrimental effect on the reputation of the organization, its standing among its constituents and international actors, and the security of the territory under its control.

An official at one embassy in Rangoon that formerly regarded the KIO as a "good" armed group—that is, one not allied with the government or involved in narcotics production—has stated that recent activities by the KIO increasingly look like those of "bad" Wa and Kokang groups; it is receiving logging deals and tracts of land from Tatmadaw regional commanders and, as a result, is in the debt of the government.[33] This appears to be supported by the recent coup against General Zau Mai, chairman of the KIO, which was reportedly triggered by discontent among many ordinary Kachin and KIO officers over Zau Mai's business dealings with Burmese generals and businessmen in the southern Chinese province of Yunnan, involving gold and jade mining, and logging concessions in Kachin state from which only he and his family have profited.[34] Although the local population is relieved that, thus far, there has been no resumption of fighting, neither has there been economic development in the region on the scale that had been hoped for.[35] Grievances over exclusion from the benefits of business deals and of broader development, while an advantage to central control, may lead to new violence and instability.

Karen State: The Democratic Karen Buddhist Army

In Karen state, logging was a primary source of revenue for Mon, Karen, and Karenni insurgent groups until 1988, when the SLORC attempted to gain control of the timber trade along the Burma-Thai border. The DKBA split off from the KNU in 1994 and signed a cease-fire returning it to "the legal fold" of recognized ethnic minority groups. According to the Karen Human Rights Group, "The DKBA no longer has clear political objectives or a strong command structure at the higher levels."[36] As a result, officers have been left to find their own means of financing and profit-seeking. Economic self-interest has become, by some accounts, a greater priority than political objectives for many within the DKBA. Recent recruits are reportedly attracted to the DKBA by the power and financial opportunities it provides. The DKBA has sold timber rights in areas under its control to both Burmese and Thai logging companies, in addition to operating its own extraction operations and sawmills. In a pattern seen elsewhere in Burma, local communities are frequently restricted from cutting trees for themselves, and are instead forced to work for the DKBA. Additional income is generated from the taxation of sawmills operated by local communities and by Thai companies—a practice shared by the KNU and the SPDC—and from increasing involvement by some DKBA units in drug production and trafficking, without discouragement from the SPDC.[37]

Shan State's "Narco-Armies"

The most compelling evidence of economic incentives facilitating the signing and maintenance of cease-fires is seen in the activities of the armed groups in Shan state that control the lucrative narcotics trade. Due to inconsistent control efforts by the British colonial administration to place limits on opium production in Burma, the largest poppy cultivation areas in Kachin, Trans-Salween, and Shan states, as well as in the Naga Hills, were left virtually unaffected. Consequently, a thriving illicit trade in opium existed prior to independence, particularly between these areas of legal production and outlying areas where opium was illegal.[38] By the time of independence, control of the industry had moved from local feudal lords and colonial bureaucrats to the proliferating insurgent and counterinsurgent armed groups.

By the late 1970s, the Communist Party Burma had become the largest and best armed of the opposition groups in Shan state—if not the whole of Burma. It controlled large areas of Shan state and, consequently, 80 percent of Burma's opium harvest.[39] After the CPB fractured in 1989, the former CPB forces, particularly the UWSA, could negotiate their cease-fires from a position of strength, as both the NDF forces and the Burmese military competed for their support. The five main emerging factions—the UWSA, the MNDAA, the 768th Military Regional Division (Shan People's Liberation Army), the 815th Military Regional Division (National Democratic Alliance Army), and the 101st Regional Military Division (New Democratic Army)—eventually signed agreements with the military, which offered incentives that the rival NDF was unable to match.[40] In its eagerness to outbid the NDF, the government granted former CPB factions tacit permission to engage in "any kind of business deal needed to sustain themselves"—including opium production, the right to trade inside Burma without interference, and army support for drug trafficking—in exchange for "joining hands with the government." In this fashion, the SLORC secured the cooperation of the former CPB factions under conditions that not only provided a significant degree of political autonomy, but also precipitated an explosion in opium and heroin production.[41]

Initially the CPB and the KMT became involved in narcotics as means of financing military operations, but revenue from drug processing, and the transport and commercialization of narcotics, provided for massive capital accumulation among leaders and various middlemen. Control of narcotics revenue has since transformed the priorities of former CPB factions. As Martin Smith notes, the successors of the CPB and the Ka Kwe Ye (KKY) defense militias "started out with varying degrees of political sincerity, but have inevitably become tainted by the endemic corruption of the international narcotics trade."[42] Under the cease-fires, the lucrative profits of heroin and methamphetamine production in northeast Shan state have in effect become armed business ventures rather than political movements.[43]

Whereas the majority of Burma's armed insurgencies have continued to subordinate economic activity to the goal of securing greater political and cultural autonomy, the insurgencies by armed groups such as the UWSA, the Shan State National Army (SSNA), and the MNDAA, although justified on grounds of ethnic identity and security,[44] have become first and foremost about protecting the highly lucrative black-market trade in narcotics. These cease-fire arrangements have resulted in de facto control over a sizable portion of Burma by private armies engaged in narcotics production.

In general, the leadership of Burma's various armed groups are not accountable to either the rank-and-file members or the local populations they claim to represent. Autocratic leadership is characteristic of nearly all the armed groups in Burma, whether pro- or antigovernment. There is no provision for participatory decisionmaking within any of the armed groups, partly because of personal leadership styles and partly because self-financing through black-market activities has freed these groups from the need to bargain with local populations for their support.[45] This is not to say that these groups cannot claim to have the support of the people, particularly where there is no viable alternative. But the lack of accountability does leave their leadership free to engage in deal-making at the latter's expense, particularly where the alternative is prolonged guerrilla war, if not military defeat. Most ethnic minority armed groups have signed cease-fires under tremendous duress. However, across almost all cease-fire groups, these arrangements have been accompanied by some form of economic incentive—including the promise of economic development and, more immediately, specific business deals to key elites. Based on the subsequent behavior by the leadership of some groups, preserving or securing these economic benefits appears to be a significant incentive for maintaining, if not accepting, the cease-fires.

The Official Unofficial Economy

In 1948 the Union of Burma was widely considered the Southeast Asian country most likely to achieve early economic success. By the end of the Ne Win government in 1988, the "Burmese Way to Socialism" had instead led Burma to the brink of economic collapse. When the SLORC took over in 1988, Burma had less than U.S.$15 million in foreign exchange reserves and it has faced a regular threat of bankruptcy since. Burma's external debt grew steadily between 1989 and 2001 to U.S.$5.85 billion, fueled by increased defense spending and the cessation of most international development assistance and foreign lending. Despite the apparent liberalization of the economy and a 5–10 percent growth in real gross domestic product over the last half decade, today the country faces high inflation, gross overvaluation of the exchange rate, declining foreign investment, export stagnation, and a balance-of-payments crisis.[46] Overall foreign direct investment (FDI) continues to decline—in 1999, FDI amounted to a scarce U.S.$54 million. However, the regime has attracted an estimated U.S.$2.5 billion in oil and gas investment (via the Yadana and Yetagun oil pipelines) since 1988.[47] Burma's financial crisis has been accelerated by Western consumer boycotts, U.S. and the European Union trade sanctions, and the denial of financing, credit, or insurance from the International Monetary Fund and the World Bank.

These circumstances have forced the national government to develop alternative sources of revenue. First, it has increased exports of natural resources, particularly to China; oil, timber, and mining now compose the primary source of government revenue. Much of Burma's resource wealth is believed to be illegally extracted, and at unsustainable levels. Second, the government has expanded its reliance on uncompensated "people's contributions"—or forced labor—to build and maintain energy, irrigation, and transportation infrastructure projects. Third, it has developed greater ties to narcotics producers and channeled revenue from narcotics into formal-sector development projects, facilitated by lax money-laundering legislation.[48] It has been estimated that in 1996, "illegal" activity constituted more than half of Burma's domestic economy. Inflows of funds from exports of opium and heroin alone were worth as much as all legal exports.[49]

Under the SPDC, Burma's economy has been transformed into one of rampant economic opportunism. Control of the national economy, including all formal economic enterprises and much of the organized black market, is concentrated in the hands of a small circle of elites, including military officers, drug warlords, and regional businessmen. Burma has "become home to a growing array of trafficker-linked investments and commercial enterprises, often in overt partnership with the ruling military junta."[50] The cease-fire program has hastened this trend. The UWSA has invested narcotics revenue into Burma's formal economy, in hotels, real estate, transportation infrastructure, and banks.[51] These profits are also believed to have funded large-scale development projects in order to compensate for the shortage of foreign direct investment.

Although certain cease-fire groups engage in narcotics production and trafficking with the apparent permission of the ruling junta, there is no consensus on the degree of actual state complicity. The SPDC officially denies any involvement in the drug trade and has stepped up eradication and interdiction efforts against several producers and traffickers.

Although the U.S. State Department maintains that there is no evidence of any *institutional* involvement by the Burmese government in the drug trade, it does note that there are "persistent and reliable reports . . . that officials, particularly corrupt army personnel posted in outlying areas, are either directly involved in drug production and/or trafficking or are paid to allow others to engage unhindered in drug activities."[52] According to some sources, Burmese military forces provide protection to methamphetamine and heroin production labs, military intelligence escorts trafficking convoys, and border patrol and customs officials that permit them to cross into Thailand.[53]

The government has limited control over large regions of Shan state. Consequently, the UWSA and other major trafficking organizations are largely immune from government action and their territory functions as an autonomous economic zone within the state proper in which they engage in narcotics refining and trafficking. In addition to areas of active insurgency by the Shan State Army–South (SSA-S), MNDAA- and UWSA-controlled territory has remained effectively outside the sphere of central government control under the cease-fire agreements.[54] In 1999 the government called for the eradication of all narcotics activity over the next fifteen years and secured "opium-free" pledges from each armed group involved. These pledges continue to be honored in the breach. Since 2001, when many of these pledges came due, the SPDC has increased pressure on individual traffickers and trafficking groups.[55] The UWSA, however, has escaped law enforcement efforts by the government, in part because its deadline is not until 2005 and because Burmese troops are still reluctant to enter UWSA territory—known as Special Region No. 2—without permission, as this would violate the cease-fire and threaten national security.[56] However, given the alleged involvement of senior military personnel in narcotics, it is also possible that the government has made a calculated decision to crack down on drug-related activities outside of UWSA-controlled territory, publicly demonstrating to the international community that it is "doing something" to control narcotics while continuing to benefit from ongoing narcotics activities inside UWSA areas. The government's lack of territorial control over vast areas of Shan state would enable it to disavow responsibility for narcotics activity by the UWSA, while continuing to benefit. However, if the SPDC is in fact committed to narcotics eradication, the stage seems set for an eventual collision with the UWSA.

One explanation for these divergent assessments is the existence, on the one hand, of a distinct "collective army" strategy, and on the other hand, of individual strategies of members of the military. Whereas collective army interest is based on a shared ideology, common opposition to the claims of the ethnic minority groups, and a desire to unify the country, the latter is based on the economic self-interest of individual officers: "The army strategy is not the sum of the individual strategies. Rather the two overlap in some places."[57] Until recently, the Tatmadaw's twelve regional commanders have wielded enormous power and influence within the regions they control and are well situated to capitalize on economic activities in their territories, including direct and indirect involvement in timber and mining concessions, as well as taxation and provision of security for narcotics production.[58] Indeed, the 1997 reorganization of the SLORC into the SPDC—and the more recent reshuffle—may have been carried out in part to control corruption. However, in a system where corruption is endemic, the reforms appear to have served to consolidate the power of the ruling triad and to "curb the large political and military power bases, which included lucrative and illicit activities, enjoyed by the military regional commanders since 1988."[59]

The regional commanders have also wielded considerable influence within the SPDC ruling circle. The support base of the SPDC is built entirely upon the military. Prior to the reshuffle, the regional commanders held twelve of nineteen SPDC positions as ex officio members. The SPDC acknowledges that a certain amount of corruption is needed to "grease the wheels" of the military and keep it unified on overall policy. In other words, military involvement in narcotics may represent a quid pro quo on the part of the SPDC command. According to one observer, the government as a whole cannot be said to be motivated by this corruption; it would prefer a system of "systematic enrichment"—rather than the existing "messy" system of resource exploitation and the drug trade, which require breaking the law and attracting the ire of the international community. Nonetheless, in the absence of any viable alternative, drug corruption is, at a minimum, tolerated, provided it does not undermine the overall strategy of the military government.[60]

Whether directly or indirectly, the SPDC is dependent on money generated by illicit economic activity, notably to finance—and expand—the Tatmadaw. At present, the military is estimated to comprise 350,000–450,000 personnel, with plans to increase the size of its armed forces to 500,000 by 2004. Burma's defense expenditures currently are equivalent to around 14 percent of its gross national product, the defense sector accounts for 40 percent of public-sector spending, and arms are estimated by the UN Development Programme to account for 20 percent of all imports.[61]

As the SPDC was unable to meet the requisite expenditure for supporting the military, the armed forces were directed in 1997 to become self-financing. Under this economic self-reliance policy, the armed forces are authorized to conduct all types of "business" ventures. For example, all foreign business ventures in Burma must be undertaken as a joint venture with the Union of Myanmar Economic Holdings (UMEH), 40 percent of which is owned by the Defense Ministry's Department of Procurement. A portion of all FDI is thus directly used for weapons acquisition by the military. Yet military finances are believed to extend to illicit economic activities as well. Thai intelligence sources have reported that Burmese units have become increasingly involved in the drug business since the imposition of the self-reliance policy.[62] This raises fundamental questions about the prospects for the success of government efforts to crack down on corruption and narcotics trafficking, as well as the implications of military self-financing for the long-term coherence of the Tatmadaw and any eventual peace. If the military is dependent on its business ventures, then the self-interest of those who benefit financially is likely to perpetuate these relationships. This raises the possibility of future internal divisions within the military should official government policy clash with these interests, particularly in the event of an agreement on government transition between the SPDC and the NLD, which is unlikely to tolerate such activity. The inclusion of ethnic minority groups in this process may further upset these business relationships as the groups seek to reassert greater political and economic autonomy over their territories.

Trade-Offs: Conflict Resolution Versus Political and Economic Participation

The cease-fires have unquestionably benefited Burma's government; in the past five years, overt military challenges to Rangoon's authority from the ethnic insurgents have eased considerably. At the same time, the impact of the cease-fires on economic, political, and security conditions for participating (and nonparticipating) ethnic minority armed groups and, by extension, ethnic minority populations, varies considerably. Generally speaking, the cease-fires have improved physical security in some former conflict zones. Still, promised political dialogue and economic development have not been forthcoming, and thus the deeper causes of conflict remain unaddressed.

　　As one would expect, the reasons underlying decisions by ethnic minority armed groups to cease hostilities are complex and involve many trade-offs. When measured against the political, economic, and social conditions in non–cease-fire areas, the cease-fires have provided varying levels of security and space for engaging in economic activities, the initiation of health and development schemes, and at least the promise of eventual political inclusion, rather than continued repression and intensified military attack. In the last ten years, a growing number of ethnic minority organizations have come to see the provision of basic economic development as a priority equal to that of democracy, and only achievable if they make peace with the government.[63] The sentiment of many ethnic minority groups is that while these conditions are not ideal, they are better than outright war. For armed groups facing the erosion of their military and economic strength, few alternatives to the cease-fires exist. Thus, in the absence of an inclusive process, the current cease-fires may represent the best available hope for a minimum of peace and economic development within the participating ethnic minority states.

The SPDC has affirmed its commitment to the "Master Plan for the Development of Border Areas and National Races," the economic development program intended to increase standards of living within ethnic minority areas. It portrays the development programs as a well-intentioned attempt to improve education, health care, transportation and communications infrastructure, and economic opportunities in areas that have typically been denied such programs.[64] The government lacks adequate funds to fully initiate development programs, though it is clear from recent budget allocations that broad border-area development is not its priority. Following five decades of armed conflict, health care and education remain woefully inadequate in most ethnic minority areas. In contrast, military expansion has continued apace, facilitated by the construction of roads and bridges in minority areas.[65]

The government-sponsored "development" plan is little more than an extension of SPDC counterinsurgency policies. Some ethnic groups have received formal economic opportunities under the cease-fires, including business opportunities with the ruling junta that have not been extended to either the Burman majority or other ethnic minority groups. For example, the Pa-O National Organization has engaged in non–drug-related businesses, including tourism, operating hotels, garlic farming, and jade mining. Elsewhere, however, it appears that border development programs, like the cease-fires, are intended to strengthen the position of the government and its control over the state by dividing and subsequently weakening its opposition.[66] The development programs are "administered by army officers, implemented by soldiers and overseen by the head of the military junta and other top ranking, ethnic Burman military officers whose experience in the border regions is limited to warfare."[67]

Kachin state is illustrative of this phenomenon. Since the KIO and KDA cease-fires in 1994, the overall incidence of forced labor by the Burmese army in Kachin state has reportedly decreased, but other human rights violations have continued, if not widened.[68] Inhabitants of rural areas "have become landless and forced to seek a livelihood in the extractive natural resources sectors or in the service sectors in urban areas."[69] The number of Burmese army troops stationed in Kachin has increased more than tenfold; the KIO, with 4,000 soldiers, now faces fifty Tatmadaw battalions.[70] New communications infrastructure has enabled the government to more effectively locate and monitor its opponents.[71] Indeed, while the government claims that "the city of Yangon [Rangoon] has now become more easily accessible to border regions,"[72] Rangoon also has easier access to the border regions through new and upgraded roads, which enable more effective penetration of armed forces into the border regions.

The cease-fires have resulted in the effective consolidation of state control over formerly contested and "liberated" zones. Military presence has increased not only in territories previously controlled by smaller ethnic minority armed groups, like the New Mon State Party (NMSP) and the PNO, but also in that of the more sizable KIO—though the UWSA-held areas in Shan state remain an exception. The overwhelming majority of cease-fires have held, the oldest of them for nearly twelve years. To date, the 1995 Karenni National Progressive Party (KNPP) cease-fire is the only one to have collapsed and cease-fire violations are infrequent.[73] Nonetheless, tensions between the SPDC and many cease-fire groups—including allied groups like the UWSA and the DKBA—remain high.[74] Simmering tensions are due to efforts by the SPDC to perpetuate fractiousness between rival ethnic minority groups, real and perceived encroachments by the SPDC on groups' territory, its limitations on their economic activities, and above all, the continuing failure to redress underlying reasons for insurgency, including initiation of promised economic development and either local autonomy or a political stake in the central government. The government's consolidation of military strength has resulted in mounting frustrations, yet fewer means of addressing these grievances, as a resumption of military actions is for most groups not a politically or economically viable option.

Paradoxically, the separation between the Wa region of Shan state and the rest of Burma may be increasing at the same time that the business activities of the drug warlords are becoming more integrated into the national economy through the laundering of drug profits into legitimate businesses. Cooperation between the UWSA and the government under the cease-fires has provided the government with some influence in Wa-controlled territory, but continued narcotics activity, as well as forced resettlement and displacement by the UWSA, suggest that it remains beyond the control of the government.[75]

Finally, cease-fires have been neither universally offered nor accepted. Violence persists in southern Shan state, in Karen, Kayah, Arakan, and Mon states, and in the Tenasserim and Sagaing divisions. Anti-insurgency campaigns—both by the military and allied groups—continue over large areas where non–cease-fire groups operate, and consequently continue to directly and indirectly affect civilian populations living in both contested areas and those under the control of the Tatmadaw. The SPDC has threatened to resume fighting with certain Karenni cease-fire groups and the NMSP. In southern Shan state, intra–narcotic group competition over control of trafficking routes and supply chains is particularly acute. Many members of these minority communities believe that violence is part of a larger pattern of state-sponsored ethnic cleansing and genocide. Violence is exacerbated by disputes over territory and control of business among the military and cease-fire groups.[76] The few remaining non–cease-fire groups consequently continue to view any agreement with the government with skepticism.

The persistence of non–cease-fires groups does not imply an unwillingness of these groups in principle to negotiate, but rather a failure—or unwillingness—of the SPDC to provide adequate political and economic incentives to these armed groups. Unlike earlier agreements between the government and the former CPB forces in 1989 and the NDF defectors in 1991, in which the armed groups were allowed to remain armed and to control their forces and territory pending a new constitution, Rangoon has repeatedly demanded that groups more recently seeking cease-fires lay down arms and abandon armed struggle. Both the KNU and the SSA-S sought cease-fires, but were unable to secure them due to demands by the SPDC that the groups disarm—a position the non–cease-fire groups view as tantamount to surrender.[77]

This may indicate the overall success of the cease-fire policy in enabling the SPDC to divide, isolate, and weaken those groups that maintain insurgencies. The state is now selective in its deal-making, and in some cases has little interest in negotiating terms of settlement. For example, given the historical animosity between the Burmese government and the KNU, the military has been fairly consistent in its efforts to defeat the KNU outright. Hence the setting of cease-fire conditions unfavorable to the KNU may reflect a "take it or leave it" attitude on the part of a military that senses its enemy is running out of options and has little to offer.

Ultimately, many ethnic minority leaders would like to see a nation-wide cease-fire accompany the dialogue between the NLD and the government. According to Martin Smith, "they see the ceasefire movement . . . as their own historic contribution to bringing peace and reconciliation to Burma. For as long as the insurgencies continue, the countryside state of tension and insecurity will exist. In the meantime, they point out, their people are no longer needlessly dying."[78]

Conclusion: Implications for Policy Responses

The relatively rapid signing of cease-fires by the majority of armed ethnic minority groups in Burma, the conditions under which the agreements were reached, and the conditions in which they have resulted for ethnic minority communities in Burma have important implications for conflict resolution and sustainable development, both in Burma and more generally.

It is commonly accepted that combatants will seek a negotiated settlement when the costs of war become too great, when available resources are exhausted, or when they reach a stalemate; in other words, when combatants stand to gain more from bargaining than continuing to fight.[79] Yet this insight has not fully informed prevailing theories of "resource war," which view competition over lucrative natural and other resource wealth as a driver of conflict and which posit that conflict will only end once combatants are denied access to these resources.

In Burma, the available evidence suggests that the cease-fires have been driven and maintained both by a desire to avoid conflict and its humanitarian impact, as well as by the economic self-interest of leaders from rival sides, for whom *increased* access to resource wealth is a key motivation for ceasing hostilities. This indicates that, contrary to the prevailing wisdom, the prospect of reaping the financial benefits of natural and other resources may aid rather than hinder conflict reduction. Where combatants have benefited from the control of production and trade of narcotics, timber, and other natural resources in the course of conflict, they may be more susceptible to deal-making to protect their accumulated assets.

In other contemporary armed conflicts, such as Sierra Leone, combatants have been seen to seek temporary, ad hoc arrangements to avoid conflict where there is a mutual interest—such as in deriving economic benefit from the exploitation of natural resource wealth. In most cases, however, these arrangements have been informal and highly localized affairs, rather than a considered strategy of combatant parties. They have also been a symptom of continuing state collapse rather than a source of state consolidation.[80] The cease-fires in Burma, however, do not fit this pattern. They are not unsanctioned arrangements between isolated combatants seeking temporary economic gain. Rather, they are quasi-formal agreements sanctioned by the state that have proven to be both a relatively more durable means of ending hostilities and a means of revenue generation for ethnic armed groups and the state alike. Most important, the Burmese junta has managed to parlay these cease-fires into the consolidation of its economic and military power in territories where previously the state had little effective reach. Here the key determinant appears to be the capacity of the SPDC government to exploit the cease-fires and to back them with the threat of renewed coercion. In this respect, Burma more closely fits the historical pattern of state formation, whereby peripheral areas are incrementally incorporated through a mix of coercion and co-optation.[81]

In Burma, the cease-fire policy has proven a successful—if crude— tool for conflict reduction, having eliminated active armed conflict in much of the country, and without the assistance of international or third-party mediation. But the cease-fires are not formal peace settlements; the parties are neither disarmed, demobilized, nor reintegrated, nor have the underlying issues of political and ethnic exclusion and economic underdevelopment been redressed. Rather, permanent settlement has been deliberately and indefinitely deferred. At best, the result is a "negative peace," punctuated by persistent levels of violence and human rights violations.[82]

As past attempts to fashion a rough and ready peace through economic incentives have elsewhere shown, this strategy is not without serious pitfalls. In Sierra Leone, the Lomé Peace Accord offered Foday Sankoh, leader of the Revolutionary United Front (RUF), chairmanship over the country's strategic resources, thereby permitting him continued exploitation of diamonds. But this did not prevent a return to conflict.[83] Likewise, in Afghanistan, peacebuilding has been accompanied by efforts to co-opt rival warlords with guns and money, thus far resulting in no more than an "ordered anarchy."[84] Thus the economic interests of combatants may provide a basis for ending hostilities, but only if the right economic incentives can be identified and only if economic interests trump the other political and security objectives of combatants. In most cases, however, there are more than economic interests at stake, and the difficulty of identifying the right economic incentives is thereby compounded by the challenge of integrating them into a wider package of political and strategic inducements. In such cases, agreements reached on the basis of economic interests do not lead to sustainable peace because they fail to address the root causes of conflict. As Burma also shows, such cease-fire deals encourage corruption and criminality, exacerbating existing grievances while also creating secondary rivalries, both of which may contribute to new cycles of violence.

The strategic manipulation of the economic incentives of insurgent groups may provide a means of reducing intractable conflicts, but it is unclear whether or not conflict reduction can become a basis for durable conflict resolution. Indeed, as Burma demonstrates, these bargains involve serious trade-offs for sustainable peace and reconstruction. First, they have isolated legitimate actors and further entrenched the social consequences of conflict, including human rights violations, corruption, political exclusion, and underdevelopment. Second, the cease-fires not only condone illicit economic activity, but also create perverse incentives for the pursuit of violence. Groups who are left out of the negotiating process or who believe they have received inadequate gains may continue or resume fighting in hopes of securing lucrative arrangements. A perception of inadequate gains also risks sparking intragroup or intergroup competition. Finally, in many instances, the cease-fires have consolidated the position and power of armed groups, allowing the possibility of resumed violence in the future.

Without the right combination of pressure and persuasion, armed groups are unlikely to give up voluntarily their lucrative involvement in production or taxation of trade in drugs, minerals, timber, weapons, and other commodities or their investments in the formal economy. A key question, therefore, is how to make this activity support a legitimate, productive economy. Where operations are legitimate, but unregulated, incentives for responsible natural resource management must be found. Where operations are criminal, combatants should be given incentives to "go legitimate," such as by maintaining some, if not all, control of their legitimate economic assets, giving them an economic stake in sustained peace. Creating conditions favorable to the pursuit of legitimate economic opportunities may in turn provide the necessary condition for reforming the current formal but still predatory economy through improved political and economic governance, in effect transforming "bandits into bureaucrats." Just as the cease-fires provided a means of separating the pursuit of conflict from the pursuit of profit, driving a "wedge" between the illegal and legal financial agendas of these groups may be one available strategy for curtailing illicit activities.[85]

Burma's cease-fires are neither power-sharing arrangements nor legally guaranteed concessions of autonomy. They have provided ethnic minority groups greater security in the short term, but they do so without significant improvement in political status. Government accountability to ethnic minority groups—and in turn, of these groups to their constituents—remains absent, as does the foundation for long-term, sustainable economic development. For ethnic minority groups dissatisfied with the results of the agreements, there is still no effective recourse beyond the use of armed violence.

To date, the dialogue between Aung San Suu Kyi and the SPDC has not included discussion on the future of ethnic minority areas, nor have the representatives of ethnic organizations been invited to participate in the highly secretive talks.[86] The government claims that it has no mandate to enter into a political dialogue with ethnic groups on the terms of comprehensive peace and power-sharing, because, as an "interim government," it does not have the legal, constitutional authority to negotiate final status.[87] The groups have been invited to participate in the national convention, but the process—now over ten years old without tangible results—is widely regarded as a farce.

Ultimately, ending both the decades-long conflict in Burma and its legacy will require a nationwide cease-fire between the remaining non–cease-fire groups and the SPDC, a resolution of the current standoff between the SPDC and the NLD over the 1990 democratic elections, and the creation of a transparent process to redresses chronic underdevelopment, lack of political representation, and severe human rights violations throughout Burma. Otherwise, violence and insecurity will persist. Under the current regime, such change is unlikely to come about without greater and more directed international pressure and involvement.

Notes

Thanks are due to the many individuals who agreed to be interviewed for this research and who provided comments and feedback on drafts of this chapter.

1. The presence of economic and commercial motivations in conflict is not new, but recent attention has focused on their role in generating and perpetuating "civil wars," particularly in the context of how access to the globalized economy has facilitated profit-seeking through war. Mats Berdal and David M. Malone, *Greed and Grievance: Economic Agendas in Civil Wars* (Boulder: Lynne Rienner, 2000), p. 1.

2. David Keen, *The Economic Functions of Violence in Civil Wars,* Adelphi Paper no. 320 (Oxford: Oxford University Press for the International Institute for Strategic Studies, 1998); Mary Kaldor, *New and Old Wars: Organized Violence in a Global Era* (Stanford: Stanford University Press, 1999); and Berdal and Malone, *Greed and Grievance.*

3. David Keen, "War and Peace: What's the Difference?" in Adekeye Adebajo and Chandra Lekha Sriram, eds., *Managing Armed Conflicts in the Twenty-First Century* (London: Frank Cass, 2001), p. 2.

4. Examples of combatants reaching an equilibrium between conflict and commercial activity include gem, mineral, and timber trading in Sierra Leone, Liberia, Angola, the DRC, and Cambodia. Likewise, in the Balkans, war profiteers reportedly sold fuel across enemy lines.

5. Most notably by Bertil Lintner, *Burma in Revolt: Opium and Insurgency Since 1948* (Bangkok: Silkworm Press, 1999); and Martin Smith, *Burma and the Politics of Insurgency*, 2nd ed. (New York: Zed Books, 1999).

6. As Kimberly Maynard points out, "what peace represents is a contentious question." Kimberly Maynard, *Healing Communities in Conflict: International Assistance in Complex Emergencies* (New York: Columbia University Press, 1999), chap. 6, available online at www.ciaonet.org/access/maynard/maynard06.html (accessed September 23, 2002).

7. There is no absolute distinction between Burman and non-Burman nonviolent and armed struggle. For most of the armed minority groups, the original underpinnings of the conflict had their origins in issues of ethnic autonomy or ideology. However, the events of the late 1980s and early 1990s pushed many of the ethnic armies and prodemocracy groups together, finding common cause in their opposition to the government. Prodemocracy ethnic organizations also exist in above-ground or legal/electoral politics, most notably the United Nationalities League for Democracy (UNLD).

8. Smith, *Burma and the Politics of Insurgency*, p. 39.

9. Lintner, *Burma in Revolt,* pp. 73–76. These groups included the Karen National Union, unhappy with the lack of constitutional provision for a Karen state, and several small movements in the Karenni states and in Arakan.

10. According to the National Coalition Government of the Union of Burma (NCGUB), there are twenty cease-fire groups and twenty-one non–cease-fire groups (NCGUB information sheet, on file with author). A reliable but confidential source lists twenty-three cease-fire groups. It is difficult to determine not only how many and which of the ethnic nationalist groups have signed cease-fires, but also how many groups exist overall. This is compounded by the splitting and merging of factions, many of which are small in size (fewer than 100 troops).

11. Successive military governments—from the BSPP to the SPDC—have been both antifederalist and opposed to ethnic rights, concerned that both would lead to disintegration of the country.

12. Of Burma's 16 million ethnic minority people, Shan and Karen groups make up about 10 percent each, while the Akha, Chin, Chinese, Danu, Indian, Kachin, Karenni, Kayan, Kokang, Lahu, Mon, Naga, Palaung, Pa-O, Rakhine, Rohingya, Tavoyan, and Wa peoples each compose 5 percent or less. The Soros Foundation Burma Project, "Ethnic Groups: Overview," www.soros.org/burma/index.html (accessed April 30, 2000).

13. The Panglong Agreement, quoted in Lintner, *Burma in Revolt,* p. 71.

14. Chao-Tzang Yawnghwe, "Burma: The Politicization of the Political," in M. Alagappa, ed., *Political Legitimacy in Southeast Asia* (Stanford, Calif.: Stanford University Press, 1995), p. 239.

15. The Karen were present as observers.

16. Smith, *Burma and the Politics of Insurgency,* pp. 147, 188, 191.

17. Distinguishing between insurgent groups and opposition parties is still a primary national security concern of the Burmese government, and remains a pretext for government intervention in national political affairs. See Smith, *Burma and the Politics of Insurgency,* p. 174.

18. Author interview, New York, May 14, 2001.

19. Smith, *Burma and the Politics of Insurgency,* p. 441.

20. The NDF remains the best-known insurgent front in Burma, comprising eleven different ethnic armies. Serious differences have always existed within the NDF, including the groups' differing relations with the CPB, and their position regarding narcotics.

21. Shelby Tucker comments that the combined force strength of the remaining insurgents totaled less than 5 percent of the Burmese army, that this strength was scattered and likely incapable of coordinated strategy, and that these insurgents only threatened each other. Shelby Tucker, *Burma: The Curse of Independence* (Sterling, Va.: Pluto Press, 2001), p. 180.

22. This is ironic, given that of the over 10,000 students and civilians who fled to insurgent-controlled territory following the military crackdown in 1988, "an estimated 5000 went to the KNU, 2000 to the KIO and 1300 to the NMSP, but only a few hundred to the CPB. . . . [I]n fact, most of these did not even join the CPB, but its allies the KNLP and SSNLO." Smith, *Burma and the Politics of Insurgency,* p. 371.

23. These included the Karenni State Nationalities Liberation Front (KSNLF), the Karen/Kayah New Land Party (KNLP), the Shan State Nationalities Liberation Organization (SSNLO), all in mid-1994; the KNU-breakaway Democratic Karen Buddhist Army (DKBA), in December 1994; the Karenni National Progressive Party (KNPP), in March 1995, though this cease-fire rapidly disintegrated; the New Mon State Party (NMSP), in June 1995; the Mong Tai Army (MTA)–breakaway Shan State National Army (SSNA), in June 1995; and the MTA itself, founded by drug warlord Khun Sa, which surrendered in January 1996. Several other small groups, not always listed by the government, have also signed cease-fires.

24. Smith, *Burma and the Politics of Insurgency,* p. 445.

25. For example, the Kachin Defense Army (KDA) split from the Kachin Independence Organization (KIO), the Democratic Karen Buddhist Army (DKBA) from the Karen National Union (KNU), and the Karreni National Defense Army (KNDA) from the Karenni National Progressive Party (KNPP).

26. In 1988 the World Bank estimated the value of this trade at U.S.$3 billion, or 40 percent of Burma's gross domestic product. Smith, *Burma and the Politics of Insurgency,* p. 25.

27. Smith, *Burma and the Politics of Insurgency,* p. 94.

28. I would like to thank Global Witness for its generous contribution of background material for this section.

29. Logging by these groups predates the cease-fires, with competition between government and insurgent forces periodically fueling conflict. Yet the rate of deforestation has dramatically increased since the cease-fires. Following its cease-fire, the KIO lost control of Hpa-kan jade mines, which previously provided most of its income, forcing the organization to rely exclusively on timber concessions from the SPDC. John S. Moncreif and Htun Myat, "The War on Kachin Forests," *The Irrawaddy* 9, no. 8 (October–November 2001), available online at www.irrawaddy.org/database/2001/vol9.8/cover.html (accessed November 12, 2001).

30. Burma Ethnic Research Group (BERG), "Internal Displacement in Burma," *Disasters* 24, no. 3 (September 2000), cited in Norwegian Refugee Council Global IDP Database, "Profile of Internal Displacement: Myanmar (Burma),"

version of July 20, 2002, p. 37, available online at www.db.idpproject.org/sites/ idpsurvey.nsf/wcountries/myanmar+(burma)/$file/myanmar%20_burma_ %20-july%202002.pdf?openelement (accessed July 31, 2002).

31. Timber harvested in Kachin is sold exclusively to China at relatively low prices (600–3,600 yuan [U.S.$75–430] per cubic meter) by the cease-fire groups. Author personal communication, July 11, 2002.

32. Author interview, New York, May 14, 2001.

33. Author interview, Rangoon, July 20, 2001.

34. "Myanmar Rebel Group Changes Leadership; Talk of Mutiny," *Associated Press,* February 27, 2001. See also Aung Zaw, "Quiet Coup in Pajua," *The Irrawaddy* 8, no. 2 (February 2000), available online at www.irrawaddy.org/ news/2001/february-1.html (accessed, November 12, 2001).

35. Author interview, Rangoon, July 20, 2001.

36. Karen Human Rights Group, *Consolidation of Control: The SPDC and the DKBA in Pa'an District,* KHRG #2002-U4, September 7, 2002, available online at www.ibiblio.org/freeburma/humanrights/khrg/archive/khrg2002/ khrg02u4.html (accessed November 6, 2002).

37. Ibid.

38. UNDCP, *Global Illicit Drug Trends 2001,* p. 46, available online at www.undcp.org/adhoc/report_2000-09-21_1/prod_opium.pdf (accessed September 29, 2001).

39. Lintner, *Burma in Revolt,* p. 292.

40. Smith, *Burma and the Politics of Insurgency,* pp. 378–379.

41. Burma is the second largest supplier of opium and heroin in the world (after Afghanistan). UNDCP, *Global Illicit Drug Trends 2001,* p. 34. In the first year of the cease-fire, Burma's opium production increased by 37 percent. Production remained relatively stable throughout the 1990s, until 1998, when production began to decline rapidly. Some credit the eradication efforts of the government, which according to the UNDCP has doubled its seizures and arrests. Burma still accounted for 30 percent of world opium production in 1998. In 2000, however, this trend reversed. UNDCP, *Global Illicit Drug Trends 2001,* p. 49. While the increase is not drastic relative to pre-1998 levels, it does raise questions about the cause of the decline and the effectiveness of government eradication efforts, as well as the stated commitment of groups like the UWSA to work toward eradication by 2005.

42. Smith, *Burma and the Politics of Insurgency,* p. 315.

43. In addition to heroin, Burma has become a center for the production and trafficking of amphetamine-type stimulants (ATS)—particularly methamphetamine (or *yaa baa*). Some former insurgent groups involved in opium and heroin production are diversifying into methamphetamines because they are easier to produce and conceal than heroin, yet just as lucrative. An estimated 600–700 million tablets, at the time worth 40 Thai baht (U.S.$1) apiece, were smuggled into Thailand from Burma in 1999. In July 2001, Thai army intelligence sources confirmed the existence of about fifty-five factories in Shan state, run predominantly by the UWSA and MNDAA/Kokang Chinese. Aung Zaw, "New Drug Factories in Laos," *The Irrawaddy,* News Alert, July 17, 2001, www.irrawaddy.org/news/2001/july-11.html (accessed July 17, 2001).

44. Catherine Brown, "Burma: The Political Economy of Violence," *Disasters* 23, no. 3 (1999): 246.

45. Author personal communication, April 17, 2001.

46. Economist Intelligence Unit (EIU), "Myanmar Country Report, 2001–2002"; and EIU, "EIU Country Risk Outlook, June 17, 2002." The SLORC stopped publishing a full breakdown of annual national accounts data in 1998.

47. Xinhua News Agency, "Foreign Investment in Myanmar's Oil, Gas Sector Tops 2.5 Bln Dollars," March 5, 2002, via *BurmaNet News* no. 1977, March 5, 2002.

48. Burma recently passed a new "Control Money Laundering Law" (Law no. 6/2002) intended to prevent individuals from controlling assets purchased with money from illegal dealings, but outside observers regard it as highly flawed. Ko Thet and Ko Cho, "Junta Introduces Money Laundering Law," *The Irrawaddy,* available online at www.irrawaddy.org/news/index.html?#jun (accessed July 2, 2002); B. K. Sen, "Burma's Toothless Money Laundering Law," *Mizzima News,* July 5, 2002, via *BurmaNet News* no. 2038, July 3–5, 2002.

49. U.S. State Department, *1996 International Narcotics Control Strategy Report,* March 1997.

50. U.S. State Department, *1997 International Narcotics Control Strategy Report,* March 1998, www.ibiblio.org/freeburma/drugs/laundry.txt (accessed April 17, 2001).

51. Ibid. For example, in addition to controlling the Mayflower Bank, the UWSA owns one-third of Burma's only GSM (global system for mobile communications) telephone company, gem mines, and probably nightclubs. Pao Yu Chang, the UWSA head, personally controls Yangon Airways. William Barnes, "Burma Tribe Takes Over Bank," *Financial Times,* April 30, 2001. The Asia Wealth Bank, one of the largest banks in Burma, is allegedly run by two former drug lords. Burma's generals are believed to favor laundering their money through the rival Kanbawza Bank, which has close ties to SPDC vice chairman Maung Aye. Maung Maung Oo, "Above It All," *The Irrawaddy* 9, no. 2, February 2001, available online at www.irrawaddy.org/above%20it%20all.html (accessed March 13, 2001).

52. Author interview, Rangoon, July 21, 2001.

53. Des Ball, quoted in "Junta Caught Dealing Drugs," *The Nation* (Bangkok), June 20, 2001.

54. Author interview, New York, May 29, 2001.

55. U.S. State Department, *2000 International Narcotics Control Strategy Report,* March 2001, "Burma, Sec. III.—Country Action Against Drugs in 2001, Law Enforcement Measures," available online at www.state.gov/g/inl/rls/nrcrpt/2001/rpt/8483.htm (accessed September 5, 2001). The MNDAA, the KDA (the former KIO Fourth Brigade), and the MDA in Shan state—under pressure from the SPDC—vowed to create opium-free zones in their territories by 2000. This deadline passed unachieved and was reset for 2001, which also expired with little progress.

56. U.S. State Department, *Narcotics Control 2000.* The SPDC has gradually established a limited police and intelligence presence in the Wa territories, a sign of potentially more assertive pressure on the UWSA to comply with its promise to eradicate opium in its territory by 2005.

57. Author interview, New York, May 29, 2001.

58. In the most extensive shake-up of the regime since 1997, seven senior SPDC members were recently dismissed, two of whom—including Third Secretary Win Myint—were arrested for endemic corruption. An additional ten

regional commanders have been "promoted" from the field to Rangoon. The relocations are likely to give the commanders more privileges, but decrease their power and autonomy. See "Myanmar Revamps Military Hierarchy After Sacking Senior Officials," *Associated Press,* November 13, 2001; "Two Sacked Myanmar Generals Under Interrogation, De Facto House Arrest," *Agence-France Press,* November 13, 2001.

59. International Crisis Group (ICG), *Burma/Myanmar: How Strong Is the Military Regime?* ICG Asia Report no. 11, Bangkok/Brussels, December 21, 2000, p. 4. The government has pursued narcotics-related corruption in the police and armed forces. Although several officers, including one major, were arrested in 2001, the majority of arrests are of rank-and-file personnel. U.S. State Department, *2001 International Narcotics Control Strategy Report,* March 2002, available online at http://www.state.gov/g/inl/rls/nrcrpt/2001/rpt/ (accessed April 1, 2002).

60. Author interview, New York, May 29, 2001.

61. ICG, *Burma/Myanmar,* p. 12.

62. See "Wa and Burmese Commanders Strike New Deal," S.H.A.N., via *Burma Net News* no. 1889, October 1, 2001.

63. See Smith, *Burma and the Politics of Insurgency,* pp. 450–451.

64. "Myanmar Says Lack of Development Aid Is Causing Migration," *Associated Press,* April 2, 2001.

65. Public expenditure declined from 62 percent of GDP in 1985–1986 to 27 percent in 1995–1996, largely in an effort to control fiscal deficits. The social sectors have been hard hit: expenditure on health and education declined by half during this time period. Translated into per capita spending, in 1995–1996 this amounted to less than U.S.3¢ per year for healthcare and roughly U.S.10¢ for education. By contrast, defense spending has remained consistently double that of social sectors, or around 4 percent of GDP, or 222 percent of combined health and education expenditure. UN Working Group, "Human Development in Myanmar," Rangoon, July 1998, pp. 30–33.

66. See "From Scorched Earth to Flooded Earth: The Generals' Dam on Burma's Salween River," Salween Watch Submission to the World Commission on Dams, March 31, 2000.

67. Curtis Lambrecht, "Destruction and Violation: Burma's Border Development Policies," *Watershed,* November 1, 1999, p. 6, available online at www.probeinternational.org/index.cfm?dsp=content&contentid=95 (accessed April 2, 2001).

68. Zaw, "Quiet Coup in Pajua"; and Project MAJE, "Ashes and Tears: Interviews with Refugees from Burma on Guam," available online at www.projectmaje.org/rep0301.htm (accessed July 11, 2002).

69. BERG, "Internal Displacement in Burma," p. 37.

70. Zaw, "Quiet Coup in Pajua."

71. Lambrecht, "Destruction and Violation," p. 5.

72. Quoted in ibid., p. 1.

73. The 1995 cease-fire with the KNPP allegedly broke down over government troop placement, but the SLORC justified the deployment of its troops as necessary to control illegal logging and exports by the KNPP, thus ensuring that it was cut off from both its supplies and the local population. The KNPP maintained its right to extract and sell resources under its control, but SPDC policy gave the state-owned Burma Timber Enterprise a monopoly over all teak

trade. See Vicky Bamforth, Steven Lanjouw, and Graham Mortimer, *Conflict and Displacement in Karenni: The Need for a Considered Approach* (Chiang Mai, Thailand: Burma Ethnic Research Group, May 2000), p. 42; "SLORC Employing Scorched-Earth Policy, Say Rebels," *The Nation* (Bangkok), June 7, 1996, via *Burma Net News* no. 436, June 7, 1996, available online at www.burmanet.org/burmanet/1996/bnet436.txt (accessed October 1, 2001).

74. For example, the NMSP agreed to a cease-fire with the SPDC in June 1995 in response to pressure from both Rangoon and Bangkok. Since that time, there has been little economic progress, and security in Mon state has gradually deteriorated as the Tatmadaw has encroached upon NMSP-controlled territory and several splinter groups from the Mon National Liberation Army (MNLA, the armed wing of the NMSP) have taken up arms. The agreement was accompanied by permission to engage in certain business ventures, including logging and mining, but most of these concessions were canceled by 1998. See Tony Broadmoor, "Precarious Peace in Monland," *The Irrawaddy* 10, no. 2 (February–March 2002), available online at www.irrawaddy.org/cover4.html (accessed April 2, 2002).

75. Under the UWSA's three-year program to relocate 50,000 households, or approximately 250,000 people, since late 1999, 90,000 ethnic Wa have been forcibly displaced from the northern opium-producing Wa region to the Mong Yawn area across the border from Thailand's Chiang Mai province. As many as three in ten of these relocated individuals may be ethnic Chinese from Yunnan province. This resettlement is profoundly altering the demography of areas under Wa control, and shifting the economic, political, and cultural orientation of the region away from Burma and toward China. See Anthony Davis, "China's Shadow," *Asiaweek,* May 28, 1999.

76. "Fireworks of Peace," *The Irrawaddy* 7, no. 8, October 1999, available online at www.irrawaddy.org/database/1999/vol7.8/fireworks.html (accessed April 14, 2001).

77. "The New Face of the KNU," *The Irrawaddy* 8, no. 2, February 2000, available online at www.irrawaddy.org/database/2000/vol8.2/cover.html (accessed April 4, 2001).

78. Smith, *Burma and the Politics of Insurgency,* p. 451.

79. I. William Zartman, "Conflict Resolution: Prevention, Management, and Resolution," in Francis M. Deng and I. William Zartman, eds., *Conflict Resolution in Africa* (Washington, D.C.: Brookings Institution, 1991), pp. 299–319.

80. William Reno, "Shadow States and the Political Economy of Civil Wars," in Berdal and Malone, *Greed and Grievance,* pp. 43–68.

81. Charles Tilly, "War Making and State Making as Organized Crime," in Peter Evans, Dietrich Rueschemeyer, and Theda Skocpol, eds., *Bringing the State Back In* (Cambridge: Cambridge University Press, 1985); and Karen Barkey, *Bandits and Bureaucrats: The Ottoman Route to State Centralization* (Ithaca, N.Y.: Cornell University Press, 1992).

82. Maynard, *Healing Communities in Conflict.*

83. See John Hirsch, *Sierra Leone: Diamonds and the Struggle for Democracy,* International Peace Academy Occasional Paper Series (Boulder: Lynne Rienner, 2001), pp. 81–89.

84. Michael Ignatieff, "Nation-Building Lite," *New York Times Magazine,* July 28, 2002, p. 30.

85. Phil Williams and John Picarelli, "Organized Crime, Conflict, and Terrorism: Combating the Relationships," paper prepared for the IPA conference "Policies and Practices for Controlling Resource Flows in Armed Conflict," Bellagio, Italy, May 20–24, 2002.

86. On March 1, 2001, six groups—the New Mon State Party, the Palaung State Liberation Party, the Shan State Peace Council (Shan State Army and Shan State National Army), the Shan State Nationalities Liberation Organization, the Karenni National People's Liberation Front, and the Kayan New Land Party—signed a joint declaration calling for their inclusion in Burma's political process, particularly in the ongoing talks between the SPDC and Aung San Suu Kyi. In contrast, in January 2001, the UWSA, the MNDAA, the PNO, the KDA, and the New Democratic Army—all considered "friendly" to the regime—were invited to meet with the EU Troika as "ethnic minority" representatives.

87. According to the SLORC, "political problems will have to be solved by the future government and the current National Convention is not meant for solving political problems, but only to set the foundation for a basic political structure." Available online at www.tawmeipa.org/organisation/third_negotiation (accessed November 13, 2001).

PART 3

Conclusion

10

Beyond Greed and Grievance: Reconsidering the Economic Dynamics of Armed Conflict

Karen Ballentine

THROUGH A CONSIDERATION OF THE POLITICAL ECONOMY OF SELECTED CONtemporary conflicts, the chapters in this volume seek to contribute to improved analysis as well as to the strengthening of policy measures for preventing and resolving armed conflicts. Indeed, one of the guiding assumptions of this approach is that a clearer understanding of the economic incentives and opportunities that shape the dynamics of violent conflict can help to identify more precise points for effective policy interventions and to develop a more refined set of tools and strategies for doing so. Such progress, however, critically depends on a considered appraisal of what role different economic factors play in shaping the onset, duration, intensity, and character of particular conflicts. Access to lucrative resources and key global markets may explain how a particular conflict is being fought or it may help explain why. These are, however, distinctly different propositions, with different implications for policy.[1] In drawing out the key findings of these studies, this concluding chapter will focus on what they reveal about the importance to conflict of economic incentives, opportunities, and grievances relative to other political, ideological, and strategic factors. It will also examine what lessons they offer for improved conflict resolution and prevention efforts.

The Contribution of Economic Factors to Internal Armed Conflict

Taken together, the findings of this volume indicate a variety of ways in which economic factors shape the incidence and dynamics of armed intrastate conflicts. Most broadly, they suggest that very few contemporary conflicts can be adequately captured as pure instances of "resource wars" or conflicts caused by "loot-seeking," on the part of either insurgents or state actors. Economic incentives and opportunities have not been the only or even the primary cause of these armed conflicts; rather, to varying degrees, they interacted with socioeconomic and political grievances, interethnic disputes, and security dilemmas in triggering the outbreak of warfare. However, these studies also suggest that, in certain circumstances, combatant access to economic resources has been a salient factor shaping a permissive opportunity structure for sustaining hostilities and has had important effects on the duration, intensity, and character of conflict.

Incidence

In none of the cases studied were economic factors the sole cause of conflict. This observation holds true whether the specific explanatory linkage was the way that the access to economic resources helped shape the incentives of combatants or contributed to the opportunity for insurgent mobilization, or the way that distribution of economic resources provoked popular grievances in support of armed protest. This said, the cases demonstrate a variety of ways in which economic factors combine with political factors to facilitate the outbreak of hostilities.

In the ethnoseparatist conflicts of Kosovo, Sri Lanka, and Bougainville, the main drivers of conflict were the grievances and insecurity bred by the systematic exclusion of ethnic minorities from political power and an equitable share of economic opportunities and benefits. In the first two cases, poor natural resource endowments precluded them from contributing either to the opportunity or to the incentive for rebellion. In the case of Bougainville, as discussed by Anthony Regan in Chapter 6, resentment over the operations of the Panguna copper mine was a prominent factor in the emergence of the Bougainville Revolutionary Army (BRA), but was fused with growing separatist aspirations and a history of anticolonial protest that had shown violence to be a successful strategy for wringing concessions from otherwise indifferent authorities. In conformity with Michael Ross's analysis of the role of nonlootable resources in separatist conflicts in Chapter 3, the central causal dynamic was the way that perceptions of inequitable revenue distribution fueled armed mobilization and reinforced a deep-rooted sense of ethnic exclusion.[2] As Regan underscores, in the absence of security and capital to keep the mine operating, the mine could not and did not yield any immediate economic benefits to the BRA that made rebellion more economically feasible or attractive for those who participated in it. But as Regan also observes, the BRA's ambivalent approach to closing the mine does not fully conform with Ross's assertion that separatist movements will seek to claim ownership of nonlootable natural resources in order to make independent statehood a more viable prospect. Despite the centrality of the mining dispute to the outbreak of armed violence, the conflict in Bougainville, like those in Kosovo and Sri Lanka, was one in which political and socioeconomic "justice-seeking" objectives were prominent.

The cases of nonseparatist insurgencies likewise reveal a more qualified understanding of the ways that economic grievances, opportunities, and incentives may contribute to the incidence of conflict. As in Kosovo, poor resource endowments in Nepal precluded them from contributing to the opportunity or incentive for the Maoist insurgency to begin. Again, accumulated socioeconomic grievances, here emanating from extreme levels of landlessness and exacerbated by the burdens of the bonded labor system upon the lower castes, appear as the most prominent factors shaping the objectives of the insurgencies and their initial ability to recruit supporters.[3] In Colombia, as in Angola, civil war had its origins in the Cold War era as a struggle aimed at state capture that was profoundly shaped by competing ideological visions as to how political power should be constituted and economic wealth distributed. In both cases, contests over lucrative natural and other resources became salient only in the 1990s, as the União Nacional para a Independência Total de Angola (UNITA) lost its former superpower patron and as globalization provided insurgents in both countries new access and opportunities to generate funding through the illicit trade in precious gems and illegal narcotics. As will be discussed below, although playing no significant role in the onset of these conflicts, the engagement of these insurgent groups in the exploitation of economic resources has shaped the subsequent course and character of fighting.

Perhaps most surprising, the cases of Sierra Leone and the Democratic Republic of Congo (DRC)—both commonly viewed as paradigmatic examples of resource-driven or loot-seeking conflicts—reveal a more complex picture. As predicted by the loot-seeking model, both cases featured a high level of primary commodity dependence, which would put them at high risk of civil conflict. However, as Charles Cater finds in Chapter 2, while contests over resources have certainly played a more prominent role here than elsewhere, significantly contributing to the desirability and feasibility of rebellion, the evidence suggests that these insurgencies were not undertaken simply to capture lucrative economic assets. In both cases, the war was rooted in decades of political misrule and corruption by a parasitic state elite and exacerbated by ensuing socioeconomic deterioration and institutional decay. These conditions made the respective Momoh and Mobutu regimes targets of both popular discontent and the ambitions of rebel and external actors at a time of profound regime vulnerability. While capture of lucrative diamond and other natural resources was an early objective of both the Revolutionary United Front (RUF) and the Kabila insurgencies, as well as some of their external allies, so too was a determination to remove unwanted regimes. The salience of this political objective was most clearly borne out by the RUF leadership's decision to forego the lucrative economic benefits of the Lomé Peace Accord in favor of a wholesale offensive to capture the capital of Freetown in 2000, and likewise by Laurent Kabila's takeover of Kinshasa in 1997.

These findings caution against reducing the causes of armed conflict to their putative economic motivations. In all cases, political motivations appear to have been predominant factors in the origin of insurgent and ethnoseparatist movements. Where access to lucrative resources has obtained, combatant motivations appear to have been shaped by a mix of continuing aspirations for political power or independent statehood as well as a desire to capture resources. While some insurgents—such as the Liberation Tigers of Tamil Eelam (LTTE) in Sri Lanka, the RUF in Sierra Leone, UNITA in Angola, and both the leftist insurgents and the right-wing paramilitaries in Colombia—have profited enormously from the economic assets they have acquired through combat, they have also used them to finance military campaigns initiated for other reasons.

While qualifying the loot-seeking theory of rebellion and armed conflict by highlighting the continuing salience of political objectives and socioeconomic grievances, these studies nevertheless underline the important role of opportunity in the incidence of armed conflict. As Paul Collier and others have stressed, objective grievances are not sufficient to impel, let alone sustain, large-scale collective action, such as is required for armed conflict.[4] Much depends on the degree to which the prevailing opportunity structure creates conditions permissive to mobilization.[5] Although Collier places greatest emphasis on the way that the availability of lucrative natural resources shapes opportunity, his model also identifies a number of other economic factors, including low levels of income and education, high levels of unemployment, economic decline, and the availability of diaspora remittances, as well as noneconomic factors such as mountainous terrain that provides rebel groups staging areas relatively secure from counterattack.[6] Virtually all of the cases examined in this volume confirm a positive correlation between economic decline, high levels of poverty and unemployment, and the incidence of armed conflict. More difficult to determine with any empirical certainty is whether these factors operate by reducing the relative opportunity costs of joining an insurgency, as postulated by Collier, or whether they contribute indirectly by fueling grievances among disadvantaged or excluded groups, thereby rendering them more susceptible to recruitment for justice-seeking mobilization. As suggested in the cases of Nepal, Bougainville, Sierra Leone, and Angola, among others, it is likely that both dynamics are at work simultaneously.

The linkages between diaspora remittances and armed conflict have taken on greater salience as the international community has stepped up efforts to suppress terrorist financing in the wake of the attacks of September 11, 2001. Collier's own research has found a significant correlation between the risk of civil war and the size of a country's diaspora relative to the remaining resident population.[7] As indicated by Rohan Gunaratna's analysis in Chapter 8, however, the dispositions of diaspora communities toward homeland conflicts are highly variable. The direction and intensity of homeland attachments are shaped not only by the relative size of the disapora, but also by the circumstances under which individuals emigrated and the prevailing conditions in which they find themselves in their new countries. Among the Tamil diaspora, the most militant supporters of Tamil separatism come from the more recent waves of immigrants and refugees generated by the conflict. In contrast, the earlier waves of largely economic migrants have manifested little solidarity or active support for the LTTE's militant brand of nationalism. The ability of politicized diaspora groups to extend moral and material support to homeland struggles is also shaped by a range of factors, including geographic concentration, socioeconomic status, and the policies of host states regarding citizenship and minority rights as well as the host state's stance toward the homeland conflict itself. Thus Gunaratna finds that diaspora capacity to extend support for homeland struggles is greater where host-country policies of multiculturalism provide political and financial support to immigrant and minority cultural and other self-help organizations.

The role of diaspora remittances likewise can have an ambivalent impact on the opportunity structure favoring conflict. Much depends on the ability of armed groups to capture these remittances. In the case of Kosovo, for example, as long as diaspora remittances remained under the control of Ibrahim Rugova's moderate "Kosovo Republic," they mitigated some of the economic hardships facing Kosovo Albanians as a result of both general economic decline and the exclusionary employment policies Belgrade imposed on Kosovo Albanians after 1989. In underwriting badly needed social welfare services and enhancing the attraction of Rugova's nonviolent approach to independence, diaspora remittances appear to have played a conflict-averting role. Once captured by the militant Kosovo Liberation Army (KLA), however, diaspora remittances helped to finance armed struggle. As this variation suggests, the impact of diaspora remittances on the opportunity for conflict appears to be mediated by other factors. According to Alexandros Yannis in Chapter 7, the factors that shaped the opportunity space for the KLA insurgency were derived from two contingent events: the signing of the Dayton Accords—which encouraged Albanian militancy by rewarding those who had forcibly redrawn the ethnic and political map of Bosnia-Herzegovina, while also discrediting Rugova's strategy of nonviolent separatism—and state collapse in neighboring Albania, which provided the KLA ready access to large stores of military equipment.

These cases also suggest that the opportunity structure favoring insurgent and ethnoseparatist mobilization is shaped by variables that do not figure prominently in Collier's model but that have been identified elsewhere as consequential.[8] Ethnic and other forms of communal solidarity can provide a potent basis for political mobilization when ethnic identities overlap with and are reinforced by salient territorial, political, social, and economic cleavages.[9] In some cases, the social capital generated by ethnic belonging has made armed struggle viable even in the absence of powerful economic incentives and opportunities. In Kosovo, for example, ethnic solidarity, reinforced by political and economic exclusion, not only provided the social capital necessary to sustain a shadow government for the better part of a decade, but it also was sufficiently compelling to attract KLA volunteers from the relative comfort of émigré communities in Western Europe and North America. In Bougainville, where the Bougainville Revolutionary Army had few economic or financial resources to draw upon, ethnic solidarity not only provided a powerful political rationale but also generated the manpower and the matériel necessary for its successful guerrilla campaign. Even in cases such as Burma and the DRC, in which combatant exploitation of lootable resources has figured so prominently, ethnic identity and ethnic capital have been important sources of insurgent mobilization.[10] In these and other multiethnic settings, where economic underdevelopment and political mismanagement have arrested or reversed the process of state formation, one facet of state weakness is the failure to incorporate ethnic minorities into full political and economic citizenship. As one scholar has observed in the African context, ethnic belonging in such cases is not simply a source of identity, but is also a source of livelihood: "ethnic capital ensures . . . the provision of services that a modern state has taken over in rich countries, including security, social insurance, education, norms of behavior, contract enforcement and justice."[11] The overlapping political, economic, and psychological functions of ethnic identity make group mobilization relatively easier. From a methodological standpoint, however, these overlapping dynamics also render efforts to separate economic from other causes of ethnically shaped insurgencies highly problematic.

The opportunity structure for rebellion is also deeply influenced by the relative strength of the state being challenged. In general, the weaker the state, the lower the opportunity costs borne by challengers and the better the prospects of successful insurgency. In Kosovo, Nepal, the DRC, and Sierra Leone, the outbreak of rebellion occurred at moments when both the legitimacy of the state and its military capacity were severely diminished, whether by broad geopolitical shifts, the direction of military assets to conflicts elsewhere, or internally generated corruption and decay that impaired both regime credibility and the coherence and discipline of state militaries in their capacity to fend off challengers. In both Sierra Leone and the DRC, state militaries were in such an advanced state of internal decay that they proved incapable of mounting a credible defense of the state. In the latter case, mass defections of Zairian soldiers allowed Laurent Kabila to take Kinshasa virtually unopposed.

The opportunity structure for rebellion is also a function of the relative capacity of the state to ensure just and effective economic governance. As indicated by Charles Cater, Michael Ross, and Anthony Regan, in natural resource–dependent countries, effective governance is the critical variable mediating the relationship that Collier has posited between natural resource dependence and the opportunity for rebellion. According to Collier's statistical findings, the risk of conflict is greater where the level of a country's dependence on primary commodity exports is around 32 percent of gross domestic product (GDP); the risk is least where there is no significant dependence or where dependence is very high. On his account, where the level is lower, there is less incentive to capture rents. Where the level is higher, he speculates that the reduced likelihood of conflict may be due to the fact that abundant resource wealth provides the government with the means for building a stronger military capacity and thereby making rebellion militarily infeasible.[12] As the Bougainville–Papua New Guinea (PNG) conflict suggests, however, state capacity may be less a function of its resource base than its ability to manage resources effectively. In PNG, revenues from mining, petroleum, and agriculture have been above 40 percent of GDP for over two decades. Yet this revenue did not automatically translate into a more robust capacity of the PNG government to avert or reduce violent conflict (see Chapter 6). Indeed, regardless of its resource base, Port Moresby appears to have been singularly ill equipped to anticipate or respond effectively to the guerrilla campaign of the BRA, despite past episodes of violent unrest.

These studies reveal an additional dimension of state weakness that contributes to the opportunity structure for rebellion. Almost by definition, where economic governance by the state is weak or absent, the greater is the size and relative importance of informal or shadow economies in the life of the societies so affected. In almost all cases examined here, the opportunity for rebellion was facilitated by the prior existence of a sizable informal or shadow economy, whether it was the product of sudden economic decline or of chronic underdevelopment. In conditions of underdevelopment, informal economic activities are typically a critical source of livelihoods, especially for the very poorest members of society, and compensate for the state's incapacity for or neglect of social service provision. Because these activities are, again by definition, unregulated, untaxed, and unrecorded, however, they are highly susceptible to exploitation and capture by criminal organizations as well as insurgent groups. In contexts such as Burma, Sierra Leone, and the DRC, informal trade and commercial networks provided a ready means for insurgents to transform captured natural resources into military finance and matériel.

Finally, the spatial dimensions of state weakness also play a contributing role. Here the opportunity for rebellion is not just shaped by rebel access to mountainous terrain, but also by the limited reach of state authority and capacity in other peripheral areas. The state's coercive capacity is particularly weak in remote border regions, especially those covered by jungle or rainforest. This was the case, for example, in Sierra Leone, where the RUF could wage its guerrilla war from the forests bordering Liberia. Similarly, in the DRC the eastern Kivu province's geographical distance and historical isolation from the central government and coercive state apparatus provided the opportunity for the two successive insurgencies of the Alliance des Forces Démocratiques pour la Libération du Congo/Zaire (AFDL) and the Rassemblement Congolais pour la Démocratie (RCD) to quickly gain ground. In the Bougainville-PNG conflict, the spatial dimension of state weakness was even more pronounced, as the separatist province's remoteness from the mainland capital and its fragmentation into a group of islands made it difficult for the PNG defense forces to subdue the BRA and secure the Panguna mine's operation. Not only does the spatial aspect of state weakness provide insurgents a functional geographical equivalent to mountainous terrain, permitting them relatively safe staging areas, but, as suggested above, it can also provide rebel groups easy access to cross-border trade routes. Taken together, these findings suggest the need for a broader conceptualization of the opportunity structures that favor mobilization for large-scale, organized violence, one that more systematically includes the military, political, sociological, and economic characteristics associated with weak states.

Duration

A major finding shared by several of these studies is that access to lucrative economic resources has figured more prominently in the duration of armed conflicts than in their onset. In Sierra Leone, Angola, and the DRC, continued access of combatant parties to financial resources served to strengthen peace spoilers, thereby sabotaging hard-won peace agreements, while in Sri Lanka and Colombia, the growth of income-generating opportunities available to all combatants—growth that was facilitated by the rapid liberalization of global commerce in the 1990s—provided a major disincentive to good faith negotiations on comprehensive peace settlements. Given the obvious connection between financial and military capacity of combatants, these findings are far from surprising. According to the greed account, economic resources prolong conflict by creating incentives for rebel self-enrichment; that is, wartime profits become so attractive to rebel groups that they prefer the continuation of war to a speedy settlement, which by restoring government control over their territories or demanding redress of their ill-gotten gains may expose them to a net financial loss.[13]

However, this is only one of several possible explanations of how economic resources serve to prolong conflict. First, and most obviously, quite apart from whether they permit rebel self-enrichment, continued or increased rebel access to resources may simply allow them to continue wars being fought for other reasons. Second, the duration of conflict depends to some extent on both the relative accessibility of the resources in question and the way that they are redistributed among rebel cadres. Ross finds that lootable resources, which can be accessed directly by rebel cadres rather than through their chain of command, can prolong conflict by creating discipline problems that make it difficult for leaders to impose a settlement on followers (see Chapter 3). Alternatively, because lootable resources are labor-intensive, they are more likely to benefit a wider segment of the population, a factor that might impact upon the duration of conflict by increasing the dependence of local communities on the illicit exploitation and trade networks controlled by insurgent groups. Third, combatant predation of economic resources may generate second-order grievances and new incentives for predation that multiply the points of conflict, thereby adding to the duration of hostilities. These patterns have been particularly manifest in the DRC and Colombian conflicts, where illicit coca cultivation and coltan mining by combatants have led to significant land displacement.

As both Cater and Ross suggest, the economic resources available to the state are often as important to the duration of conflict as those available to armed challengers. As with rebel groups, these resources may provide either the means for continued combat, the incentive of elite self-enrichment under cover of war, or both. As Ross details further in his comparative study of the role of natural resources, different natural resources have varying effects on the duration of conflict, depending on whether or not they are lootable and/or obstructable, whether the conflict is an insurgency or a separatist struggle, and whether the state or the challenger is the stronger party. Based on this analysis, he finds the duration of insurgent conflicts to be prolonged in those cases where rebels are the weaker party but have access to lootable or obstructable resources, and also in cases where both sides in a conflict have access to these types of natural resource.

Significantly, Ross observes that while separatist conflicts, on the whole, last longer than insurgencies, there is no strong relationship between lootable natural resources and separatist conflicts. This finding is supported by the case of Bougainville, where ethnoseparatist militants managed to sustain an effective guerrilla campaign for nearly a decade without the benefit of lootable or obstructable resources, and in conditions of a fairly robust economic embargo imposed by the PNG government. As this suggests, the duration of separatist conflicts is largely attributable to other factors. In the case of Bougainville, the key factor appears to have been the social capital afforded by ethnic solidarity, a factor that allowed the BRA to supplement the military matériel acquired from battles with PNG security forces with in-kind donations from coethnic sympathizers. In the case of Sri Lanka, the ability of the LTTE to sustain its fight against the well-equipped and highly disciplined Sri Lankan military has been primarily due to its skillful use of coercion, propaganda, and extortion to capture significant amounts of remittances from the Tamil diaspora.[14]

Intensity

Regarding the impact of economic factors on the intensity of armed conflict—as measured by the scope of conflict, the number of battles, and the number of casualties they claim—the findings of these studies are mixed. In Colombia, the 1990s saw a massive increase in the revenues of both the Fuerzas Armadas Revolucionarias de Colombia (FARC) and

Ejercito de Liberación Nacional (ELN) insurgents as well as by Autodefensas Unidas de Colombia (AUC) paramilitaries. As Alexandra Guáqueta observes in Chapter 4, this increase in nonstate armed groups' revenues was directly related to expanded opportunities for combatant self-financing in the illicit trade of narcotics and in the extortion of oil companies operating in remote and poorly defended areas of the country. As she demonstrates further, by the late 1990s these resources had transformed what was previously a relatively contained, low-level conflict between leftist insurgents and the Colombian government into a full-scale war between insurgents, government forces, and right-wing paramilitaries, all of which became larger and better equipped. Indeed, the 1990s saw the ELN insurgents reemerge from the brink of oblivion to become a formidable fighting force with over 5,000 armed men. The escalation of this conflict has been evidenced by its geographic spread from the rural to the urban areas of Colombia, as well as across its borders to neighboring states, and by the increased number of casualties and internally displaced persons. In Sri Lanka, too, the LTTE's control of diaspora remittances and its sophisticated manipulation of opportunities to engage in legal and quasi-legal business ventures both inside and outside Sri Lanka enabled it to purchase more sophisticated and deadly firepower, with a consequent rise in the number of casualties and displaced persons.

In other cases, however, increased access to resources during conflict does not appear to correspond directly with increased intensity. In Angola, for example, the conflict intensified sharply between 1992 and 1994—a period when both UNITA and the government were deriving greater revenues from their respective diamond and oil assets. However, the subsequent four years were marked by sporadic, low-intensity conflict, despite the continuing high levels of financial resources available to both sides. As Cater explains, this shift from total warfare to low-intensity conflict was particularly evident in the diamond-mining areas. This may reflect a tendency noted by other observers of conflicts in Sierra Leone and the DRC, in which the impossibility of any one side securing a full monopoly over lootable resources has, in some instances, offered putative adversaries a compelling incentive for collusion rather than competition.[15]

Character

No conflict is static. There are a wide range of structural and situational factors that can transform the objectives of armed struggle, the strategies and tactics deployed to achieve them, as well as the identity and coherence of combatant forces, state as well as nonstate. As concerns the discrete impact of combatant access to or dependence on lucrative economic resources on the character of armed conflict, however, the key question is whether conflicts that "have begun with political aims have mutated into conflicts in which short-term economic benefits are paramount."[16] Quite clearly, how this question is answered for a particular conflict is a matter of signal importance for the selection of appropriate strategies to resolve it; to the degree that economic priorities have overtaken political ones, combatant parties may prove responsive to interventions that target their cost-benefit calculus.

From a comparative perspective, these cases suggest that the nature and amount of financing available to combatants can shape the evolving character of armed conflicts in consequential ways. In contrast to the state-supported insurgencies typical of the Cold War era, contemporary insurgencies are less centralized and less territorially contained, and are more prone to internal fragmentation.[17] To varying degrees, similar sorts of debilitating effects have been observed on the coherence of state militaries that have increasingly had to fend for themselves. As Ross suggests, how extensive these characteristics are depends upon the type of resource that combatants exploit and the nature of the conflict in question. Specifically, it is access to lootable resources that seems to have made combatant groups more susceptible to problems of internal coherence and discipline. Like states, insurgent and paramilitary groups that derive the bulk of their financial means from the clandestine exploitation of lucrative natural resources and the trade in illegal narcotics may be prone to their own variant of "the resource curse." As in the case of rentier states, where windfalls from abundant natural wealth relieve governments from the need to finance expenditures through taxation, thereby removing a key incentive for accountable governance, nonstate armed groups that are dependent upon lootable resources may have less of a need or incentive to generate and maintain social capital among putative supporters and fewer constraints against indiscriminate forms of civilian predation. Further, as both Alexandra Guáqueta and Jake Sherman observe of insurgent groups in Colombia and Burma, increased combatant access to economic capital may have worked to undermine their acquired social capital, both by enabling quicker rates of recruitment, which may strain a combatant group's ability to socialize new recruits to the group's ideological cause, and by attracting recruits for whom the prospect of financial benefit is more important than ideological conviction or political aims (see Chapters 4 and 9). In either case, these dynamics can alter the political identity and undermine the internal coherence of combatant groups. The corrupting influence of lootable resources may be one reason why the RUF in Sierra Leone and various rebel groups in the DRC—mirroring the regimes they have opposed—have so demonstrably failed to generate a coherent political program or to attract sustained popular support. Conversely, it may also explain the relatively higher level of indiscriminate violence perpetrated against civilians by these groups.[18]

The degree to which these characteristics obtain depends on the conflict in question. Not all rebel groups suffer the same degree of internal fragmentation and decay. And there is a notable variation in the strength and nature of the relationship between rebel leaders, their cadres, and the communities in whose names they claim to be fighting. On the whole, ethnoseparatist rebellions feature higher degrees of coherence, discipline, and popular support over time. One reason may be that ethnoseparatist conflicts tend to be associated with nonlootable resources—resources that, if they are to be exploited at all, require a much greater degree of coordination and social capital. Another may be that ethnoseparatist groups place a higher value on political legitimacy. Indeed, the indispensability of international recognition for their claims to separate statehood to succeed acts as a powerful incentive for these groups to demonstrate domestic legitimacy and support, to exercise a modicum of discipline and self-restraint, and to cultivate and maintain social capital. In some cases, such as in the Shan state in Burma and in some LTTE enclaves, they do so by redistributing wealth they have gained via crude taxation and predation of rival and enemy groups to their own constituents, providing them both physical protection and rudimentary social services.[19]

In general, then, nonseparatist conflicts in which lootable resources figure as a predominant source of combatant financing appear to be the most prone to mutate over time. Whether this tendency also indicates the mutation of erstwhile political struggles into conflicts in which short-term economic interests are paramount is, however, difficult to establish with any confidence. As the studies in this volume suggest, ascertaining either the precise balance of combatant groups' economic and political priorities at any given time or the changing balance of these priorities over time can be highly problematic. Elsewhere, Collier has noted the methodological problems associated with basing these judgments on combatants' self-described purposes.[20] In particular, he argues that rebel discourses cannot be trusted, because combatants always seek to justify their behavior using a "narrative of grievance."[21] But the alternative approach of inferring combatant preferences from their behavior has its own shortcomings. Most certainly, the mere fact of combatant engagement in predatory economic activities is seldom a reliable guide to their central dispositions. In most cases, it is difficult to discern when these economic activities are indeed a paramount concern, and are undertaken for the sole purpose of combatant self-enrichment, or whether they are being pursued strategically, either to finance military campaigns or to redistribute wealth among those they claim as their constituents. Take again the example of the Revolutionary United Front of Sierra Leone. Among analysts, the RUF is often held as the prototypical example of a politically inspired insurgent movement that, when faced with the opportunity to exploit Sierra Leone's lucrative diamond fields, transformed into something more akin to a well-armed, if particularly brutal, criminal gang. In the eyes of many observers, the clearly predatory behavior of the RUF and its incoherent political program together suggested that it was, or had degenerated into, an armed group driven solely by economic self-interest. However, as Cater observes, Foday Sankoh's abandonment of the Lomé Peace Accord, together with its lucrative economic benefits, and his attempt to capture political power in 2000, suggest a more complicated picture in which the balance of RUF priorities shifted "from political to economic back to political." From a certain perspective, the behavior of the RUF still could be construed as consistent with a predominantly economically driven insurgency. Insofar as political power is itself an instrument of economic accumulation and distribution, insurgents may seek to seize power in order to capture wealth as well as deprive rivals of access to it. This may be particularly relevant in settings such as Sierra Leone and the DRC, where the state already has been extensively penetrated and "privatized" by particular patron-client relations and where, in the absence of a robustly institutionalized private economic sphere, the state is not only the chief arbiter of "who gets what, where, and how," but also a direct source of wealth.[22] That said, to view attempts at state capture simply as an economic agenda would deprive the concept of much of its explanatory utility, while also ignoring the degree to which political and economic agendas may in reality be mutually reinforcing.

These observations caution against characterizing rebel groups and the conflicts in which they are engaged as a simple function of their economic activities. All too often, however, an emphasis on the largely illicit nature of rebel self-financing has invited casual assertions that, in the words of one recent study, "much of what has been called war during the past decade—especially in places like Sierra Leone and Angola—is merely an extreme form of criminality."[23] To be sure, while many of the economic pursuits that combatant groups engage in are illicit if not clearly illegal, and borrow from the methods of organized criminal groups, this does not necessarily mean that combatants are "mere criminals" and should be treated accordingly. What distinguishes combatant groups from criminal organizations is not the economic activities pursued nor even the methods employed. Rather, it is the purposes to which these activities are directed. Whereas criminal organizations employ violence in the pursuit of profit, combatant groups employ both violence and predation in the pursuit of military and political goals.[24] Only where armed insurgencies have fully abandoned their political and military objectives in favor of economic self-enrichment can they be characterized as having transformed into a criminal enterprise.

As the studies in this volume show, however, there are no cases in which this organizational transformation can be said to have occurred unequivocally. Despite their extensive involvement in criminal economic activities, for example, neither the KLA in Kosovo nor the LTTE in Sri Lanka have wavered in their pursuit of ethnoterritorial dominance. In the case of the KLA, the economic assets and degree of organization it had developed during the conflict remained intact through the immediate postconflict period, despite the KLA's reconstitution into the Kosovo Protection Corps (KPC). As the subsequent role of former KLA militants in the unrest in neighboring Macedonia and southern Serbia indicates, however, this change did not imply an abandonment of their ethnonationalist program. Likewise, in Colombia, the pursuit of criminal economic activities has not significantly altered the commitment of either insurgent or paramilitary groups to their respective political programs. For this reason, these groups may be more accurately characterized as "hybrid organizations" that combine both political and economic agendas to varying degrees.[25] While their economic concerns may at times complicate or compromise their political and military campaigns, they have not supplanted them entirely.

Policy Implications

As Charles Cater observes in Chapter 2, policy choices for conflict resolution and prevention are deeply influenced by the way a given conflict is characterized. While this may seem an obvious point, it highlights the importance of considering what analyses that posit the primacy of contests over resources or loot-seeking motivations for conflict have indicated for policy action. First, and most generally, they suggest that resource or loot-seeking conflicts may be relatively more amenable to resolution than are other types of conflict. As one analyst has put it:

> At least in one sense, money or financial resources, is a physical entity that can be traced, manipulated, and halted. Economic incentives can fundamentally be influenced and adjusted to serve a given political purpose—be it to tempt a child soldier out of the jungle through a compensation package or depleting the sources of funding for main parties to a civil war. What a welcome news, finally, to be able to substitute the intractable historical myths, obscure cultural differences and frozen ethnic loyalties for something real, tangible, and more easily subject to political manipulation.[26]

Unlike ethnic, religious, or ideological conflicts, which involve nondivisible values such as identity and belonging, conflicts over resources are interest-based contests over divisible goods. Accordingly, if economic incentives are driving combatants to fight, then altering those incentives by measures that move their cost-benefit calculus in favor of peace may also induce them to cease fighting. Such an approach may be particularly apt in cases where combatants have already accumulated significant and identifiable economic assets; insofar as these assets are vulnerable to counterinsurgency and sanction, combatants may seek to cut their losses by negotiating peace.[27] This suggests that there is greater room for third-party mediators to strike bargains for peace. Where such bargains effectively satisfy the acquired assets or vested economic interests of key parties, there would also appear to be a greater likelihood that they will be sustained.

Second, this approach suggests that peace can best be achieved not by long and arduous efforts to negotiate a political compromise, nor by the even more risky approach of direct intervention, but rather by implementing technical measures that, in the short to medium term, will reduce both the accessibility and the profitability of lucrative economic resources to combatant groups.[28] These technical measures encompass the full range of targeted sanctions, including commodity embargoes, aviation bans, and freezing of financial assets, as well as strategies of interdiction developed to deal with transnational organized crime. By denying combatants access to lucrative economic resources, these measures would affect the opportunity for rebellion by raising both the economic and the military costs of fighting to the targeted groups, thereby inducing them to settle.[29]

However, there are a number of reasons to believe that resource-driven conflicts may be less amenable to resolution that this optimistic prognosis suggests. First, as has obtained in some of the cases studied here, combatant groups that are heavily dependent upon lootable resources are more vulnerable to fragmentation, incoherence, and lack of internal discipline. Particularly in cases where soldiers are remunerated indirectly through natural resource concessions or a license to loot, rather than through direct payment of commanders, there will be a high incentive for individual combatants to cut their own deals. The more such defection there is, the greater the number of potential spoilers and the more difficult it will be for combatant leaders to ensure the commitment of followers to peace accords. Second, by definition, lootable natural resources—which these cases indicate are the most closely associated with armed conflict—are inherently difficult to regulate. The ease with which combatant groups in Sierra Leone, Angola, and Colombia have circumvented embargoes on conflict goods and international narcotics interdiction regimes underscores the abiding technical challenge of international sanctions enforcement, particularly in regions where technical and regulatory capacities are weak or nonexistent. Third, even where such efforts do succeed in reducing the volume of trade in conflict goods and the revenue streams they generate, they may not yield the anticipated results. As is well known, sanctions have the effect of raising the value of the targeted activity, thereby increasing the economic incentive for less scrupulous profit-seekers to engage in it. Likewise, rather than inducing combatants toward negotiated settlements, the reduction in revenues from established sources can intensify intragroup competition over spoils, while also encouraging increased predation of available civilian assets to compensate for lost revenues. In either case, there is a distinct possibility that these sorts of supply-side policies will exacerbate both criminality and conflict, at least in the short term.

In several of the conflicts examined here, one or another variant of a policy approach aimed at resolving conflict by influencing the economic incentives and assets of insurgents was adopted by international or state actors. As some of these conflicts have since ended or have been put in abeyance by negotiated cease-fires, there is some basis on which to evaluate the contribution such policies made to these outcomes. UN sanctions against UNITA in Angola and the RUF in Sierra Leone, in particular the embargo on the "conflict diamonds" from which the two rebel groups derived huge revenues, were perhaps the most explicit attempt to resolve conflict by influencing the economic incentives of combatants.[30] Because of the lucrative and lootable nature of these commodities and the lack of regional will and capacity to implement sanctions, they continue to be violated with impunity. However, they did lead to significant reductions in the flow of rough diamonds from these countries and the revenues accruing to rebel forces. While restrictions on these commodities clearly affected the profit margins of these groups, for example by forcing them to sell at below-market rates, their contribution to the subsequent conclusion of peace was far from definitive. In Angola, depriving UNITA of diamond revenues helped weaken its military capacity, but it is arguable that the parallel UN arms embargo, in conjunction with increased supplies of U.S. military training and matériel to the Angolan government, were more important to shifting the military balance in favor of the latter. In any case, as Cater explains, the immediate effect was to transform UNITA from a potent conventional army into an increasingly predatory and defensive guerrilla force. Peace became possible only with the death in combat of UNITA leader Jonas Savimbi in 2002. A similar pattern occurred in the case of Sierra Leone. Neither internationally sponsored efforts to secure peace by offering RUF leader Foday Sankoh continued access to diamond revenues nor subsequent UN sanctions against the RUF induced greater compliance with the orphaned 1999 Lomé Peace Agreement. Ultimately, the RUF's commitment to peace was secured by the serial military interventions of Nigerian and British forces.

Sanctions, in the form of a comprehensive naval blockade, were also applied early on against the Bougainville Revolutionary Army. While unilaterally imposed by the PNG government, Bougainville's complete dependence on sea access made the blockade remarkably effective in preventing flows of arms and money from reaching the insurgents. This comprehensiveness notwithstanding, however, the blockade had little effect on improving the balance of military power in favor of Port Moresby, nor did it help to shorten the conflict. The BRA proved quite proficient in the arts of guerrilla warfare, capitalizing on military resources and other assets made available by the popular support it enjoyed in key regions of the island. As Regan details, the negotiated peace accord of 2001 was the product of a combination of factors, including the accumulated war-weariness on all sides, the ability of the BRA to negotiate from a position of strength, and the mounting economic crisis that confronted the PNG government after 1994. Perhaps most critical was the gradual recognition by the PNG government that its inept use of force to secure the Panguna copper mine had been counterproductive and that the legitimate economic and political grievances of Bougainvilleans could no longer go unaddressed.

With a cease-fire concluded only in February 2002 and still fragile, it would be premature to announce a definitive end to the separatist conflict that has rent Sri Lanka for the last two decades. In the context of ongoing negotiations, there is still insufficient information to offer more than a speculative assessment of the factors that finally led to sustained peace talks. The conflict had already reached the point of a "hurting stalemate" in which no side could expect to gain by further military escalation. On the part of the government, accumulated weariness with the human toll had already led to several abortive efforts to negotiate with the LTTE. A renewed commitment to genuine power sharing was made in 2001, as the economic costs of continuing the war were exacerbated by the regional financial collapse of the late 1990s. Until then, the economic vitality of Sri Lanka outside the LTTE areas had been unaffected by war. By 2001, however, the Sri Lankan economy had shrunk for the first time since the conflict began, mobilizing a perceptible support for peace on the basis of broad autonomy from within the influential Sri Lankan business sector. While the motives of the LTTE still remain obscure, there is reason to believe that their unprecedented willingness to entertain a peaceful resolution of the conflict was partly a strategic response to decisions by Britain, Canada, and Australia to follow the lead of the United States in designating the LTTE a terrorist group.[31] While these policy shifts did not immediately imperil the extensive economic activities of the LTTE, in the wider context of the war on terrorism, a significantly reduced flow of diaspora remittances and revenues from international investments appeared likely, as did increased international support for a more robust Sri Lankan counteroffensive. From this perspective, the LTTE leadership may have calculated that it stood to obtain greater political gains at the bargaining table, or at least bide its time, by entering a cease-fire and negotiating from its present position of strength.

A common supposition of the resource-driven view of armed conflict is that economic incentives of combatants are uniformly conflict-promoting. As long as combatants "do well out of war," they will have an interest in perpetuating conflict and the convenient disorder it brings for their illicit economic pursuits. As Sherman observes, however, these same interests may also provide a basis for the cessation of hostilities. In Burma, conflict reduction has occurred without denying insurgents their base of resource accumulation. The ruling State Peace and Development Council (SPDC) has managed to secure cease-fire agreements from at least twenty ethnic insurgent groups since 1990, most of which remain in place today. In all cases, these cease-fires have been accompanied by economic inducements to insurgents. As long as the insurgents ceased attacks on SPDC forces and in some cases shared their revenues with SPDC members, they were granted lucrative natural resource concessions, tacit allowance to undertake the production of and trade in illegal narcotics, and de facto autonomy over the territories under their control.

Notably, these agreements were not accompanied by any requirement that insurgents disarm or demobilize. Nor were they part of any comprehensive political settlement, which the SPDC has deferred indefinitely. While the success of this strategy of economic co-optation may suggest the predominance of economic motivations and interests among the insurgents so co-opted, it is worth stressing that the incentives of insurgent groups were also shaped by other factors. As Sherman concludes, the use of economic incentives to end active hostilities depends on getting the mix of incentives right. In Burma, the economic inducements to accept a cease-fire were combined with the tacit threat of resumed SPDC counterinsurgency operations. In contrast to Sierra Leone, where the RUF proved impervious to an economic peace dividend, the will and capacity of the SPDC to make credible this threat may have been as important as the prospect of economic gain in securing the acquiescence of insurgent groups. As Sherman also explains, however, the result of this strategy is a negative peace at best. While the SPDC has managed to extend its territorial and political reach and economize its previously overstitched military forces, and while both the SPDC and insurgent elites have derived significant economic wealth from these arrangements, they have done so at the expense of political and economic justice, human rights, and sustainable development. Whether these cease-fires provide the basis for an enduring settlement that will result in a peaceful and prosperous Burma remains very much an open question.

Policy Lessons

Taken together, these studies offer several general lessons to those concerned with improving policies of conflict resolution as well as of conflict prevention. First, the self-financing nature of contemporary insurgency complicates and prolongs conflicts, while creating serious impediments to their resolution. This is particularly true in cases where insurgents have access to lootable resources. Improved international efforts to curtail the illicit supply of these lucrative conflict goods are therefore both warranted and necessary. As the mixed record of such efforts to date would suggest, however, the very lootability of these goods, which renders them susceptible to criminal and rebel capture, also makes them highly resistant to effective regulation. For this reason, regulation that seeks to affect the financial networks underpinning the illicit conflict trade may be more effective than measures aimed at controlling their physical movement. This will require more sustained engagement and coordination between the UN and international financial institutions and law enforcement agencies

Policymakers should also anticipate the unintended negative consequences that sanctions and other supply-side controls may engender.

By raising the value of targeted commodities, sanctions increase the incentives for criminal behavior. This outcome is impossible to avoid. It can be mitigated, but only where policy responses are sustained over time and are as creatively adaptive as the criminality they seek to target. Further, as Ross observes, the labor-intensive and unskilled nature of lootable resource extraction means that, even while yielding massive revenues to combatants, this activity is the basis of survival for large numbers of civilians. Care must be taken to ensure that efforts directed at the former do not harm the latter. Beyond its critical humanitarian value, providing civilians with alternative livelihoods compatible with development may enhance the prospects for peace, by releasing them of their dependence on rebel-controlled enterprises. A similar lesson would apply to diaspora remittances; rather than engage in blanket freezes of all diaspora remittances, policy efforts should aim to deny these funds to combatant groups while allowing them to support humanitarian—and conflict-preventive—ends. This may require governments to be more proactive in creating effective mechanisms for identifying, supporting, and engaging pacific and transparent diaspora organizations, while sanctioning those that fund violence.

Based on the findings of these studies, even the most robust policies of curtailing resource flows to insurgent groups are unlikely to have a decisive or a wholly positive effect on outcomes. Rather than lead directly to a peaceful compromise between rival parties, denying insurgents access to resources serves to shift the military balance in favor of government forces, often intensifying violence in the short term. Tellingly, in those instances where a denial of economic resources has contributed to peace, it has done so not simply by reducing insurgents' profit margins, but by supplementing more direct efforts to undercut their military coherence and capacity, rendering them more vulnerable to government counterinsurgency, and sometimes outright military defeat. In considering this option, then, policymakers should understand that, far from being a neutral, nonviolent alternative to force, the use of economic sanctions in many instances is a highly coercive and partisan instrument.[32]

A related lesson that emerges from these studies is the danger of characterizing insurgent goals and preferences or the wider struggles in which they are engaged by the illicit economic activities they pursue. Undoubtedly, there are insurgents who profit from war, just as surely as there are some for whom personal enrichment is a major objective of armed violence. Even where economic predation is most egregious, however, the political dimensions of the conflict are not entirely overtaken by criminality. Casting insurgents as mere criminals may lead to a profound mischaracterization of what is really at stake, may foreclose opportunities for positive diplomatic engagement, and—at the very extreme—may reinforce existing aversions of the international community to undertake humanitarian interventions. Policymakers should respond by criminalizing the activities, not the groups.

Thus far, efforts to affect the economic dimensions of armed conflict have focused narrowly on the activities of rebel groups. As we have seen, however, both the state-as-institution and the state-as-actor form part of the political economy of armed conflict. In the context of socioeconomic underdevelopment, weak institutional capacity and the corruption of state elites create a permissive opportunity structure for conflict. The high correlation between lucrative natural resources and violent conflict underscores the critical role played by poor governance, not only in fueling political and economic grievances, but also in reducing the costs of undertaking violent challenges. Particularly in natural resource–dependent settings, breaking the vicious cycle of state corruption, rebel predation, and violence will thus require complementary efforts to systematically address the demand side of the problem, both through the creation of more effective, just, and accountable systems for managing natural resource revenues and through longer-term strategies of economic diversification and poverty reduction.

Most of today's conflicts are a complex amalgam of economic, political, ethnic, and security dynamics, in which contests over resources intersect with and often reinforce contests over identity and power. Given the complex and shifting constellation of motivations and interests that sustain conflict, finding the right mix and balance of policy responses remains an abiding challenge for those who seek the resolution and prevention of armed violence. Examining conflicts in terms of their economic dimensions yields important insights into the way that underdevelopment, state weakness, lucrative resources, and the forces of unregulated globalization can exacerbate conflict and impede its resolution. This approach also underscores the urgency of designing more holistic policies of conflict prevention and resolution that integrate economic, political, military, and diplomatic measures. As these studies caution, no conflict can be reduced to its economic aspects. Neither should policy.

Notes

1. As Mats Berdal and David Keen have stressed: "Without a better understanding of the interaction between the political and economic agendas of the parties, the conflict-mitigating efforts of outside actors may have the opposite

effect of what is intended. They may prolong conflict rather than prepare the ground for lasting peace." Mats Berdal and David Keen, "Violence and Economic Agendas in Civil Wars: Some Policy Implications," *Millennium: Journal of International Studies* 26, no. 3 (1997): 807.

2. According to Ross's definition, the lootability of a resource is a function of the ease with which it can be extracted and transported by small teams of unskilled workers. Drugs, alluvial gemstones, agricultural products, and timber are relatively lootable, whereas oil, natural gas, and deep-shaft minerals—the extraction of which requires sophisticated technology and a larger capital investment—are unlootable.

3. By early 2003, however, there were growing reports that the Maoist insurgents have begun to rely on the kidnapping of children for use as soldiers—a sign of the movement's limited ideological and social appeal and possibly also a sign of wider transformation into a predatory force. Amy Waldman, "Nepal: Conflict's Toll on Children," *New York Times,* January 16, 2003, p. A10.

4. Paul Collier, "Doing Well Out of War," in Mats Berdal and David Malone, eds., *Greed and Grievance: Economic Agendas in Civil Wars* (Boulder: Lynne Rienner, 2000), pp. 96–99; Charles Tilly, *From Mobilization to Revolution* (Reading, Mass.: Addison-Wesley, 1978); Ted Robert Gurr, *Minorities at Risk* (Washington, D.C.: U.S. Institute of Peace Press, 1993); and Sidney Tarrow, *Power in Movement: Social Movements and Contentious Politics* (Cambridge: Cambridge University Press, 1994).

5. Tarrow defines opportunity structures as "consistent—but not necessarily formal or permanent—dimensions of the political environment that provide incentives for people to undertake collective action by affecting their expectations of success or failure." Opportunity structures work in combination with internal group attributes, including identity, leadership, and organizational and economic resources. Tarrow, *Power in Movement,* p. 85.

6. Paul Collier, "Economic Causes of Civil Conflict and Their Implications for Policy," in Chester A. Crocker, Fen Osler Hampson, and Pamela Aall, eds., *Turbulent Peace: The Challenges of Managing International Conflict* (Washington, D.C.: U.S. Institute of Peace Press, 2001), pp. 143–162.

7. Ibid.

8. Doug McAdam, John McCarthy, and Mayer Zald, "Towards a Synthetic, Comparative Perspective on Social Movements," in Doug McAdam, John McCarthy, and Mayer Zald, eds., *Comparative Perspectives on Social Movements: Political Opportunities, Mobilizing Structures, and Cultural Framings* (New York: Cambridge University Press, 1996).

9. Donald Horowitz, *Ethnic Groups in Conflict* (Berkeley: University of California Press, 1985).

10. See Koen Vlassenroot, "Citizenship, Identity Formation in South Kivu: The Case of the Banyamulenge," *Review of African Political Economy* 29, nos. 93–94 (2002): 499–515.

11. Jean-Paul Azam, "The Redistributive State and Conflicts in Africa," *Journal of Peace Research* 38, no. 4 (2001): 429–444.

12. Paul Collier and Anke Hoeffler, "Greed and Grievance in Civil War," World Bank Policy Research Working Paper no. 2355 (Washington, D.C.: World Bank, October 2001).

13. David Keen, "Economic Incentives and Disincentives for Violence," in Berdal and Malone, *Greed and Grievance,* pp. 24–25.

14. In Kosovo, the key factor to the speedy termination of hostilities was the robust intervention of the North Atlantic Treaty Organization (NATO) and then the UN Interim Administration Mission in Kosovo (UNMIK). As evidenced by continuing interethnic enmities and the elusive agreement as to Kosovo's final status, it remains to be seen whether peace could be sustained in the absence of international guarantors.

15. Periodic collusion among erstwhile enemies has been a prominent feature of conflict in Sierra Leone, Angola, and the DRC. See Adekeye Adebajo, *Building Peace in West Africa: Liberia, Sierra Leone, and Guinea-Bissau,* International Peace Academy Occasional Paper (Boulder: Lynne Rienner, 2002), chap. 4; and United Nations, "Final Report of the Panel of Experts on the Illegal Exploitation of Natural Resources and Other Forms of Wealth of the Democratic Republic of Congo," UN Doc. S/2002/1146, October 16, 2002. On the relationship between resource predation and the level of violence, see Michael L. Ross, "How Does Natural Resource Wealth Influence Civil War? Evidence from 13 Case Studies," paper presented at the World Bank conference on "Civil Wars and Post-Conflict Transition," UC Irvine, Irvine, Calif., May 18, 2001.

16. David Keen, *The Economic Functions of Violence in Civil Wars,* Adelphi Paper no. 320 (Oxford: Oxford University Press for the International Institute for Strategic Studies, 1998), p. 12.

17. Jean-Christophe Rufin, "Economics of War: A New Theory for Armed Conflicts," in International Committee of the Red Cross (ICRC), *War, Money, and Survival* (Geneva: ICRC, 2000). The AUC in Colombia, the Communist Party of Burma, and the Congolese rebel movements, for example, have experienced various degrees of fragmentation over resource-related disputes.

18. Theodore Triton, "The Political Economy of Sacrifice: Kino's and the State," *Review of African Political Economy* 29, nos. 93–94 (2002): 483.

19. As Sherman also points out, however, internal resentment and competition over the opium trade combined with interethnic resentments of the lower-level recruits to split the Communist Party of Burma in 1989.

20. Collier, "Doing Well Out of War," p. 92.

21. Ibid.

22. Jean-Francois Bayard, Stephen Ellis, and Beatrice Hibou, eds., *The Criminalization of the State in Africa* (Bloomington: Indiana University Press, 1999), p. 8.

23. International Consortium of Investigative Journalists (ICIJ), *Making a Killing: The Business of War* (Washington, D.C.: ICIJ, 2002), p. 2. This view, however, is not limited to journalistic accounts. According to Collier, "Economists who have studied rebellions tend to think of them not as the ultimate protest movements, but as the ultimate manifestation of organized crime." *Economic Causes of Conflict and Their Implications for Policy,* World Bank Study (Washington, D.C.: World Bank, June 15, 2000), p. 3.

24. Phil Williams and John Picarelli, "Organized Crime, Conflict, and Terrorism: Combating the Relationships," paper prepared for the conference on "Policies and Practices for Controlling Resource Flows in Armed Conflict," sponsored by the International Peace Academy, Bellagio, Italy, May 21–23,

2002, pp. 1–3.

25. Ibid., p. 3.

26. Leiv Lunde, *Economic Driving Forces of Violent Conflict,* Econ Report no. 27/01 (Oslo: Econ Center for Economic Analysis, 2002), p. 12. See also Don Hubert, "Taking the Profit Out of War," *Ploughshares Monitor,* June 2000.

27. Marie-Joëlle Zahar, "Is All the News Bad for Peace? Economic Agendas in the Lebanese War," *International Journal* 56, no. 1 (Winter 2000–2001): 123–128.

28. "If economic gain is a prominent motivation for armed conflict, the very basis for the resolution of violent conflict through negotiation is undermined and the search for a political settlement may be futile." Hubert, "Taking the Profit out of War."

29. Collier, *Economic Causes of Conflict and Their Implications for Policy,* p. 20.

30. UN Security Council Resolutions 1173 (1998) and 1306 (2000).

31. The UK undertook this policy change in January 2001; Canada and Australia did so after September 11, 2001, in the wider context of the global war on terrorism.

32. For a fuller discussion of economic and military incentives, see Jeffrey Herbst, "Economic Incentives, Natural Resources, and Conflict in Africa," *Journal of African Economies* 9, no. 3 (2000): 270–294.

Acronyms

ABSDF	All Burma Students Democratic Front
AFDL	Alliance des Forces Démocratiques pour la Libération du Congo
AFRC	Armed Forces Revolutionary Council (Sierra Leone)
AMF	American Mineral Fields
ARI	Andean Regional Initiative
ATS	amphetamine-type stimulants
AUC	Autodefensas Unidas de Colombia
BAT	British American Tobacco
BCA	Bougainville Copper Agreement
BCL	Bougainville Copper Ltd.
BERG	Burma Ethnic Research Group
BIG	Bougainville Interim Government
BIPG	Bougainville Interim Provincial Government
BKI	Babbar Khalsa International
BRA	Bougainville Revolutionary Army
BRF	Bougainville Resistance Forces
BSPP	Burma Socialist Program Party
CIAA	Commission for the Investigation of Abuse of Authority
CIVPOL	Civilian Police (UN)
CPB	Communist Party Burma
CPC	Constitutional Planning Committee (Bougainville)
CPN-M	Communist Party of Nepal–Maoist
CRA	Conzinc Riotinto Australia Ltd.
DAB	Democratic Alliance of Burma
DFID	Department for International Development
DKBA	Democratic Karen Buddhist Army (Burma)

DRC	Democratic Republic of Congo
ECOWAS	Economic Community of West African States
ECOMOG	Economic Community of West African States Cease-Fire Monitoring Group
ELIAMEP	Hellenic Foundation for European and Foreign Policy
ELN	Ejercito de Liberación Nacional (National Liberation Army, Colombia)
EO	Executive Outcomes
ESP	Enabling State Programme
FACT	Federation of Associations of Canadian Tamils
FAR	Forces Armeé de Rwanda
FARC	Fuerzas Armadas Revolucionarias de Colombia
FDI	foreign direct investment
FNLA	Frente Nacional para a Libertação de Angola
GAULA	Unified Action Group for Personal Freedom and Anti-Extortion (Colombia)
GDP	gross domestic product
GNP	gross national product
HDI	Human Development Index (UN)
ICG	International Crisis Group
IDAS	International Defence and Security
IFI	international financial institution
ILO	International Labour Organization
IMF	International Monetary Fund
INGO	international nongovernmental organization
INTERFET	International Force in East Timor
IRA	Irish Republican Army
ISAP	Immigrant Settlement and Adaptation Program
ISS	Institute of Social Studies
JIAS	Joint Interim Administrative Structure (Kosovo)
KDA	Kachin Defense Army (Burma)
KFOR	Kosovo Force
KIO	Kachin Independence Organization (Burma)
KLA	Kosovo Liberation Army
KMT	Kuomintang
KNDA	Karenni National Defense Army (Burma)
KNLP	Karen/Kayah New Land Party (Burma)
KNPP	Karenni National Progressive Party (Burma)
KNU	Karen National Union (Burma)
KPC	Kosovo Protection Corps
KPS	Kosovo Police Service
KSNLF	Karenni State Nationalities Liberation Front (Burma)

LTTE	Liberation Tigers of Tamil Eelam
M-19	Movimiento 19 de Abril (Colombia)
MAS	Muerte a Secuestradores ("Death to Kidnappers," Colombia)
MCC	Maoist Coordination Centre
MIOT	Medical Institute of Tamils
MLC	Mouvement de Libération du Congo
MNDAA	Myanmar National Democratic Alliance Army
MONUA	UN Observer Mission in Angola
MONUC	UN Organization Mission in the Democratic Republic of Congo
MPLA	Movimento para a Libertação de Angola
MTA	Mong Tai Army (Burma)
MUP	Ministarstvo Unutrasnjih Poslova (Ministry of the Interior, Serbia)
NATO	North Atlantic Treaty Organization
NC	Nepali Congress
NCGUB	National Coalition Government of the Union of Burma
NDAK	New Democratic Army, Kachin (Burma)
NDF	National Democratic Front (Burma)
NGO	nongovernmental organization
NLD	National League for Democracy (Burma)
NMSP	New Mon State Party (Burma)
NSPG	North Solomon Provincial Government
NUP	National Unity Party (Burma)
OFERR	Organization for Eelam Refugee Relief
OPM	Organisasi Papua Merdeka (Indonesia)
OSCE	Organization for Security and Cooperation in Europe
P-5	permanent five members of the UN Security Council
PESI	Programme for Strategic and International Security Studies
PGK	Provisional Government of Kosovo
PKK	Kurdish Workers Party
PLA	Panguna Landowners Association
PMG	Peace Monitoring Group (Papua New Guinea)
PNG	Papua New Guinea
PNGDF	PNG Defense Forces
PNO	Pa-O National Organization (Burma)
PPP	purchasing power parity
PWG	People's War Group
RCD	Rassemblement Congolais pour la Démocratie

RIM	Revolutionary Internationalist Movement
RNA	Royal Nepal Army
RPP	Rastriya Prajatantra Party
RTL	Rio Tinto Ltd.
RUF	Revolutionary United Front (Sierra Leone)
SLORC	State Law and Order Restoration Council (Burma)
SPDC	State Peace and Development Council
SPLA	Sudan People's Liberation Army
SSA	Shan State Army (Burma)
SSA-S	Shan State Army–South (Burma)
SSNA	Shan State National Army (Burma)
SSNLO	Shan State Nationalities Liberation Organization (Burma)
SSPP	Shan State Progress Party (Burma)
TCC	Tamil Coordinating Committee
TCG	Tamil Coordinating Group
TES	Tamil Eelam Society of Canada
TNC	transnational corporation
TRO	Tamil Rehabilitation Organization
UCPMB	Liberation Army of Presevo, Medvedja, and Bujanovac
UMEH	Union of Myanmar Economic Holdings
UML	United Marxist-Leninist
UNAMSIL	UN Assistance Mission in Sierra Leone
UNAVEM	UN Angolan Verification Mission
UNDCP	UN International Drug Control Programme
UNDP	UN Development Programme
UNHCR	UN High Commissioner for Refugees
UNITA	União Nacional para a Independência Total de Angola (Union for the Total Independence of Angola)
UNLD	United Nationalities League for Democracy (Burma)
UNMIK	UN Interim Administration Mission in Kosovo
UNODCCP	UN Office for Drug Control and Crime Prevention
UNOMB	UN Observer Mission on Bougainville
UNU	United Nations University
UTO	United Tamil Organization
UWSA	United Wa State Party/Army (Burma)
VDC	Village Development Committee
VJ	Vojska Jugoslavije (Army of Yugoslavia)
WIDER	World Institute for Development Economics Research
WTCC	World Tamil Coordinating Committee
WTM	World Tamil Movement

Selected Bibliography

Addison, Tony, and S. Mansoob Murshed. *From Conflict to Reconstruction: Reviving the Social Contract*. UNU/WIDER Discussion Paper no. 48. Helsinki: UNU/WIDER, 2001.

Addison, Tony, Philippe Le Billon, and S. Mansoob Murshed. "Finance in Conflict and Reconstruction." *Journal of International Development* 13, no. 7 (October 2001): 951–964.

Adebajo, Adekeye. *Building Peace in West Africa: Liberia, Sierra Leone, and Guinea-Bissau*. International Peace Academy Occasional Paper. Boulder: Lynne Rienner, 2002.

Adebajo, Adekeye, and Chris Landsberg. "Back to the Future: UN Peacekeeping in Africa." In Adekeye Adebajo and Chandra Lekha Sriram, eds., *Managing Armed Conflicts in the Twenty-First Century*. London: Frank Cass, 2001, pp. 161–188.

Amnesty International. *Making a Killing: The Diamond Trade in Government-Controlled DRC*. London: Amnesty International, October 2002.

Ayoob, Mohammed. "State Making, State Breaking, and State Failure." In Chester A. Crocker, Fen Osler Hampson, and Pamela Aall, eds., *Turbulent Peace: The Challenges of Managing International Conflict*. Washington, D.C.: U.S. Institute of Peace Press, 2001, pp. 127–142.

Azam, Jean-Paul. "The Redistributive State and Conflicts in Africa." Journal of Peace Research 38, no. 4 (2001): 429–444.

Bamforth, Vicky, Steven Lanjouw, and Graham Mortimer. *Conflict and Displacement in Karenni: The Need for a Considered Approach*. Chiang Mai, Thailand: Burma Ethnic Research Group (BERG), May 2000.

Barkey, Karen. *Bandits and Bureaucrats: The Ottoman Route to State Centralization*. Ithaca, N.Y.: Cornell University Press, 1992.

Bayard, Jean Francois, Stephen Ellis, and Beatrice Hibou, eds. *The Criminalization of the State of Africa*. Bloomington: Indiana University Press, 1999.

Bennett, D. Scott, and Alan C. Stam III. "The Duration of Interstate Wars, 1816–1985." *American Political Science Review* 90, no. 2 (June 1996): 239–257.

Berdal, Mats, and David Keen. "Violence and Economic Agendas in Civil Wars: Some Policy Implications." *Millennium: Journal of International Studies* 26, no. 3 (1997): 795–818.

289

Berdal, Mats, and David M. Malone, eds. *Greed and Grievance: Economic Agendas in Civil Wars*. Boulder: Lynne Rienner, 2000.

Bergesen, Helge Ole, Torleif Haugland, and Leiv Lunde. "Petro-States: Predatory or Developmental?" *CEPLMP Internet Journal* 7, no. 20a (2000). Available online at www.dundee.ac.uk/cepmlp/journal/welcome.htm.

Bildt, Karl. "The Balkans' Second Chance." *Foreign Affairs* 80, no. 1 (January–February 2001): 148–159.

Brown, Michael E. *Nationalism and Ethnic Conflict*. Cambridge: MIT Press, 1997.

Caplan, Richard. "Crisis in Kosovo." *International Affairs* 74, no. 4 (October 1998): 745–761.

Chabal, Patrick, and Jean-Pascal Daloz. *Africa Works: Disorder as Political Instrument*. Oxford and Bloomington: International African Institute, James Currey, and Indiana University Press, 1999.

Christian Aid. *The Scorched Earth: Oil and War in Sudan*. London: Russell Press, March 2001.

Clapham, Christopher, ed. *African Guerrillas*. Oxford: James Currey, 1998.

Clarke, Colin, Ceri Peach, and Steven Vertovec, eds. *South Asians Overseas: Migration and Ethnicity*. Cambridge: Cambridge University Press, 1990.

Collier, Michael W., and Eduardo Gamarra. "The Colombian Diaspora in South Florida." Latin American and Caribbean Center Working Paper no. 1. Miami: Florida International University, May 2001.

Collier, Paul. "Doing Well Out of War." In Mats Berdal and David M. Malone, eds., *Greed and Grievance: Economic Agendas in Civil Wars*. Boulder: Lynne Rienner, 2000, pp. 91–111.

———. "Economic Causes of Civil Conflict and Their Implications for Policy." In Chester A. Crocker, Fen Osler Hampson, and Pamela Aall, eds., *Turbulent Peace: The Challenges of Managing International Conflict*. Washington, D.C.: U.S. Institute of Peace Press, 2001, pp. 143–162.

Collier, Paul, and Anke Hoeffler. "Greed and Grievance in Civil War." World Bank Policy Research Working Paper no. 2355. Washington, D.C.: World Bank, 2001.

———. "On the Economic Causes of Civil War." *Oxford Economic Papers* 50, no. 4 (October 1998): 563–573.

Connell, John. "Compensation and Conflict: The Bougainville Copper Mine, Papua New Guinea." In John Connell and Richard Howitt, eds., *Mining and Indigenous Peoples in Australasia*. Sydney: Sydney University Press, 1991, pp. 55–76.

Cortright, David, and George A. Lopez. *The Sanctions Decade: Assessing UN Strategies in the 1990s*. Boulder: Lynne Rienner, 2000.

Cortright, David, and George A. Lopez with Linda Gerber. *Sanctions and the Search for Security: Challenges to UN Action*. Boulder: Lynne Rienner, 2002.

Council of Europe, Economic Crime Division. "Report on the Planning and Assessment Mission on Corruption, Organized Crime, and Money Laundering in Kosovo (Pristina, 1–4 February 2000)." Strasbourg: Economic Crime Division, Directorate General I, February 11, 2000.

de Silva, K. M. *A History of Sri Lanka*. Berkeley: University of California Press, 1981.

de Soysa, Indra. "Natural Resources and Civil War: Shrinking Pie or Honey Pot?" Paper presented at the International Studies Association annual convention, Los Angeles, March 2000.

Denoon, Donald. *Getting Under the Skin: The Bougainville Copper Agreement and the Creation of the Panguna Mine.* Melbourne: Melbourne University Press, 2000.

Dietrich, Christian. "Power Struggles in the Diamond Fields." In Jakkie Cilliers and Christian Dietrich, eds., *Angola's War Economy: The Role of Oil and Diamonds.* Pretoria: Institute for Security Studies, 2000, pp. 173–194.

Dinnen, Sinclair, Roy May, and Anthony J. Regan, eds. *Challenging the State: The Sandline Affair in Papua New Guinea.* Canberra: Australian National University Press, 1997.

Dove, John, Theodore Miriung, and Melchior Togolo. "Mining Bitterness." In Peter G. Sack, ed., *Problem of Choice: Land in Papua New Guinea's Future.* Canberra: Australian National University Press, 1974, pp. 181–189.

Duffield, Mark. *Global Governance and the New Wars: The Merging of Security and Development.* London: Zed Books, 2001.

———. "Globalization and War Economies: Promoting Order or the Return of History?" *Fletcher Forum of World Affairs* 23, no. 2 (Fall 1999): 21–38.

Elbadawi, Ibrahim, and Nicholas Sambanis. "How Much War Will We See? Estimating the Prevalence of Civil War in 161 Countries, 1960–1999." *Journal of Conflict Resolution* 46, no. 2 (June 2002): 307–334.

Ellis, Stephen. *The Mask of Anarchy: The Destruction of Liberia and the Religious Dimension of an African Civil War.* New York: New York University Press, 1999.

European Commission/World Bank. *Toward Stability and Prosperity: A Program for Reconstruction and Recovery in Kosovo.* November 3, 1999.

Fairhead, James. "The Conflict over Natural and Environmental Resources." In E. Wayne Nafziger, Frances Stewart, and Raimo Värynen, eds., *War, Hunger, and Displacement: The Origins of Humanitarian Emergencies,* vol. 1. Oxford: Oxford University Press, 2000, pp. 154–159.

Fearon, James D. "Why Do Some Civil Wars Last So Much Longer Than Others?" Paper presented at the Civil Wars and Post-Conflict Transitions Workshop organized by the World Bank and the University of California at Irvine, Irvine, May 18, 2001.

Fearon, James D., and David Laitin. "Ethnicity, Insurgency, and Civil War." Paper presented at the annual meeting of the American Political Science Association, San Francisco, Calif., August 30–September 2, 2001.

Filer, Colin. "Resource Rents: Distribution and Sustainability." In Ila Temu, ed., *Papua New Guinea: A 20/20 Vision.* Canberra: National Centre for Development Studies, 1997, pp. 222–260.

Ghai, Yash, and Anthony J. Regan. "Bougainville and the Dialectics of Ethnicity, Autonomy, and Separation." In Yash Ghai, ed., *Autonomy and Ethnicity: Negotiating Competing Claims in Multi-Ethnic States.* Cambridge: Cambridge University Press, 2000, pp. 242–265.

Glenny, Misha. *The Balkans 1804–1999: Nationalism, War, and the Great Powers.* London: Granta Books, 1999.

———. *The Fall of Yugoslavia.* 2nd ed. London: Penguin Books, 1993.

Global Witness. *All the President's Men: The Devastating Story of Oil and Banking in Angola's Privatised War.* London: Global Witness, March 2002.
———. *A Rough Trade: The Role of Companies and Governments in the Angolan Conflict.* London: Global Witness, December 1988.

Gomel, Giorgio. "Migration Toward Western Europe: Trends, Outlook, Policies." *International Spectator* 27, no. 2 (April–June 1992): 67–80.

Gunaratna, Rohan. "Impact of the Mobilised Tamil Diaspora on the Protracted Conflict in Sri Lanka." In Kumar Rupesinghe, ed., *Negotiating Peace in Sri Lanka: Efforts, Failures, and Lessons.* London: International Alert, 1998, pp. 301–328.

Gurung, Harka. *Nepal Social Demography and Expressions.* Kathmandu: New Era, 1998.

Gurr, Ted Robert. *Minorities at Risk.* Washington, D.C.: United States Institute of Peace, 1993.
———. "Containing Internal War in the Twenty-First Century." In Fen Osler Hampson and David M. Malone, eds., *From Reaction to Conflict Prevention: Opportunities for the UN System.* Boulder: Lynne Rienner, 2002, pp. 41–62.

Harden, Russell. *One for All: The Logic of Group Conflict.* Princeton: Princeton University Press, 1995.

Hare, Paul. *Angola's Last Best Chance for Peace: An Insider's Account of the Peace Process.* Washington, D.C.: U.S. Institute of Peace Press, 1998.

Hechter, Michael. *Principles of Group Solidarity.* California Series on Social Change and Political Economy no. 11. Berkeley: University of California at Berkeley, August 1988.

Hedges, Chris. "Kosovo's Next Masters." *Foreign Affairs* 78, no. 3 (May–June 1999): 24–42.

Hegre, Håvard, Tanja Ellingsen, Scott Gates, and Nils Petter Gleditsch. "Towards a Democratic Civil Peace? Civil Change, and Civil War, 1816–1992." *American Political Science Review* 95, no. 1 (March 2001): 17–33.

Hellman-Rajanayagam, Dagmar. "The Politics of the Tamil's Past." In J. Spencer, ed., *Sri Lanka: History and Roots of Conflict.* London: Routledge, 1990.

Herbst, Jeffrey. "Economic Incentives, Natural Resources, and Conflict in Africa." *Journal of African Economies* 9, no. 3 (2000): 270–294.

Hirsch, John L. *Sierra Leone: Diamonds and the Struggle for Democracy.* Boulder: Lynne Rienner, 2001.

Hislope, Robert. "The Calm Before the Storm? The Influence of Cross-Border Networks, Corruption, and Contraband on Macedonian Stability and Regional Security." Paper prepared for the annual meeting of the American Political Science Association, San Francisco, August 30–September 2, 2001.

Hoffman, Bruce, and Donna Kim Hoffman. "The Rand–St. Andrews Chronology of International Terrorist Incidents, 1995." *Terrorism and Political Violence* 8, no. 3 (Autumn 1996): 87–127.

Holbrooke, Richard. *To End a War.* New York: Modern Library, 1999.

Horowitz, Donald. *Ethnic Groups in Conflict.* Berkeley: University of California Press, 1985.

Hubert, Don. "Taking the Profit Out of War." *Ploughshares Monitor,* June 2000.

Human Rights Watch. *Angola Unravels: The Rise and Fall of the Lusaka Peace Process.* New York: Human Rights Watch, 1999.

———. "Federal Republic of Yugoslavia: Abuses Against Serbs and Roma in the New Kosovo." *Report Series* 11, no. 10 (D) (August 1999).

———. *The "Sixth Division": Military-Paramilitary Ties and U.S. Policy in Colombia.* New York: Human Rights Watch, 2001.

Humphreys, Macartan. "Economics and Violent Conflict." Harvard University, August 2002. Available online at www.preventconflict.org/portal/economics/login.php.

International Consortium of Investigative Journalists. *Making a Killing: The Business of War.* Washington, D.C., 2002.

International Crisis Group (ICG). "Disarmament in the Congo: Investing in Conflict Prevention." Africa Briefing Paper. Brussels: ICG, June 12, 2001.

———. *Kosovo: A Strategy for Economic Development.* Balkans Report no. 123. Pristina: ICG, December 19, 2001.

———. "Trepca: Making Sense of the Labyrinth." ICG Balkans Report no. 82. Washington, D.C.: ICG, November 26, 1999.

Judah, Tim. *Kosovo: War and Revenge.* New Haven, Conn.: Yale University Press, 2000.

Kagwanja, Peter Mwangi, and Gloria Ntegeye. "Regional Conflict Formations in the Great Lakes of Africa: Dynamics and Challenges for Policy." Summary Report of the Nairobi Conference, November 2001. New York: Center on International Cooperation. Available online at www.nyu.edu/pages/cic/pdf/rcf_nairobi.pdf.

Kaldor, Mary. *New and Old Wars: Organized Violence in a Global Era.* Stanford: Stanford University Press, 1999.

Kaputin, J. R. *Crisis in the North Solomons Province: Report of the Special Committee Appointed by the National Executive Council.* Port Moresby: Department of the Prime Minister, 1992.

Karki, Arjun K. "The Politics of Poverty and Movements from Below in Nepal." Ph.D. diss., Norwich, UK, University of East Anglia, 2001.

Keen, David. *The Economic Functions of Violence in Civil Wars.* Adelphi Paper no. 320. Oxford: Oxford University Press for the International Institute for Strategic Studies, 1998.

———. "Economic Incentives and Disincentives for Violence." In Mats Berdal and David M. Malone, eds., *Greed and Grievance: Economic Agendas in Civil Wars.* Boulder: Lynne Rienner, 2000, pp. 19–41.

———. "War and Peace: What's the Difference?" In Adekeye Adebajo and Chandra Lekha Sriram, eds., *Managing Armed Conflicts in the Twenty-First Century.* London: Frank Cass, 2001, pp. 1–22.

King, Charles. *Ending Civil Wars.* Adelphi Paper no. 308. Oxford: Oxford University Press for the International Institute for Strategic Studies, 1997.

Klare, Michael. *Resource Wars: The New Landscape of Global Conflict.* New York: Metropolitan Books, 2001.

Klare, Michael, and David Andersen. *A Scourge of Guns: The Diffusion of Small Arms and Light Weapons in Latin America.* Washington, D.C.: Federation of American Scientists, 1996.

Larmour, Peter. "The Politics of Race and Ethnicity: Theoretical Perspectives on Papua New Guinea." *Pacific Studies* 15, no. 2 (1992): 87–108.

Lawyers Committee for Human Rights (LCHR). *A Fragile Peace: Laying the Foundation for Justice in Kosovo.* New York: LCHR, October 1999.

Le Billon, Philippe. "The Political Ecology of War: Natural Resources and Armed Conflicts." *Political Geography* 20, no. 5 (June 2001): 561–584.

———. "The Political Economy of Resource Wars." In Jakkie Cilliers and Christian Dietrich, eds., *Angola's War Economy: The Role of Oil and Diamonds.* Pretoria: Institute of Security Studies, 2000, pp. 21–42.

Lintner, Bertil. *Burma in Revolt: Opium and Insurgency Since 1948.* Bangkok: Silkworm Press, 1999.

———. "The Drug Trade in Southeast Asia." *Jane's Intelligence Review,* London, 1995.

Loescher, Gil. *Refugee Movements and International Security.* Adelphi Paper no. 268. Oxford: Oxford University Press for the International Institute for Strategic Studies, 1992.

Lunde, Leiv. *Economic Driving Forces of Violent Conflict.* Econ Report number 27/01. Oslo: Econ Center for Economic Analysis, 2002.

Malcolm, Noel. *Kosovo: A Short History.* London: Macmillan, 1998.

May, R. J., and Matthew Spriggs, eds. *The Bougainville Crisis.* Bathurst: Crawford House Press, 1990.

Maynard, Kimberly. *Healing Communities in Conflict: International Assistance in Complex Emergencies.* New York: Columbia University Press, 1999.

McAdam, Doug, John McCarthy, and Mayer Zald. "Towards a Synthetic, Comparative Perspective on Social Movements." In Doug McAdam, John McCarthy, and Mayer Zald, eds., *Comparative Perspectives on Social Movements: Political Opportunities, Mobilizing Structures, and Cultural Framings.* New York: Cambridge University Press, 1996.

Mikesell, R. F. *Foreign Investment in Copper Mining: Case Studies of Mines in Peru and Papua New Guinea.* Baltimore: Johns Hopkins University Press, 1975.

Murshed, S. Mansoob. "On Natural Resource Abundance and Underdevelopment." Background Paper for the *World Development Report 2003.* Washington, D.C.: World Bank, 2002.

Mwanasali, Musifiky. "The View from Below." In Mats Berdal and David M. Malone, eds. *Greed and Grievance: Economic Agendas in Civil Wars.* Boulder: Lynne Rienner, 2000, pp. 137–153.

Naylor, R. T. *Economic Warfare: Sanctions, Embargo Busting, and Their Human Cost.* Boston: Northeastern University Press, 2001.

Ogan, Eugene. "The Cultural Background to the Bougainville Crisis." *Journal de la Société des Océanistes* 92–93, nos. 1–2 (1991): 61–67.

Pashko, Gramoz. "Kosovo: Facing Dramatic Economic Crisis." In Thanos Veremis and Evangelos Kofos, eds., *Kosovo: Avoiding Another Balkan War.* Athens: Hellenic Foundation for European and Foreign Policy (ELIAMEP) and the University of Athens, 1998, pp. 329–355.

Peleman, Johan. "Mining for Serious Trouble: Jean-Raymond Boulle and His Corporate Empire Project." In Abdel-Fatau Musah and J. 'Kayode Fayemi, eds., *Mercenaries: An African Security Dilemma.* London: Pluto Press, 2000, pp. 155–168.

Pluchinsky, Dennis A. "Ethnonational Terrorism: Themes and Variations." In Gunnar Jervas, ed., *FOA Report on Terrorism.* Stockholm: Defence Research Establishment, 1998.

Porto, João Gomes. "Contemporary Conflict Analysis in Perspective." In Jeremy Lind and Kathryn Sturman, eds., *Scarcity and Surfeit: The Ecology of Africa's Conflicts.* Pretoria: Institute of Security Studies, 2002, pp. 1–49.

Quodling, Paul. *Bougainville: The Mine and the People.* Sydney: Centre for Independent Studies, 1991.

Rangel, Alfredo. "Parasites and Predators: Guerrillas and the Insurrection Economy of Colombia." *Journal of International Affairs* 53, no. 2 (Spring 2000): 577–601.

Reeve, Ros, and Stephen Ellis. "An Insider's Account of the South African Security Forces' Role in the Ivory Trade." *Journal of Contemporary African Studies* 13, no. 2 (1995): 227–244.

Regan, Anthony J. "Current Developments in the Pacific: Causes and Course of the Bougainville Conflict." *Journal of Pacific History* 33, no. 3 (1988): 269–285.

———. "Why a Neutral Peace Monitoring Force? The Bougainville Conflict and the Peace Process." In Monica Wehner and Donald Denoon, eds., *Without a Gun: Australia's Experience of Monitoring Peace in Bougainville, 1997–2001.* Canberra: Pandanus Books, 2001, pp. 1–18.

Renner, Michael. *The Anatomy of Resource Wars.* WorldWatch Paper no. 162. Washington, D.C.: WorldWatch Institute, 2002.

Reno, William. *Corruption and State Politics in Sierra Leone.* Cambridge: Cambridge University Press, 1995.

———. "The Real (War) Economy of Angola." In Jakkie Cilliers and Christian Dietrich, eds., *Angola's War Economy: The Role of Oil and Diamonds.* Pretoria: Institute for Security Studies, 2000, pp. 219–236.

———. "Shadow States and the Political Economy of Civil Wars." In Mats Berdal and David M. Malone, eds., *Greed and Grievance: Economic Agendas in Civil Wars.* Boulder: Lynne Rienner, 2000, pp. 43–68.

———. *Warlord Politics and African States.* Boulder: Lynne Rienner, 1998.

Reyes, Alejandro. "La expansión territorial del narcotráfico." In Bruce Bagley and Juan G. Tokatlian, eds., *Economía y política del narcotráfico.* Bogotá: Ediciones Uniandes CEI and CEREC, 1990.

Rohde, David. "Kosovo Seething." *Foreign Affairs* 79, no. 3 (May–June 2000): 65–79.

Ross, Michael. "How Does Natural Resource Wealth Influence Civil War? Evidence from 13 Case Studies." Paper presented at the World Bank conference on "Civil Wars and Post-Conflict Transition," UC Irvine, Irvine, Calif., May 18, 2001.

Rudrakumaran, Visuvanathan. *The Tamil's Quest for Statehood in the Context of the Birth of New States in the Former Soviet Union and Yugoslavia.* Camberley: International Federation of Tamils, 1991.

Rufin, Jean-Christophe. "Economics of War: A New Theory for Armed Conflicts." In *War, Money, and Survival.* Geneva: ICRC, 2000.

Rupnik, Jacques. "Yugoslavia After Milosevic." *Survival* 43, no. 2 (Summer 2001): 19–30.

Sandole, D. *Capturing the Complexity of Conflict: Dealing with Violent Ethnic Conflicts in the Post–Cold War Era.* London: Pinter, 1999.

Schatzberg, Michael. *The Dialectics of Oppression in Zaire*. Bloomington: Indiana University Press, 1988.

———. *Mobutu or Chaos: The United States and Zaire, 1960–1990*. Lanham, Md.: University Press of America, 1991.

Schnabel, Albrecht, and Ramesh Thakur, eds. *Kosovo and the Challenge of Humanitarian Intervention: Selective Indignation, Collective Action, and International Citizenship*. New York: UNU Press, 2000.

Schwarz, Walter. *The Tamils of Sri Lanka*. London: Minority Rights Group, 1975.

Seddon, David, Jagannath Adhikari, and Ganesh Gurung. *Foreign Labour Migration and the Remittance Economy of Nepal*. Norwich, UK: Overseas Development Group, University of East Anglia, 2000.

Shawcross, William. *Deliver Us from Evil: Warlords and Peacekeepers in a World of Endless Conflict*. London: Bloomsbury, 2000.

Shearer, David. "Aiding or Abetting? Humanitarian Aid and Its Economic Role in Civil War." In Mats Berdal and David M. Malone, eds., *Greed and Grievance: Economic Agendas in Civil Wars*. Boulder: Lynne Rienner, 2000, pp. 189–203.

Silverstein, Josef. "Fifty Years of Failure in Burma." In Michael Brown and Sumit Ganguly, eds., *Government Policies and Ethnic Relations in Asia and the Pacific*. CSIA Studies in International Security. Cambridge: MIT Press, 1997, pp. 167–196.

Smillie, Ian, Lansana Gberie, and Ralph Hazleton. *The Heart of the Matter: Sierra Leone, Diamonds, and Human Security*. Ottawa: Partnership Africa–Canada, January 2000.

Smith, Anthony. *The Ethnic Revival*. Cambridge: Cambridge University Press, 1981.

Smith, Martin. *Burma and the Politics of Insurgency*. 2nd ed. New York: Zed Books, 1999.

Spriggs, Matthew, and Donald Denoon, eds. *The Bougainville Crisis: 1991 Update*. Canberra: Australian National University in association with Crawford House Press, 1992.

Stedman, Stephen John, *Implementing Peace Agreements in Civil Wars: Lessons and Recommendations for Policymakers*. IPA Policy Paper Series on Peace Implementation. New York: IPA, May 2001.

Stedman, Stephen John, Donald Rothschild, and Elizabeth M. Cousins, eds. *Ending Civil Wars: The Implementation of Peace Agreements*. Project of the International Peace Academy and the Center for International Security and Cooperation. Boulder: Lynne Rienner, 2002.

Stewart, Frances. "Crisis Prevention: Tackling Horizontal Inequalities." *Oxford Development Studies* 28, no. 3 (October 2000): 245–262.

———. "Horizontal Inequalities as a Source of Conflict." In Fen Osler Hampson and David M. Malone, eds., *From Reaction to Conflict Prevention: Opportunities for the UN System*. Boulder: Lynne Rienner, 2002, pp. 105–136.

———. "The Root Causes of Humanitarian Emergencies." In Wayne E. Nafzinger, Francis Stewart, and Raimo Väyrynen, eds., *War, Hunger, and Displacement: The Origins of Humanitarian Emergencies*, vol. 1. Oxford: Oxford University Press, 2000, pp. 1–41.

Swanson, Philip. *Fuelling Conflict: The Oil Industry and Armed Conflict*. Fafo Report no. 378. Oslo: Fafo Institute for Applied Social Science,

Programme for International Co-operation and Conflict Resolution, March 2002.

Tambiah, S. J. *Sri Lanka: Ethnic Fratricide and the Dismantling of Democracy.* Chicago: University of Chicago Press, 1986.

Tarrow, Sidney. *Power in Movement: Social Movements and Contentious Politics.* Cambridge: Cambridge University Press, 1994.

Thompson, Herb. "The Economic Causes and Consequences of the Bougainville Crisis." *Resource Policy* 17, no. 1 (1991): 69–85.

Tilly, Charles. *From Mobilization to Revolution.* Reading, Mass.: Addison-Wesley, 1978.

———. "War Making and State Making as Organized Crime." In Peter B. Evans, Dietrich Rueschemeyer, and Theda Skocpol, eds., *Bringing the State Back In.* Cambridge: Cambridge University Press, 1985, pp. 169–225.

Triton, Theodore. "The Political Economy of Sacrifice: Kino's and the State." *Review of African Political Economy* 29, no. 93/94 (2002).

Tucker, Shelby. *Burma: The Curse of Independence.* Sterling, Va.: Pluto Press, 2001.

United Nations. "Report of the Panel of Experts Appointed Pursuant to Security Council Resolution 1306 (2000), Paragraph 19, in Relation to Sierra Leone." UN Doc. S/2000/1195, December 20, 2000.

———. "Report of the Panel of Experts on the Illegal Exploitation of Natural Resources and Other Forms of Wealth of the Democratic Republic of Congo." UN Doc. S/2001/357, April 12, 2001.

———. "Final Report of the Panel of Experts on the Illegal Exploitation of Natural Resources and Other Forms of Wealth of the Democratic Republic of Congo." UN Doc. S/2002/1146, October 16, 2002.

———. "Report of the Panel of Experts on Violations of Security Council Sanctions Against UNITA." UN Doc. S/2000/203, March 10, 2000.

———. "Report of the Panel on United Nations Peace Operations." UN Doc. A/55/305-S/2000/809, August 21, 2000.

———. "Report of the UN Secretary General Pursuant to Paragraph 10 of Security Council Resolution 1244 (1999)." UN Doc. S/1999/672, June 12, 1999.

United Nations Development Programme (UNDP). *Human Development Report 2001: Poverty Reduction and Governance.* New York: UNDP, 2001.

———. *Nepal Human Development Report.* Kathmandu: UNDP, 1998.

United Nations International Drug Control Programme (UNDCP). *Global Illicit Drug Trends 2001.* Vienna: UN Office for Drug Control and Crime Prevention (UNODCCP).

U.S. Department of State. *2001 International Narcotics Control Strategy Report.* Washington, D.C.: U.S. Department of State, 2002.

Valluvan, T. *The Ethnic Conflict in Sri Lanka: Economic Aspects.* London: Tamil Information Centre, 1987.

Vlassenroot, Koen. "Citizenship, Identity Formation in South Kivu: The Case of the Banyamulenge." *Review of African Political Economy* 29, no. 93/94 (2002).

Vlassenroot, Koen, and Hans Romkema. "The Emergence of a New Order? Resources and War in Eastern Congo." *Journal of Humanitarian Assistance,* October 28, 2002. Available online at www.jha.ac/articles/a111.htm.

Waldman, Amy. "Nepal: Conflict's Toll on Children." *New York Times,* January 16, 2003, p. A10.

Wallensteen, Peter, and Margareta Sollenberg. "After the Cold War: Emerging Patterns of Armed Conflict, 1989–1994." *Journal of Peace Research* 32, no. 3 (August 1995): 345–360.

Walter, Barbara F. *Committing to Peace: The Successful Settlement of Civil Wars.* Princeton: Princeton University Press, 2001.

Wechsler, William. "Follow the Money." *Foreign Affairs* 80, no. 4 (July–August 2001): 40–57.

Weiner, Myron. "Bad Neighbors, Bad Neighbourhoods: An Inquiry into the Causes of Refugee Flows." *International Security* 21, no. 1 (Summer 1996): 5–42.

Weinstein, Jeremy. *The Structure of Rebel Organizations: Implications for Post-Conflict Reconstruction.* Conflict Prevention and Reconstruction Unit Dissemination Notes no. 4. Washington, D.C.: World Bank, June 2002.

Weller, Marc. "Resolving Self-Determination Conflicts Through Complex Power Sharing: The Case of Kosovo." Draft paper prepared for the project on "Resolving Self-Determination Disputes Through Complex Power-Sharing Arrangements" of the Carnegie Corporation, the Centre of International Studies, the Lauterpacht Research Centre for International Law of Cambridge University, and the European Centre for Minority Issues, April 2001.

————, ed. *The Crisis in Kosovo 1989–1999: From the Dissolution of Yugoslavia to Rambouillet and the Outbreak of Hostilities.* Cambridge: Cambridge University Press, 1999.

Wesley-Smith, Terence. "The Non-Review of the Bougainville Copper Agreement." In Matthew Spriggs and Donald Denoon, eds., *The Bougainville Crisis: 1991 Update.* Canberra: Australian National University in association with Crawford House Press, 1992, pp. 92–111.

Whall, Helena J. *Repatriation of Displaced Tamils: Voluntary or Mandatory? Victims of War in Sri Lanka.* London: Medical Institute of Tamils, 1995.

Wilkinson, Paul. *Terrorism and the Liberal State.* London: Macmillan, 1986.

Williams, Phil. "Transnational Criminal Organisations and International Security." *Survival* 36, no. 1 (Spring 1994): 96–113.

Williams, Phil, and John Picarelli. "Organized Crime, Conflict and Terrorism: Combating the Relationships." Paper prepared for Policies and Practices for Controlling Resource Flows in Armed Conflict conference, sponsored by the International Peace Academy, Bellagio, Italy, May 21–23, 2002.

Wilson, A. Jeyaratnam. *The Break-Up of Sri Lanka: The Sinhalese-Tamil Conflict.* London: C. Hurst, 1988.

Wolfers, Edward P. "Politics, Development, and Resources: Reflections on Constructs, Conflict, and Consultants." In Stephen Hennigham and R. J. May, eds., *Resources, Development, and Politics in the Pacific Islands.* Bathurst: Crawford House Press, 1992, pp. 238–257.

Woodward, Susan L., *Economic Priorities for Peace Implementation.* IPA Policy Paper Series on Peace Implementation. New York: IPA, October 2002.

World Bank. *Kosovo: Economic and Social Reforms for Peace and Reconciliation,* no. 21784-KOS, February 1, 2001.

————. *The Road to Stability and Prosperity in South Eastern Europe: A Regional Strategy Paper,* March 1, 2000.

Yannis, Alexandros, *Kosovo Under International Administration: An Unfinished Conflict*. Geneva: Programme for Strategic and International Security Studies (PESI) and the Hellenic Foundation for European and Foreign Policy (ELIAMEP), 2001.

Zahar, Marie-Joëlle. "Is All the News Bad for Peace? Economic Agendas in the Lebanese War." *International Journal* 51, no. 1 (2000–2001).

Zartman, I. William. "Mediating Conflicts of Need, Greed, and Creed." *Orbis: A Journal of World Affairs* 44, no. 2 (Spring 2000): 255–266.

Zartman, I. William, and Saadia Touval. "International Mediation in the Post–Cold War Era." In Chester A. Crocker, Fen Osler Hampson, and Pamela Aall, eds., *Managing Global Chaos: Sources of and Responses to International Conflict*. Washington, D.C.: U.S. Institute of Peace Press, 1996, pp. 445–462.

The Contributors

Karen Ballentine is senior associate for the International Peace Academy's Economic Agendas in Civil Wars (EACW) program. From 1994 to 2000 she was a research associate at the Carnegie Corporation of New York, where she undertook a variety of research projects for both the president emeritus and the corporation's grant-making program on Preventing Deadly Conflict. In addition to leading research on the political economy of armed conflict, she has written widely on democratization, contemporary nationalism and self-determination, ethnic conflict, and conflict management and prevention.

John Bray is director of analysis at the Control Risks Group, an international business risk consultancy. Until 2002 he was political risk specialist with the same organization. He is also a member of the Private Sector Working Group of the International Peace Academy's Economic Agendas in Civil Wars program. His professional interests include conflict analysis, the politics of business and human rights, and anticorruption strategies. His links with the Himalayan region date back to 1978, when he taught in northern India. His recent publications include *Facing Up to Corruption: A Practical Business Guide.*

Charles Cater is a doctoral candidate in international relations at St. Antony's College, University of Oxford. Previously he worked for the Zimbabwe Human Rights Association, the International Rescue Committee, and the International Peace Academy. He is also coauthor, with Elizabeth Cousens, of *Toward Peace in Bosnia: Implementing the Dayton Accords.*

Alexandra Guáqueta is analyst in the department of government affairs for Occidental Petroleum in Colombia. She holds a doctor of philosophy degree in international relations from the University of Oxford, where she completed a doctoral dissertation on U.S.-Colombian relations and the war against illegal drugs. From September 2001 to August 2002 she was senior program officer for the International Peace Academy's Economic Agendas in Civil Wars program. She has worked for the Congressional Research Service in Washington, D.C., the Colombian Pacific Economic Cooperation Council at the Colombian Ministry of Foreign Affairs, and the Universidad de los Andes in Bogotá. She tutored in international relations at the University of Oxford and is author of several articles on international relations and Colombian foreign policy. She also writes on Latin American security and political risk for *Jane's Sentinel Security Assessment.*

Rohan Gunaratna is associate professor at the Institute of Defence and Strategic Studies, Nanyang Technological University, in Singapore. Previously, he was a research fellow at the Centre for the Study of Terrorism and Political Violence at the University of St. Andrews in Scotland and an honorary fellow at the International Policy Institute for Counter-Terrorism in Israel and principal investigator of the UN's Terrorism Prevention Branch. He has served as a consultant on terrorism to several governments and corporations, has lectured widely on terrorism in Europe, Latin America, North America, the Middle East, and Asia, and has addressed the United Nations, the U.S. Congress, and the Australian Parliament in the wake of September 11, 2001. He is the author of six books on armed conflict and terrorism, including *Inside Al Qaeda.*

Leiv Lunde is senior policy analyst at the ECON Centre for Economic Analysis in Oslo and chair of the Private Sector Working Group of the International Peace Academy's Economic Agendas in Civil Wars program. He has broad experience in research, policy analysis, and consulting/project management and has conducted policy research in a wide range of areas, including environmental policy, development cooperation, humanitarian policy and conflict resolution, human rights, and corporate social responsibility. He has worked with a variety of UN organizations, the World Bank and regional development banks, as well as a number of governments, companies, and nongovernmental organizations. From 1997 to 2000 he served as state secretary (deputy minister) for international development and human rights in the Norwegian Ministry of Foreign Affairs.

S. Mansoob Murshed is associate professor of international economics and conflict studies at the Institute of Social Studies (ISS) in the Hague. Previously he worked at the United Nations University (UNU) World Institute for Development Economics Research (WIDER) in Helsinki, where he directed research programs on globalization and low-income countries, and why some countries avoid conflict while others fail. His most recent edited publications include a special issue of the *Journal of Peace Research on Civil War and Underdevelopment* and a volume titled *Globalization, Marginalization, and Development.*

Anthony Regan is a constitutional lawyer who lived and worked in Papua New Guinea and Uganda from 1981 to 1996. Since 1997 he has been a fellow in the State, Society, and Governance in Melanesia project at the Research School of Pacific and Asian Studies at Australian National University in Canberra. He has been a constitutional adviser to the Bougainvillean parties to the negotiations with the Papua New Guinea government on the political future of Bougainville (1999 to 2002). He has also served as adviser to the Solomon Islands peace process and the East Timor constitution-making process. He has published extensively on decentralization, autonomy, and the Bougainville conflict and peace process.

Michael L. Ross is assistant professor of political science at the University of California, Los Angeles. He is currently a consultant for the World Bank's Governance of Natural Resources project. His research has focused on the political economy of the resource curse, including the impact of natural resource extraction on poverty reduction, governance, and armed conflict. He received his Ph.D. in politics from Princeton University in 1996. He is the author of *Timber Booms and Institutional Breakdown in Southeast Asia.*

Jake Sherman is political affairs officer in the office of the Special Representative of the Secretary-General, United Nations Assistance Mission in Afghanistan (UNAMA). From 2001 to 2003 he was senior program officer for the International Peace Academy's Economic Agendas in Civil Wars program. Previously, he worked for Physicians for Human Rights in Boston and Bosnia-Herzegovina. He is the author of several reports for the IPA on economic dimensions of armed conflict.

Alexandros Yannis is a research fellow in the Programme for Strategic and International Security Studies (PSIS) in Geneva and in the Hellenic

Foundation for European and Foreign Policy (ELIAMEP) in Athens. He studied law and international relations in the Law School of Athens University, the Graduate Institute of International Studies (IUHEI) in Geneva, and the School of International and Public Affairs (SIPA) of Columbia University in New York. From July 1999 to December 2000 he served as a political adviser to Bernard Kouchner, the first UN Special Representative of the Secretary-General in Kosovo. He is the author of *Kosovo Under International Administration: An Unfinished Conflict.*

Index

About the Book

Globalization, suggest the authors of this collection, is creating new opportunities—some legal, some illicit—for armed factions to pursue their agendas in civil war. Within this context, they analyze the key dynamics of war economies and the challenges posed for conflict resolution and sustainable peace.

Thematic chapters consider key issues in the political economy of internal wars, as well as how differing types of resource dependency influence the scope, character, and duration of conflicts. Case studies of Burma, Colombia, Kosovo, Papua New Guinea, and Sri Lanka illustrate a range of ways in which belligerents make use of global markets and the transnational flow of resources. An underlying theme is the opportunities available to the international community to alter the economic incentive structure that inadvertently supports armed conflict.

Karen Ballentine, senior associate at the International Peace Academy, directs the IPA's Economic Agenda's in Civil Wars Program. **Jake Sherman** is political affairs officer in the office of the Special Representative of the Secretary-General, United Nations Assistance Mission in Afghanistan (UNAMA).